EVERYTHING I HAVE IS YOURS

Also by Eleanor Henderson

The Twelve-Mile Straight

Ten Thousand Saints

EVERYTHING
I HAVE
IS YOURS

a marriage

ELEANOR HENDERSON

FLATIRON
BOOKS
NEW YORK

EVERYTHING I HAVE IS YOURS. Copyright © 2021 by Eleanor
Ann Henderson. All rights reserved. Printed in the United
States of America. For information, address Flatiron Books,
120 Broadway, New York, NY 10271.

www.flatironbooks.com

Design by Donna Sinisgalli Noetzel

Library of Congress Cataloging-in-Publication Data

Names: Henderson, Eleanor, author.
Title: Everything I have is yours : a marriage / Eleanor
Henderson.
Description: First edition. | New York, NY Flatiron Books,
2021.
Identifiers: LCCN 2021008170 | ISBN 9781250787941
(hardcover) | ISBN 9781250787958 (ebook)
Classification: LCC PS3608.E5259 E84 2021 |
DDC 813/.6—dc23
LC record available at https://lccn.loc.gov/2021008170

Our books may be purchased in bulk for promotional,
educational, or business use. Please contact your local
bookseller or the Macmillan Corporate and Premium Sales
Department at 1-800-221-7945, extension 5442, or by email
at MacmillanSpecialMarkets@macmillan.com.

First Edition: 2021

10 9 8 7 6 5 4 3 2 1

For Aaron, still

The lover ultimately, willingly, takes on
the afflictions of the beloved.

MIKHAIL BULGAKOV

AUTHOR'S NOTE

This is a true story. However, some names and details have been changed. It is not an endorsement of any medical professional, diagnosis, or treatment.

EVERYTHING I HAVE IS YOURS

BAD NIGHT

I am trying to get Aaron to sleep.

It's close to midnight on a Sunday, the bedroom dark but for one low lamp, the air purifier purring. He is struggling, crying out, his eyes squeezed shut in pain. I rub his back. I kiss his forehead. "It's okay," I whisper. "You're okay." Across the bridge of his nose are the freshly flecked scars on his swollen sinuses, like the scratches sleeping babies inflict on themselves with their tiny fingernails. How many nights have I spent rocking babies to sleep, how many hours waiting for the weight of their limbs to fall with the gravity of the dead, then laying them in the crib, sliding my hands out from under their diapered bottoms one knuckle at a time, praying *please please please*?

But Aaron is not a baby. He is my husband.

Two hours ago, he was in our older son's room, putting him to bed for the second time. I'd taken the boys to the apple harvest festival— Aaron hadn't been in shape to go—where they had encountered a clown in the funhouse. Later, the memory of the clown kept Nico awake, and Aaron got him to calm down by telling him about the painting of a clown that had hung in his house growing up, how much it had scared him, and how messed up it was that his parents had refused to take it down. Before long Nico was laughing, and then sleeping, and then the two of us stood as we do most nights in his doorway and said to each other, "What a beautiful boy," and then stood in Henry's doorway and said it again.

Now we are in our room. It's the first night of October in Ithaca,

New York. Last week it was in the nineties, and the portable fans are still gathered around the room, blank faced, needy, bearded in dust. It's a narrow room, once a sleeping porch, still poorly insulated, and any day now we will need to turn on the heat. I'm in my flannel pajamas, wrapped in the bare, slightly sour-smelling duvet, but Aaron is in his underwear, no blanket, no sheet, because even though he's cold, the contact hurts his skin.

"Did you take your medicine?"

He plunges his hand into the little basket of orange pill bottles arranged on his nightstand. He knows by size and shape which are the right ones. He rattles out two Seroquel, then two Aleve PMs—four years ago, he developed D-grade esophageal ulcers after a steady diet of Ibuprofen—and I help him find the baby-blue pills that have spilled onto the bed. His hands are shaking. He chases them with a swig of Smirnoff Ice. I try not to worry what the sugar will do to his teeth.

Four months ago, he'd been sober for four years. Then he decided that the pain of being inside his own skin was worse than the pain of addiction—and was he really an alcoholic anyway? My sister-in-law was making mojitos that night. She offered Aaron one and he said yes, and we all laughed about her bad influence, the powers of her mixology, but only Aaron and I understood what we were toasting, what we were risking.

"Let's take off your glasses, honey." I slide them off his blistered nose and find a place for them beside the bed. There is not a spare inch of space on the nightstand—a tissue box, nasal spray, a drawing pad, three alarm clocks, books upon books, a pencil cup Henry made for him from a frozen orange juice carton in kindergarten last year.

His body is seizing up, each wince piling on the last. "I don't know what's happening," he cries.

I rest my head against his armpit, where I don't think I'll hurt him. "Shhhhh." I don't know, either. He is having a fit. It is kind of familiar, though I can't be sure. Is it his skin? Or something deeper? The last two days, his body has issued a red, angry rash, one that evades language as fiercely as it evades diagnosis. (Although what is diagnosis but language?) On his left arm, above the bird tattoo and below the eyeball-sun tattoo, across the tattoo that says ELEANOR, it's more like a third-degree sunburn. The one on his chest and ribs—a new place, in recent months—might be called a rash. ("Doesn't it look like a penis and balls?" he asked me earlier today.) The one on his right shin—the one I am very careful not to rub up against in our bed—might best be called a boil. It is faintly blue, the color of the blood inside, though the skin around it is the electric pink of infected skin. Both ankles are slightly swollen. It is bad, though not emergency-room bad. Not even urgent-care bad. At least I don't think so.

Should I have taken him to urgent care? Despite the old fights about it, our tired cycle of neglect and blame? *We wouldn't need to go to urgent care if you'd called your doctor for a refill!* He needed antibiotics three days ago, but he refused them. Tomorrow—Monday—he has promised, he will call his dermatologist for antibiotics, and—while he's at it!—his psychiatrist, for a refill on the Maxalt. Will she prescribe migraine medicine? It's related to the mind, right? He will even call his gastroenterologist, he says, for that long-overdue checkup on those ulcers.

I will not call any of these doctors. It was part of our pact four years ago, after I got into Al-Anon, after I learned the word "codependency," pronounced it like a woman with a new language in her mouth.

Now we have new language, every year a little more. The latest is *schizophrenia*, at least according to the latest psychiatrist. It's a diagnosis he's trying on, a jacket that still needs tailoring. Earlier tonight, from the schizophrenia handbook that hides in the toothpaste drawer, he read me two new words: "executive function." I tapped the letters into my phone and read him the definition: "a set of mental skills that help you get things done." Like? "Managing time. Paying attention." We looked at each other, eyes wide. It has been a half joke among us for years, that Aaron is allergic to finishing things. The dishes. A song. A career. Starting things also! The middle part? He's good at that.

I think of these words as I'm rubbing his back in our bed. Codependency. Executive function. Does my husband have schizophrenia, and if so, is it a spousal crime to fail to call the doctor on behalf of your executively dysfunctional husband? Is it like expecting your baby to pick up the phone and dial?

He's on his stomach now. Every few seconds, his legs swing back and then he brings them down hard, one at a time, thumping the mattress.

"You're kicking the bed again," I say helpfully.

"Sorry. I know that sucks." He is almost laughing, as anyone might when their body is out of their control—a shaking hand, a foot asleep. "I can't help it."

He has a long, broad surfboard of a back. A beautiful back. When he was a teenager and surfing all day under the Florida sun, his body tanned and lean, you could count—I've seen pictures—the marbles of his spine. Now it is the back of a forty-five-year-old man who still lifts weights every day, despite the pain. *Fuck it.* When I am lying beside him in bed, it is a dune, a whole beach between us. It is the only plane of his body that is not covered in tattoos, or sores.

I watched the tattoo artist put the ELEANOR tattoo on his arm. I was nineteen, half the age I am now. Aaron was twenty-six. In Burlington, Vermont, the city where my parents had fallen in love, I sat in the corner of the tattoo parlor and watched my name appear, letter by capital letter. *Eleanor,* even though he, like my family, called me Nell. So formal! And crooked, I was sure. *Say something,* I willed myself. But was it really crooked? Or was it just my angle? And wasn't it too late anyway?

In our bed, he thrashes. He looks as though he's being attacked by a hundred invisible needles.

Or is he being attacked by a hundred invisible demons? Are they outside, or inside?

"He's always had his demons," his best friend Derek told me on the phone, the night I called him four years ago. I nodded, knowing how much Aaron hated that fucking phrase, like he was an aging rock star on a VH1 documentary.

On the bedside table, my phone pings. I reach to turn off the volume. Beside the phone, splayed facedown and open, is a book. Part of my mind is still in that book. Part of my mind is scanning my phone—who is texting at this hour?

But I don't pick it up. I put my lips to Aaron's forehead. It's clammy, though his cheeks are hot.

Maybe he just has a fever. Maybe he's shivering. Maybe his body is fighting the infection in his limbs. It is almost poignant to me, the way his systems continue to rally, to fight off their threats, despite all of the ways they are broken.

But the struggling seems deeper. Tonight it is inside. His skin is burning, but he is burning somewhere else, too. He drives his head into the pillow. "Breathe," I say. "Don't fight it." I say this with conviction, though I have no idea if it is the right advice or the exactly wrong advice. It's the kind of thing the midwives told me when I was giving birth—don't fight the labor, work with your body, not against it. And in fact my husband reminds me of a laboring woman, the pain that extra-terrestrial, the desperation that whole. Any minute now he might expel eight pounds of life force. What would it look like, the foreign matter that is fighting so hard to break through his skin? I think of *Gremlins*, which we've just introduced to our kids. I think of Gizmo, splashed with water, writhing in anguish, and picture Aaron popping three viscous Mogwai out of his back. Pop! Pop! Pop!

What is it with that horror-movie goo? That ectoplasm of *Gremlins*, *Ghostbusters*, *Alien*. Last year, in this bed, we binge-watched the first season of *Stranger Things*, where that goo is nothing less than a portal to another world, the secretion of some dark birth canal that leads to the Upside Down.

I cried when it was over and I didn't know why. I wasn't just scared. I wasn't just exhilarated. I was devastated. I felt so helpless, so sad.

It was the unkillable-ness of that monster. It would not die. It lurked in the darkness, never showing its face. It went away, and then it came back. And as hard as those kids tried to kill it, with shotguns and bear traps and Christmas lights, it returned to haunt them. And now, just when it seemed to be gone, it bubbled up its black tar from that poor boy's throat. The monster was inside him now.

Here we are, Aaron and I, in the middle of the night, in our Upside Down. How did we get here? How do we get back?

"It's bad," Aaron says, his face in the pillow.

"Breathe," I say, and I can hear him trying. He is trying.

It's bad, but not bad-bad. It's not guzzling-the-Nyquil bad. It's not fighting-all-night bad, or crying-all-night bad, or hallucinating-bugs bad, or sitting-on-his-hands bad, or beating-himself-up-with-a-baseball-bat bad. It's not call-our-therapist bad. Another night, when I don't know better, I might have my phone in my face, rage-researching every symptom. Another night, he might punch himself in the face. Another night, in a cruel and illogical rage, I might smack *him* in the face. *Stop it! Stop doing this to yourself! Wake up! Come back to me! Help!*

Not hard enough to hurt him, I think, though I will feel the tarry shame in the morning and apologize. *I'm sorry. I'm so sorry.*

The worst nights are not the ones where he suffers beside me. The worst nights are the ones where he suffers alone. The worst nights, he sleeps on the couch downstairs, despite my begging. *I don't want to keep you up. I can tell it's going to be a bad night.*

Or: *It's too much.* Or: *I'm fine.* Or: *You didn't sign up for this.*

The worst nights, I can hear his soft voice down the stairs. It's the early hours of the morning and he's on the phone. For a moment I let myself hope he is talking to a friend. I let myself worry he is talking to a woman. But I know he has called the suicide hotline. A faceless, professional voice on the other end of the phone. And because what I fear more than anything is that my husband will try to kill himself again, and because what I want more than anything is to be the one to save him, it is the worst kind of betrayal. I go back to our room and sleep alone. I toss and turn, desperate and furious and hurt. Short of saving him—I am reasonable enough to know I can't save him—I want all his pain to myself. Is that too much to ask?

Tonight, though, he is in our bed. Tonight, my touch is gentle. I spoon his beautiful back. "Stop hunching your shoulders," I say. "Let me get in there."

He relaxes his shoulders a little. I find the warm crease of his neck. I lay the kisses along his collarbone. His shoulders relax some more. He purrs. His feet thump the bed softly.

His skin: that tender membrane between inside and outside. What nerve endings is my mouth reaching, and what chemical reaction is happening below the surface? How do my kisses slow the beating of his heart, and ease the breath in and out of his lungs, and turn the fretful moan in his chest to the even rasp of sleep?

Maybe it's the Seroquel. But I like to think it's love.

I slide my left hand out from beneath him and place it on his back, soft, firm.

I sigh.

Tomorrow morning, I know, we will stand in the kitchen while the Keurig heats up, and he'll be warm and solid and upright, and we'll hold each other and we'll say, "I'm sorry it was a bad night."

But now, with my left hand on my husband's back, I reach for my book with my right. His snoring is the loveliest sound on Earth. Peace has been restored. The monster has been banished. The portal, for to-night, has been sealed. And I read by the lamplight, far longer than I should.

SICK HOUSE FAMILY

n Nico's backpack, in a wrinkled pile of fourth-grade homework—fractions and energy transfer and Susan B. Anthony—I find a worksheet about feelings. *When I feel angry, I can take a deep breath*. Nico finds this series boring and babyish, and half the blanks are empty, or answered with a sloppy *I don't know*. I'm kind of proud of his bullshit detector, though his dad and I tell him, "Sometimes you just have to bullshit."

But I keep reading.

I feel anxious about _____.

On the line he has written three words: *sick house family*.

I swallow.

I find him in his bed, reading a comic book. "Nico," I say, trying to keep my voice open, steady. I show him the paper.

He takes it, balls it up, and throws it under his bed.

Last year, in kindergarten, with the pencil cup made from the orange juice carton, Henry brought home a drawing of Aaron for Father's Day. On the other side, a worksheet about his dad.

> *My dad is a _____. My favorite thing to do with my dad is _____.*

His teacher's handwriting completes the blanks. One line says:

My dad is really good at <u>putting medicine on his boo-boos.</u>

Henry asks me in the car, "Were Dad's boo-boos there when I didn't exist?"

I tell him yes, he was in my tummy when Dad got sick.

The summer of 2011. I was seven months pregnant and on tour for my first novel, leaving Ithaca for a week, then coming home for the weekend, then going out on the road again. Aaron was home taking care of Nico, and our dog and cats. He texted me pictures of our son asleep in our bed in his Batman pajamas.

Maybe it was the stress of solo parenting a three-year-old. Maybe it was the lack of sleep. One night on the phone, he said, "I have this weird rash." He texted me a picture: little red bumps on his back and the back of his arms, around his elbows. "Weird," I said. "Go get it checked out." We both expected it to go away. But he didn't go to the doctor for another few weeks, until I was home for good, and by that time the rash had spread into painful, dime-sized lesions that wouldn't heal.

When Henry was born a month later, it had been diagnosed as a staph infection. We had to get special permission for Aaron to be in the delivery room. The lesions spotted his torso, his legs, his concave temples. He was fatigued and he was in pain. He'd dropped from 163 pounds to 138. In the pictures of him holding our newborn, he is frightfully skinny. For most of my labor, Aaron slept in a chair while I rocked back and forth with contractions in the shower, he in his private pain, I in mine.

Aaron's skin didn't heal. It wasn't a staph infection, his GP said. But he wasn't sure what it was.

The first dermatologist, the head of dermatology at the state university hospital, said, "Prurigo nodularis!" with such conviction that later Aaron said he looked like he expected a high five. He took a biopsy that turned up nothing. He gave him some steroid creams that didn't help.

The second dermatologist said, "You say it flares up with stress? Maybe you should look into that." And stood to leave.

The third dermatologist took another biopsy and confirmed it. Prurigo nodularis. It means, basically, "itchy nodules."

I'm not sure what those doctors saw under the microscope. Prurigo nodularis isn't a bacteria or a virus or a parasite. It's the body's response to scratching, to self-excoriation.

"But he doesn't scratch them," I told the fourth dermatologist, who wasn't a dermatologist but a physician's assistant, but looked like he could play a dermatologist on a soap opera. "They just erupt that way. Spontaneously."

"I understand. A lot of people scratch them in their sleep."

"But his skin doesn't itch. It *hurts*."

"Well," he said, not unkindly, "you have to understand. Ninety percent of patients with this disease deny itching and scratching."

"Deny itching," I said, "or scratching?"

"Both," he said, and turned to write down something on a chart. Then he turned back. "I see. Scratching," he said. "That's true. Most patients don't deny that they itch."

As we left, he told Aaron, "You gotta relax. Enjoy life!"

Some doctors looked at his skin and dismissed it as scratching. Some looked at his skin and dismissed it as drug use.

"These almost look like track marks."

"I have to ask. Have you used intravenous drugs?"

One GP looked at a nasty rash on the inside of Aaron's elbow. It looked like he'd been burned with a blowtorch. But over the head of one of our children who sat in Aaron's lap, she whispered: "Needles?"

He closed his eyes. I wanted to hold his pain for him, like a purse.

THEORY 1

Needles are the only thing he didn't use. He did do drugs, of one kind or another, for a very long time. He medicated his feelings. Then he stopped doing drugs, and his feelings burned through his skin.

THEORY 2

A few months after the rash broke out, after the visits to the GP and the dermatologists, we went to an acupuncturist and herbalist, Dr. Chang, who counted Aaron's pulse, examined his sores, and asked him to stick out his tongue. She concluded, "Too much fire."

I made a sound somewhere between a gasp and a laugh. Too much fire! Were there three truer words to describe my husband?

IXORA CIRCLE

1997

He was the guy behind the counter at CD Warehouse. I had bought *Sweet Relief* from him, and *Stop Making Sense*, and on my break from my job at the movie theater, *Physical Graffiti*. He was older and so fearsomely good-looking that it was painful for me to behold him. He had full lips and dark brows and warm smart eyes with brown and green in them, ringed with a thread of violet. He had this way of aligning a stack of CD cases together before he bagged them—neat, competent, comfortable in his world—tapping it against the desk like a deck of cards. Sometimes he would flirt with me and I would think, *There is no way he's flirting with me.* Once I bought a Temple of the Dog album from him and he teased me for it, even when I told him it was for my brother. "But you *are* wearing a fuchsia shirt with cows on it," he said, "so I guess it's okay."

It was the spring of 1997, my senior year. I'd spent high school getting straight A's, avoiding parties in favor of concerts. I was the editor of my school newspaper, but by senior year all I really wanted to write were album reviews, on Hole and Tori Amos and *Melon Collie and the Infinite Sadness*. I'd started smoking pot. I'd stopped shaving my legs. One day at lunch, while I sat in my overalls with my ankles crossed on the courtyard table (my calculus teacher was always telling me to sit like a lady), Jason Murphy, who had beaten me for class president in the sixth grade, told me I'd never get a boyfriend with hairy legs. I gave him the finger as he walked away. "Yell for Nell!" he called. It had been my presidential campaign slogan. My mother had hand-stenciled the fliers with me, and after I handed them out to kids before school, Jason had collected them, one by one.

I was counting the days to college, when I could get the fuck away from Florida, from all its Jason Murphys, from its unimaginative weather and poor taste in music, and start my life and fall in love with a dark-haired guy who played guitar. For three years, I'd had a Middlebury College brochure by my bed. On the cover, a girl with a tote bag stood at an intersection of sidewalks on the quad, talking casually to a guy paused on his bike. I imagined my way onto that campus, hologrammed myself into an Adirondack chair. Every day after school, I checked the mailbox for a letter from Middlebury.

The summer before, I'd had my heart broken. He was a boy who worked at the movie theater, a poet on the cross-country team who loved Led Zeppelin. I'd watch him stand at the podium where he tore tickets while I nibbled on popcorn behind the concession stand as irresistibly as I could, until finally he asked me out. In the months between his seventeenth birthday and mine, we went on dates to the thrift store and *Clueless* and the Pink Floyd laser light show, both of us in our cardigans and Converse and delicate metal-framed glasses. With our matching chin-length hair, we had successfully fashioned ourselves into the androgynous versions of each other, Kurt Cobain on *MTV Unplugged.* Maybe our twinning should have sounded an alarm. Instead, I felt that we were made for each other.

Then I left for a trip to my family's cabin in Vermont, a tour of college campuses on the way. I lay in a canoe on the lake in my forest-green bikini, seeing my future form above me in the clouds. We'd lose our virginity to each other, go to the same college, take the same poetry workshops, and be madly in love forever.

When I got home, he broke up with me over the phone. I took the call in my father's office, on the corded phone, standing at the desk. I stared at the buttons of the fax machine, dusty and stupid.

Nine months later, I was looking for the heartbroken voice of Vic Chesnutt and nothing more when I walked into a record store downtown and the guy in the giant shorts flashed me a smile. The shorts were more like pants. His calves were hairy and tanned and tattooed. He did not look like Kurt Cobain, or me. He looked like someone I hadn't thought to imagine. I was wearing thrift-store bell-bottoms, Birkenstocks, and a white tank top with no bra.

Sweet Relief II had just come out, a collection of Vic Chesnutt covers by bands like R.E.M. and Indigo Girls and Garbage, and I'd had it on repeat. There'd been no Vic Chesnutt albums at CD Warehouse, where the other guy who worked there, Derek, was talking on the cordless phone with his long-distance girlfriend. There were definitely no Vic Chesnutt albums at Record Town or Sam Goody at the mall. So I'd driven down to Okeechobee Boulevard, to a West Palm Beach record store called Sound Splash.

It was a real record store—with records, and patchouli. The cute guy from CD Warehouse was chatting with the gray-bearded guy who stood behind the counter. I went over to the C's and assessed them. No Vic Chesnutt.

Then there he was, crossing the store to me, smiling with recognition. "Hey!" he said.

"Hi," I said.

We'd had conversations before, but here we were in a new store, a new space; this required an introduction, we seemed to agree.

He extended a hand to me. "I'm Aaron."

"I'm Nell."

We shook. The one and only time, it is odd to think, we ever shook hands.

His teeth were as white as his T-shirt. Around his neck, a string of wooden Krishna beads was wound three times, tight as a choker. "What are you doing down here?" he said.

"Looking for Vic Chesnutt."

"Who?"

"Vic Chesnutt. They just put out that new album with his songs? He's in a wheelchair. They raise money for musicians with health problems. But the money isn't for him. It's just his songs." I was babbling.

"Can't find anything here?"

I shook my head.

"Well, come into the store later tonight. I'll be working. I'll order you whatever you need."

That evening, I went to CD Warehouse and Aaron hauled out a phonebook-sized catalog, which in 1997 was how you ordered an obscure album. He ordered me every Vic Chesnutt album listed. A week later, he called to tell me they were in. A CD and two cassettes—that was the only way he could get them. "Come on in and pick them up."

It was just Aaron working that night, but another customer was in the store, an older guy in a shirt and tie, and Aaron was chatting with him. (So much chatting! How friendly he was! How capable of good customer service.) Aaron nodded and smiled hello at me but kept on chatting. It was a small store, neat and minimal and fluorescently lit, less warehouse and more your nerdy dad's garage. I pretended to browse. I picked up a used copy of *Staring at the Sea* and popped it in the CD player at the listening station, popped on the headphones. Who was this guy and when would he stop talking? Any longer and I couldn't hang around without looking like I was hanging around. So I took off the headphones and brought the Cure case to the counter, where Aaron had gathered the Vic Chesnutt albums.

"Thank you *so* much," I said as he rang me up.

Halfway home, at a red light, I leaned over and opened the Cure case. No CD. I turned the car around. When I got back to the store, the guy was gone. It was just Aaron, smiling.

"Forgot my CD in the player," I said, going over to retrieve it. Aaron still says I left it there on purpose.

"Hey," he said as I turned to leave. "Do you have a boyfriend?"

I bit my lips to hide my smile. "No. I don't have a boyfriend."

He wrote his phone number on the back of a CD Warehouse business card. Capital N. AaroN.

A few days later, in the mailbox, a letter waited for me from Middlebury, fat and full, promising a scholarship. I sat in the living room with my parents and cried with joy. Then I went to my room. Beside my bed was the well-worn Middlebury brochure. I'd wanted to escape into that future, and it was close enough to touch. Now, another future, even closer, was presenting itself. This was not in the brochure.

I dialed Aaron's number for the first time and told him the news.

"Wow! Congratulations," he said, but I could hear the disappointment in his voice. How did you start to date someone when she was going away to start her life?

Our first date was the mini-golf course and Chili's and Dunkin' Donuts and the beach. I knew what it meant when a boy said, "Let's go to the beach." We stood in the dark parking lot and leaned against the dirty grill of his Pathfinder, both of us in white T-shirts, the ocean wind whipping toward us. "Your shirt's getting messed up," he apologized, and I said, "Don't worry. I've got more." He laughed. I waited for him to kiss me. I asked him what he liked to read, and when he said Arthur Rimbaud, I pretended to know who that was. He asked me what I liked to read, and when I said Toni Morrison, he admitted he hadn't read her. Then he said, "I have to feed my cats. Want to come with me?" I thought, I know what it means when a boy says, "I have to feed my cats."

But I didn't, actually. When I'd made out with boys in high school, it was at the beach, or in cars, or in the stolen minutes before our parents came home. Aaron wasn't like other boys. He wasn't even a boy! He was a man! We drove from Juno Beach south to Lake Worth and he let us into the quiet house on Ixora Circle. His dad owned it, and he lived there with his friend Derek, who wasn't home. In the darkened living room, I could see an electric guitar, mahogany, handsome, alert on its stand. "Is that yours?" I asked, my heart speeding up, and he nodded. There were no roommates, no parents, nothing hanging over us but a distant and halfhearted curfew.

He introduced me to the cats. Ratboy, the girl, a springy little white one. Human Furnace, the boy, tiger-striped, grumpy, and fat. Aaron had this hand gesture, pulsing his fist open and closed, as he called to them: *Pssht pssht pssht.* They came. He kissed at them then petted them and they wound their tails around his ankles. Their food bowls were full of kibble, but he set out two cans of wet food, and they ate happily.

"Well," he said. "I better get you home."

On the half-hour drive back to my parents' house in North Palm Beach, a police car began to follow us. "What the fuck," he said. The cop idled at the corner while he pulled into my driveway. My mother was peeking out the living room blinds. Aaron didn't kiss me good night.

Did he like me? I had wanted, expected to be kissed. I liked him so much. I liked his Krishna beads. I liked his Swatch watch and his silver hoop earrings and even his giant pants. I liked the way he seemed not to be able to stop smiling. I liked the way he seemed to know everything about everything. I liked the way he opened doors for me, gave me a hard time, and ordered vegetable soup for dinner.

But we already had a date for the next day, at a craft show we'd seen advertised on our first date. Tomorrow I'd wear a blue tank top and no bra, and afterward Aaron would insist that we play pool, and I'd spend the whole time shooting pool while standing perfectly straight, so as not to expose my A-cup cleavage. He didn't see my cleavage and he didn't kiss me on that date, either. But it was, I would recognize later, the nicest thing a boy could do, to tell a girl he liked her: make a second date before the first one was over.

I went home and looked up Rimbaud's "The Drunken Boat." A record of all the beauty and heartache glimpsed on ocean journeys. All the romance! All the melancholy!

I have seen the low sun spotted with mystic horrors . . .

I thought, I want to see what this guy has seen.

When he was seven years old, my future husband thought to himself: my future wife could be a baby right now. She could be being born. That's what he told me later.

But we didn't know how extreme our age difference was, not at first. It was the first of our willful denials. It was kind of like this: I didn't know what his last name was. He hadn't written it on the business card he gave me. I didn't ask him on our first date, and I forgot to ask him on the second. By the third date—the date he finally kissed me—it would have been strange. *Hey, what's your last name? And how old are you, anyway?*

On the phone he told me that he'd graduated high school the same year my brother had. Later, he revised this story. Well, he hadn't actually *graduated*. But if he had graduated, it would have been the same year. It wasn't until a month into our dating, on his birthday, that I finally learned his age: he was turning twenty-five.

My mother met him when he came to pick me up for my second date. She was blowing her nose as she answered the door. "Hi, Aaron! I'm Ann." I was a little embarrassed, but not much. Aaron came in and looked around the living room, which was crowded with books and art and newspapers, my father's drafting table in the corner covered with sketches, markers, bills, pipe tobacco. He told me later about the shock of familiarity he'd felt—my dad's space was as messy as his dad's.

Our parents, our dads in particular, had a good deal in common. Each set of parents was twelve years apart. Both of our fathers had been in accidents as teenagers. My father, Bill, was fifteen when he flew through the windshield of a car that he was driving around a curve in a country road in Georgia. His hip was broken, his ears were torn down to the lobes, and his body was sliced down each side like a paper doll. The other passengers didn't have a scratch. Aaron's father, Morris, was nineteen, a radio operator in France during World War II, when his Jeep went over a landmine and his body was thrown straight up into a tree. The driver was killed instantly. Morris was in a full-body cast for a year. He received two Purple Hearts, one for the shrapnel in his back, one for the shrapnel in his arm, but it was his legs that were the most damaged. Aaron's dad had raised him alone from the time he was six, first in a mansion on Long Island, then in a retirement condo in Florida.

Aaron was eleven when they moved. He'd had to leave behind his mom, his best friend, Ashmat, his beloved streets of the Lower East Side, where he'd spent weekends. No children under twelve were allowed in his father's building in Florida, so his father had lied about Aaron's age. No pets were allowed, either. He'd lied about that, too.

Morris still lived in the condo. Aaron drove me over one day. "I have to pick up some mail," he said. It had been a fancy building when they'd arrived in the early eighties, but now it was outdated and sun-bleached, the sidewalks paved with AstroTurf. At the mailboxes, an old woman with a walker eyed us warily. When Aaron produced a key for the elevator, her expression softened. "Hello," he said to her, not warmly.

In the elevator, he shook his head. "Every time," he said. "What do they think I am? A cat burglar?"

"Why would they think that?"

"Because I'm under eighty years old."

As the elevator rose, he cheered up. "I once brought a burning mat-tress down this elevator," he told me. When he was a teenager, he'd fallen asleep with a cigarette and his bed caught on fire. He'd dragged the mattress out the front door and tried to access the fire hose, but it was broken. Now the elevator opened on the seventh floor, and he pointed to the little box with the hose. *In case of fire, break glass.* "It's probably still busted," he said.

"What happened to the mattress?" I wondered, following him to the apartment door.

"I put it out eventually." He fit his key in the lock. "The elevator kept stopping so people could get on."

"Maybe that's why they give you looks," I suggested.

He waved his hand. "This fucking place."

His father's apartment was the bachelor pad of a seventy-three-year-old Jewish war veteran. "Eccentric" is how Aaron had described him. The place smelled powerfully of cats. Everywhere were dusty history books and cardboard boxes and little figurines and too much furni-ture, as though a mansion had been downsized into a two-bedroom apartment, which it had. Aaron found a stack of mail among the many stacks of mail on the glass dining table. His bedroom was pretty much as he'd left it. The dresser and shag carpet and the vanity in his bath-room were all the same faded piss-yellow and had all been there since 1983. But out the sliding glass door was a narrow balcony with a view of the swimming pool, the marina, the Intracoastal Waterway, and the Atlantic Ocean beyond it, water as far as the eye could see.

"Wow," I said. "Beautiful."

Aaron was holding tight to the doorway. "I used to sleepwalk as a kid," he said. "I was always scared I'd sleepwalk out here in the middle of the night and fall seven stories to my death."

While Aaron used the bathroom, I snuck a peek at the mail he'd picked up. On the top was a credit card bill addressed to him.

It was a strange sensation, learning my boyfriend's last name. It felt like I was uncovering a secret.

Aaron returned from the bathroom, grabbed the stack of mail. In the other bedroom, shirtless, sitting in bed, was Morris. He held a newspaper in front of him. One cat was curled at his feet. Another sat nibbling at one of the little saucers of dried cat food that littered the floor around his bed. Another he called to him—*Pssht pssht pssht*—and I recognized the hand gesture, the way he tapped his thumb, as though pushing a button. The cat came and forced its forehead into his fist.

"Hey, Pop," Aaron said. We stood just outside the doorway. "This is Nell."

"Hello," I said, waving.

He lowered his newspaper and lifted a hand, eyeing me over his glasses. "Hello." He sounded tired. How many girls had Aaron presented in this doorway?

On the elevator down, I said, "He seems nice."

"He's a little crazy," Aaron apologized. "Kind of a mess. That's why I can't leave Florida."

The elevator opened. He looked at me. "Well. It's why I haven't left yet."

When I eventually admitted to my parents how old Aaron was, they feigned shock. Then they shrugged. "Who are we to judge?" my mom laughed. They had a larger age difference than we did. I was the third child, months away from leaving the house; they were old and they were tired. I was *this close* to eighteen. They trusted me. And they liked Aaron.

But Aaron didn't yet know how young I was. How did we not talk about what I did with my day—go to AP Calc and Lit and Art, stay

after school until dark to lay out the newspaper? We talked about music, about movies, about our families, our friends, our jobs. He knew I
was going away to college, he knew I still lived with my parents, but he
didn't want to believe I was so young.

I didn't ask him to my senior prom. I didn't go. I didn't invite him
to my graduation—though I did, finally, tell him that I was graduating.

"Like, from high school?"

"Yes," I said.

"Wow."

"You didn't know I'm in high school?"

"I don't know. I thought maybe you went to community college."

After graduation, he took me out to dinner at TGI Friday's to cele-
brate. His friend's girlfriend waited on our table. She was in the grade
above me; we'd played softball together. See? She was dating an older
guy, too. "Congratulations!" she said to me. "I heard your speech was
awesome." She turned to Aaron. She must have seen his blank face.
"Your girlfriend is the valedictorian," she said approvingly.

When she'd walked away, he looked at me, proud and scolding at
once. "Valedictorian?"

I looked at my plate. "Yeah, I guess."

Why hadn't I told him? Was I scared that he wouldn't want me? Did
I already sense, somehow, that our worlds were not aligned, what an act
of will it would take, for us to fit the facts of our lives together?

We tried to make the most of our summer together. We went to
the beach, the mall, the movies, so many restaurants. He surprised me
on my break at the movie theater, and we sat in his car and ate free
popcorn and talked. We met each other's friends. A friend of mine
started dating his friend Derek, and we went on double dates. It wasn't
so weird, dating an older guy! Everyone was doing it. At night, Aaron
and I put on our bathing suits and snuck into the hot tub at the condo.
We danced to Santana at SunFest, then went home and had sex in his
bed. We had sex in his bed and sex in the hot tub and sex in my parents'
Honda Accord, parked at the beach. He was my first. I did not know
then that there wouldn't be a second.

We spent a lot of time in the car, driving around, Aaron driving me home after a late night at his place. I wanted to wake up next to him. My parents had pushed back the curfew, and pushed it back some more. I begged my mother to let me sleep over. "What can we do at eight in the morning that we can't do at two in the morning? Wouldn't you rather know I'm safe than driving home on I-95 in the middle of the night?" She wasn't stupid. She knew I wasn't going to let up.

"Fine," she said finally. I leapt up and hugged her.

That night, out at dinner, I took a toothbrush out of my purse and presented it to Aaron. His face lit up in a smile.

Then it was our room, our bed.

"I love you," he told me in that bed. His face was hanging close to mine.

I laughed. "I love you, too, you know."

On my eighteenth birthday, I was brushing my teeth when there was a knock at the door. My brother presented with me a giant vase of roses that had been delivered. I smiled around my toothbrush and brought the flowers into the bathroom with me. It was weird, performing our courtship in front of my family, but we were oddly unembarrassed. I still have those flowers, dried, in a glass box in my office.

We drove around. The windows open, driving up the beach, down the highway, in circles, listening to Ween, the Lemonheads, Dinosaur Jr., all the music Aaron was teaching me. One of us would accidentally bring it up—my impending departure—and the car would fill with a sad silence, like a held breath.

"Maybe you should come with me," I said.

I don't know why we chose Colorado. Neither one of us had been there before. It was a kind of test run for Vermont: a weeklong vacation in the mountains. I had taught him, on the desktop in my bedroom, how to use a mouse, and he found a cabin for rent in the Rockies. The executive functioning required to plan this trip was no small task. It required phone calls, mailed checks, plane tickets.

The moment we landed in Denver Aaron started getting sick. He'd had headaches his whole life, terrible ones, but not like this. "That altitude will do it every time," said Richard, the owner of the cabin, as he drove us the hour from the airport. The cabin was sweet and quaint and covered in an outrageously ugly paisley carpet, orange and purple and vomit green, which became the psychedelic background to Aaron's headache. While the rain came down outside, he lay naked in the fetal position in the bed, and I learned to freeze a washcloth for ten minutes and to lay it in a crunchy crown on his forehead, then after he'd melted it, to switch it out for another washcloth in another ten minutes, and so on. I rubbed his back, kissed him, and while he intermittently slept, retreated to my bed to read *The Bluest Eye*. While it pained me to see him in so much pain, I also felt spiritually nourished, wildly in love, and deeply connected to my boyfriend. I was the powerful minister to his pain. I was high. Maybe it was the altitude. I did not know that it was a ritual that we would perform night after night in the years ahead—Aaron moaning along to the mystery that had befallen him, me cooing beside him with a book half-open: *there, there; there, there.*

After twenty-four hours, the headache eased, and he returned to me. Between rainstorms, we hiked. We watched *Seinfeld* on VHS. We washed our clothes in the cast-iron sink and hung them up outside the back door, and nothing had ever made me happier than the sight of our shared laundry—his boxers and athletic socks, my tank tops and bras—the colorful banner of our domestic coupleship.

One morning in the middle of sex, a knock came on the door. It was Richard, who had promised to drive us up to Mount Evans as soon as the rain cleared. The rain hadn't quite cleared, but it had tapered off, a fog hanging heavy behind him. Richard drove us in his little pickup up the steepest, narrowest, crookedest, windiest—and at 14,265 feet—the highest paved road in North America, Aaron and I cramped in the cab beside him, Aaron in the middle, I pressed against the door, the wild and intrepid mountain goats inches from my face, the passing trucks rattling the windows, the road almost entirely pillowed in fog, no guard rails to catch us, just green giving way to August ice and snow and the rock face of our death. Every time another car's headlights approached,

Aaron squeezed my thigh and I squeezed his, not a sweet or tender squeeze but the squeeze of someone trying to extract something difficult to extract, and I thought, if I die on this mountain, my parents will kill me, all while Richard piloted the pickup with the heel of one hand, narrating, pointing. When we got to the top and parked, the fog was so dense we couldn't see a thing. "It's usually a spectacular view," Richard said. He took a picture of us anyway, Aaron shivering in his shirt sleeves, the wind whipping my hair. We looked both miserable and ecstatic to be alive.

And then we had to get in that car and drive back down the mountain.

Later, we lay under the blankets of our rented bed. We were alive, warm, healthy.

"I don't want to say good-bye to you," he said.

"Me neither," I said.

"So let's not."

We laid out the way our life would look together. I would leave for Vermont in a few weeks, and he would let me settle in for a semester before he followed me. My heart bounced around the bed. What about his job? He would quit. (He reminded me that I had said, during our first phone conversation, "What, you don't want to work at CD Warehouse the rest of your life?") What about the cats? He would bring them. He'd find an apartment. He'd find a job. He'd enroll in classes at the community college. He'd always wanted, he said, to be a kindergarten teacher.

A kindergarten teacher! I pictured him in his big pants and a cardigan and a bowtie, a little boy on his knee, a book open before them.

My heart was floating over the bed now, looking down at us. It was joy, it was innocence, the rush of a life glimpsed at its beginning, from the first colorful square on the board. It was also a righteous satisfaction: that I would get him out of Florida. That I would change his life. That I would save him.

We had an early flight back to Florida, so we spent the night at an airport hotel. After Aaron went to bed, I filled the tub and got into the water and cried. I had spent the week desperately happy. I was going to spend, it seemed, the rest of my life with this person; he would be the only man I ever loved. But how could I do that—how could I give him everything—when he had already been in love before?

"I *thought* I was in love before," he'd told me. "Three times."

There were many more girls in his past. But in the bed in Ixora Circle, he'd told me about those three girls he'd thought he loved. The girl with the glasses, who owned the same baby doll dress I did, a patchwork of faded plaids from Contempo Casuals, like a dress that might be worn by a barefoot girl in a factory during the Great Depression. I'd found a picture in a drawer: the girl with the glasses, sitting in a driveway with a bunch of other kids while Aaron and his band tuned up in a garage. They had been engaged, he told me. For a while she had even lived with Aaron in his dad's condo with his dad and his dad's little saucers of cat food, but they had fought a lot, and they called off the engagement and she moved back in with her parents.

There had been another girlfriend, when he was in high school. There was a picture in a drawer of them sitting together on a couch, Aaron in a white Robert Smith shirt, buttoned to his neck, the girl blond and blue-eyed, with hair-sprayed bangs the height of a heavy metal drummer's. Aaron had gone on camping trips with her family, had gone to more than one prom with her, and though their relationship had been innocent, was that maybe even worse, that he had loved her so purely?

The third girlfriend was dead. She had been bipolar. She had been prescribed lithium, which I knew only as a Nirvana song I really liked. The lithium—why did he tell me this?—had increased her sex drive. After they broke up, they were friends. She was working as a stripper in Lake Worth, and one night after work she was raped and murdered. Her body was found in a field behind the strip club, her throat slashed. She was wearing nothing but a pair of sneakers. Her murderer was arrested but never convicted. Soon after, her sister died, and her mother. She had a three-year-old daughter.

There were no pictures of her, but her initials were tattooed on Aaron's wrist.

It had been building for months, this sadness I did not know what to do with. All those girls! He still had the number of a girl whose number he'd gotten at TGI Friday's the week before we met. He'd never called her, but he'd shown me the slip of paper in a fit of hyper-honesty: *Lisa del Rio,* in fat, loopy cursive. A girl who lived in this neighborhood, that neighborhood. Girls who worked in record stores. Brunettes, blondes, the Black Puerto Rican waitress from his mother's restaurant, years older. I had gone to a couple of bases with maybe a dozen zitty guys, ages twelve through seventeen. He had been going to bed with girls for years. How many years? How many girls? Sometimes I tried to torture myself, imagining the number. I would never, ever ask him. I still don't know it.

In the bathtub in Colorado, I cried as loudly as I could, until Aaron woke and came to me and sat on the edge of the tub. I babbled out my teenage sorrow. "I can't take it," I said. "I can't stop thinking about them."

I had wanted and expected him to be consoling, to tell me again that his love for me was beyond what he'd felt for any of them. But I think I already knew that. I wasn't afraid that I would be another girl in a photo in a drawer. I was afraid that I would be with Aaron for the rest of my life and that drawer of photos would follow us. I understood that this was the fate I was choosing. The truth was, as much as I hated Aaron's past lives, I needed them. I needed someone who was carrying around all that heartbreak, all that history, so I could warm my own hands near its flame. That drawer of photos, it felt combustible.

But Aaron sighed. He was tired; he had been sleeping and wanted to go back to bed. "It was a long time ago," he said. "That me didn't have anything to do with you."

Only now do I suspect that he wasn't just tired; he was jaded. It was not the first time he'd had to reassure a girl that he loved her the most.

I packed for college. We sat on the couch and told my parents Aaron was coming with me. They tried caution.

"What happens if you break up?" my mother worried.

I hugged Aaron around the ribs. "We won't."

Middlebury was blazingly beautiful, and I adored all my classes, but I didn't make friends right away. Everyone else seemed to fall in love with their roommate. Everyone else seemed to come from the same New England prep school. On the first night of college, I watched a girl jump on a boy's back and howl across campus together like some mythic eight-foot beast, and I thought, *You just met an hour ago.* For orientation, I chose the three-day hike in the mountains, lacing up the boots I'd bought for Colorado. I struggled to keep up. I told the group leader, a senior, about my boyfriend back home, and she laughed. "I give it until fall break," she said. When we stopped the first night, I asked her to cut my long hair to my chin, and she did, with the first-aid scissors, and I packed out my hair in a Ziploc bag.

I missed Aaron. He sent me a cassette on which he'd taped one track, Billie Holiday's "Everything I Have Is Yours." On a Post-it note, a hand-drawn heart and instructions: *Listen to this on your headphones before you fall asleep tonight.*

I did, while my roommate slept, smiling at his handwriting.

> *Everything that I possess, I offer you*
> *Let my dream of happiness come true*

"I love it," I told him.

We didn't really discuss it. It just became our song.

I listened and listened to it, and cried and cried.

After two weeks, I called him and said, "I want you to come up now." I found an ad for an apartment in the local paper and called to make an appointment, the first call I would make on his behalf. A few days later, my dorm room phone rang at six in the morning, and I pulled on shoes and a sweater and ran out into the September dawn, where Aaron's Pathfinder was idling in the fog. We drove to the closest motel, had sex in the motel bed, and then I cried and cried, not the performative tears of the bathtub but tears of joy, because my love had come to me and because I wasn't only saving him, he was saving me.

He brought me a warm washcloth and pressed it to my face. "I love your haircut," he said.

The next week, I asked a guy in my dorm to buzz what was left of it, and he did. Between my scalp and the coming winter were a few millimeters of hair.

We mailed a picture to my parents. On the phone, that same delight dressed up as shock. "You don't mind that she has no hair?" they teased Aaron.

He told them, "I'd love your daughter if she had no head."

My mother laughed hard. Later she told me that was when she knew he was the one.

DISTEMPER

When performing an image search of "skin disease," "rash," or "lesions," it is best to hold your head as far from the screen as possible, which depending on the length of your arms is approximately three feet. If possible, close one eye. Squeeze the other one shut until you almost can't see out of it. Then scroll fast and don't stop until you've seen all that you cannot unsee. There will be children, just so you know. They live in another country, another time. Their faces aren't even faces anymore.

Compare your husband's lesions to the lesions on the screen. That one's too crusty. This one's too oozy. That one's too uniform, too stippled, too oblong, too yellow.

Conclude that there is no one on the planet with your husband's disease. He is both too original and too damaged to share in anyone else's symptoms—he is above and below others' suffering. Except for the children, whose suffering you scroll by as fast as you can.

This is six years ago, when it started.

Watch him go out to the shitty little AstroTurf porch to smoke and pet the stray cats he's adopted, Prego and Lobster. Count the hours he's out there. When he comes in, smelling of smoke, with a Ziploc sandwich bag full of things coming out of the sores on his body, examine them from a distance of approximately three feet. They look like tiny twigs, like something he might have found on a mulch playground or pulled off the wing of a moth. They look like dust, lint, thread. They look like splinters and ash and bone. Some of them are white. Some of them are red and blue. Sometimes you think you see these things on or in your husband's skin. Mostly you see them once they have already been collected.

Watch him tape them to Post-it notes. Watch him slip them into matchboxes. You have no idea what they are. Find them on the coffee table, in the tool drawer, taped to the inside of the kitchen cabinet.

"Look!" he will say. "Look at this." He holds a tiny magnifying glass to a knuckle. Suddenly he is a person who owns many types of magnifying glasses, loupes, scopes. You peer through the even tinier glass within the glass. "Do you see it?"

"Do I see what?"

"I don't know what! Something! Right there!"

"Stay still."

"Do you see it?"

"I don't know, honey. I see skin."

"That's not skin!"

"I mean, it's a sore. It's not normal skin. But it's skin. I think?"

What is normal? What is foreign? Best to nod, or shrug, or both. Best to say, "I don't know."

It's his mother who first tells you about Morgellons disease. For years she lived in New York but she's in Santa Fe now, in a little adobe house filled with crystals and herbs. She has not been much of a mother to your husband, but she sends gifts to the kids on the holidays—books, birdhouses, cowboy hats—and she tucks in little salves and sachets for her son, sensing, perhaps, some looming malady. She is either supernaturally attuned to the body or she knows nothing; you're not sure. "Look it up," she says, and spells it: M-o-r-g-e-l-l-o-n-s. "Joni Mitchell has it. I'm sending you some emu oil."

You look it up, and there it is. The microscopic fibers, blown up to ten times their size, appear on the screen in full color, as clear as the red and blue wires on a car battery. In forum after forum, patients complain of the same symptoms that have plagued your husband: the pain, the fatigue, the stubborn skin lesions that appear overnight and sprout mysterious fibers in all the colors of the rainbow.

"Oh, my God," you both say, staring at the screen. The lesions look exactly like Aaron's.

You read on. You can't stop reading. It is the jackpot you've been waiting for. There is the interview with Joni Mitchell. "I have this weird, incurable disease that seems like it's from outer space," she says. "Fibers in a variety of colors protrude out of my skin like mushrooms after a rainstorm: they cannot be forensically identified as animal, vegetable or mineral." Yes! you think. You can't resist the imagery, the flattery: your husband is without category, paranormal, an outlier. There is the Charles E. Holman Foundation for Morgellons disease page. There is the story, again and again, of the mother who named the disease, who revived it from a seventeenth-century letter from the English physician Sir Thomas Browne describing an "endemial distemper of little children" in France. Endemial distemper! You don't know what this means but it sounds like your husband.

But then, on page after page, is doctor after doubting doctor, who say that Morgellons disease is a fiction. The symptoms are in the patients' heads. There is the *Washington Post* article, the CNN coverage, and finally, in January 2012, the CDC study, which concludes—again, try to read the words as far from the screen as possible—that these patients don't have fibers in their skin, or bugs, or bacteria. They have delusional parasitosis. The recommendation? Psychiatric care. Antidepressants.

Notice your stomach dropping. Take a deep breath.

You try to read the skepticism with skepticism. Look at your husband. He's not well. He's not himself. And yet look at the things his body is producing. He didn't make them up!

You must make a choice. Are you with the deluded patients? Or the unfeeling doctors?

You are a writer and a professor of fiction—you love a good sci-fi monster; you love, too, a good underdog: your imagination believes the world is bigger than what we know of it.

But you are also a professor of rhetoric and composition. You believe in science. You believe in research. What is it you're always telling your students about supporting their arguments with evidence?

As it happens, your husband is the one to decide for you. He makes his choice quickly, chastened. He does not want to be with the crazy people. He stops collecting the fibers. He throws away the quart-sized bottles of emu oil that have sat unopened in the cabinet, because he definitely does not want to be with his mother.

Still, his skin doesn't heal. Knowing what it isn't doesn't help.

The only thing that seems to help? Alcohol. "You need to relax, honey," your father tells him one day when he comes to visit and pours Aaron a glass of bourbon. He hasn't been much of a drinker since you met him, but he accepts the glass, and then another. He doesn't love bourbon, but he falls back in love with gin. The quart bottles begin to appear in the cabinet, in the recycling bin, on the kitchen counter. Blue gin the color of mouthwash.

Watch him relax. Watch the sores fade to rosy scars. Watch his belly stretch wide and hard. Watch him sleep on the couch, on the cot he has set up downstairs. Give him some space. Sleep in your bed with your baby, nursing him all day and night. Nurse him while you half-sleep, while he half-sleeps. Watch the wall grow between you and your baby's father, too tall to scale. Stand in the kitchen with your husband. Almost without words, agree that you need to return to couples counseling. The first time, in Charlottesville, didn't really count.

You choose the first man's name you see in the yellow pages. Stu. On his voice mail recording, he has a voice like a game show host's.

In the waiting room there is a chocolate-covered suede love seat, a bottle of Cherry Almond Jergens, a well-maintained selection of *People* magazines, and more M&M paraphernalia than you have ever seen. Inside the office are M&M pillows, M&M candy machines, M&M cups and salt shakers and picture frames. Your homework was to bring a list of ten things you like about the other, and ten things you are unhappy about. The first item on your first list is *He makes me laugh*. The first item on your second list is *Chaos*. You can barely articulate further. It is written on a sheet of your son's Spider-Man note paper.

Who knows if it helps? You keep going. Your insurance doesn't cover acupuncture but, praise be, it covers every cent of couples counseling. Instead, you spend the money on a sitter, every Wednesday at three o'clock. Stu has a salt-and-pepper beard, a Queens accent, white sneakers, and a gold chain. On the stereo he plays the Grateful Dead. He tells you he was a medic at Woodstock. "He definitely did mad drugs," your husband jokes in the car on the way home, because doing mad drugs is something you still joke about.

Watch your husband drink. Watch your husband sleep on the cot. Watch your husband grow so big that, one night, he breaks it. Watch him rage and cry in shame.

Watch *The Bachelor*. The sexiest thing about the Bachelor is that he owns a vineyard. Drink red wine, but just a little. Your son is nursing, always, at your open bathrobe. You have an excuse, because suddenly your mother is dying of lung cancer. Your mother, who smoked a pack a day while pregnant with you. A little glass of wine can't be so bad.

Your father turns eighty. At your brother's house in Virginia, where your parents live, the whole family surprises him, grandsons running around like puppies, your other brother sitting with your baby in his lap, letting him hold his empty beer bottle. Watch the hospice nurses come with their oxygen and meds. Wash your mother's hair. Cut it. Slice off a crescent of your left thumb. She would have been the one to clean the wound, if she were all there. But she isn't all there. She is going. She is breathing on one lung. You want to breathe for her, to inflate her lung through the nipple, like a balloon. "Good-bye," she says before you leave. "You are wonderful children."

Come back the next week, after she's gone. Find your father sitting on the couch eating pistachio ice cream. Find your baby book. "13 months. Weaned Nell. She's mad at me." Sleep with your baby in her bed, his body an anchor against your ribs, a bullet-proof vest. Nurse him. Drink in the vinegar sweat of his matted hair on the damp sheet.

When your mother dies, your husband quits smoking. He loved her, your mother. And you love him for quitting. But he does not quit drinking. Your husband is no longer diseased, but he is an alcoholic. "You're an alcoholic," you tell him, realizing as you say it that this is what he is.

Watch him realize it, too. Watch him rage and cry. Listen to him admit it. Watch him pour the blue gin down the drain. Listen to his promises.

It brings you some comfort that the therapist is as surprised as you are.

Well, your husband has taken pains to mask it. There had been so many drugs before you were in the picture—acres and acres of drugs. Cocaine and mushrooms and LSD, liquor bottles carpeting his teenage bedroom. You had thought, silly girl, that they were in the past tense. You had seen the tattoo artist affix the straight edge tattoos!

The first stash you found was in college. Pot. "Just don't hide it from me" became the refrain, so for a while he didn't. For ten years, he smoked his pot in the open. He said it made him less sad, so it made you feel less sad, too.

Then, the text messages. You don't even want to touch his phone in the first place. But your own phone is dead or broken or lost when you pick his up from the bookshelf to set the alarm for the next morning and discover the texts from a woman with an abbreviated name, an alias, it seems. You don't know what her name is, but you know that your husband is calling her *sweetie* and planning to meet up with her, for he's gotta get out of this house soon.

You drop the phone. It may as well be a gun. Always something else. Always some other secret, ready to discharge in your hands.

You wake him, present him with the evidence. He begs forgiveness but does not explain. He is actually down on his knees. He didn't get down on one knee to propose, but here he is now, begging. It feels appropriate. You say *maybe*. You are in your bathrobe.

Go to Boston for a conference. Cry on the phone to your friends. Is there any forgiveness? You feel as though you've been drowned.

On the phone in your hotel, listen to your husband admit who the woman was. Is? The ex-girlfriend with the glasses. Married to someone else now but still knocking on the door.

You've always suspected that the reason your husband didn't get down on one knee is because he got down on one knee for her. That it would feel dishonest, or something.

Listen to your husband try out the phrase *emotional affair*. There are still unresolved feelings there. There is guilt and blame, wounds to heal, and forgiveness, yes. A door reopened. He will close it now.

You aren't still that teenage girl, are you, so jealous of those exes you can't see straight? You are a full-grown woman in a conference hotel, with a dead mother and a hangover. Think about going downstairs to try to pick up a guy in the bar. So many writers hooking up with other writers, fish drawn to fish. How do you even do that? You feel like Ruth in Lorrie Moore's story "Real Estate": "The idea of taking her clothes off and being with someone who wasn't a medical specialist just seemed ridiculous." You don't want to have a revenge affair. You miss your babies and your bathrobe. You don't want anyone else. You just want things—everything—to be different.

Return home. Drop your suitcase at the door. How can you not try, with these beautiful boys you've made together, hugging your knees?

For a few weeks, there is peace. He carries your suitcase up the stairs. He does the laundry, the dishes. He gives you space. He sleeps on the couch.

And then, weeks after he's poured the gin down the sink, you find something else. Your heart has learned to seize up. It recognizes the fear like an old enemy. Not a text message, but a stash. Buried in the back of the bathroom drawer is a darling little balsa-wood box, and inside is a metal cigarette and a lighter and some little straw scraps—you are such a square—that look to you like pot.

"It's not pot," he says. "It's an herb. I got it online."

"Then why were you hiding it?"

"Because you'd be mad!"

For a week he stays at the hotel by the mall with the ugly turquoise roof. It's the first time you worry, really worry, that he will kill himself. It's a feeling of panic in the stomach. He comes home to visit the kids, and then you drop him off in the hotel parking lot, and you scream alone in the car, sure he will die. So you ask him to come home. Anyway, the money has run out. You can no longer afford the hotel.

Why is he spending so much time in the bathroom? You can't find another balsa-wood box, but it almost doesn't matter. You have become a crazy woman, searching everywhere, trusting no one, a small forest rodent, vigilant of every predator, every sound. One night you are sitting at the kitchen table in your bathrobe with a towel on your head when you see him smile weakly from across the room. It is a smile he puts on. The smile of a child who hopes his mother will feed him. He wants forgiveness, or affirmation, but you realize you have neither. "I have nothing left to give," you tell him.

You are planning to leave town tomorrow to visit your family in Virginia. Tell your husband, "You can stay here. I'll take the kids with me." But he doesn't want to stay here. His smile turns to rage. He grabs his jacket and keys and is gone before you can stop him, peeling out of the driveway in your shitty little Kia.

All night, all bad night, in bed in your bathrobe with your baby, you have that feeling you had while he stayed in the hotel with the turquoise roof. Is that where he is now? You call all night. Finally, in the morning, he picks up the phone. That fucking phone. He sounds half dead. "I just want to make sure that it's true," he says.

"That what's true?"

"That it's over," he says.

"Yes," you recite. The words are like wax. "I'm sorry. It's over."

He hangs up the phone.

You dress yourself. You dress your children. You invite Emily over for lunch. She lives in the apartment in your house. She brings over her daughter. You make peanut butter sandwiches. You busy yourself, your stomach a pit of worry. When he bursts in the door, the children are playing with Play-Doh in the kitchen. Emily takes one look at him and shepherds the kids upstairs. He won't look at you. He rummages, he rages. He finds his backpack. He pushes into the kitchen. He's standing at the sink when he turns and looks at you, his eyes wide with black joy. The word you think is "monster." "I'm going to do it," he says.

"No," you say. "No no no no no!"

But he is outside before you can stop him. You know what he's going to do but you don't know how he's going to do it. So you make a choice. Follow him, or stay in the house with your children. When he comes back to the door, the door to the kitchen on the shitty AstroTurf porch, and jiggles the knob, he will find that you have locked it. He looks at you through the glass. You shake your head. He looks back at you with hate. And then he is gone again.

The 911 operator wants to know how your husband is trying to kill himself. You say, "I think he's taking pills." You can't see him through the door. He has the car door open in the driveway, and he's hidden behind it. It's the middle of the morning on a Saturday in April.

The ambulance is there within minutes, the police cars, the fire truck. You watch through the window as they load him into the back and drive him away. He looks, you think hopefully, alive.

Emily comes downstairs and holds you and now that it's over you let yourself cry. "Thank God for you," you say. The children have seen nothing.

And Emily whispers to you then that her ex-husband, her daughter's father, tried to do it once, tried to hang himself from a shower rod. "Don't worry," she says reasonably. "It's hard to kill yourself." And it's true—it's hard to overdose on antidepressants. If he'd come back into the house for the Ativan, he might not have been so lucky.

Put the kids in the car. Drive the six hours to your brother's house. Sit in the backyard in the sun, because even though it's still winter in Ithaca, spring has arrived in Virginia. Tell your eighty-year-old father what has happened. Listen to him tell you about the time he ended up in Bellevue after a woman left him and he tried to kill himself, too. His friends found him days later in his apartment, OD'd on pills, nearly dead. Your gentle, brilliant father, shirtless in a lawn chair, his sun-stretched skin. Watch the backyard spin. Think how your father lived a whole life before he met your mother. Think how close you were to not being.

Imagine the first time your father told your mother this story. Did it make her love him more?

Call your husband's mother and tell her. Listen to her say, "I knew this would happen." Listen to her say, "It's that Morgellons. It's destroyed his brain."

Don't correct her. Don't remind her that she abandoned him at six years old, leaving him with a father who destroyed him. Don't say, "You might as well have dumped those pills down his throat."

Try not to pay attention to your love for him. Remember that he's transformed into a monster. Don't wonder if he can transform back.

Leave your kids with your family. Say, "Thank God for you." Drive home and spend the week looking for an apartment. Bring your friend Katie. Thank God for her, for all the women in the world.

Visit him in the psych ward. Tell him he looks nice in his scrubs. Already the weight of the gin is vanishing from his body, but there is his body, he has one, blood washing through his veins. His skin is clear and healthy. His eyes sparkle and fizz. When he says, "I want to kiss you," don't let him yet. First, remember the way he looked at you when you were seventeen, over the counter at the record store. Wonder if the monster has been, somehow, killed. Wonder if he didn't kill himself but killed the monster.

A few weeks later, your husband is alive and out of the psych ward and in a rehab program and back in the house, and then a few weeks later, back in your bed. You make dinner for your family. You invite Emily and her daughter and her ex-husband, who is back in her bed, too. There is soup and bread and blueberry pie, which your baby smudges over his lip in a mustache in his high chair. The kitchen shakes with laughter. Your baby laughs back. You think how lucky you are, to have made it intact. To have a second chance. For years afterward, you will pass by the streets you might have moved to, without him. Your ghost lives there, in all those houses. You don't tell your husband you've been inside.

And then one night a few weeks later still, after Emily has moved out of the apartment in your house and into a new one, after she argues with her ex-husband and leaves his house, her ex-husband hangs himself again, and this time he does it right. Their daughter, four years old, now has no father. It's days later, but you rush to her new apartment as though there still might be flames to put out. There are women there already, a team of them, washing the dishes, brushing Emily's hair, reading to her daughter. What is this, the suicide response team? It's her friends from AA, you realize. An evil part of you is jealous that they have beat you here to demonstrate their love and support. Another evil part of you is relieved, so relieved—this little tableau could have been yours. Hug her. Feel sick. Say, "I'm sorry. I'm so sorry." You have switched nightmares.

SEYMOUR STREET

1997

n Vermont, when I was in college, we lived in three apartments in three years, all of them on Seymour Street. The first was a one-bedroom in a yellow house above an architect's office, around the corner from the post office. It was brand-new, with A-frame walls and baseboard heaters and a clean white kitchen where we made spinach and feta quesadillas every night. We weren't supposed to have cats, but we did. I sent my parents a picture of our bedroom, the queen mattress on the floor, the light coming through the lavender tapestry I'd hung in the window. "Why would you send me that?" my mother asked.

One day I came home from class and climbed the outdoor steps and found Aaron sitting on the floor—we didn't yet have a couch—with a stack of Toni Morrison novels beside him. He'd spent the last three days reading every one of them.

Another day, I came home from school and found a white Pottery Barn couch sitting in our living room. Aaron had had it delivered as a surprise.

It's safe to say it was a happy time.

It wasn't that I hadn't tried to live in the dorm. My roommate was nice enough. But she had a boyfriend, too, and they had ostentatious sex in her twin bed. When I knocked, her boyfriend would say, "Don't worry! We're definitely not having sex in here!" At least an hour a day, my neighbor played Third Eye Blind at full volume. And then there was the whole part about going to the bathroom beside other people and wearing flip-flops in the shower. None of it appealed to me when presented with the alternative of a Pottery Barn couch.

I made a choice. A nice guy from my freshman seminar showed up at my door one evening and asked if I wanted to hang out at his dorm and drink some wine with friends. "I don't really drink," I said, and closed the door.

Within a few weeks I was living permanently at Aaron's. He was both a comfort from my home life and a promise of something more exciting than the campus life I thought I'd wanted.

It was a year of firsts. We bought our first dining room table. We got our first email addresses. We almost got in our first car accident and traded the rear-wheel-drive Pathfinder for a used gold Range Rover. One weekend morning, I woke up, walked to the bathroom, and looked out the window to see that it had snowed overnight. The sun was shining, and the tree limbs were glassed in white. It was my first snowfall, and it was magical. Us two Florida kids dressed in our parkas and went downstairs and built our first snowman in front of the architects' door.

We buried our first cat, a calico stray we'd adopted that I'd let out late at night and forgotten to call inside. I spotted her through the window the next morning, dead in the snow on the side of the road. We borrowed a shovel from the architects and drove out in the woods. We couldn't dig very deep; the ground was too frozen. We cried a lot. My tears were tears of grief and also guilt.

I got my first college job. In high school, I'd taken art classes at the local community center, where I stood around with senior citizens drawing strangers. If seeing nakedness as art made one an adult, then *being* that naked art seemed a mark of even more advanced maturity. So in my first weeks of college, when I was looking for a job on campus, I circled the ad for "nude model." Plus, how cool would I look, a nude model with a shaved head?

But Aaron got mad when I said I wanted to apply. (What would the application process look like, though? Do you have a body? Can you stand for a long time?) He didn't want me standing naked in front of a bunch of college boys.

I raged at the injustice, his small-mindedness and chauvinism.

I also understood and craved his protectiveness. I needed him to need me all to himself. I wouldn't want to share his naked body, either.

Instead, I got a job at the local bakery. Anyway, it was our first fight.

When I'd first arrived, I had scoped out the retail options for Aaron. For some reason I'd pictured him working at the army surplus store downtown, selling backpacks and hats and hiking pants. But he didn't like something about the guy who owned the place. Aaron had asked him who the owner was so he could get an application, and the guy said *he* was the owner, rather rudely, Aaron thought. Young and entitled, was Aaron's estimation.

Meanwhile Aaron's rich aunt had given him an old diamond ring with which to propose to the girl with the glasses, and when they broke off the engagement, the girl with the glasses had given him the ring back, and his aunt had let him keep it. I didn't know this until he'd sold it for $6,000, an amount of money that made me ill to contemplate. I didn't like knowing that we were dining out on the money acquired through his ex's engagement ring. Then again, I didn't want the engagement ring around, either. I certainly didn't want him to recycle it on *me*. Two thousand dollars of the money he spent on a new keyboard. He said he thought he deserved it. His father was sending him $500 a month, which covered the rent. It seemed to be a temporary allowance until it wasn't. It seemed a generous gesture, that his father covered the rent, and then odd, and then embarrassing. It was the least his father could do, Aaron said. I remember thinking that it was an odd thing to justify, and yet also sensing that he was right—that he'd been wronged somehow by his family—and that this keyboard, this rent money, was his compensation.

For months, I circled the ads in the Classifieds. I left them on the dining room table, in the magazine basket in the bathroom. I pointed out the HELP WANTED signs in the windows. Aaron always had an excuse. He would apply eventually, or the job wasn't quite right, or he didn't want to go back to retail, or there were no good options in this tiny town. He wasn't angry, exactly. He seemed to be nursing some greater injury, some resentment for what the world owed him. I couldn't tell what the source of it was, only knew from instinct that I had to walk on eggshells. In this way, we managed to avoid conflict for a while. I observed his pain and respected it, even if I hadn't begun to understand it.

"We don't really fight," I tried to explain to my friend Jen on the phone. "We just kind of get sad."

That fall, I helped him study for the GED. Look how smart he was, when he applied himself! When given the tools! He passed the test and got his certificate in the mail, and that spring he enrolled in two classes at the community college, on his father's GI Bill. He started out strong. We did our homework side by side on the couch. Then he fell behind in computer science. He got pissed at his English teacher for implying that his Middlebury girlfriend might be writing his papers for him.

I wasn't writing them for him. I was maybe helping him find his voice.

Then one day I found some porn videos in the closet. I felt my stomach drop. I put them back, shut the door. I tried to unsee what I'd seen.

It wasn't really the porn. I was mature enough not to be shocked that my boyfriend owned pornography. I was angry and hurt that he'd hid them. I felt the rug pulled out from under me: that we'd shared everything, that I knew him inside and out. And yet he'd had a secret.

Okay, it kind of was the porn. When I looked at the pictures on the back of the VHS, what I saw was all the girls he'd been to bed with. Copulation and its attendant positions were not in fact the sacred invention of me and my boyfriend but had a long and colorful history to which I was an innocent latecomer.

I wasn't mature enough to tell him so. I couldn't even confront him. Instead, I huffed and puffed through his paper that night, guilt-tripping him, making him feel inferior, making him need my help. Finally, in the morning, I said, "I found your porn." It was an accusation. I had been simmering all night. I was pissed. I'd wanted the upper hand: not only had he lied to me; now I could lord it over him that I'd spent all night sweating over his paper.

"Jesus," he said. "Tim sent me those! It was a joke!"

Oh. "Then why'd you hide them?"

"So you wouldn't get mad like you are now! Jesus, it's just porn. All night I thought you were mad because you didn't want to help me!"

We fought, yelling at each other, accusing each other of betrayal, sabotage, manipulation. I had a class to get to, and we fought as he drove me to campus. I slammed the car door, slipping, spilling my thermos of coffee in the snow. "Go find a college boy!" he yelled at me and drove away.

Okay, so we did fight.

He didn't accept my help with any assignments after that. He was a few weeks from finishing his first semester when he stopped going to class.

But that spring, he finally found a job, in the afterschool program of an elementary school. For three hours every afternoon, he helped kids with their homework, played kickball on the playground, and made friends with the farm kids of Vermont. It seemed one step closer to his dream of being a teacher. I was relieved.

"What's he do the rest of the day?" my boss asked me. She was looking for someone for the lunch shift.

I loved my job at the bakery. I washed and dried the dishes, returning all the utensils to the special jars and drawers where they lived. I took sandwich orders and made them—*whole wheat, honey oat, sourdough, rye, or French?* I shook the rugs and rolled the croissants and made cappuccinos with just the right amount of foam. But Aaron had made it clear he didn't want our work worlds to collide.

"He writes music," I told my boss. I didn't say that he hung out at the coffee shop. That he copied videos of hardcore shows he'd taped in Burlington and sold them online. That he drove his Range Rover through the woods, and tended to it, moisturizing its leather seats, bottle-feeding it high-octane fuel, memorizing its exotic British parts.

When he got a second job, at a TV station, I felt like I could breathe. It was still just part-time, but we were both, more or less, pulling our weight. We drove to Burlington. We watched *Days of Our Lives.* We

ate at every restaurant in town. All of the waitstaff had crushes on him.
The waitress at the Mexican restaurant, who'd been in his class, once put
black pepper on my black bean pizza. And the waiter at the place with
open-faced sandwiches once rubbed Aaron's back as he took his order.
Aaron stopped wearing his silver hoop earrings after that, and I started
growing my hair out.

Sometimes I snuck him into the dining hall on campus. We ate in
the lobby downstairs on our orange trays. We always felt like we were
trespassing, because we kind of were.

It was easier to be in our universe on Seymour Street. We were out-
liers. Our litter box overflowed.

Sophomore year, I chose a dorm based on its proximity to a parking
lot, which meant my boyfriend could drop me off with ease. No one
really lived off campus, and certainly not sophomores, so I had to keep
a room. It was a single, but I never used it, except to store stuff I didn't
need.

My mother's cousin, at my mother's urging, had invited us to
Thanksgiving dinner in New Hampshire. We'd accepted the invitation,
but then the Rover was in the shop again. We were on a first-name basis
with the rental place down the street called Lemons 4 U. No lemons
were available the week of Thanksgiving, so my mother's cousin had
kindly arranged for a family friend, who was driving from Burlington,
to swing by and pick us up in Middlebury. I was wearing a new dress
Aaron had bought me after I'd seen it in the window of Banana Repub-
lic, purple velvet with a V-neck. My hair was in the Chia pet phase, but
that dress made me feel pretty.

I wasn't really sure what was bothering Aaron. He didn't want to go
to Thanksgiving dinner. I thought it was very clear and very obvious
that we had to go, that we should go. What else were we going to do? "I
don't know how to be around family," he said. And we were vegetarian.
What were they serving? The whole idea seemed miserable to him.

The family friend picked us up and we cruised along. Aaron was silent in the backseat. The friend was a nice guy, young and long-haired, a Burlington kid you could almost smell the weed on. He seemed not much more familiar with the family we were going to see than we were. We were strangers driving into the unknown.

Perhaps thirty miles from Middlebury, the family friend pulled over to get gas. Aaron saw his opportunity. "I'm leaving," he said, getting out of the car.

"What do you mean, you're leaving?"

"Don't worry. I'll find my way home."

"Don't do this," I said.

"I'm sorry," he said.

And my future husband walked down the highway and disappeared.

"Where's he going?" the family friend asked, getting back in the car.

"I don't know." I sat in the passenger seat in my velvet dress and began to cry. "I'm sorry. I don't know what just happened."

"Should we go after him?" he asked. But it was too late.

We began to drive. The Vermont landscape passed by our windows, leafless and gray.

The family friend shrugged with understanding. "Relationships are hard."

It was a great kindness he extended to me, the little bit of language he offered to describe the indescribable abandonment, bafflement, and embarrassment I felt just then. We drove along, chitchatting. I felt that I had left my heart on the highway. And yet I was safe in the car, sniffling and listening to the radio and talking to a person I'd met an hour before. I trusted him to get me where I needed to go.

The next day, my mother's cousin drove me back to Middlebury. Like my grandfather, he was a political science professor. Was I registered to vote? Did I know what an exciting time it was in politics now, with a socialist Vermonter named Bernie Sanders in the Senate? I wasn't and I didn't, I was ashamed to admit. My mother's cousin's arm was amputated above the elbow. When he was a kid, he had grabbed an electric wire while climbing a tree. When I was a kid, I had rebuilt a beaver dam with him at the lake where our family had a cabin, and that was how I remembered him, swashbuckling through the water, heaving logs with one arm and a stump. I didn't know how to build a beaver dam and I wasn't registered to vote and my boyfriend had left me with a stranger and hitchhiked home. I felt so clueless.

We pulled up to the little yellow house. My mother's cousin had to pee. So he came upstairs, shook Aaron's hand, and went in to use the bathroom. Aaron and I stood awkwardly outside the door. I didn't know where to begin. *Where did you go?* might have been a good start. *What the fuck is wrong with you?* would have been something.

Then my mother's cousin hurried out and drove away, and only then did I see that the shower curtain was open and at the bottom of the shower was a giant cat turd.

That fall, I was enrolled in Intro to Drawing. A nude model came in from time to time to pose for us. She was a freshman named Eleanor. I wondered if she had a boyfriend.

For one assignment, I created four paper and fabric collages. It was a knockoff of Matisse's paper cut-outs and of my mother's acrylic paintings of figures in bed. Each of the four pieces of paper depicted a couple in the same bedroom—sometimes in embrace, sometimes with distance between them—and a season revealing itself in a window. Snow, flowers, sun, leaves. I connected the four collages with tape, like four images on a strip of film, and then I shaped them into a cylinder, so there was no beginning and no end.

When it was my turn to present my creation to the class, I said, "I wanted to show the perennial nature of love."

To my professor's credit, he didn't laugh. He didn't cringe or raise an eyebrow. Instead, he thoughtfully critiqued my method. Was the sculpture to be viewed from the outside, or inside? It was like a wheel, but you could see the inside, the seams, the tape. Here he did cringe.

What did that nineteen-year-old know about the perennial nature of love? My professor must have wondered. I want to laugh at that girl, critique her method. I didn't know the details of what the next twenty years would bring. But after living through one cycle of seasons with my future husband, I already knew the story. He will go away, and return, go away, and return.

Aaron was straight edge when we met. His body was covered in straight edge tattoos. In Burlington, I watched more straight edge tattoos go on his body. In Burlington, we went to straight edge matinees. I wasn't really straight edge, but I didn't drink or do drugs, either. I'd let my senior-year experimentation fade when I met Aaron. I wasn't trying to escape my life anymore; I was living the life I'd wanted to escape into.

Like a lot of straight edge kids, Aaron came to the scene—and then left it, and then got into it again—after doing a lot of drugs. He'd done all the drugs, to be exact. Well, everything but heroin, he clarified. Nothing like that. There were some he liked more than others. But all of them were packaged in the distant cubby of the past. Straight edge was a narrative—a savior narrative, the story of saving oneself—that allowed him to see his life to that point, his twenty-something years, as containing a Before and After.

I found the weed in his desk drawer. I was looking for some papers. It was in a plastic baggie with a lighter in a hanging file folder. As soon as I saw it, I closed the drawer, walked to the bedroom, and forgot it.

Maybe part of my brain didn't register what it was. I was the naïve girl, after all, who had once carried a large bong-shaped box into the Bob Marley music festival for my friends while they snickered behind my back. But most of my brain knew what my eyes had seen. It's just that my brain didn't want to see it. I was like a possum playing dead. We call this "denial," or sometimes "survival."

A few hours later I woke up from my possum death and a curtain rose in my head. I walked back to the desk drawer and opened it. There it was, hanging in the file folder. I hadn't imagined it.

That evening, I heard him on the phone. I listened to him from across the house. My brain didn't want to listen, so I made my ears do it. He was soft-spoken, pleading, matter of fact. He had run out of something, and he needed it.

"Who were you talking to?" I asked when he hung up.

"A friend," he said.

"What were you talking about?"

He paused for just a beat. "VHS cases."

"VHS cases? You've run out of VHS cases?"

He looked at me and knew I knew.

"I found your pot," I said.

We didn't fight that time. He didn't deny it. He was defeated. He was sorry he'd lied to me. He had been smoking pot. He felt that he needed it. He was sad all the time. It made him feel better.

I thought of the Rimbaud poem I'd read after our first date. All the exclamation marks, all the O's.

It had appealed to me, this sadness, when it had been merely figurative. I liked thinking of Aaron as a lost boat. I could steer him to shore.

But now I didn't know what to do.

"I'm sleeping in the dorm tonight," I said.

"Why?"

"Because you kept something from me."

"But I kept something from you because I'm sad."

I rode my bike to the dorm and cried and slept in my lonely bed.

We had to break up, I reasoned. He'd lied to me and now we would break up.

FAMILY OF ORIGIN

like to think I came by my denial honestly.

I liked growing up in my house, because we didn't have to go to church and could swear. My mom was an artist and a secretary at the elementary school and later a teacher. My dad was an architect and a photographer. He built every piece of furniture in the house. In Gainesville, where we lived until I was eight, they had a studio in our garage, where my dad smoked a pipe and sketched buildings, and my mom smoked cigarettes and painted canvases of figures with no faces. "Can't you put just a nose on one?" I wondered. Our bathroom was a darkroom where my father developed his photos. My friends were always scared to go in there. Many of them told me years later that they had watched their first R rated movie at my house. We farted freely. That was enough openness to fool me into thinking we were a functional family. A little weird, but functional.

I mean, we functioned. We paid the bills, went to school, made art, shot hoops in the driveway. We decorated the Christmas tree. We ate macaroni and cheese and hot dogs, sometimes in the same dish. We rode bikes all over the neighborhood. We drove from Florida to Vermont in a Volkswagen Rabbit, our stinky dog, Wheezer, at our feet, our parents smoking the whole way. We loved each other and often said so. All of the things we said were well and good, but we were not saying all of the things.

When the things were hard, I think it was hard for my parents to talk to us. They tried. When I was eleven, my mom gave me the puberty talk as we floated in our swimming pool, our elbows resting on a raft between us. Around the same time, she took me on a walk and told me that her brother, Peter, was dying of AIDS. Around the same time, in the pool—what was it about that neutral, watery territory that would seem to protect us?—my father told me he was thinking about moving out. I was shocked. I'd had no idea, and no idea how to respond. I stepped out of the water in my leopard-print one piece and ran inside, sobbing, or pretending to. That night, I told him I didn't want him to go, and he hugged me and told me that maybe he just needed to hear that. He didn't move out, and I didn't hear anything else about it.

My parents' reticence was practiced and well-intentioned. My brother had been adopted at a week old, when my parents assumed they couldn't have children. When it turned out my mother could get pregnant—only one of her fallopian tubes was blocked—my other brother was born, and then me. We were born into the universe of my parents' making, and that included the fact that Pete was their child as much as Sam and I were. Of course he was. Somehow we all knew Pete was adopted, and somehow we all knew that to acknowledge it was to risk his belonging. It was a kind of radical acceptance.

Sometimes silence doesn't feel like a gift, though. Sometimes it feels like shame.

When Uncle Peter died, I found out sideways. For weeks my mother was tied up on the phone, sitting at her desk and talking to him, talking to her other siblings. He was a country away in San Francisco, but all of their other siblings went to see him one last time. "You'll hate yourself if you don't come see me," he told her. I rarely saw her cry, but she cried when she told me this. Why didn't she go? I wondered. Then one day my friend was over and we were looking at the family photographs hanging over my mother's desk. My mother pointed to the one of her brothers and said, "He just died this morning."

I looked at her, startled. "He died, Mom?"

She nodded.

"How'd he die?" my friend wanted to know.

My mother told her, "AIDS." She pointed to the picture of my uncle's "lover," as she called him.

"Gross," my friend said.

For the life of me, I did not know what to say, to reprimand my friend, to comfort my mother, though I have thought of a few things since then.

When our dog died a few years later, it was the same. "Where's Wheezer?" I asked, looking under beds and tables.

Sam told me, "They put him down two days ago."

In this way, my mother taught me how to avoid conflict, and death, and difficulty. How to tolerate the differences of others, the sadness of others. You don't question it. You don't talk about it. You give it a very wide berth. Otherwise, you insult their legitimacy. You threaten the order.

Where did she learn that unquestioned loyalty? From her own mother? Her alcoholic father?

If you want to talk to your father, my grandmother told her children, *do it before noon.* After that, he was too far gone.

My grandmother, who suffered from psoriasis. Her hands were covered with it. Immediately after my grandfather died, my mother told me, it cleared.

She had stood by her man, her sick and brilliant man, as my mother did when it was her turn.

Four years before my father told me in my brother's backyard that he'd once tried to kill himself, I sat with my mother on the same patio. She was smoking a cigarette at the table under the hood of an umbrella. It was dark, our voices were hushed, the baby was sleeping inside. Aaron was back home in Charlottesville. We were having a hard time. I was as desperate as I'd ever let myself be in front of my mother. I admitted to her that we'd just started seeing our first couples' counselor. I saw her make a calculation as she breathed in a lungful of smoke.

"Your father and I were in therapy at one time."

I sat up straight. "Really?"

"Well. Not really a therapist. We saw Simon Katz."

"Simon?" He was my friend's father. Their family had lived next door to us in Gainesville. "Wasn't he just a regular doctor?"

"We wanted someone we knew. It was different then. This was after we'd both moved." For months, she said, they had driven the hour from North Palm Beach to Ft. Lauderdale to meet with their trusted friend.

"When was this?"

"You were maybe eleven."

"Was it when Daddy said he was leaving?"

My mom whipped her head toward me. "He told you that?"

I told her what he'd told me that day in the pool. "He didn't tell me why," I said. "What was that all about?"

She took a careful puff. "Your father had an episode."

"What kind of episode?"

"A paranoid schizophrenic episode."

I looked at her. With the hand that wasn't smoking the cigarette, she ran her finger over her lips.

"Paranoid about what?"

She gave her head a shake toward the night sky. "Oh, I could never say."

I tried to get my head around it. She couldn't say because she didn't know? Or she *wouldn't* say? It was the first I'd heard of any mental imbalance on my father's part.

I tried to remember what our house had been like when I was eleven. Where was I when my parents were in secret therapy? Did they go while I was in school? Did my brothers babysit?

"Your Uncle Peter was dying," she said.

"Oh." I saw the memories slide into place. My leopard-print bathing suit. My mother on the bone-colored telephone. "It was then."

"It was why I couldn't go see him." She stubbed out her cigarette. It gave a little white fizz in the dark. "I had to choose. I chose to stay with you kids. And with your father."

THE PINK CLOUD

sat in the circle, looking at everyone's shoes. It was summer in Ithaca: Keens, Tevas, Crocs. A fan churned in the corner. The slurp of iced coffee.

"Is there anyone here for their first Al-Anon meeting?"

I was there with Katie. We gave each other nervous smiles as we half-raised our hands. "Hi." My voice sounded like a child's. "I'm Eleanor."

"Hi, Eleanor," said the room. It was the singsong cadence of schoolchildren greeting their teacher. But they were like the schoolteachers, older women mostly, mothers and grandmothers with white-blond hair in practical bobs, books and purses and thermoses balanced in their ample laps. It had been four months since my mother had died, and two months since my husband had tried to overdose in the driveway. "Welcome," they said, and already I was crying.

These women! They had been coming to Al-Anon meetings, some to this very room—*the rooms,* they said—for ten, twenty, thirty years. The rooms had saved their lives. They had grown children who were addicted to alcohol, meth, heroin, who were in rehab, or jail, or finally coming home. They had custody of their grandchildren. They had brothers and mothers and husbands and wives who were alcoholics. Some were active alcoholics. Some were in recovery. They had left spouses and stayed with them. It almost seemed irrelevant, whether they had stayed or left. The point was, you could stay, or leave. You still came to the rooms. The important thing was to *detach with love.*

If I'd had a notebook, I would have written it down. *Detach with love.* If I'd been able to raise my hand, I would have asked, "Um, how do you do that?"

The answer came about on its own, slowly, Saturday morning after Saturday morning.

You detached with love by hanging up the phone. By saying, "I love you, but . . ." By saying, "I can talk for five minutes." By not sending money. These were called *boundaries.* When you didn't set boundaries? That was when you were on the roller coaster. Or in the hurricane. With your *qualifier.* That was called *codependency.*

Codependency! So that was what that was. There were more C words, the three C's. You didn't *Cause* it, you can't *Control* it, and you can't *Cure* it. Alcoholism, that is. They were the fixers, solvers, nurses, sandwich-makers, doctor-callers. No more. They had stepped out of the chaos. Mind your own hula hoop. Take care of yourself. *Self-care!* Can you imagine a time when we didn't have this handy phrase? Those women taught it to me. Oh. And something else? Maybe take a look at your own *family of origin.*

And of course: *One day at a time.*

And of course: the serenity prayer.

I had never, ever prayed in my life.

The first time I said it, it was like a little cairn of stones balanced on my tongue. Then, soon, there was the thrill of learning a foreign language, the words coming to my mouth before I'd prompted them:

> *God, grant me the serenity to accept the things I cannot*
>   *change*
> *The courage to change the things I can*
> *And the wisdom to know the difference.*

I had memorized the words, but that didn't mean I knew what to do with them. They were like a spell I had no wand for.

I kept coming back. Sometimes with Katie, sometimes alone. At the meetings, I shared a little of my story, then a little more. My husband had been in the psych ward, I said. A suicide attempt. Now he was in outpatient rehab. A ten-week program. He'd been an addict since I met him, I said, but it was the first time he was getting help. It was hard to see he'd been an addict. It was pot for a while. Then it was alcohol. And he was sober in between. I didn't realize!

Oh, yes, the women said. *Changing seats on the* Titanic. They nodded. They made approving noises. Afterward, they hugged me to their bosoms.

"You're still in the pink cloud," more than one explained to me, smiling. "Early recovery." The words were uttered with some discomfiture, by these mothers who had achieved the wisdom of a necessary but private milestone, like menstruation. Teasing, blushing. It was part congratulations, part warning.

Aaron had gone to a handful of NA meetings before I met him, but the first AA meeting he attended was in the psych ward. When he'd gotten out, he kept going. Every day, he went to meetings in the brick building downtown, the alcohol and drug council on one floor (he'd been assigned a drug counselor, Rich), and the mental health clinic on another. He was clear-headed, clear-skinned, remorseful, steady, thankful. "Thank you," he said, when I went to my first Al-Anon meeting. "Thank you for going." We'd bought a new house downtown, far from the miserable scenes of the last one. The house was an indeterminate color I loved—greenish bluish gray—and Aaron walked down the steep hill to the clinics early each morning, his backpack heavy on his back like a kid going off to school for the first time. The weight of the alcohol melted off of him. The weight melted off of us.

When the person you love tries and fails to end his life, you are glad that he is still living. That he failed.

There is a kind of embarrassment in that failure, though: embarrassment in the company of others who love people who successfully ended their lives. Embarrassment that the person you love is still living. Embarrassment that he did not succeed. He did not go about suicide seriously. His anguish was not deep enough.

You don't have much time for embarrassment, though, because

another thing that happens when someone you love tries and fails to end his life is that you spend the rest of your life trying to keep him from trying again. Trying to create a world in which he will not want to try again. When someone you love tries to end his life because you took your love away from him, you will spend the rest of your life trying to keep him alive with your love.

You keep thinking of what your father said about the time he swallowed those pills. "Being on crutches all your life . . . It does something to your sense of manhood." What he didn't say: when a woman leaves you, it does something to your sense of manhood.

What is it with men? you think. Are they all this way? Is it just straight white men? Little boys at their mothers' knees, begging to be loved? Or have you managed to find one just like your father?

The problem is: trying to keep someone alive with your love is the exact wrong thing to do. The rooms make this much clear. Still, you go to the meetings. You repeat the prayer. *Detach with love,* you remember. *He has his own higher power.* Your higher power is the room. The rooms. *That's fine,* they say, the women. *Your higher power can just be the rooms.*

Maybe if I just found a sponsor. It was the next step, apparently. Everyone talked about having a sponsor: someone to guide you through the trying moments. Someone who would always take your call. It sounded a little like a benefactor to me, a godmother. *Will you sponsor me?* As though I were a hungry orphan on a commercial.

One week toward the end of the summer, I watched the women carefully. *Will those who are willing to serve as sponsors please raise their hands?* Up the hands went. I eyed the woman with the short salt-and-pepper hair, the wire-framed glasses, the sensible clogs. She always shared these effortless little stories of grace: a trial, a moment of doubt, a higher-power intervention, a miraculous metaphor—all without getting too God-y, and with a humble humor that sent an appreciative laugh through the room that you could feel under your feet. And all under three minutes! Her name was Kate. She was like a minister in a church I'd want to go to.

After the meeting, I approached her. I asked her if she'd be willing to sponsor me.

"Of course," she said. She didn't really have much of a bosom, but she had a bony shoulder the same height as my mother's and a cozy quilted vest.

Every couple weeks, I met Kate in the Wegmans café for coffee. She drank a small black cup of decaf. I had a towering twenty-ounce, drowned with soymilk. I took mental notes: *Don't be afraid. The coffee will not run out.*

We talked about my two sons. Her two sons. My work, her work. It turned out she actually *was* a minister. She had been a social worker for years. Then she'd gone back to school. She had just been assigned to a Methodist church.

What we didn't talk about: my husband, her husband. I knew she had one. They weren't technically married; they'd both been married twice before. But we didn't talk about them. Irrelevant! It was just the two of us, drinking coffee, being women, being mothers, taking care. Whenever I'd open my mouth and start talking about Aaron—or worse yet, when I would begin to answer the question *How are you?* with *Aaron*—she would gently course-correct me. Once she complained about another Al-Anon-er who talked incessantly about her qualifier. *She's missing the point!* Kate said. Oh. Got it. I would not miss that point!

So I didn't talk about Aaron. I talked about missing my mom. I talked about teaching and writing. I talked about trying to keep my kids happy and safe.

They were, I thought, happy and safe. They had mostly been pro-tected from Aaron's hurricane. We didn't lie about it. We just gently reshaped the truth. When he was in the psych ward, he'd been "in the hospital." True. He was "sick." Also true. When he was going to rehab, he was going to "a meeting," or to "class." True and true. Was this how it started? Was this what my parents had done, when they kept their marriage problems a secret? Would my kids be in their thirties before they learned that their father struggled with mental illness? With ad-diction? That their parents were in therapy?

But they were still so little! Nico had just turned five. Henry was almost two. They loved their dad unconditionally. They didn't have the language for understanding what he was going through. Henry was just babbling out little clutches of words. I had weaned him that spring, but he still walked around in his footed pajamas with my bra in his hand like a blankie, muttering "Milk, milk, milk." Meanwhile Nico had taken to coming down the stairs in the morning with five T-shirts on.

Kate laughed. Pick your battles, she told me. Except she didn't give me advice. In Al-Anon, we spoke from our own *experience, strength, and hope*. "I tried to remember to pick my battles," she said, remembering her own sons, now grown, one with a baby of his own. "I tried to say yes as much as possible."

I tried this. I tried to say yes as much as possible. Who cared if Nico walked around with five T-shirts on? He was fine. His father was alive. He was healthy. We were all healthy. I walked around, knocking on all the wood. In the rooms, and in the Wegmans café, I did not talk much about Aaron. This was difficult, and also a relief. It removed Aaron from the center of my story and also gave him the space to struggle on his own.

I saw, from my side of the room, that he was still struggling. I could see how hard he was on himself. From the moment he'd come out of the psych ward, it seemed to me he'd wanted to do recovery perfectly. A meeting every day, push-ups and meditation and wheat-grass smoothies. It wasn't new to him, after all, recovery—it was just a new word for the straight edge kid's inexhaustible reserve of reinvention. All or nothing. That was what I would have said about Aaron, if I had been talking about him.

"Sometimes I just had to remember to do the next right thing," said Kate, sensing, perhaps, all I wasn't saying. "Whatever was in reach. Sometimes all I could do was read my kids a story."

That worked. I took it literally. Henry would be crying, or Nico would be whining, or I would be yelling, and I would sit down on the floor where I was standing, reach out my arm until it touched the nearest book, and pull them into my lap. I couldn't save their dad. At least I thought I wasn't supposed to. Or I wasn't supposed to want to. But anyway, Elephant and Piggie? What were those two fellows up to?

We did talk, Aaron and I, at Stu's. Stu was so pleased with us! Going to AA, to Al-Anon. On his big yellow pad he wrote down all the programs Aaron was going to. CBT. DBT. Aaron had a drug counselor, a therapist, group therapy. *Group*, it was called, just *Group*. Stu was proud but he was kind of unsettled, seeing as he'd had no idea Aaron was an alcoholic. He ran a Drug and Alcohol group for men on Wednesday nights! And still, he had not seen it coming. "You and me both!" I said. We laughed. We were in good spirits. He was an alcoholic! An addict. Of course. He'd just needed a program.

Stu was part of our program, too. We saw that now. Why did people only go to marriage counseling when they were in a crisis? When they wanted to know if they should get a divorce? We were rising from the ashes of our crisis, and yet we knew we still needed Stu. I was resolved to be one of the white-haired ladies in Al-Anon in thirty years. It would be a lifelong program. Marriage counseling would be part of the program.

That had been our problem, I saw. We had not had a program.

Now we had a program.

I'd started to say it, to some of our friends: "Aaron's in recovery." He was doing well, on track, on program. I was grateful for this handy phrase, which gave these uncertain months a structure, a story: a road to recovery.

I told my family about rehab, therapy, medication. I told them we were making a fresh start in a new house and attached a picture of it, along with a picture of Nico and Henry smiling in the bath. My brothers and sisters-in-law responded with support and love. My dad wrote back:

> Good show, guys.
> Looks like a great house.
> Where is the smoking porch?
> Love, Pops.

Maybe the reason my dad didn't say much wasn't because he didn't understand. Maybe he understood all too well what life looked like after

you'd tried to end it. You could take away the alcohol. You still had to be
the person you were. Now you just had to deal with it.

The rooms were in a stately brick building that had once been an
orphanage, and then a Church of God, and now it was supported by
the community as a recovery center. On the white board in the little
lobby was a calendar listing every kind of meeting you could dream
of. Recovering Couples Anonymous, RCA, was held on Sunday evenings in the big room downstairs. It was where Aaron attended AA.
When we stepped into the room together, it felt like we were crossing
a threshold.

When Kate had mentioned the meeting, I didn't know what to
expect. Couples who were in recovery: What did that mean? Did they
both have to be addicts? Is that the way it worked for other people:
addicts found each other, and then got sober together? Or had they
gotten sober before? Had they all met and fallen in love in AA? Was
that the fatal, stupid flaw in our marriage: we were mismatched, addict
and codependent, forever on opposite sides of the fence?

All of this was in my head as Aaron and I stepped into the room.
There was Kate, grinning, waving us over. "Welcome!"

I went over and gave her a hug. I started to introduce her to Aaron,
but Aaron was hugging the man sitting beside her. Her partner! He was
calling him by the name of his drug counselor, Rich. My sponsor's partner was Aaron's drug counselor! We all laughed at this. I shook Rich's
hand. Aaron shook Kate's. It was like one of her little cosmic stories. It
was like a double date. I felt dizzy with belonging. Aaron's recovery and
my recovery slipped beside each other like two canoes. We were all in
the rooms now. They had opened up before me, these rooms, invisible
to me before but now as big as a secret Wegmans. In fact, I think I recognized some of these people from Wegmans. I looked around. They
were welcoming us, shaking hands.

And before long I would see that these couples were, like me and
Aaron, mismatched, codependent, unmanageable, two trees tangled
around each other from the roots. A lawyer and a chemist, together

since high school, on the brink of divorce when they'd started coming to meetings eight years ago. Eight years! An EMT and a kindergarten teacher. A massage therapist and an opera singer. A midwife and a—well, he didn't work. He was in recovery! In some couples, both were addicts. In some, only one was. Some weren't married. Some didn't even live together. Some had been together for decades, some for just months. Some were young, some were old. Most were straight. Most were white. There was a lesbian couple, two Italian women with a small daughter who sat between them, coloring. How did they get her to sit so very quietly?

"Hi," one half of the couple would say. "I'm so-and-so, and I'm in recovery with so-and-so."

And then everyone would greet them as a couple.

They went around the table, introducing themselves, ten couples or so. When it came to our turn, I looked at Aaron. We raised our eyebrows at each other.

"Hi." I sounded out the words slowly. "I'm Eleanor, and I'm in recovery with Aaron."

"Hi." His turn. "I'm Aaron, and I'm in recovery with Eleanor."

"Hi, Eleanor! Hi, Aaron!"

We traded little smiles. Under the table, I squeezed his knee. He squeezed mine back.

The couple leading the meeting sat at the front of the room, a book open in front of them. Kate handed us a guest copy, and we found the right page. The wife began to read:

> Ours is a fellowship of recovering couples. We suffer from many addictions and dysfunctions, and we share our experience, strength, and hope with each other that we may solve our common problems and help other recovering couples restore their relationships. The only requirement for membership is the desire to remain committed to each other and to develop new intimacy.

I was practically shaking with recognition. On the table in front of the couple sat a candle on a hand-carved three-legged stool. The three legs, they read, represented my recovery, my partner's recovery, and the couple's recovery. Or commitment, communication, and caring.

Three more C's! I tried to see it all with some critical distance, these Ithacans with their candles and prayers and alliteration, their ceramic brown mugs of chamomile. I tried to spin it into a joke.

But I suddenly felt dead serious. What was this feeling of icy heat, like Vick's VapoRub on my chest? Was this what fellowship felt like? Was this faith? Was this my shame, leaving me?

THEORY 3

t's stress, stupid. The stress caused the rash. The alcohol suppressed the stress.

MADNESS OF TWO

When cancer returns to the body, when the old cancer cells you thought had been killed haven't been killed, it's called a recurrence. With autoimmune diseases, when the symptoms come back, it's called a flare-up, or a flare.

Which is the weird disease your husband had? (Has?) A cancer—a foreign invader? Or is it his own body, turning on itself?

When you think that the weird disease that has almost ruined your husband has been killed, is capable of being killed, has been gone for a year, you imagine yourselves victors. Survivors of a deadly combat. He runs the Ithaca Festival Mile with your six-year-old and he might as well be running a marathon, so healthy and handsome he looks in his black running tank, his toned biceps flashing down Cayuga Street. From the sidelines, you cheer like a soccer mom.

When the disease has been killed not through radiation or chemotherapy but through some murky combination of luck and will and alcohol, you both remain, even in remission, in submission to the fickle beast, lest he wake from his cave. Be nice to your skin. Pet it. Moisturize. Exfoliate. Meditate. Avoid stress. Stay on program. Pray to the beast. You cannot feed the beast alcohol anymore. The alcohol will kill your husband if the pain doesn't first.

Was it really ever dead, or have the cells just been sleeping? One afternoon in 2014 at the end of that first year of recovery, that long, lovely pink cloud, your husband will have to make a phone call. He has to call a doctor's office and make an appointment. You go out. He stays home. He finds that he can't do it. He finds himself locked in the bathroom with his phone in his hand, panicked. He paces. He sweats. When you come home, he emerges from the bathroom, and the sores on his forearms—the ones that had faded to scars the camouflaged color of chewed bubble gum—are on fire. A flare. The blood has bloomed to the surface. He walks out of the bathroom like a zombie, arms floating in front of him, like they belong to someone else. He walks out of the bathroom like Teen Wolf. The transformation is that swift, that complete.

"No," you say. "No no no no no."

You had been on guard for the return of the wrong monsters. It was suicide you were worried about, and alcohol. Relapse. Your army was divided, weakened. While you weren't looking, the other beast has awoken. It's the beast's fault, and yet it's your husband who has called him back.

This is the way you see it, this is where your fear goes. It fights. It blames. How not to blame your husband, when it lives inside him? What's so hard about making a fucking phone call? And how does it lead to this?

There is nothing to be done. Keep coming back to the rooms. Buy him the apricot exfoliating soap he likes. Cry.

Going back to the rooms is hard when Aaron's skin is on fire, though. You go to your own room. More and more, he stays home. He has been tiring of the AA meetings, anyway. Always a personal agenda, always the horror stories that trigger his nightmares. Sometimes he meets with Rich, who has become his sponsor. Mostly he stays in bed. His skin boils and bakes and heals. It feels like things are crawling inside it, he says. It goes away for a few weeks. And then it flares again. Recurs. "He had a breakout," is how you put it to the doctors, to friends, which makes him sound like a teenager with unfortunate acne.

You go back to the internet. You search for "rash," "skin disease," "lesions." Scrolling the images is like playing a slot machine, pulling the handle and begging for the symbols to line up. No matches.

Except there they are again, the pictures of Morgellons disease. The same chocolate-chip pattern of lesions across a forearm. You recognize them the way you'd recognize the pattern of freckles on your child's face.

The literary festival I'd been invited to was in the fall, in a sleepy, green New England town with a white steeple and a dust-colored river rushing with rain. All weekend, the rain came down. I left Aaron and the boys in the hotel. The kids had their own adjoining room with twin beds, topped with Halloween gift bags when we arrived—spider rings, skull tattoos. Aaron wasn't feeling great, but the kids were content watching Scooby-Doo and eating candy corn when I took my umbrella and ventured out to the library, where Leslie Jamison was reading from her new book, *The Empathy Exams*.

I'd seen it everywhere, the beating heart on the cover with its opened arteries. After the reading, I bought a copy, asked her to sign it, and sat in the coffee shop next door, waiting for the rain to pass and shuffling through the book. I paused on the first page of the second essay, "The Devil's Bait."

> For me, Morgellons disease started as a novelty: people said they had a strange ailment, and no one—or hardly anyone—believed them. But there were a lot of them, reportedly 12,000, and their numbers were growing. Their illness manifested in many ways, including fatigue, pain, and formication (a sensation of insects crawling over the skin). But the defining symptom was always the same: fibers emerging from their bodies. Not just fibers but fuzz, specks, and crystals. They didn't know what this stuff was, or where it came from, or why it was there, but they knew—and this was what mattered, the important word—that it was *real*.

I looked up from the book. Through the window, the festival-goers were bravely dodging the easing rain. I had never seen the word *Morgellons* outside of the glowing screen of my laptop, and it seemed odd and earthly—*real*—printed with ink on the page.

Real, I thought. Maybe it *is* real.

I followed Leslie Jamison into the essay, through the short, contentious history of the disease, and to a Morgellons conference at a Baptist church in Austin, where she meets scores of people who say they have stuff coming out of their skin. They look at the stuff under microscopes. They share pictures on their phones, finding comfort in each other's symptoms. Their lesions look like all the others' lesions. They show them to Jamison, too, and she nods, confused: she can see they're suffering, but she can't see the bugs.

"*Folie à deux,*" she writes, "is the clinical name for shared delusions. Morgellons patients all know the phrase—it's the name of the crime they're charged with. But if *folie à deux* is happening at the conference, it's happening more like *folie à* many, *folie en masse,* an entire Baptist church full of folks having the same nightmare."

Across the street, the white church steeple was bright under the parting clouds. The rain had stopped. I thought of the boys back at the hotel, felt the restless distance between us, the familiar tug of them. Were they okay? I wasn't a wife and mother who lounged in coffee shops without a decent excuse. And yet the book was keeping me there. The moment felt seizable; it felt important that I sit and read it out. I thought of what it would be for Aaron to be in that room with those people, the disbelieved. To be believed by each other—would it be enough?

And then, halfway through the essay, this.

> This isn't an essay about whether Morgellons disease is real. That's probably obvious by now. It's an essay about what kinds of reality are considered prerequisites for compassion. It's about this strange sympathetic limbo: Is it wrong to speak of empathy when you trust the fact of suffering but not the source?

I looked up again. *That's probably obvious by now.* What was "that"? Clarify your antecedent! I reread the sentence before it. Was it obvious that the essay wasn't about whether Morgellons disease was real, or was it obvious that Morgellons disease wasn't real?

I could feel the answer in my chest. It was the latter. My heart felt like the heart on the cover of the book, fat and sloppy, pumping out shame.

I had wanted the essay to render my husband's suffering real, to be delivered the diagnosis no doctor would, but Jamison expected the reader to see with reason and clarity what the CDC saw, and the patients couldn't: it was all in their heads.

It went on like that for months, years: believing, not believing, hoping, not hoping, praying. Not praying. Could my whole life up to this point be captioned "Not praying"? When I didn't need to pray, when the curse lifted, I stood and ceased praying. I believed when I needed to believe. Witnessing Aaron's agony was the closest thing to a spiritual crisis I'd undergone, the closest to a test of faith.

One night, Aaron woke me in the middle of the night, absolutely certain that he knew what was wrong with his skin. He'd been up for days, unable to sleep, his arms and legs sleeved with a fiery rash.

"What is it?" I asked.

"Scabies."

His laptop lay open, the keyboard wet with droplets of his sweat. I put on my glasses and studied the images of the blood-colored bugs on the screen. "Mites! Parasitic mites. They're *burrowed* in my skin." His voice was shrill with panic and delight. "They've been laying *eggs* under my skin!"

I looked between the screen and the shin he'd thrust in front of my face.

"Look! See them moving?"

I thought I maybe saw something moving. Or was it the light? "I don't know, babe." It was hard to tell. He couldn't sit still.

"*All* this time. Scabies!" He laughed. "The *mange!*" He was almost joyous.

Maybe it was that joy I wanted to believe in. The allure of identifying a foreign invader. The warm relief of trusting my husband. He was as confident as a general with binoculars, watching the enemy march in.

"It's *highly* contagious," he said. "It's a miracle the kids haven't gotten it."

I looked down at my left forefinger, which the day before had sprouted a ridge of white, itchy bumps. Did they look mite-shaped?

I could practically feel my guard falling, our minds fusing, as I stepped over to the other side. All this time! He'd not been infected but infested.

Aaron's regular GP, Dr. Das, wasn't available the next day, so we saw a nurse practitioner, who looked skeptically at Aaron's shins. She didn't see any evidence of mites, but to be on the safe side, she prescribed Permethrin cream. "You'll both have to do a full treatment," she said. "Just in case." I nodded my head, as though accepting my religious duty.

Before we left, I asked her, "Can you please, please give him something to sleep?"

That night, we stripped to our underwear and painted our bodies with insecticide, neck to toes. We laughed, squirmed. It was a science experiment, a mating ritual. Aaron took one of the Ambien he'd been prescribed. Carefully we lay ourselves down on the clean sheets, palms to the ceiling, sunbathers slathered in holy oil. We waited for the rapture. We waited to be transformed.

My friend Anna had once taken half an Ambien and it had knocked her out so completely that she woke up the next morning on the bathroom floor. My husband, he didn't sleep one wink that night.

I slept but woke up sticky with confusion and shame. What had I just done? Had it worked? I remembered the line from "The Devil's Bait." *That should be obvious by now.* My husband was still my husband, moody and sleepless and in pain. I took a shower.

The next week, when his rash had not healed, he went back to the doctor's office and saw Dr. Das. He pointed to the bug crawling in the sore on his shin. His doctor looked at him and said with absolute certainty, "There are no bugs in your skin."

"Oh," Aaron said.

Folie à deux. It means, literally, "madness of two."

I'd done more research on folie à deux after reading about it in "The Devil's Bait." It was once known as Lasègue-Falret syndrome, named for French physicians Charles Lasègue and Jean-Pierre Falret in the mid-nineteenth century. They identified two kinds. *Folie simultanée* is when two people, each vulnerable to psychosis, simultaneously undergo a similar delusion. The other, *folie imposée,* is when one person, the "inducer," undergoes a delusion and imposes it on another person, the "acceptor." Without the inducer, the acceptor would not have been susceptible to delusion. She consents to madness.

Perhaps every marriage is a madness. To agree to see the world the way another sees the world—what is that vow but a shared delusion?

When I rinsed my body of that insecticide, though, I stepped back onto the other side, and I left Aaron there, alone. No matter how much he showered, he could not wash off the evidence of his folly.

THEORY 4

got on intrauterine birth control and stopped getting a period. Then Aaron started getting it for me. Between vomiting and shitting and bleeding from his skin, I'd say he loses about seven teaspoons of blood every month, the same amount the average menstruating woman loses. His cycle is about as regular as mine ever was, which is to say, not very regular. The body must shed its excess. It must shed what is not biologically useful.

Say this is impossible, or say it is witchcraft, but what do we call it when women under the same roof begin to bleed at the same time? How are their bodies listening to each other? How is my body, lying next to Aaron's, listening to his? How is his body listening to mine?

THEORY 5

Or perhaps there is no such thing as disease at all. There is no diagnosis. Why should I assume that any pain I feel approximates the pain you feel? The field of medicine relies on the idea that understanding one person's body will help me understand another person's body. But it seems to me as unreliable a concept as looking inside a radio, or a flower, or a black hole, or a frog, and expecting to see a human heart there.

But the thing is, you kind of can.

Have you ever seen a glass frog? Its skin does not reflect light. You can see everything inside it, and everything reminds you of something else. Its green-spotted back is a city viewed from an airplane at night. Its limbs are the sticky hands your kids get from gumball machines and toss at the windows. Its glowing belly is a translucent rice paper roll, and wrapped inside it are the sweet-pea caviar of its organs, the white cocoon of its intestines, or maybe it's an electric spiraling light bulb, and its brave little berry of a heart pumps blood through a vein that looks like a red blade of grass. The glass frog dares you not to get metaphorical.

"My willingness to turn Morgellons into metaphor," Leslie Jamison writes, "—as a corporeal manifestation of some abstract human tendency—is dangerous. It obscures the particular and unbidden nature of the suffering in front of me."

Dangerous, sure. All suffering is not alike. All bodies are not alike. I don't want to define my husband's pain against my own.

But doesn't the glass frog long to be compared to its opaque cousin? To the amphibious and the mammalian? To the electric and the synthetic? Doesn't the universe ask to be analogized? Isn't that all it asks? You are like me. I am like you. I am another mortal creature.

You better believe I dream that my husband is that beautiful glass frog.

I dream I see his heart pumping, tar black. And then I give him my own.

HOT MESS

n our bedroom is a broken mirror. It's one of the panels of our sliding closet door, installed a few months ago by an overpaid handyman. For years, a curtain hung in place of it. For years, the bedroom ceiling hung low and rotten along one edge, where an ice dam had damaged it. We could afford to replace the roof but not the drywall, and so the place where the ceiling met the wall was a foaming mouth of insulation and mold. We learned not to see it. When we finally fixed it, we had the overpaid handyman open up the whole wall of the room to reinsulate it, and we discovered that, as we suspected, our bedroom had once been a sleeping porch. The porch posts were still buried there in the wall, sheetrocked over.

For a few months the room was intact again, the ceiling replaced, and while we were at it, a closet door hung. But now the bottom third of one of the doors is smashed through, like a mirror in a fairy tale, and as much as we vacuum we still find shards of glass in the fibers of the carpet.

Tonight Aaron is not in the bed. I sleep on one side, in case he comes back.

He doesn't come back. He sleeps the night—five hours, a good night—on the daybed in the playroom. I find him there when I come downstairs. He didn't want to keep me up, he says. The skin on his left bicep was tightening all night, as though squeezed by a blood pressure cuff. "It was like catcher's gear," he says, gesturing from his bare chest to his belly. Now it's better, he says; it's just blotches of burns. They look like the lesions that have long spotted and scarred his torso, except for one, a slick little steak the size of a rose bud, shaped like Ohio. A few days ago, in bed, it sucked and smeared on my belly. "Sorry," he said. "Want me to put a shirt on?" I shook my head no.

Now these recurrences are as regular as rain. It's weather. You see it like a storm, from far off. It will come eventually. There is little to be done.

This time, he'd been called in for jury duty. His second summons; he'd ignored the first. For the second one, he was ready. He had asked his psychiatrist, Dr. Friedlander, to write him a note, like a kid who'd lost his homework, but she encouraged him to go. It would be good for him to try. It could be a fraud case, drug possession, and he probably wouldn't even be selected. I'd been dismissed last year for a case involving a stolen flat-screen television. Yesterday morning, though, at the dentist's office, I'd spotted an article on the front page of the local paper: "Jury still being filled for murder trial." A man had been accused of killing another man over some marijuana plants. I had the bright idea of taking a picture of the article and texting it to Aaron. "Fuck that," he texted back. But he walked down to the courthouse that afternoon, stood a few feet from the alleged killer, and when asked if anyone believed they were not fit to serve, he stood.

"I don't think I'm in the right mind," he said.

They dismissed him. On the walk home, he threw up, then walked some more and threw up again. By that evening, the Ohio-shaped burn had appeared on his stomach, ghosting the E and D in STRAIGHT EDGE, a rash that no amount of professional-proof vodka could abate.

Now, the next morning, I'm on the phone with the dermatologist's office. I'm not on his HIPAA, apparently. So I hand him the phone. There is an appointment tomorrow at three. We'll make it work, I whisper. I can cancel Henry's OT session. But he takes the appointment on November 6, two weeks away. In two weeks his skin could look like Ohio, California, Alaska. His ankles could be swollen. He could be infected. Or he could be fine.

"I need to prepare," he says.

"I'm going to have to watch you suffer for two weeks."

He looks at me. "I'm going to have to suffer for two weeks."

Nothing to do but wait. And read.

I can't think of schizophrenia without thinking of the song by Sonic Youth, which tells me that alternative bands of the eighties and nineties were really into mental illness metaphors. Does this say something about them, or about me? One morning I sit down at the dining room table and play *Sister* on my laptop while I page through the book that I've rescued from the toothpaste drawer. I keep the volume low so I don't wake Aaron, who has gone back to bed.

We like to use the adjective "schizophrenic" metaphorically. A whole with two parts that don't belong together. People with schizophrenia don't have multiple selves inside them, though, any more than other people do. They have hallucinations, delusions, paranoia. Often, the book tells me, they hear voices. Thoughts, emotions, and behavior are fragmented. From the Greek *skhizein*, "to split" and *phrēn*, "mind," schizophrenia is a psychosis. The mind is split—not split into parts but split from reality.

Is my husband's mind split from reality? And if so, when did it begin? People don't really develop schizophrenia in their forties. For most, it emerges in early adulthood—late teens, twenties. Has it been there since I've known him? Is it possible to be with someone for twenty years and fail to notice?

I close the book. It's the part of "Schizophrenia" where Kim Gordon is sing-talking over the swaying, rumbling, about-to-go-insane guitar:

My future is static

Static, as in: my future is over? Nothing to be done?

Or static, as in: a buzzing. The music itself is a kind of static. A white noise.

When I asked Aaron if he thought he had schizophrenia, he was resolute.

"I've always heard things," he said.

When he was about twelve, he told his father, "It sounds like there's a radio playing."

There was no radio playing.

His father, alarmed, took him to the doctor. Nothing was concluded that Aaron can recall. His hearing was fine.

Now his ears are damaged from years of live shows. His ears ring with tinnitus.

But it's more than ringing. It's not voices, per se. It's that radio of his childhood. Sometimes it's the snowy murmur between stations. Sometimes it's full songs, complete with lyrics that come with the clarity of a dream, like a song he has written himself, except he hasn't.

Aaron steps into the dining room now, a look of panic on his face. Is that a real radio, or in his head? I turn up the volume. The wailing white-noise guitar surges through the tinny laptop speakers. He sighs with relief. Hand to chest. This exchange requires no words.

"A diagnosis is a thing that helps doctors describe symptoms," Dr. Friedlander tells us. We are sitting in her office in her vine-covered stone house, Aaron and I on a couch, she far from us in a chair in the corner, where the morning light coming through the window won't blind her. This is the room where Aaron has sat once every few weeks for the past seven months. Seven months ago, when I first pulled into the driveway to drop him off, there was a foot of fresh snow on the ground, and Dr. Friedlander was shoveling the driveway. Aaron, introducing himself, took another shovel and helped her clear a path to the door. An hour later, he emerged from that door, shaking, shaken.

"How did it go?" I said.

"It's bad," he said. "It's scary."

I knew then what it was. What other diagnosis could strike that kind of fear?

Now I am here to meet her. I will give her some insight into Aaron. She will give me some insight into Aaron. My twenty years of insight, her twenty hours. I feel both hopeful and defensive, skeptical and cowed, as though I am at a parent-teacher conference, a parent-teacher conference where the teacher takes off one Birkenstock and sits with her bare foot tucked under her. She is sipping tea from a large mug. In the waiting room are bowls of rocks, framed photos of lily pads, and a knee-high stack of *Poetry* magazines. I am pleased by how closely she adheres to my fantasy of a psychiatrist practicing in Ithaca, New York.

"A diagnosis is just a word," she says. Psychiatrists like to argue about whether there are genes that determine these diseases. But right now there's no test for schizophrenia. Any diagnosis, she says, is going to describe a wide range of symptoms. "If you have schizophrenia," she says to my husband, "you're an outlier."

If.

It's a comfort to me. Not because I am afraid of the diagnosis, not because I'm ashamed of it, but because it does not adhere to my understanding of who my husband is. Not all of who he is. It is a piece in an incomplete puzzle. What he is—she is right about this—is an outlier.

"You're articulate, bright, thoughtful, socially engaged." I am nodding, proud mother. "You don't present as most people with schizophrenia do. You wouldn't know by looking at you that you have schizophrenia."

I watch Aaron. Is he disappointed? Would it be better, easier, to reflect the textbook? Seven months ago, when he got into the car on that snowy day, he was shaken, but he was also relieved: a diagnosis.

"When I took your history," she says, "it seemed clear to me that you had problems organizing yourself. You suffer from hallucinations. You hear things, see things. You second-guess yourself. You distrust yourself."

"Yes!" I say. "He distrusts himself. He distrusts everyone."

"And yet you're exceptionally good at describing your feelings."

"He is!" I agree.

"Which could actually make it more difficult for you to live with this disease, because you are so emotionally attuned."

"Not while it's happening," he says. "It's like I'm being bombarded by my feelings. I'm being tortured."

"That's what I'm most worried about," I say. "This emotional agony he's in." Dr. Friedlander is studying me carefully. Schizophrenia—maybe,

I say. But I don't think that's what's happening when he's up at night, convulsing in invisible pain. "The nights," I say. "They're really bad. He looks like he should be in a straitjacket."

"Why do you say that?"

"Because he has to lie on his hands to keep from hurting himself."

"I don't want to hurt myself," he says. "I just want the pain to end. I just want to put my lights out." In the morning, he says, he can see behind him, see what happened. But not while it's happening.

Dr. Friedlander nods. "That's what you have to practice. Identifying the feelings while they're happening. It won't happen overnight. You might get good at it in five or ten years." She smiles. *"Oh, there's my terror. There's my dread. There's my feeling. There's my symptom. And"*—is she looking at me?—*"I don't have to fix it."*

Before we leave, she asks if there's anything else we want to talk about.

"I just wanted her to understand," Aaron says, "that I can't control this. That it's not my fault that I can't do some basic things."

She sits up and slips her right foot back in her Birkenstock. "I had two preconceptions about your wife before you came in. One is that she'd be patient and calm. The other is that she must love you very much." She looks back at me. "Is that right?"

I nod, blinking back tears. I have passed the test.

"I think she understands. Maybe she's pulling the wool over my eyes." She looks me up and down. "But I don't think so."

That afternoon, I leave the kids with Aaron and go downtown for a meeting. I turn off my phone. When I come out an hour later and turn it back on, there are three missed calls and seven texts from Aaron's phone.

> I just 0uked ebryehtrt ypu need to come home
> This is nico dad just puked out blood all over the seconed floor
>   please come home
> Nell im teally sick you need to come home

Im pukinkubf blood
Please come home now
MOM GET HOME NOW dad might pass out!!!!!!
Please mom

I call back. I'm coming. Put Nico on. Tell me what happened. Nico is crying. It's okay, I say. Dad will be okay. I'm coming home and we'll take him to the doctor. Get your shoes on. Get your brother's shoes on. Bring your homework. You did great, I say. I hang up and make the ten-minute walk up the hill in five minutes.

"Dad threw up!" Henry says when I come in the door. "Nico was crying!"

"Shut up, Henry!"

"He throwed up *everywhere.*"

Aaron is on the couch, moaning under a blanket. Last week he had a bloody nose, was coughing up blood, and now there is blood on his jeans, on his white socks. Upstairs, the house looks like a crime scene. I follow the trail of blood-colored vomit from the bedroom to the bathroom. It's on my office floor. It's on the bathroom floor. It's blasted across the toilet and walls, and there are several inches of it in the bathroom sink, along with what looks like a brain. Upon closer inspection I see it is a nest of undigested ramen noodles. Three-minute, spice-packet, Oriental ramen noodles, the only flavor that is vegan, if the ingredients inside could be judged as actual food. It is Halloween—will the kids be able to trick-or-treat?—and for a moment I think of the Halloween festival at my elementary school, where I stuck my hand in a box to feel spaghetti brains—what a sick thrill that was!—and I wonder if this is some Halloween prank. A trick.

Not a trick. "But I did drink a lot of cranberry juice," Aaron remembers.

He is delirious, and his left arm still hurts, so everyone piles in the car and we drive to urgent care, where last week we left without being seen because of the hour wait. Today they see him right away. The kids are now elated: they can stay in the waiting room with the retro Pac-Man arcade game and unlimited play! The nurse asks a thousand questions. Family history? Medications? What does he take the Sero-quel for?

We look at each other.

"I have issues," Aaron says.

"Depression?" the nurse asks.

"It's a drug prescribed for schizophrenia," I say.

"That's okay!" the nurse says sweetly. "Did you throw up that blood on your shirt?"

No. That's blood from his skin. He lifts his T-shirt to show them. The Ohio-shaped steak is scabbing over. He has been wearing the shirt for a week straight because why ruin seven shirts? Then the doctor comes in and asks the questions all over again. She is kind, ponytailed, smiling with concern while we take turns repeating the details. "Any other medical issues?"

"Oh, hell yeah," he says. By the time he's done, finishing with the knot on his head he got while closing the car trunk that morning, she says, "Well, you're just a hot mess, aren't you?"

We laugh. It's another diagnosis that brings the comfort of truth. It's a feminized moniker, borrowed by the ponytailed doctor and applied to the helpless male who lies trainwrecked, trapped on his back on the butcher paper, half Amy Schumer, half Gregor Samsa. This is what we will write on the medical form next time. So much more accurate than *schizophrenia*. Any medical issues? *Hot mess. Outlier. Too much fire.*

They do an EKG. Normal. No fever. Last week he had chest pains, couldn't breathe, but now, this moment, he is okay. She prescribes oint-ment for his sore arm and physical therapy. The blood, she is pretty sure, is cranberry juice. Who knows what caused him to spontaneously vomit all over the house? Other than ramen noodles? It is a body's sensible response, we conclude, to expel it.

I take the kids trick-or-treating and Aaron stays home in bed. It's not the first Halloween he's missed, so we're not surprised but we're sad. The boys are Ghostbusters. They aren't sad for long. They are shriek-ing down the street with their friends, fluorescent bands circling their wrists in the dark.

When the kids are asleep in their candy comas I use an entire plastic canister of Seventh Generation antibacterial wipes on the bathroom. I don't mind. It is satisfying, scrubbing each honeycomb tile, the blood-vomit disappearing as if in slow-mo rewind, and then the bathroom is clean and white again.

SEYMOUR, AGAIN

1999

We didn't break up. But after two years, in the summer, the lease on the yellow house came to an end. The architects were expanding their business upstairs.

Down Seymour Street, we found another one-bedroom apartment, this one in a slate blue house above the apartment of an aging cat lady named Linda who wore a comb in her hair. Aaron said she reminded him of Julie Hagerty. Out back was a garage turned into a hostel. Our apartment was a square with the stairway rising in the center. There were more slanted ceilings, and a gas stove you had to ignite with a barbecue lighter, a claw-foot tub with a shower curtain that went all the way around. We had our first dinner party in that apartment, inviting our friends Esther and Eva, sisters who worked at the bakery with me. I made: potatoes.

Linda owned four cats, and so didn't mind when we adopted a new kitten we named Blue. We kept her in the bathroom while Ratboy hissed through the door. Once we'd introduced them, the kitten slept in our bed. I was a fretful co-sleeping parent. That first night, I was awake more than asleep. At some point, the kitten squirmed out of my reach to nestle on my grandmother's quilt at the end of the bed, and managed to pounce between my legs, one of her new claws impaling the inside of my right butt cheek.

Linda, did, however, mind when we asked a friend to house-sit for us. We were going to visit our family in Florida that summer, and Esther had offered to stay there to take care of the new kitten.

"I've looked at the lease," Linda said, "and it doesn't have anyone else's name on it." She would be happy to take care of the cats herself, she said.

Aaron was pissed. Fine, he said. But he vowed to me that, when we got back, we'd look for another place. "I've looked at the lease," he told me, "and it doesn't have an end-date on it."

Aaron's father had a psychiatrist, Dr. Delano. He worked for Veterans Affairs. It was decided that Aaron, when we went to Florida, would see this psychiatrist.

It wasn't therapy, per se. He was seeking medication. For the first time, I thought, *My boyfriend is depressed.*

He had lost so much. His mother, in the divorce. His ex-girlfriend, who had been killed. His best friend, Ashmat, who died when they were twelve, shortly after Aaron moved to Florida. Another friend, who died in his twenties of cerebral palsy. I had always thought of Aaron as haunted by these ghosts. Seeing him as clinically depressed was less romantic, but I wanted desperately for him to feel better.

We returned to Florida and the two of us slept in my twin bed. There were my old posters and books and photos, the collection of ceramic elephants, the peace-sign collage I'd made from magazine clippings, the SAVE THE RAINFOREST poster. There were my old sheets, the turquoise ones with red flowers. I don't know if it was the safety of being outside of our regular life, like the magical pool water that made my parents so loquacious. Maybe he was trying to explain the appointment with the psychiatrist. But it was there, late one night, that he told me, quite out of the blue, that he'd been abused.

"Like, sexually abused?"

He nodded. He was a man in my bed and he was also a little boy.

"Oh, honey," I said. I held him.

"For a while, I didn't remember it," he said. "And then it came back." For all those years he'd been on drugs, he'd pushed the memory to the back of his mind. Then, when he got off them, the memories had nothing left to cloud them.

Oh. I'd thought I understood the appointment, the weed.

"Who was it?"

"I can't tell you."

"You won't tell me?" I asked. "Or you don't remember?"

"I remember." He squeezed his eyes shut. "But I'll never ever tell you."

We met his dad at the VA hospital. We spotted him in the cafeteria on his motorized scooter, in the sea of other old men in turquoise suit jackets. He was a volunteer.

Downstairs, for some reason, Morris and I waited for Aaron outside Dr. Delano's office. Morris sat quietly on his parked scooter. I had the absurd recollection of my mother waiting outside the bathroom door while I, at thirteen, tried to insert a tampon for the first time. I could hear her whispering to my father. I was furious.

What did Aaron's father know about why he was there? About what had made him depressed? I wished he could share his secret with his father. I thought it would make things better, bring them closer.

It was not a long visit. Soon Aaron emerged from the office. He had a white paper bag in his hand. The psychiatrist had, in a few minutes, dispensed Aaron's first antidepressant. Zoloft.

For the life of me, I cannot remember one word I exchanged with his father in that hallway. I remember only Aaron's nervousness, his face edged with anger, as he emerged from the room: that we were waiting for him, worrying about him, together.

IRONY 1

The pain inflicted on my husband as a child prevents him from sharing the bed with our sons.

Sharing the bed with our sons would be, perhaps, the best medicine for the pain inflicted on my husband as a child.

SEYMOUR, AGAIN

1999, STILL

The third apartment on Seymour Street, which we moved into at the end of that summer, was the downstairs of a rambling cream-colored house with porches falling off in every direction. One porch looked out at the barn-shaped garage. Another looked over the Otter Creek, and the tall, otter-eaten trees that threatened to fall on the house. From another you could see an honest-to-goodness covered bridge.

The rent was $750 a month. Fifty percent more than what we'd been paying. The amount staggered me. My father told me it was a foolish idea. What was wrong with the one-bedroom apartment with the cat lady?

Here, our landlords would live in another state, oblivious to our cat-sitters and our comings and goings. Above us lived a recent Middlebury graduate who wrote for the local paper. She left a note on our door when we moved in. *Come up for drinks sometime! Or tea for the teetotalers.* I pretended I knew what the word meant, but I had to look it up. Teetotalers! That was what we were. Well, sort of. Was I a teetotaler if I wasn't technically old enough to drink? Was Aaron a teetotaler if he was smoking pot pretty much every day?

We had made, somehow, a pretty little life for ourselves. In the morning, Aaron would drop me off on campus, or I'd ride my bike. I'd go to class, study in the library. I wrote papers and went to office hours and filled notebooks with notes. I read Virginia Woolf and William Carlos Williams and Ralph Ellison and Virgil and Shakespeare. I learned Ancient Greek. In warm months, I liked to find an Adirondack chair and write under a tree, and for a moment I'd be the girl in the college brochure I'd always wanted to be.

In winter months, I'd retire my bike, and more than anything, I remember walking through the snow. On those short winter days, it always seemed to be dark. The silent march over the dark, icy sidewalks, across campus, to campus, from campus to home. On weekends, I'd wake up at five thirty in the morning and walk through the snow to work, rounding the corner where the post office sat dark, following the dead-quiet streets of Middlebury. Sometimes I'd pass some college kids stumbling home from their parties. It wasn't what I'd pictured in the college brochure. But it was mine. All of Main Street, at six o'clock, was mine. And then there was the warm, yellow glow of the bakery windows at the far end of the street. You could smell the bread baking from a block away.

Then, after class, after work, I went home. I cooked with Aaron, watched TV, did homework. I had my wisdom teeth removed, and Aaron drove me home, loopy on anesthesia, and helped me to the couch. He helped me change the bloody gauze on my gums. He gave me the Vicodin, then held my hair when I threw it up. He made me chana masala, then put it in the blender and spoon-fed it to me. My mouth was still numb. It dribbled down my chin, and Aaron cleaned it. I was laughing because I was still high and laughing because I loved my boyfriend and loved the way, when I let him, he took care of me.

It was a compartmentalized life. Aaron dipped into my worlds occasionally. He attended a lecture, or stopped by the bakery to refill his mug with hazelnut coffee. But largely he existed, to me, in a domain sealed off from the rest of my life.

It was not exactly a case of split personality. I was me in every domain. But I could adapt to what each world asked of me, adopt a language, a culture, a vocabulary. I prided myself on this, the way I could read a room and be what it wanted me to be.

But such division tires the mind. The mind does not want to collate itself. The mind longs for integration.

I wanted to fuse with Aaron's world, to puncture its membrane, get under its surface. But I was scared to. As well as he might have appeared to the outside world—he had two jobs and a Range Rover, two cats and a girlfriend—his interior world, I was beginning to suspect, was a place of chaos and distress. Since confessing his childhood abuse to me in my childhood bed, he hadn't shared much of that world with me, and I didn't ask for much access. I wanted to respect his trauma. He played the keyboard. He played the guitar. He recorded songs on minidiscs and sent them back to his old bandmates in Florida. He smoked a lot of pot. He took the Zoloft. Whether it was working, I didn't know.

In a computer lab at school, I wrote a letter to my friend Esther. I wrote down all the sadness I felt for Aaron and with him, all my disappointment and worry and regret. It felt like an unspeakable betrayal, that letter. I must have chosen the computer lab because my own desktop at home felt too unsafe. I printed it out on the lab's laser printer and sealed it in an envelope, and after carrying it around like a bomb in my backpack for two days, I went back to the computer lab and ran it through the shredder.

I could handle it, I thought. I had control of my worlds, of my access into each of them. We were behind on the bills, despite his father's continued allowance. That $750 rent was beginning to weigh on us. I was managing a lot. I was working almost as much as Aaron, and I was in school full-time. Finally I worked up the nerve to say something about it. One winter night, we sat in the dark living room, Aaron playing with a flashlight against the wall. We watched our shadows. Maybe it was the safety of that darkness. I said, "I see you working twenty hours a week, and I wonder why it's not more. It's not enough."

The beam of the flashlight dropped to the floor. It was exactly as though a light had been switched off—or on? I had crossed a threshold.

Here was his disbelief, his anger. Who was I to question his work? His integrity? Who was I to say what was enough for him? It was the same as the fight about finding his pot. It wasn't his fault; he was depressed.

We fought, yelled, cried. For months, years, we'd held it all in. Then it came tumbling out.

Sniffling, I held my ground. I didn't have a dorm room to return to. The residential life director, short on housing, had approached me at the bakery the previous summer. Are you still living with that boyfriend? My parents had been glad to save the money on an unused room.

Instead, I spent the night on the futon on the floor of my office. We didn't have a second blanket, and I was too cold, too worked up, to sleep.

In the morning, I walked to campus and went to the residential life director's office. Were there any rooms left on campus? She handed me a box of tissues. "Aaron and I are going to spend some time apart," I said. I could barely get the words out.

There was a room in Hepburn Hall, on the fifth floor, and it was mine if I wanted it. I did. I dialed Aaron's number from the pay phone of Bicentennial Hall. I was serious about spending time apart. I would hold my ground.

There was his voice, bright and solid and apologetic. Light was streaming in the massive windows of the building. Outside the window, a cluster of yellow campus bikes was capped in snow.

How was it that my lives were split too rigidly and also that, at twenty, my life had become so entangled with my boyfriend's that I couldn't tell them apart? We call this paradox "codependency," but I didn't know it then. My dorm room in Hepburn Hall was the first nervous step I took out of that tangled nest.

But, okay, I still loved him. I admitted it on the phone. Given the distance, the morning, the fresh coat of snow, it felt possible to love him and to be me at the same time.

"Good," he said, relieved. I could hear him smiling. "'Cause I think I'm a pretty good guy."

He drove me to Ames and we bought a lavender sheet set, twin XL, to fit the bed in the dorm. I arranged the framed pictures of me and my boyfriend on the dresser. I stacked my CDs in my CD tower. Aaron bought me a stereo with a minidisc player and a white TV with a built-in VCR, and I thought both were the most impressive devices ever made. I was exultant, moving into that dorm room. It was a hundred

square feet that belonged to me. My parents may have been less exultant, scrambling to find a credit card for room and board again.

"Sorry, dude," my brothers said when I called to tell them I'd moved
out. They were shocked and sad. For Thanksgiving they'd visited us
at the house on Seymour Street. They'd played Sega Dreamcast with
Aaron and took turns shooting a BB gun at the otter-eaten trees in the
backyard. We went out to eat for Thanksgiving dinner, and they'd peer-
pressured him into eating turkey, and I'd shaken my head at them, bad
influences pushing my boyfriend off the vegetarian wagon.

"No, it's good," I said. "I'm happy. We're still dating. We're just not
living under the same roof."

It was good. I was happy. After class, nearly every day, Aaron picked
me up in the parking lot behind Hepburn Hall, and I'd climb into
his car, the heat roaring, and kiss him. We went on dates. We went to
Woody's and Amigo's and Fire & Ice. At the little second-run movie
theater on Main Street, we saw *Rushmore*. We saw *The Blair Witch Project*. We rented movies from the video store and watched them at his
place—it was his place now; he paid the rent—and then he drove me
back to my dorm. We were proud of ourselves. We had found a way to
be together. My hair had grown out to a cute and respectable bob.

One Saturday in March, I answered the phone at the bakery, expecting someone to ask about our hours or to order a cake. I could barely
understand the voice on the other end, but eventually I realized it was
Aaron. "My dad had a stroke," he cried.

At home, I found Aaron sitting on the bed, the phone to his ear.
When he hung up, he told me what the doctors had said. His father had
had a massive stroke. He'd been discovered on his scooter at the Palm
Beach Zoo—the zoo!—and rushed to the hospital, where he was now.
There wasn't much they could do but stabilize him.

"This is why I didn't want to leave," he said, sobbing. It wasn't really
an accusation, unless it was aimed at himself.

IRONY 2

His father suffered from posttraumatic stress syndrome. He did, after all, get shot into a tree by a landmine when he was not much more than a child. He watched his commanding officer killed in front of him. He killed a man, and his dog.

IRONY 3

Our older son worships his grandfather. He's obsessed with World War II. His favorite book is *Maus*. Every time we go to D.C., he asks to visit his grandfather's grave at Arlington. He will inherit Morris's Purple Hearts as well as the Nazi armband in our attic, which his grandfather removed from the uniform of the man he killed. When he was in first grade, Nico brought home from school a picture he had drawn of his grandfather at war, swastika armband and all. Luckily, he wasn't a very good artist then.

GEOGRAPHICAL CURE

How many houses have you and Dad lived in?" Nico asks.

"Together?" I count them up. I run out of fingers. "Eleven. This will be twelve!"

We are moving to a new house. We are tired of living among college kids, the lawn littered with red Solo cups, the electric lines strung with shoes. We chose the Aurora house in haste, fleeing the haunted Etna Road, and we've been there for four years. We've graduated, done our time. Time to move on—not to flee, but to put down roots. In the summer, we found a half-built house on a couple acres eight miles south, long past where Aurora Street becomes Danby Road. It's on the farthest edge of the county: the kids can stay at the same school, take the bus. There's a beautiful view of the mountains, a tiny creek, a strip of trees. The house is all windows and angles and French doors. Aaron and I fell in love with it immediately. "Contemporary as fuck" is how he put it. When we bought it, the only thing inside was a massive salvaged beam from a dairy barn, ancient, sturdy. The old thing in the new house feels like a blessing, like my grandmother's pearls that I wore at our wedding: something old, something new.

"Why not?" we said, arms around each other's waists. "Let's do it." I loved that about us, that we could make spontaneous decisions together, that we could change our lives if we wanted to.

It will be a couple of years before I'll hear the phrase, uttered by another codependent at an RCA retreat, "geographical cure." I won't need to look it up. I'll know exactly what it means.

November in Ithaca is like settling into a long fatal illness. I distract myself from winter, from Aaron's symptoms, with giddy plans for the new house. I research ceramic tile and wood grains, slate and concrete and quartz. All of the sturdy materials we will build our wolf-proof house with. Nothing will get to us there. Not by the hair on my chinny-chin-chin!

The kids are not excited about the new house. What was wrong with the old one? They don't care about Caesarstone countertops. They feel comfortable here, in this hundred-year-old house with its vinyl floors and stucco walls.

Every week or so, we drive down the road to check in on the progress. We try to visit when the kids are at school. We have a key, and today the house is empty. There are wood planks on the ceilings now, whitewashed, new. The walls are primed. In the highest windows, trapped flies butt against the glass.

Behind the house, the leaves have fallen off the trees in the woods, and now we can see in plain sight that the rocks leaning against the tree trunks are headstones. We investigate, boots crunching over the leaves. We can barely read the names on the stones, but there are a dozen corpses buried a hundred feet from the house, and they've been there for two hundred years. We have bought a cemetery.

We say it at the same time. "No fucking way we're telling the kids."

But what is there to do? We go back inside and make love on the stairs of our new house, because there is sawdust on the floor, and a cemetery in our backyard.

A week later, I wake to a strange sight: daylight. No school today, I remember. It's a parent-teacher conference day. Aaron isn't in our bed. He has turned on the air purifier so I can sleep in.

On the dining table downstairs are several versions of the same drawing he draws almost every night, two people bent toward each other, viewed from behind. At age forty-five, deep into illness, he has started drawing. At first, it was cartoons for the kids. Now, twists and turns and faces and figures. Some nights he fills a whole notebook, like he's making up for lost time.

The kids are awake, and Aaron is singing a song he's made up for them, called "The Lookaway":

> *Have you heard the news about the brand-new dance?*
> *It's got everyone moving like they peed their pants!*

The kids show me the dance, tossing their chins over their shoulders. I laugh hard.

He says, "I have the most useless skills."

On another November day, he says, "I want to take a long nap and wake up when all this is over." He says, "It's not worth it. I hate to tell you that. But right now I feel like it's not worth it."

The kisses, the sex, help. A blow job helps like nothing else. It cools the beast in his belly, in his brain.

"I want to feel something good," he says.

He says, "This feels good."

Spoiler alert.

In season two of *Stranger Things*, what happens to the boy with the Upside Down inside him is they have to burn it out of him.

He lies in the bed in the woods, writhing in pain, the thing choking him from within. The black vines crawl up his throat. He takes his mother by the throat.

I would do it. I would strap him to the bed, blast all the heaters, and press the hot poker to his belly.

In a note on my phone, Nico has composed a Christmas list while following me around Target. He has developed a code. The items with a crown emoji next to them are the ones he really wants. Most of the items are video games and most of them are marked with one crown. Then, at the bottom:

A cure for dad

Next to this item he has tapped out 107 crowns.

"Mom?" he asks in the car on the way home. "Are there doctors who are trying to find a cure for what Dad has?"

I think about it. "Not exactly. We don't know exactly what's wrong with Dad. We're kind of trying to find a cure ourselves."

It sounds outlandish when I say it, like I'm Jane Goodall or Erin Brockovich. Why do I think I can find a cure that dozens of doctors can't? And why is a cure what I'm looking for?

Back home, Nico helps me carry in the shopping bags. Aaron is moaning faintly on the couch. "You okay, Dad?" Nico asks. He goes to him and strokes his face.

I like to think he's imitating me, performing the loving care he has seen me give his father. Maybe he is. Maybe he is just a baby bonobo acting the part of a baby bonobo. What percentage of my own loving care is performance? Nico's affection is natural, innate.

"I'm okay, buddy," Aaron says.

"I want to be sleeping or dead."

We are at Stu's. When asked for clarification, he says, "I don't want to kill myself. I just want to be dead." I don't cry at this. It's not the first time I've heard it in this room.

For six years, we've sat beside each other on the chocolate suede love seat in the waiting room, but I sit across from him today. This is how the fight starts. Aaron says to me, "You're such a child."

We aren't fighting when Stu goes to fetch us some water. We are

fighting when he returns and we fight for perhaps half the session before he puts up a forefinger and says, "My turn?"

The fight is about my being defensive. I am defensive about that. We
fight and fight. I defend myself.

And then Aaron says, "You still don't understand me! You don't want
to understand me!"

This makes me defensive. I say, "Understanding you is my fucking
life's work!"

"Look," Aaron says. He sits with one elbow over the back of the
chair, the other hand gesturing at Stu. He is trying to explain me to our
therapist. "I still don't believe she really believes me." He is still looking
at Stu when he says, "I know my own body, honey."

We all laugh at the same time.

"You can call me honey if you want," Stu says.

It's an inside joke among the three of us, so twice as funny. We like
to quote the line from *What About Bob*, when Bill Murray tells his therapist, "You can call me Boob if you want!"

It helps, or doesn't help, that Aaron and I are simultaneously reminded of another slip-up of his, earlier in the day, when we were on
speaker phone with our builder and Aaron let out a not-subtle fart. We
are snickering conspiratorially now and we've lost the train of our anger.
It's running around the room like a poodle with its leash trailing.

"That's how much I care about you," Aaron tells Stu. "To me, you're
honey." And we both tell him how, last week when I told Aaron to pick
me up a pregnancy test—it was negative, that familiar twin of disappointment and relief—Aaron told me, "If it's a boy, his middle name
will be Stu."

Stu is touched, but the clock is ticking. He tries to get us back on
track.

"You just don't accept that I'm sick," Aaron says, looking at me now.
"I get one diagnosis, and you can't accept it. I get another diagnosis,
you still don't accept it. You're still trying to fix me on your own terms!"

That's when I stop being defensive and start to cry. "You're right," I
say. "You're right, you're right."

It's an unseasonably warm day, fifty degrees and sunny. In Ithaca, any day in November when the sun is out is powerful enough to heal rifts between warring nation-states and spouses.

"Go put your face in the sun for five minutes," Stu says.

So we stop at the park on the way home and walk along the lake under the willows. He looks for driftwood to draw. I put my hands inside his jacket. It's like the rush of oxytocin after giving birth, the hormones washing away my body's memory of pain. Stu's waiting room is far behind us, and we are only here in the sun, and through my gloves I can feel my husband's blood beating beneath his ribs.

In the new house, we will not leave dirty dishes piled in the sink. We will not leave Lego creations on the dining room table. We will not yell at the children to brush their teeth, put on their shoes, stop touching each other, stop saying, "Kiss my ass," stop saying "Look at my nuts!" In the new house, I will use all five burners of the gas range to make soups with root vegetables, all of the vegetables no one wants from the farm share. We will get a farm share. None of the food in our French-door refrigerator will go bad. The kids will get water for themselves from the dispenser. This will increase my productivity by twenty percent. We will be productive, patient, loving, free. Even our messes will be beautiful— colorful blocks on the shag rug, red wine stains on the concrete counters. We will eat all our meals in the same room. Aaron will not sleep through breakfast. Aaron will not sleep through dinner. I will not whisper-yell, "Don't wake your father!" We will build plywood furniture from plans we find on YouTube. We will build a new life. We will buy new sheets and rugs and pillows, and none of them will be stained with his blood.

"Can I tell you something?" Aaron asks me.

I am full of plans for the new house. My mind is on pendant lamps and fiberglass doors, backsplashes and built-ins. But when I show him the catalogs, the Pinterest pins, he shrugs.

"I know it's crazy," he says. "But part of me thinks I'll never live in that house."

I tell him that breaks my heart. I tell him I have no idea what that means.

Actually, I have two ideas. He believes I will leave him, or he believes he will be dead.

The first weekend of December, Aaron drops me off at the local arts colony so I can write for a few days. I pack two reusable grocery bags of books. If I get stuck writing, I can read. Yiyun Li's *Dear Friend, from My Life I Write to You in Your Life.* Ron Powers's *No One Cares About Crazy People.* Leslie Jamison's *The Empathy Exams.* I unpack my books, my index cards, my ear plugs, my soymilk. Settling in is the hard part. One half of my brain is trying to focus on my desk. The other half is thinking about my boys—whether Aaron will feel well enough to take them out of the house, whether he'll feed them noodles for breakfast.

I still haven't gotten past "The Devil's Bait" in Jamison's book. My brain is stuck on it. But I slide out the book and open it up. It feels like touching an old bruise to find the line I read in that coffee shop in Vermont:

> This isn't an essay about whether Morgellons disease is real. That's probably obvious by now.

The shame of believing, the shame of being fooled.

I close the book. It's been five years since I researched Morgellons disease with any seriousness, but I find myself typing the words into the search bar. Am I trying to recover evidence, looking for clues to some forgotten crime? To find a definition that will confirm Jamison's claim? Or that will refute it? There are the familiar photos, the CDC report, the link to Jamison's essay, published in *Harper's* and illustrated with a black-and-white hellscape: a skeletal figure, more insect than man, with fingers distorted into rakes. What I don't expect to find is a new scientific paper, published in 2016. "Morgellons disease: A filamentous borrelial dermatitis." Authors: Marianne J Middelveen and Raphael B Stricker. I read the first line of the abstract:

> Morgellons disease (MD) is a dermopathy characterized
> by multicolored filaments that lie under, are embedded
> in, or project from skin. Although MD was initially con-
> sidered to be a delusional disorder, recent studies have
> demonstrated that the dermopathy is associated with
> tickborne infection, that the filaments are composed of
> keratin and collagen, and that they result from prolifer-
> ation of keratinocytes and fibroblasts in epithelial tissue.

I'm sitting on the carpet, cross-legged in front of the coffee table. I increase the size of the font, blow it up. I read the words again. Then I scroll on, past a photo of a hand that could be Aaron's.

> The distinguishing feature of MD is the appearance of
> skin lesions with filaments that lie under, are embedded
> in, or project from skin (Figures 1 and 2). Filaments can
> be white, black, or brightly colored. Furthermore, MD
> patients exhibit a variety of manifestations that resemble
> symptoms of Lyme disease (LD), such as fatigue, joint
> pain, and neuropathy. A study found that 98% of MD
> subjects had positive LD serology and/or a tickborne dis-
> ease diagnosis.

I sit up, kneel in front of the screen, stare into it like a face. The part of my brain that is persuaded by scientific language is lighting up with hope: dermopathy, neuropathy, serology.

Here I fall deep, deep down the rabbit hole.

I open links, chase leads, research publications, Google scientists, define terms. Bovine digital dermatitis, Borrelia burgdorferi, histopathology, microspectrophotometry. I know there are standards for publishing scientific articles, but I don't really know what they are. "It has to be peer-reviewed!" I tell my students. There are more new studies, more new papers. They seem to be peer-reviewed? All of them are published on Dove Press. What is Dove Press? "Open access to scientific and medical research." Open access is good, right?

Except you have to pay to have your papers published there. Except Dove Press was kicked out of the Open Access Scholarly Publishers Foundation for "lax standards for accepting manuscripts."

The author consistent across the articles is Marianne Middelveen. A veterinary microbiologist.

Who is on the board of the Charles E. Holman Morgellons Disease Foundation.

I scroll to the bottom of the first article.

> Funding for open access publication was provided by the
> Charles E. Holman Morgellons Disease Foundation,
> Austin, TX, USA.

God, what a dummy.

I have been reading at an arm's length, but still, I feel that I've fallen from a great height, splayed hideously on the carpet. My jaw is tense. I close the computer.

Phone reception is weak at the colony, so the next day I have to step out onto the balcony in my scarf and jacket and socks to hear Aaron's voice on the other end of the line. He has taken the kids out for breakfast and they've watched *Robin Hood: Men in Tights* and now he is calling from the school playground, where he is tossing a Frisbee around with them.

He is okay. The children are okay.

He sends me a video. I press play. Henry throws the Frisbee and yells, "In your nuts!" His voice echoes across the empty playground.

I put down the phone. The electric kettle is warming and the table is scattered with my coffee grounds and some other artist's dried paint. The light is paling in the tall windows above the desk. There is a long winter ahead of us, but now December is young, the woods brown and gray, and there has been little snow yet.

IRONY 4

A person who brings others such joy finds his own joy so elusive.

BOMB CYCLONE

The bomb cyclone, the first storm of 2018, has covered the Northeast in snow. Ithaca is just on the edge of it, but here it is always cold. We send the kids to school on January 4th, bundled, waxed in lip balm, but on the 5th the wind chill is below zero, and school is canceled. In two weeks, we'll move to the house down the road. We stay home and pack boxes and watch *Naked and Afraid,* and the kids build a box fort that would provide expert-level shelter on any croc-infested island. They hunker down in it and do Mad Libs by the light of Aaron's camping flashlight, then fall asleep in it, bundled in his sleeping bag.

Upstairs in bed, Aaron swipes between two pictures—one of Henry in his room in front of his massive grown-up shadow, and one of his own leg in the shower, snapped earlier that day, gushing clotty blood into the drain. "Stop looking at that," I suggest.

Both pictures bring him to the edge of crying. He swipes back to Henry, his shy smile, two teeth lost last week.

"I have such a good life," he says. "It kills me that I can't enjoy it."

On *Naked and Afraid,* there is always a survivalist who's too tough to cry, until he isn't anymore. Then his partner tells him it's okay to show emotion.

"Hell yeah it is," Aaron says to our young survivalists. "I cry at least once a day."

This is not news to our kids, who are mostly interested in the blurred, bug-bitten backsides of the contestants.

That night, at one in the morning, I wake up to Aaron chewing what sounds like pretzels in the dark. He is chewing, and then he is snoring. I nudge him. "Honey, finish your food."

He laughs, chews some more, then he's snoring again.

I poke him. "Honey."

He laughs, finishes his pretzel, snores again.

I poke him. "Can you turn over please?"

"Turn over? Why would I turn over?"

"Not all the way. Like on your side."

He turns on his side. Still he snores.

I take my pillow down the hall to Henry's bedroom, closing the door so his snores won't follow me. I sleep on the bottom bunk.

At three A.M., I hear his struggled shuffling in the hall. "I need help I need help I need help."

I bolt up, go to him, hold him up by the shoulders. "What's wrong?"

"My leg. My leg." He is writhing while standing up. He is incoherent, irritable, breathing deeply. I don't understand what's happened—is it his wound? Is his leg swollen? Is he trying to go downstairs for more pretzels?

"Cramp," he says, "in the back of my knee," but as he says it, it seems to be easing. He's wincing, he's hopping, but he's quieting.

"You almost killed me," he says.

"I almost killed you?"

"I was calling for you. I was calling and calling."

I tell him I'm sorry. I didn't hear.

Now he is shivering. "I'm cold," he says, and I see that his teeth are chattering.

"You probably have an infection," I say, walking him back to our bed. He lies down, still writhing, and I cover him with the duvet. I try rubbing his arms to warm him up, but he says, "Careful of my skin."

For a few seconds I watch him struggle under the sheets. We're both helpless. Then carefully, sitting beside him, I cover the top of his body with the top of my body, offering him my warmth. The air goes out of his lungs, and on his next breath, he is snoring.

.   .   .

We do move into the new house. We do, on a mild day in late January. We write the movers a check. It's taken them two loads of their giant truck. We have twice as much stuff as we thought we did.

The first night, I climb on to the kitchen island and lie facedown on the Caesarstone counter. I kiss it. "I'm gonna sleep here," I tell Aaron.

The kids, they still aren't thrilled. They miss the old house, down the road.

"But it's so much bigger!" we say.

In February, my dad moves in. It was part of the plan: in the new house, we'll have room for my dad. It's our turn to take him, after many years of his living with Sam's family outside D.C. Sam has moved to a new house, too, and my dad's room was in the basement: no windows, steep stairs, a furnace that makes all kinds of noises in the night. Each time a visitor asks him how he likes it here, he says, "So quiet! Except for two of the loudest grandchildren in the world." He ruffles Henry's hair. The room is small, a converted foyer, big enough only for a couch and a TV. But he is easy to please. He likes the light that comes in the tall windows, the proximity to the bathroom and the coffee machine.

The only thing that feels off: he doesn't smoke anymore. Sam and Keri convinced him to quit when he moved into their new house. His pipes are gone. Every once in a while, he makes a joke about going to the tobacco shop, and I say, "Sorry, Dad." He has a ten-year-old heart bypass, and I want to keep his heart pumping.

A few days after my dad arrives, Aaron and I are back at urgent care, the one with the Pac-Man arcade game in the waiting room. The kids are sad they can't come with us. We leave them home with my dad.

We fear it's the flu. The flu is bad this year. Kids and grandparents are dying of the flu. Last week Aaron reconnected with an old friend from Florida on Facebook. They thought they both had the flu. How long does it last? the friend asked. Couple weeks, Aaron said. Within a week the friend was dead. The year before he'd nearly died from years of drinking. His immune system was shot.

Now Aaron is thinking about his own liver, what he's done to it. The scale has tipped 200 again. He has the bloated neck, the barrel belly, of the Bad Time, the months he looked like he'd drowned in gin. This time it's vodka. I know, he says before I can say it, I know. On the new season of *Stranger Things*, a character extolled the healing virtues of vodka, and Aaron raised his eyebrows. *See?* Sometimes whiskey, sometimes gin, but always vodka. "I don't care what anyone says," Aaron says. "I know myself. It's the one thing that works."

But the flu. That's what it must be now. For weeks he's been drained, throwing up, short of breath. Yesterday he tried to climb the hill behind our new house to explore the graveyard with our kids—Aaron, a little drunk, told Nico about the graveyard, and he wasn't scared—and he could barely make it. Today, late on a Friday afternoon, he spiked a fever. So: urgent care, the one in the plaza between the Chipotle and the Supercuts. Aaron jokes with the nurse that he needs a frequent-user punch card: every tenth copay should be free.

The doctor, who looks a little like Aaron's mother—the same firm, flat mouth; the sharp, slim nose; the makeup that looks painted on—does not swab Aaron for a flu test. She takes one listen to his chest and calls for a chest X-ray. "Could be bronchitis or pneumonia," she says. Aaron goes back for the X-ray, returns to the exam room. On the little TV above the sink, *Couples Retreat* is playing mutely.

We peck away at our phones. We read the news. The Winter Olympics. The Parkland shooting. Trump's playmate affairs. Aaron is feeling better after the Tylenol the nurse has given him, and sheepish: maybe all he needed was a Tylenol. He hates nothing more than looking stupid, of asking for help when he doesn't need it.

After half an hour, I go out to the desk to check on the results. The doctor is squinting at her computer. "The tech still has the chart locked," she says, confusion in her voice. That means the remote technician is reading the X-ray. "He should be done by now." She'll try to call him.

Fifteen more minutes pass before she returns to the room. I'm sitting on her rolling stool so she stands against the door, far from Aaron, as though she might want to make a quick exit. "How long ago did you quit smoking?" she asks.

"Six years," Aaron says, not hesitating. This month is six years since my mother died of lung cancer, after a dozen years with COPD. His mother, too, has died of COPD, less than a year ago.

"Your lungs show significant changes," she says. I wonder how she knows how they've changed, what they looked like before. "They show emphysema. That's why the tech took so long."

Aaron looks at me, eyebrows raised—is this a big deal?

"Fuck," I say.

He looks back to the doctor. "Fuck," he says.

"You also have bronchitis," the doctor says.

I picture the X-ray tech alone in a room somewhere peering at the gray sacks of my husband's forty-five-year-old lungs. What did he see, in those ink clouds and smudges? The twenty years of cigarettes, give or take? The two packs a day of Marlboro Reds?

"And all that pot," Aaron says from the passenger seat on the way home, staring at the windshield in disbelief. He will call his doctor for a referral to a pulmonologist. It's good they caught it now, the doctor says, while he is young. She's prescribed steroids and antibiotics until then, and we say thank you, thank you so much.

We're sitting at a red light behind Chipotle when he says, "And that's not all. I smoked heroin."

I close my eyes.

"I didn't know that," I say.

"What'd you think? You know I didn't shoot it up."

"I thought you snorted it."

"I did that, too."

The blinker ticks. We are waiting to turn left, the day turning to night in the moment before the light changes.

"It would have been really nice if you hadn't spent so many years trying to destroy your body," I point out.

We are not arguing. We are both sitting there, strapped into our seats.

"Well, for a long time I did want to kill myself," he says matter-of-factly. "Now I don't."

In March, Dad slips on the bathmat, falls, and breaks two ribs. I'm at a birthday party with Henry while he lies on the bathroom floor, calling out for help. Aaron is downstairs sleeping. Nico is in his room on the other side of the wall with his headphones on. When he finally goes into the bathroom, Dad has been lying there for thirty minutes.

"Not a great welcome, Dad." He's in his regular warm spirits, but I feel terrible. I have underestimated, it seems, what it will mean to have another body, a brittle body, in this house.

When my dad gets out of the hospital, we buy Nico a Gizmo watch. The three of them, it occurs to me, all need the same amount of looking-after: the eighty-six-year-old, the nine-year-old, the forty-five-year-old. Together, they look after each other. I'll feel better leaving them alone if I can reach Nico. The watch is red; he wears it gleefully. He can call five programmed numbers. He can text nine programmed messages: On the way. Where are you? We can program custom messages, too. I program two:

> You are a badass mom.
> Dad needs you.

It takes weeks to get an appointment with the pulmonologist. When we do, she looks at Aaron's chest X-ray and confirms it: the spot of emphysema on his lung. She orders another, to be safe.

On the second X-ray, the spot is gone. You don't have emphysema at all, she tells Aaron.

We are relieved. But confused. What do you mean, he doesn't have emphysema?

The pulmonologist cannot explain it. It was there, and now it's gone.

I wake to the slamming open of the pocket door. Aaron is yelling. He is yelling at me to get out of bed and take him to the hospital.

It's the middle of the night: 2:00 A.M.

"You have to look at this! You have to look at this!"

The lights are turned on. An arm is thrust in my face.

"Aaron, please!"

"You *have* to look at this. You *have* to look!"

"Aaron," I whisper. "You have to be quiet."

"Fuck quiet! You have to see this NOW."

I fumble for my glasses. I put them on. Aaron is in a gray T-shirt and underwear. I say, "What is it?"

"Shit is *coming* out of me. Parasites!"

His arm is a bloody mess. He is rubbing the skin, trying to force something out.

"I can't see when you're doing that."

He needs me to follow him to the family room, to see better. He shoves his arm under the lamp on the speaker, spattering blood on the white wall of our new house, and I see that there is already blood on the wall, and sweat, a steamy, bloody shower, and I understand that he has been standing under this lamp all night, staring at his arm, rubbing it unceasingly, there is blood on his T-shirt, and a hole in its hem. I fixate on this hole; it is the only thing that seems real.

In the corner, the dog stands from his bed. His collar jingles. "You're scaring Zabby," I say. "You're scaring me."

"Nell, you don't understand! You need to take me to the hospital!"

"I'm not taking you to the hospital!"

"I'll drive then."

"You can't drive like this!"

"I'll take a cab!"

"You're not going to the hospital! You're a mess. They'll send you to the psych ward, Aaron."

"They won't! They'll see I have parasites. They have to see them."

"I can't see them, honey."

"How can you not see them? Are you fucking crazy?"

He laughs maniacally. *Maniacally* is the word in my head.

"Drink some water," I say helplessly, handing him the Nalgene bottle from the coffee table.

He bats it away. "Look at this look at this look at this."

"Aaron. Sweetie. You have to calm down."

"Please please please take me. Help me!"

"Please please please calm down."

He is pacing, sweating, swearing, begging. I stand in the center of the room while he circles around me, knocking into things. Any minute the boys will be awake. They will come down the stairs and see their father, raving mad. *Raving mad* are the words in my head, this is what *raving mad* looks like. I am both in my body and out of it, looking down from above, he has passed into a new state and so have I, when I take the Nalgene bottle and dump it over his head.

He collapses on the floor, back against the couch.

"What are you doing! What have you done! You'll wash them away! You'll wash them away! They can't see them if you wash them away!"

Then I too am collapsed on the floor, and I am crying. My husband looks like a doll who has been dropped by a fickle child, his limbs bent grotesquely. *Lost his shit,* are the words I hear, in his voice.

"Okay," I say quietly. "I will take you. I will take you to the hospital, but we're going to the psych ward."

He is unreachable now, mumbling to himself, crying.

In a daze I walk up the stairs to my dad. Somehow the children have managed to sleep through it, but my dad is sitting there on the couch, waiting for me.

"I'm taking Aaron to the hospital. He's seeing things. He thinks he's covered in parasites!"

"Oh, honey." He holds me while I cry.

Downstairs, though, Aaron says, "I'm not going to the hospital."

"What?"

"I'm not going to the psych ward! I'm not crazy."

"You're seeing things, Aaron. You're not yourself."

"Fuck that."

"Please. Let's go."

"I'm not going. I'm fine."

"You're not fine. You're very sick."

"You're going to take me to the psych ward."

I realize I am very tired and do not actually want to drive to the hospital. I don't want to deal with any of this.

"Fine," I say. "We'll go in the morning."

Somehow, he lets me bring him to bed and accepts a Seroquel. His body is heavy beside me, steaming with sweat. Slowly his breathing eases into sleep. And I am envious, so envious, of those 600 milligrams of oblivion. I want to sleep until it's over.

MANHATTAN AVENUE

2001

Three days after I graduated from college, I took a bus to New York City and moved in with a very tall and very handsome gay stranger named Phillip. For a month I lived in his studio apartment on Madison Avenue, watching the beautiful pastel city through the giant window above my downy white guest bed. Everything in the apartment was white. It was a work of minimalist art—no couch, no television, no microwave. "Where's the garbage?" I asked Phillip, holding a pitiful fistful of trash.

"Oh, I don't have one," he apologized. "I just bring it out to the street."

He was the executive assistant to the editor-in-chief at a glossy lifestyle magazine, a friend of a friend, and I was to take over his afternoon shifts while he studied for the MCAT. I was living with him until Aaron moved to New York and our lease started.

Aaron and I knew we wanted to move to New York when I finished college. At first I'd planned to apply to grad schools there. Then I decided to put grad school off. Get some life experience first, every single professor advised. I felt that every year of being Aaron's girlfriend was worth seven years of real-life experience, and I was proud of this, this is what I'd wanted, but I didn't tell my professors this. "Are you married?" one of them asked before workshop one evening, as we waited for the classroom before us to empty. She pointed to the silver band on my ring finger. I was proud of this, too, that my professor would assume I was the kind of nineteen-year-old who would be serious enough to get married. "It's just kind of a promise ring," I told her. Aaron had a matching one. He'd been saying we should get married since we'd moved in together, and when I told him not yet, and he asked, "Why?" and I said, "I'm eighteen," he looked at me as though this was a ridiculous reason.

We wouldn't get married this year either, but I had begun to think about it in my last year of college, the year we spent apart, he in Florida, I in Vermont. Walking around town, I eyed the bed-and-breakfasts, the village green with the gazebo where Aaron and I had spent so many hours, now covered in snow. I imagined it come to life with wildflowers, saw a ceremony there, the eaves strung with tiny lights. At work, as I stood at the back table folding bakery boxes, I daydreamed of the dress I might wear, a sunshiny yellow, I thought, because it was the middle of winter and I was hungry for spring. I missed my boyfriend.

So we would be reunited, not in Vermont or in Florida but in New York. It had once been his home, the place he knew best. His mother was there. His memories were there. It would be a return for him; he could be more himself. And it would be a new start for me; I could be the self I wanted to be—more fashionable, funnier, with more friends. I would have material. I would have experience. I could see the two of us walking arm in arm down the street, Aaron's step both more relaxed and more alive, mine a little taller in my platform shoes.

Over spring break, Aaron and I met in the city to try to find an apartment. We hadn't heard of Craigslist; we were looking in *The Village Voice.* It seemed an impossible task. His mother urged us to call her cousin, a real estate agent in the city, but Aaron said we could find something ourselves. He didn't like relying on family. We couldn't find anything ourselves. On the last day of our visit, I broke down and cried at the Astor Place Starbucks. The idea of returning to Florida put me in a soul-panic.

Aaron broke down and called his cousin. We went to her office and immediately she found us a one-bedroom sublet in an elevator building for $1,200 a month, for a fee of $1,200. She took down our information on the application form—rental history, previous addresses, income. I told her what I'd be making at the magazine. Then she looked to Aaron. "About two thousand dollars," he said.

His cousin paused her pen. "Two thousand a month?" she asked.

"No. For the year."

"Wow," his cousin said.

His cousin owned two apartments in Greenwich Village—one for herself and one for her dogs.

While I started my new job and pretended I lived on the Upper East Side, Aaron tied up loose ends in Florida. He was needed to take care of one problem at one property, then another. A hurricane rolled through and took part of a roof off one of the houses. There were bills to pay, cats to feed, repairs to oversee. He'd picked up some shifts at CD Warehouse. Might as well. This pleased me, his return to the job he'd had when we met. We might go on indefinitely like this, us being the people we'd been before we'd complicated each other's lives.

It was a strange period of inheritance. His father wasn't dead yet. But there was little Aaron could do for him by that point. After a second stroke, he was an empty shell. Slowly it became clear he would be a resident at the VA hospital for the rest of his life, however long that would be.

Meanwhile, there was stuff. A lot of it.

His father had once been a rich man. Now Aaron had to rummage through a lot of bizarre crap to find the equally bizarre riches. Jewels. Some gold pieces. Tiny jagged pieces of meteorite, encased in beds of cotton. Mayan artifacts that belonged in a museum. The speakers his father had manufactured in his factory in the Bronx. Aaron would call me and report on the day's findings. What to save? What to trash? What to sell? His attitude about his father's stuff ranged from annoyance to disgust to nostalgia to reverence. Other days he just wanted to burn it all. "I'm afraid I'm going to find something scary," he said.

"Like what?"

"I don't know."

He had already found his father's guns. They were one of the first things Aaron sold. They went to Morris's friend from the VA. Aaron didn't want them around, and I was glad to see them go.

In other boxes, he found pictures. Pictures of his grandfather, his namesake, Aaron David. Pictures of his father's first wife, the woman he had married shortly after returning from the war. Aaron knew of her, growing up, had seen the pictures of the young wife and their baby son, who was born with his umbilical cord wound around his neck. His brain suffered such loss of oxygen that it never developed beyond his birth. He learned to walk but not to speak. As though knowing what fate lay beyond, Morris had reversed the order of the names he'd intended to give his first son: David Aaron.

David was twenty-five years older than Aaron. He might have been his father, if he had ever had a life of his own. When he was a child, too much of a burden on his young parents, his mother made the decision to commit him to an institution upstate. Morris didn't want to. At least that's what he told Aaron. That was the end of their marriage.

Still David lived in a home in Rome, New York. As a child, Aaron had never been taken to see his brother, and now he was an adult and didn't know how to start, whether he should, what it would do for him or David.

But now these were among the calls and letters Aaron managed. He was still in his twenties and the power of attorney for a seventy-six-year-old man in one home and a fifty-four-year-old man in another, both of whom were spoon-fed their breakfasts by a state-paid nurse. Insurance, social workers, medical updates. Morris had a stomach virus. David had eaten a razor blade. Morris would be moved to a room down the hall. David had eaten a comb.

There were the pictures. Then there were all the contents of his father's walk-in closet, and a storage unit across the street: cases and cases of collectibles from failed businesses. Baseball cards, coins. His father had written them off. They weren't worth much, but they weren't worthless. Aaron got to know the baseball card dealers in town, the coin dealers. He'd meet them in the parking lot of the storage unit and make a deal. And he started selling stuff on eBay. Slowly, he learned the way it all worked. How to time an auction for the best bids. How to deal with buyers. How to insure a package. He became a regular at the post office on US-1. He started researching his items on eBay, finding poorly listed auctions—inaccurate descriptions, or misspellings—then buying those items and relisting them at a profit. He hadn't signed up for it, but he was good at it. That year, for Christmas, I had business cards designed for him, which he tucked into every package.

I don't remember having a conversation about it. It was predetermined. That was what he would do in New York. He would sell stuff on eBay.

After sixteen months sleeping in his old bed, he called his father's social worker and his brother's social worker and gave them his new address. He found homes for his father's cats and he drove to New York. He would go back to visit his father every month. The condo sat, shuttered, empty of people, full of junk.

Every Sunday afternoon, we took three trains to visit Aaron's mother on St. Marks Place. In some ways we considered it our neighborhood, more than Manhattan Avenue. It was Aaron's home. We walked the block he'd walked as a kid, a whole universe between Second and Third avenues, drank egg creams at the Gem Spa, browsed music at Kim's, comics at St. Mark's Comics. That was where he'd played arcade games; that was where he'd played violin in front of his mom's restaurant; that was where he'd bought liquor for his mom's restaurant; that was the dumpster where she'd found a dead body; that was where he and his best friend, Ashmat, used to sell the Star Wars action figures they'd stolen from K-mart. In some ways, it felt like the reason we were here in New York: so we could walk up and down this block, reconstructing Aaron's childhood.

Aaron's mom had grown up in Manhattan. Her parents hadn't married; she had more half-siblings than Aaron could count. When she was a child, she had been subjected to abuses acknowledged but not detailed by the family. Her father had sent her to a boarding school in

Belgium, where she was taught by nuns. Like Aaron's father, she did not go to college.

But she learned French and Spanish and Italian. She learned to cook from her mother, a Sicilian immigrant with a restaurant in Midtown. She was married young, to a man who abused her and her two children, and divorced young. She was married again, to a millionaire and World War II vet who had struck it big with a speaker company he'd founded. She told me later he was the love of her life. He bought her a big Gatsby mansion in Manhasset (built by Raoul Fleischmann, cofounder of *The New Yorker* and heir to the Fleischmann baking company) with twenty-three rooms, chauffeur's quarters, a tennis court, and a swimming pool on Oyster Bay. In pictures from that time, family lounged around the pool, smoking, laughing, doting on her baby son, Aaron. Aaron's older half-sister and half-brother, who lived there with them, aunts, uncles, cousins. There were nanny's quarters too. It was his Dominican nanny, Eni, who really raised him, he said. His first language was Spanish. Lost now.

When Aaron was six, his mother moved out. His half-siblings, now grown, had left, too. Aaron lived in that big house with his father. Morris told him his mother didn't want to be a mother anymore. Sandra told him his father had cut her off, used his money and power to muscle her out of Aaron's life. "I couldn't fight him," she told me. After a while she moved to St. Marks Place, where she had been living now in a rent-controlled apartment for more than twenty years, half of them with a boyfriend who was thirty years her junior. As a kid, Aaron had visited on the weekends, in the summers, whenever he could, even after his father moved him to Florida. His dad kept a tight leash on him, but on his days in the city, he was free. Once, at sixteen, he skipped school, pawned his amp, got a ride to the airport, and bought a ticket to LaGuardia. He called his father that afternoon from his mom's living room. "I'm in New York," he told him. He expected his dad to be furious, but Morris laughed and laughed.

From the sidewalk, I could see a slice of that living room: the cherry cabinet lined with vases, the crystal chandelier. The apartment had once been the second-story entrance to the building; now the ornate white

French doors opened on to a tiny balcony. The next building over, the Search & Destroy vintage clothing store blasted punk, but as I approached I could hear the competing notes of a symphony. I'd duck under the Sock Man's awning and Aaron would ring the buzzer. "Hey, Ma," he'd say.

"Come on up, sweeties."

I could smell the onions sizzling as I came up the stairs. Sandra would be hustling around the kitchen when we came through the propped-open door; she stopped to air kiss each of our cheeks. "I'm making pulao," she'd say. Or dumplings, or soup—vegan, she'd promise.

"Smells so good," I'd say. She smelled good, too, floral and sharp. She was sweating over the stove, but she did so with the slightly intimidating poise of a woman who had once employed a chef herself, and often said so. She was a large woman, and the tiny kitchen she filled was a kind of extension of her body. Everything in the apartment was tiny: tiny stove, tiny refrigerator, tiny countertop that swung open to pass through to the tiny living room, and closed to double as the tiny dining table. I could reach out and touch the mirrored door to the bathroom, which was so tiny I could sit on the tiny toilet while washing my hands in the tiny sink. But the whole apartment was tall; all the tiny things were stacked neatly in long, white cupboards that stretched to the eleven-foot ceilings. A loft bed hovered overhead.

"Can I help?" I'd think to ask. I was a little scared of her, the same way I was still a little scared of New York. I was worried that I'd burn or bungle something, that I'd reveal myself to be the inept girl who could never get my MetroCard to swipe on the first try.

Sandra would wave a hand. She cooked; it was second nature; it was like asking her if I could help her walk. "It's easy. You could make it. I'll give you the recipe. Oh! I have something for you." Rarely did we come over without her pressing some cast-offs into our hands. She'd open one of the tall cabinets and pull out a handful of slightly bowed wooden spoons. "They were just going to throw them away." She cooked for a family uptown. She used to cook for George Soros and would bring home his discarded pots and pans.

At dinner, Sandra told stories about a bright and colorful ensemble cast, friends and lovers and cousins who were dancers and psychics and entrepreneurs, Bob Dylan singing on the sidewalk, Madonna eating in her restaurant, beautiful people (his sister, his niece)—they could have been models! Sandra, too, had been beautiful—"I used to be beautiful, you know," she would say, with pain. She told only a handful of stories about Aaron. "I took you to Radio City. You must have been seven or eight. You loved those Rockettes!" It was a shallow field, I realized, Sunday after Sunday, her memories of Aaron as a child.

But she was fairly absent in Aaron's stories of New York, too, a figure glimpsed from under a table at her restaurant, where he played. "She fed me well," he allowed. There was that.

She fed us well still, these Sundays, and I felt strangely full and empty, leaving the apartment, as she pressed a bag of goodies into my arms—leftovers and the wooden spoons, a silk jacket she didn't wear anymore. We walked in silent exhaustion to the subway station. I didn't tell Aaron that, after dinner, when he was in the bathroom, Sandra had leaned over to me and whispered, "You know, he could get his chin done, easy." She held her glass of sparkling water steadily in one hand, and with the other, scissored the skin under her own chin.

One night, leaving his mom's, he pointed out the building to me. A regular building on St. Marks Place he had passed a thousand times as a kid. It was the building where his mom and Ashmat's dad had owned a restaurant while they were carrying on an affair. It had happened shortly after Aaron had moved from New York to Florida. He hadn't wanted to leave his best friend. Ashmat was about twelve. When he and his siblings had come over from Afghanistan—his father, a judge back home, had sent for them—they hadn't brought birth certificates. The family wasn't sure of his exact age.

One day, one of the waitresses found herself locked out of her apartment in the building. It was her idea to tie a rope around Ashmat's waist and lower him from the roof down to the third-floor window. But she hadn't been able to hold on, and Ashmat fell to the ground. He died in the hospital.

Aaron learned the news from his father, in their condo in Florida.

Ashmat was the one in Aaron's stories of New York. Selling fire-works with Ashmat. Going to see *E. T.* in the theater with Ashmat. He still had a Snoopy Valentine's Day card from Ashmat. "He was like a brother to me," Aaron said.

Phillip had lined up another job for me. It was with another friend of his, a woman who worked as a private art dealer and bookseller and needed an assistant. This meant I went to her Tribeca studio and ordered old books and prints on eBay and put new dust jackets and frames on them so that my boss could sell them for ridiculous amounts of money. It also meant I helped her out of bed and fetched her coffee and cia-batta rolls and listened to her gossip about rich people in New York. I felt poor and dull in her presence, but never bored; feeling poor and dull was a small price to pay for proximity to a dark and dysfunctional opulence. She once bought me a $300 dress from Bergdorf Goodman, black and silky and, I realized too late, entirely see-through in the flash of a camera.

Meanwhile Aaron was at home in our apartment, selling things on eBay. He too was calculating markup and postage and insurance, timing auctions and waiting in line at the post office in our neigh-borhood, leaving with receipts long enough to touch the ground. He'd already gone home to Florida once to visit his dad at the VA nursing home and to pick up more inventory: baseball cards, coins, figures, his own versions of weird collectibles. I knew he was also picking up pot.

We were in New York City. There were drugs everywhere. It was the place Aaron had first tried pot, first tried everything. His mother had kept it in the refrigerator. But he was too shy, or paranoid, or isolated, to ask for connections. He thought about having his dealer in Florida mail him some. But we had a friend in Vermont who'd been arrested for receiving pot through the mail. Aaron didn't want to risk it. Instead, he flew down to Florida, rented a car, and drove back with a trunk full of collectibles, a big bag of pot hidden in an emptied-out Nintendo console. The uglier the car, he thought, the better. No cop was going to pull over a white guy driving a Pontiac Aztec.

I took in this information with some amusement and some worry. I still felt like a square myself, didn't really like to smoke and never smoked with him. But I'd accepted that it was a part of Aaron's life, accepted that he needed it, even if I didn't totally understand why. When I'd feel the worry nagging me, I'd tell myself, Everyone smokes pot! It's a harmless hippie drug!

Mostly, I was worried about money. The money came in, a little here, a little more there. Aaron had access to his dad's accounts, but there was less and less money in them, mortgages to cover, insurance, repairs. I was starting to feel the weight of it, money, the gravity it had in New York.

Phillip's MCAT class was coming to a close. Soon he would take back the afternoon shift at the magazine and I would be done.

Then one morning I received a phone call on my giant clamshell cell phone. It was from an editor at *Poets & Writers*. They had received my letter and résumé. As it happened, they were looking for a part-time person to edit a couple of sections of the magazine. Would I like to come in for an interview?

A few mornings later I took the 6-train downtown past St. Marks, and got off at Spring, wearing the suit and the silver sweater shell my mother had bought me at the Gardens Mall. The editors were kind and did not seem to notice how very badly I wanted the job.

We shook hands. They'd be in touch. I went downstairs to the enormous Starbucks and bought an iced latte. A splurge! I fantasized about drinking iced lattes on my breaks. I took out the giant phone and called Aaron. "How'd it go?" he asked. He was in Florida, visiting his dad. "I have a good feeling," I said. It was September 10, 2001.

It was shortly before 9:00 A.M. when my brother Sam called from D.C. Had I seen the news? I sat up in bed. More than a hundred blocks north of the towers, the sky out the window was, as everyone knows, a beautiful blue.

"Where's Aaron?" I asked.

"What do you mean?"

"Aaron's in Florida." I was confused, still half-sleeping. "He's supposed to be flying back soon."

"He's not there?"

"It wasn't his plane? That's not why you're calling?"

"No. It's not Aaron. Aaron is fine."

I tried to reach Aaron, again and again, but I couldn't get through. It wasn't a busy signal and it wasn't dead silence. It was a new kind of sound invented on that day.

The airports reopened and Aaron came home. We lay on our futon bed and held each other. Outside the bedroom window, beyond the fire escape, the leaves were changing in the trees in the neighborhood below.

One night, we were walking home from dinner on Broadway when we came across the 24th Police Precinct. A table was set up outside. Officers were recruiting for the Auxiliary Police Force. All over the city, people were signing up for the NYPD, the FDNY, the Armed Forces. "Hold on," Aaron said. He walked over and picked up a pamphlet. He gave his name and number to one of the officers. The next day, he received a call. Did he want to begin training? He signed up.

It wasn't like he was going to fight terrorism on the streets of the Upper West Side. He didn't even seem to want to. I remembered Aaron's quiet fury at the police car that had followed us home after our first date. "I fucking hate cops," is what he'd said. Now he wanted to be one?

"They're not cops," he told me. "They're volunteers. They can't arrest people. They don't have guns."

"That's even worse!"

"You want me to have a gun?"

"Well, no." I wondered what it was he felt he needed to fight.

"They're peacekeepers," he said. "I want to do *something*. I want to help."

.   .   .

Mornings, I went to the art dealer's studio in Tribeca, where the dust had been professionally cleared; afternoons, to SoHo, to the *Poets & Writers* office. Some days I still freelanced at the first magazine, stopping by the Midtown office to pick up bags of letters to answer. I didn't like to take the subway anymore—it made me panic. So I took three buses to work and three buses back, an hour and a half each way. It was far past dark when I got home.

At *Poets & Writers,* I loved having my own desk and my own email address, my own lamp that I dusted each evening. I loved the ceiling-high bookshelf full of books. I could see a glimpse of the self I'd hoped would materialize in New York: a self typing in hushed offices with extravagant plants in the windows, talking to people who loved books all day. I was safe from the city there, from all the toxic loss it endured that year, and all the toxic loss in my apartment.

New York likes to mess with you. One fall day after work, as I exited Starbucks drinking an iced coffee (I couldn't afford a latte), I saw my ex-boyfriend—the poet who had broken my heart in Florida—smoking a cigarette. We exchanged a startled hug. "You live in New York!" we each said. We worked, in fact, in the same building. I pointed upstairs to my office at the magazine. He pointed to the literary nonprofit a floor above. We caught up. "Wow, that's great," we said, congratulating each other on how far we'd come since high school, which was another way of congratulating ourselves. We no longer had the same Kurt Cobain haircut, but we had traveled practically parallel paths to find each other standing here on the sidewalk.

If we were in a Lifetime movie, we might have rekindled our romance. But he had made his choice, and I had made mine. The heavy-handed fate of our reunion only made my choice that much starker. I had chosen difference, difficulty, a wild and illogical love. A life with a person whose life was not the mirror image of mine.

I went to work. Aaron went to his cop class. I hadn't seen him sign up for anything since he'd tried college four years before. Maybe he wouldn't finish the course. It was good for him to be out, I reasoned, doing something, keeping busy.

But then sixteen weeks had passed and he hadn't missed one class, and he was given a certificate and a walkie talkie and a billy club and a blue policemen's uniform. You had to look closely to see *Auxiliary Force* lettered on the shield.

Every Monday night that spring, he worked a shift on the Upper West Side, walking Broadway with his partner. Mostly he directed traffic when the lights went out. Mondays were the nights I hosted a writing workshop in our apartment. I was taking the class, not teaching it, but I needed the tuition discount. I had gone down to the Pearl River Market on Canal Street to buy ten pale-blue coffee mugs for $1.99 each. I was playing grown-up in my way, Aaron in his.

My writing teacher would pass Aaron on her walk home, and she'd remark to me how handsome he looked in his blue police uniform, and I'd never felt such pride.

In the winter, the city started lighting the sky at night, the two white beams shooting up from Ground Zero. I could see them from the Upper West Side, and it filled me and everyone else with a sad chill and a stupid hope and you wished they'd stop doing it and that they'd never stop. It reminded you that you were small and alive.

Aaron went to Florida, returned. Went to Florida, returned. He was in a kind of purgatory with his dying, not-dying father. I started taking the subway again, and it was boiling down there, that terrible smell of burning trash and baking flesh.

I attended an info session with Aaron, for auxiliary cops who were interested in becoming real cops. There was a procedure for cops who didn't yet have a college degree. For the NYPD, you had to complete your degree and pass the test before you were thirty-five, and Aaron had just turned thirty.

The procedure involved a lot of very big paperback college textbooks with bland pastel covers. They looked like phone books. It was a kind of home college course. You read the books, you took the tests. Easy! He was pretty sure it was what he wanted to do. He ordered the starter kit: the college textbooks, the practice tests. He stacked them up on the coffee table in our apartment, where they sat, untouched, for weeks. They sat and they sat. I said nothing. I watched them, collecting dust.

They were sitting there one ordinary evening when I came home from work, sweaty, hungry, weighed down with bags, letters and notebooks and groceries I'd hauled on three buses, after three jobs, to find Aaron lying in his familiar position on the couch. A plastic box of his father's bills sat beside the stack of books. We had been in New York a year and had come so far, and had gone nowhere at all.

"How was your day?" he asked, sitting up. He turned off the TV.

I sat down on the blue couch next to him. There wasn't much room, but I made it. I was practically on his lap, the couch was so small. I felt crowded and resentful and broke and tired. I replied, for the first time, with sarcasm.

"Great. How was yours?"

"Okay."

Then I said what had been in my head all those months.

"Looks like it was hard."

In my voice, he must have heard all the times people had looked at him and thought he had it easy. All the times people had looked at his Range Rover, his waterfront condo, and thought, *Must be nice.*

He shoved me away from him. Really shoved me. It was the first and only time he shoved me.

"Do you know what it's like?" he yelled at me. His face had contorted into rage. "Do you know what it's like!"

"What?" I was yelling back at him, but my heart was racing. I really didn't know what he was talking about. Sitting here on the couch all day?

"Do you know what it's like to take care of the person who was supposed to take care of you!"

"No! I don't!"

"To pay all his stupid fucking bills?"

"No!"

"To watch him refuse to die?"

He kicked the stack of books and the box of bills and they sailed across the room and crashed to the floor.

"The person who raised you! Do you know what it's like to be fucked by the person who raised you?"

I shook my head.

"No," I said, very quietly.

I was shaking my head. "No," I said, "no, no, no, no . . ."

"Yes," he said. "It was him."

"No, no, no, no, no," I was saying.

"Yes," he was saying, calmer now. "Yes."

I'd had no idea. It had not occurred to me. I'd thought *teacher, rabbi, uncle, coach.* I had never, ever thought *father.*

"No no no no no." I realized I was hyperventilating with a distant interest: so this is hyperventilating, it's a real thing. Aaron got me a paper lunch bag from the kitchen and I breathed into it as I'd seen people do in movies. I was sitting on the floor now, and he had his hand on my back, and he was saying, "I'm sorry." Sorry that I was hyperventilating, sorry he'd yelled at me, sorry he hadn't told me. "I'm sorry I pushed you," he said. "That was fucked up," and I was saying, "I'm sorry, I didn't know, I'm sorry."

We were both crying, and I started to breathe again, and Aaron was telling me the details, what he remembered. It was in the condo. He was twelve or thirteen. Young enough to still sleep sometimes in his father's bed. It happened while Aaron was sleeping. When he woke up, he asked his father to stop. And his father did.

I kept crying. My hand over my mouth.

There were other times. The memories came back to him in bits and pieces. Mostly he felt the force of not-remembering, his childhood wiped clean.

"I don't know how many times it happened."

"Did you ever confront him about it?"

He did. Later, an older teenager, moody, stronger. Passing him in the hall, he had thrown it out in disgust, as he had done just then.

His father had said to him, "Get over it."

We talked late into the night. I sat for a long time on the floor, Aaron beside me on the couch, and by the time we had exhausted ourselves and were ready to fall into bed, we had passed through a doorway that we couldn't go back through, a threshold of horror and understanding, but I didn't know what would be on the other side.

Over the months, it had been building. Our unspoken fear, anxiety, weariness. We were broke, and broken. New York was breaking us. It was a relief to admit it.

What I wasn't ready for Aaron to say was that he wanted to leave.

"What do you mean, leave? Where?"

I wasn't ready. It felt like giving up.

He knelt on the floor, gathering the books and bills he had kicked over. I crawled over to help him.

"Back to Florida."

I thought of my desk at *Poets & Writers,* my little patch of ground. My future of book-lined offices, vanishing before my eyes. I couldn't imagine another future. Imagining another one felt like a death.

I thought of Aaron, a teenager trapped in that terrible condo in Florida, dreaming of the freedom of New York, and now he wanted to go back. Whatever he'd been looking for in returning to New York, he hadn't found it. It had vanished with Ashmat, with his childhood. And what he'd been trying to fight with his billy club wasn't in New York.

The condo in Florida sat empty. Rent-free, Aaron said. We could save some money. It would be easier to tend to his father's affairs there. His father was still alive, alone in the nursing home. I did not want to face him, not ever. I shook my head. It didn't make any sense.

"How can you want to go back to that place?"

Aaron shrugged. "He's my Pop," he said. "It's home."

DELTA RAY RADIATION

There's something wrong with this schizophrenia diagnosis. It's insufficient, a placeholder. Why is he seeing Dr. Friedlander just once a month, anyway? In April, I go back to the office with him. I'm officially that wife, the one with the little notebook and the giant handbag, the kind that makes almost everyone I meet say, "Wow, that's a *big bag.*"

Dr. Friedlander doesn't say this. We tell her about the trip to the ER, the psych eval. I ask her about schizoaffective disorder. My friend Ursula, whose husband works for McLean Hospital, mentioned it to me. "It's kind of like schizophrenia meets bipolar? Is that right?"

Dr. Friedlander shakes her head in a way that makes it seem like she's agreeing with me. "It's what we call a wastebasket term," she says. Wastebasket, as in it's trash, or wastebasket, as in it's as big as my catch-all handbag?

"What about bipolar disorder then?" I describe the nocturnal circus of his symptoms: a week of sleep, a week of no sleep, depression, mania, again and again and again. "Lately," I say, "you can set your watch to it."

She shakes her head, definitively this time. "Bipolar disorder doesn't work that way," she says. "Each phase lasts more like six months, not six days."

She prescribes him Ativan, and we take our leave.

"Fucking Ativan," Aaron says in the car.

It's one of the drugs he was on during the bad time. He let it go because he was becoming too dependent, too tolerant, but mostly because it had bad associations.

"What you need is lithium," I say. "Why will no one prescribe you lithium?!"

As soon as we're home, I pick up the phone. Screw the no-calling-the-doctor rule. I am done with waiting for him to call. Aaron's GP, Dr. Das, has left the practice, so I make an appointment with my dad's new doctor. He looks like a professional golfer. He used six different metaphors to describe what was happening to my dad's blood pressure, squeezing hoses, stopping traffic jams, as animated as a kid in a school play. He adjusted my dad's meds in five minutes and by the next day my dad had more energy than I'd seen in months. "You gotta see this guy," I said to Aaron. "I think my dad is in love."

Aaron says he'll see him. He'll try the lithium. He'll try anything.

The day of the appointment, I come home just in time to pick up Aaron and meet the school bus. Nico will stay with my dad while we pick up Henry from reading club and then go to Aaron's appointment. He's waiting on the deck, dressed and ready, but as he walks to the car, he is unsteady, lumbering. We wait in the driveway for Nico's bus.

"Are you okay?"

"I'm great," he says, goofy smile, but he can barely keep his eyes open.

"Did you take an Ativan already?"

"Yes. Maybe."

"Maybe?"

"Maybe two."

"Aaron! *Two?* I'm supposed to be dosing you."

"Where's this fucking bus?"

"That was *your* idea. I would control the meds. I don't want to control the meds. But clearly I need to control the meds."

"I needed it. I was anxious."

"Where *is* this bus?"

"There's cops out there," he slurs.

"Where?"

"There." Traffic is heavy and slow down the road, and through the trees I do see flashing lights.

"I think that's construction."

"It's cops. They're always fucking things up."

"There are no cops, Aaron."

"Wanna know why all cops are such dicks? 'Cause they all got fucked."

"Stop it."

"I wanted to be a cop," he says into his lap.

"Yeah, I know."

"I'd make a terrible cop."

"Yeah, probably."

"Cops all got CORNHOLED BY THEIR DADS!" he yells to the closed window.

"Jesus, Aaron. Are you *drunk*?"

It's two forty in the afternoon.

"Not *drunk*."

"Did you have a *drink*?"

"Yes. Maybe."

"Oh, for God's sake."

And then here is the bus—there the bus goes—past our driveway. Then it screeches to a halt. Nico hops out and has to cut through the ditch at the edge of the yard. "*Stay here*," I say to his father, and climb out of the car to greet him. It's a sub, I see. I wave to the driver who is not Harold. At least I think that's his name. Last week I yelled at him, waving Mom-style, "Thanks, Harvey!" and Nico, mortified, watching the whole bus watching us, whispered, "Mom, his name is *Harold*."

I get Nico settled inside with his grandfather, and then rage-drive down the road to town. Aaron is practically asleep in the passenger's seat. "I can't believe you got drunk in the middle of the day. How much did you drink?"

"Whatever was in the fridge."

"That bottle of wine?"

"Maybe."

"The *whole* bottle?"

"I don't remember," he says, eyes closed.

"Fucking hell." I dial the number to the doctor's office while I drive.

"What are you doing?"

"Canceling your appointment. What a fucking waste."

"Why?"

"I can't take you there like this! You're barely conscious."

"I'm fine."

"You're unbelievable, is what you are."

Then he begins to vomit on himself. On his shirt, on his seatbelt, on the dashboard.

I stop at a red light. He opens the door, vomits on the street. Like one of the college kids in this neighborhood. Then the light turns green and I drive. He vomits on himself some more. I pull over into the parking lot of the abandoned power plant. He opens the door and vomits some more. Afternoon traffic is swimming steadily up the hill. I turn the car so he's facing away from the street. He vomits for a long time. He's leaning far out of the car. His ass is hanging out of his jeans. With one hand I'm covering my face. With the other I'm holding the back of his jacket. And then he falls out of the car onto the ground.

"Aaron!"

I run around to his side of the ground. He is lying there, unmoving. For a couple of seconds, I think he's dead. The car is still running. I try to pick him up, but he's dead weight.

"You okay, ma'am?"

A man approaches in a backhoe and leans out of it. The power plant is not totally abandoned, I guess.

"I'm okay," I say.

He does not ask if Aaron is okay. Maybe he knows better than I do what is happening here.

Aaron stirs, stands with my help, and gets back into the car. I pick up Henry from school. In the teacher parking lot, Aaron has a little more to throw up.

"I'm sorry," he mumbles, half-asleep, head weaving the whole way home. "I'm so sorry."

It is a confusing time to be a woman who loves a troubled man.

In Al-Anon, the serenity prayer tells you to accept the things you cannot change. To stop trying to control, cure, resolve, outthink, outfox another's pain. To take responsibility for your own actions while also taking care of yourself.

At the Women's March in D.C.—a march you attended while your husband cared for your children six hours away, worried about him, always worried—the hand-drawn posters were everywhere, the prayer reconceived by Angela Davis: "I am no longer accepting the things I cannot change. I am changing the things I cannot accept." It becomes a godless refrain, a sigh, an anti-prayer; Angela Davis, fist in the air, her afro Sharpie'd in sharp relief, is not asking anyone to grant her anything. Who has time for serenity when there's a patriarchy to topple?

Lift your poster in the air with your right arm. Hold it there until it hurts. It's hard work with two hands, but you must use only one. With your left, rub the back of your husband. Do his dishes, do his laundry, feed his children. Hang the bookshelf, mow the lawn, eat the leftover crust of the peanut-butter sandwich. It is hard to clean a toilet with one hand. Every cell of your body wants to fight it. To resist. *I'd be happy just to spend my life / waiting at your beck and call.* You hadn't really listened to that part of the Billie Holiday song. *Everything I have is yours / My life, my all.*

"I am so tired of cleaning your shit," you apparently said to your husband. You don't remember it, but it hurt his feelings. It sounds like something you might say.

You are a smart person. You understand the difference between the personal and the political. You understand the wisdom of the serenity prayer. The serenity prayer was written for people like you—women who give everything to their men in the hope of rebirthing them. Who believe they might push them back through the birth canal and get it right this time. Alcoholism is a chaos, and the serenity prayer is your ticket out of it. The serenity prayer permits you to live outside the chaos, across the street from it. Fight the fight on the Capitol steps, but accept the limitations of the humans we live with.

But you also understand that the personal is the political. You want serenity *and* justice. When you've been taught that a woman can, must, do anything, that her place is in the resistance, you must believe that you are powerful enough to heal your husband. Curing the mental illness of your husband seems no more likely than curing the mental illness of the system—of patriarchy, poverty, racism, hate—and yet you try to do that, too. They are both devils—the devil that lives in your husband's brain, the devil that lives in your country's.

And after all, isn't the devil in your husband's brain because of the devil in his father, and wasn't the devil in his father because of the devil of the system, because of, in fact, the government, because of the country that sent him to war when he was barely a man (but haven't men been blowing each other up since the beginning of time, and didn't he help to liberate the camps?), the country that sent him to kill men and dogs in the snowy forest, because of the mine that sent his body into a tree, because of the broken body that was sent back home, his broken body begetting Aaron's broken body, then breaking it further?

This is where your mind goes when it seeks an open pathway for the blame. Like blood against a blockage, it finds another artery of logic. Your house is sick because the planet is sick, war-ravaged, warming, too much fire.

At the bookstore, I spot the book on the top shelf of the Science section. The Matisse paper cut-out catches my eye first, the black figure falling through yellow-starry space, the red oval of its heart. Then the title: *The Body Keeps the Score.* I can feel the title in my body. *Brain, Mind, and Body in the Healing of Trauma,* by Bessel van der Kolk, M.D.

What is happening to Aaron except this? His body is keeping the score.

I buy the book and read it, over breakfast, at the gym, in the bath. I carry it from room to room. I mark my place with a pencil. I underline every third sentence. "One in five Americans was sexually molested as a child." I draw stars. "Trauma affects not only those who are directly exposed to it, but also those around them." In the margins I write "Yes!"

But I tread lightly with Aaron. He is the kind of person who hates overhyped movies as a matter of principle.

"This is really interesting," I say casually, turning the pages in bed. "These people's stories . . . they sound a lot like you."

I flip back to the part about Bill. One of the first Vietnam vets Dr. van der Kolk worked with in the seventies. After the war, he returned to normal life in Boston. Everything was fine until his wife gave birth to a son. Whenever the baby cried, he heard the crying children of Vietnam.

I look to Aaron, who's drawing in bed beside me, spirals and shadows, fingers and freaks. *I draw what I see,* he has said. The boy on *Stranger Things* who sketches the monster that has hold of him? Hard not to think of that.

"Mm-hmm," he says, agreeing.

Aaron isn't a veteran of any combat war. But sometimes, when our children cry in a certain way, he is flooded with fear and panic. When they are inconsolable, lost in their own little traumas, he seems to be reliving his own torture.

"But listen to this." Dr. van der Kolk's colleagues diagnosed Bill with paranoid schizophrenia. PTSD wasn't really a thing yet. "Something about the diagnosis didn't sound right," Dr. van der Kolk writes. "I unwittingly paraphrased something Sigmund Freud had said about trauma in 1895: 'I think this man is suffering from memories.'"

"Wow," Aaron says.

My students already speak the language of trauma, of triggers. I accommodate them, as we do, with trigger warnings, alternative assignments, protecting them from their own memories. Some of my colleagues roll their eyes. "These kids and their trigger warnings. Life is a trigger!"

And yet I've seen it with my own eyes, the things a brain can do. How it corrupts itself. How it preserves itself. How it both preserves and corrupts by lying to itself. How it contains multitudes. How it is actually a piece of gray matter. How it is wired, like a car battery or a bomb. *The red wire or the blue?* How the wires can get swollen, denuded, jammed. How it can recalculate, like a GPS. This is what Dr. van der Kolk promises us: we can rebuild the brain. Broken as it is, it is plastic. It is pliable.

Last year, we got a babysitter and went to see the movie *Lion.* For an hour, we watched a boy Henry's age wander the Indian countryside. Lost, hungry, scared, alone, he fights off predators of all kinds. We had not yet reached the part where the boy, now a man in Australia, eats the jalebi that makes his mind travel back to his forgotten childhood. It was the part of the story I had been waiting for, that I needed. I had been crying for an hour and gripping Aaron's hand. I needed to see the story through to its catharsis.

Like the man in the movie, Aaron was encountering his own memory trigger. It wasn't as specific or as sweet as Saroo Brierley's jalebi or Marcel Proust's madeleine, but it was powerful enough to make him leave the theater. "Stay," he whispered. "I'll be fine." But ten minutes later I found him sitting outside in the hall, sweating, panting, his hands swollen in a new red rash.

"I'm sorry," he said. "I couldn't take it."

"*I'm* sorry," I said. It had been my idea to see the movie.

We left and went home early, startling the sitter.

A few weeks after I finish *The Body Keeps the Score* and hand it over to Aaron, he's making slow progress through it. It's interesting, he says. He sees himself in it. But most days it's hard for him to concentrate on reading for an extended time. "Maybe just skip to the part about the experimental treatments?" I suggest. "EMDR? Neurofeedback?" He's already agreed to it. To any kind of therapy. *I'll go to any therapist you want* he told me the night I drove him back from the ER, after he'd narrowly escaped the psych ward.

One day he brings the book to Starbucks and we sit there reading together. Yesterday we spent the whole day together, eating lunch from the farmer's market in the park, renting bikes and riding them around town. It's May. He's just turned forty-six. Maybe this is the year he'll get well? The trees are in bloom. The sun is out. We're pushing our luck, I know. Today we want to squeeze a little more out of this good period.

But while he sits there reading in Starbucks, I can see something come over him. His body grows restless. He keeps pressing his pen into the seam of the book, closing it, opening it again. "I can't read this," he finally says. "It's making me too upset," and I drive him home, where he takes an Ativan and goes to bed and tries to ward off the breakout, but before long it returns, as it always does.

Reading about triggers: it's triggering. Should have seen that one coming.

That night I have a dream that I am in a room with a boy with lesions on his legs. He is a college-aged boy, and I have ridden a bike to his house. He is young and vague and lovely and in his underwear. I go fetch Aaron—he is in a room somewhere in this house—and bring him to the boy. "Look," I say.

How pathetically loyal. Even in my dreams, I can't be in a room with a man without inviting Aaron to witness.

"Take off your pants," I say to my husband. He takes off his pants and then his underwear. *No*, I think, embarrassed, irritated. *Only your pants.* He stands there in nothing but a T-shirt. But then I notice something. The boy has removed his underwear, too. Their legs are twinned, scaled, their penises hanging between them, innocent, dumb. The two men look at each other, as if into a mirror, but say nothing. Perhaps there is some recognition between them. Perhaps they are performing some recognition for their dreamer.

What am I doing, waiting for him to read the damn book? I find a trauma therapist who does neurofeedback, make an appointment: easy. He's been sleeping for most of five days—I might second-guess this, if I hadn't started keeping a journal five days ago—when he rouses himself from bed and dresses himself for the appointment. "I'm not really here," he apologizes to the therapist, a woman with long white hair and a boxy frame. But I can see him in there, behind the weeks-long beard. He's wearing athletic shorts, his sores healing to a fine crust, a Band-Aid the size of a small envelope on his lovely inner thigh. There is a gameness in his face. In the therapist's narrow office are orchids, paper lanterns, a lumpy couch, a tortoiseshell puppy who sleeps in a tiny bed on the floor, and an office chair, where after looking over his intake papers, she asks Aaron to sit. While she tells us about neurofeedback, she's dipping what look like Q-tips into what looks like Vaseline. She's wasting no time! A little wick of hope lights in my chest. Some action! "The first thing that neurofeedback does is help us calm down," she says, swiping Aaron's temples with alcohol. "Now this is electromagnetic paste," she says. "Just a little zinc." Electromagnetic paste! Zinc! She pauses. "*Do* you have bipolar disorder?" We don't know for sure, we say. We rescheduled his appointment with his GP, who prescribed the lithium, but he's just started taking it. She says, "It affects where I put the sensors." Then she reconsiders. "Well, what we know is that childhood trauma trumps everything." She positions two of the sensors—they look like earbuds—at his temples, and two on what is apparently the region of the brain where childhood trauma lives, a few inches behind and below, in his dark curls. Thin white wires connect the sensors to an amplifier on the desk. "It sounds like, when you were a child, you didn't get good enough care for you to learn to calm down on your own. Not *nearly* good enough," she adds. Yes, I think, *yes*. "We can strengthen the connection between here and here"—she points to a rear sensor and a front one—"to teach the brain to do that." She flips on the computer monitor on the desk, and the screen fills with the graphic of a spaceship flying through a trippy tunnel, a series of shifting pink and purple parallelograms that makes me a little sick even from across the room. It looks like a video game Aaron might have enjoyed in the nineties. Global pop music thrums from the tiny computer speakers. Aaron's job is to keep the spaceship moving by using 0.1 millihertz of his brain. When the right amount of brainpower is used—almost none—he is rewarded with a speedier spaceship, and a billow of smoke out of its ass. "It's difficult," she acknowledges. "It's like asking a professional athlete to just flex his pinky for an hour. We naturally want to use more of our brains. This slows us down."

Whatever Aaron is doing with his brain, or whatever his brain is doing to him, the spaceship is moving steadily, devouring translucent diamonds like Pac-Man pellets. The inside is talking to the outside. The sensors are telling the monitor, *We have located the brain. It is wounded but it is working. It is brave. It is operating at .01 millihertz.* One sensor says, *Here is the place—yes—where his father wounded him.* The other says, *Here is the place where his mother didn't save him.* Here is the virtual proof of his survival, the spaceship finding the opening at the end of the psychedelic tunnel, rising now into the blank blue sky—

"It's making me a little dizzy," Aaron says. It's time to leave anyway.

At Stu's, he's restless, rocking, rubbing the sores on his shins and his calves.

"Let's try something," Stu says. "Can you count to ten for me?"

He starts counting slowly, still rocking. When did he start this rocking? He was up all night, feeling worms under his skin, collecting things from his body and looking at them under Henry's toy microscope.

When he gets to six, he speeds up, races to ten.

Stu takes notes on the sheets of yellow paper tucked into a clipboard. Where do all these notes go? How many file cabinets has he filled with our seven years of delusions and promises and medication updates?

> 300 mg Seroquel, 750 mg lithium, 5 mg Prozac, .5 mg of
> Ativan, as needed.

We talk about adjustments. Maybe more Prozac. Is the lithium doing any good? In two days, he has a sleep study scheduled, to see if he has sleep apnea. Stu asks me to imitate how Aaron snores, and I try, snorting and choking like an old man. Stu tries to convince him to try a C-Pap. It's not that bad, he says. But Aaron is skeptical. Of all the drugs, of the mask with its tubes and tentacles, of the sleep lab lady, who wants to sell him something.

"It's the latest thing," he says. "*Get a C-Pap! Everyone's getting a C-Pap!* It's like a rumpus room in the fifties. *Oh, you gotta have a rumpus room!*"

He's still rocking, rubbing his hands together. "I don't want to end up like Captain Pike," he says. "Remember him? He was *before* Kirk. He couldn't talk, couldn't walk. He was just a head coming out of this space-age wheelchair." He imitates him, lifeless, staring into space. Stu and I don't know who Captain Pike is, but we laugh. Aaron is in there! In some safe vault of his embattled brain, all the obscure TV trivia is preserved.

Stu tells him, "I want you to go home and take your Seroquel and try to sleep."

At home, I help him to sleep. Some days, when he lets me, I can fuck the devil out of him. Or maybe I'm just fucking it back inside.

When he's finally snoring his apneic snore, I Google "Captain Pike." The wheelchair is more like an iron lung. Captain Pike is like a bust of a man, and on the entire right side of his withered face is a purple scar shaped like Italy. He was paralyzed by delta ray radiation.

I imagine a doctor noting those words on a yellow legal pad. The satisfaction, at least, of the diagnosis. *Delta ray radiation.*

When they were first married, my father used to photograph my mother. In hundreds of photos, black-and-white 8 x 10s he developed in his darkroom, there she is: on a balcony, on a rooftop, in a director's chair in their studio. She wears a black turtleneck or a denim shirt or a corduroy dress. Her thick dark hair is parted down the middle. Silver hoops hang from her ears.

Did she know, as she sat for those photos, at twenty-four, twenty-five, twenty-six—what a gift they'd be to her daughter after her death? Or was she thinking only of her beloved behind the camera, posing for him alone?

It wasn't posing, exactly. It was more like not-posing. It was more like appearing not to be posing, as she watered a plant, painted a picture, smoked a cigarette. It was musing. As in the archaic definition: "to gaze meditatively or wonderingly." And in the classical one: she was the goddess inspiring the artist. In the gentle set of her mouth, her over-there eyes, there was a stillness, a consent to being seen, to being captured.

When Aaron gave me his blessing to write this book, we were sitting at a vegan restaurant in Seattle, on tour for my second book, in front of fat goblets of red wine and plates of food so good we didn't know what we were eating. He was wearing a navy blazer and white T-shirt and the black glasses I loved. He wasn't in pain. We were happy.

"Do it," he said. We held hands, smiled, kissed.

"All of it?" I asked.

"All of it." He spread his arms across the table at our bounty.

"Even that?"

I gave him a wide-eyed look. There had been a time when even a hint at his father's abuse, even a look, would have sent him out of the restaurant into the street.

He chugged his wine. He shrugged and said, "Even that."

Then he let me feed him something sweet and fatty from my fork.

Some might call this grooming.

But wasn't he consenting to being seen by me, by my camera? Wasn't he entrusting me with his story?

"I'm a person," Aaron tells me on another day. We are in bed in our new house, piles of laundry at our feet, no wine glasses in our hands. Around me are stacks of dog-eared books: *Loving Someone with Bipolar Disorder. Total Recovery. The Body Keeps the Score.* The sores on Aaron's arms look like they've been painted on by a talented but overzealous special-effects makeup artist.

"Not a project," he says. "Not a mystery."

THEORY 6

His parents made him sick.

"We now know that trauma compromises the brain area that communicates the physical, embodied feeling of being alive," Dr. van der Kolk writes in *The Body Keeps the Score*. "These changes explain why traumatized individuals become hypervigilant to threat at the expense of spontaneously engaging in their day-to-day lives."

Does it matter if the trauma isn't remembered?

Once, a dentist looked at his X-rays. He looked inside his mouth. "What kind of injury did you have as a child?" he asked.

Aaron said, "What do you mean?"

His jaw had been impacted, the dentist said, as though from a heavy blow. It was early, before he'd lost his baby teeth.

You're not the only person who had a shitty childhood, is a sentence that sometimes knocks around in my mouth, like a loose tooth. Maybe once or twice, I've said it.

I know I'm not the only person who had a shitty childhood, is a sentence I've heard him say, once or twice.

QUAY NORTH

2002

A few days after we moved from New York to Florida, to the condo called Quay North where Aaron had spent his teenage years, I went about cleaning his father's refrigerator.

It had not been cleaned for years, or maybe ever. It required Formula 409, several rolls of paper towels, and, perhaps too late, a dishcloth tied around my face, covering my nose and mouth, like a bandit's. It required great powers of distraction, as I tried not to think about the steaks that had been stacked in the freezer, tried not to wonder whether the dried, meat-colored trails of grime that were despite my best efforts now caked under my fingernails were cat food or human food or some alien fungus our planet had not seen before.

"Gross," Aaron said over my shoulder.

I narrowed my eyes at him over the dishcloth.

"I told you I'm not touching that fridge. My dad got E. coli in this kitchen once."

He had told me that before. E. coli had seemed like a mythical, abstract organism. If it was too small to see, was it real? Now I believed him. But it was too late.

Almost immediately, I got sick.

Maybe it was a coincidence. Maybe it was the change of climate, moving from smoggy Manhattan to salty South Florida. Maybe I had caught something on the plane. (We'd left in such a rush, fleeing our apartment before our lease was up, that we couldn't afford a moving truck; we'd sold our furniture to other people in our building and

FedExed everything else.) Maybe it was the stale cigarette smoke that stained the walls of his room. But that night my throat closed up and my body grew hot, and then clammy, and then cold, and I lay moaning in Aaron's old bed and thought I would die.

I'm going to die here, I thought.

I thought, *scene of the crime.* I'm living in a crime scene.

I used my powers of distraction. I tried not to think about what had happened in this apartment. I tried not to remember that Aaron had fled to this room and locked the door to keep himself safe from his father. I tried not to think of the girls he'd brought to this bed later, the one who had lived here with him in this room, all of the skin cells and fluids and microbes and ash that were trapped in the urine-colored shag carpet. In the dark, that night, I tried to forget it all; I could float for a few minutes in black un-memory, I could will myself back to New York, on a blanket with a book in Central Park, or ahead to some other future, in a house where I would have dinner parties on a long farm table, with little sprigs of herbs on the edge of each white plate, where I wasn't living in this place, but then I was here again, heavy in the bed, feeling the springs of the mattress stabbing every muscle. I dreamed dreams of dark shapes. My head felt as if it would fall off, backward, back to earth. My arms ached, my legs, and mostly my throat, which felt swollen to twice its size. I couldn't swallow. When I swallowed, I felt like I was swallowing glass. So I didn't. I didn't drink the water Aaron brought me in the night. I let him bring me a wet washcloth for my head. He did his best to care for me. In the morning, when I wasn't better, when I didn't dare open my mouth to speak, he sat on the edge of the bed. The sun was too bright, coming in the sliding glass door, shining off the too-beautiful water. How was it so beautiful out there, and so miserable in here? "I think I should take you to your parents'," he said.

"Please," I croaked.

Tucked under my turquoise sheets, against the forest-green wall I'd painted myself, under the SAVE THE RAINFOREST poster, I was as cozy as a bug. Still sick, but cozy. My mom brought me lemon tea I was too sick to drink, crossword puzzles I was too dizzy to look at, but she was there, the familiar, warm shape of her on the edge of the twin bed. I pressed my cheek to her blue-jeaned hip. She brushed my hair with her fingers. I had just turned twenty-three, but I could pretend for a day that I was thirteen again, before I had fallen in love and left home and moved into an E. coli-infested apartment.

I tried to be objective. I had once hated my house, too. I couldn't wait to move away. My parents smoked in the house here, too, it was probably in the walls and the carpet—years later, I would catch a whiff of it on an old sweater or stack of papers, and sneeze—and the dust! Did we even own a duster? I had never seen my mother mop the floors. We had ants in this house. And, once, rats! It was too horrible to even remember. They had come through the rotten walls, the wood under the kitchen sink soggy from the humid hurricane air. Nothing was sealed properly. Everything was wet. In my room, the AC unit in the window was attached to the glass with duct tape, but not enough. As a teenager, I had once been sleeping in this bed when a tree frog leapt, as though out of my rainforest poster, onto my face.

So. Others might find this place gross. I once thought it was. Still, it was what I knew. It was home. In my feverish state, I understood for one moment why Aaron, at home alone in his own childhood bed, felt safe.

My next mistake, after cleaning the refrigerator, was going to the ER.

"I'll take you in the morning," my mother said, "if you're not better." She looked down at me. I know now, as a mother, as a veteran of emergency rooms, she was assessing the emergency level. Was I being dramatic? Like when I was eight and riding my bike to school and found a baby bird fallen out of its nest on the sidewalk, and I begged to stay home, saying my stomach hurt, and please could we take the bird home? Fine, she had decided then, to my great joy.

She put her hand on my forehead now. "Or do you want to go tonight?"

I nodded.

Here is what I wasn't thinking about: health insurance. I had aged out of the plan my parents had paid for when I was in college. My part-time job at *Poets & Writers*—I would be continuing, with a new title, contributing editor! from afar—did not pay health insurance. I hadn't seen a doctor since going to my college health center. But I felt terrible and it was nine o'clock at night and I felt I needed to go to the hospital.

I lay in a hospital bed for four hours. They tested my blood and gave me an IV of fluids. You have to swallow, they told me. Don't be afraid to swallow. And then they sent me home with a diagnosis of a throat infection. A throat infection! Because it was viral, they couldn't give me antibiotics. I was on my own. I watched my mother hand over her American Express card and saw the canary-yellow receipt. $495. My parents didn't have that kind of money. I had never felt so foolish, until the next bill came in the mail, addressed to me this time, for $2,700.

I didn't have $2,700. I'd spent my last five hundred dollars FedExing everything in my apartment to myself. My parents didn't have $2,700, and Aaron didn't have $2,700. I went into the billing office and inquired about a sliding scale. By that time, my throat had gotten better on its own. I provided my income for the last year. I had made too much money to qualify for a reduced fee. Too much money! I'd left New York because I couldn't even afford to have my hair cut.

So I didn't pay the bill. And for seven years, there went my credit.

In the coming years, I would spend many late nights in the ER with my husband, and though we would be insured up to our eyeballs and lucky to have a $100 copay, I'd enter under the fluorescent lights and smell the sick, shameful tang of rubbing alcohol and remember that no matter how friendly the staff was, this was not friendly territory. It was my first adult lesson about the health care system: it sucks.

I was also learning that it was easy to blame everything on Morris.

It was the year of disgust.

I spent a lot of time trying to clean that apartment, to air it out, transform it. The main room was tiled with those almond-colored tiles with dark brown grout that tiled every other South Florida house I'd ever been in. I hated that tile, but I scrubbed them, square by square. I took Aaron's old urine-colored desk and painted it white, and set it up in the living room, overlooking the balcony and the water, and if I didn't move my head too far to the right or left, if I just sat at my white desk, looking at the ocean, working on the magazine columns, or writing—I was trying to put together an application for grad school—everything would be okay.

The cats—we still had two, but these were Morris's evil cats—had peed all over the white Pottery Barn couch. The couch was now the same pale yellow of the rest of the apartment. I removed the cushion covers and soaked them in OxiClean in the pale-yellow bathtub and Febrezed the cushions on the balcony, hoping the beachy air might cleanse them. It kind of worked. The couch was usable again, if you didn't tell anyone of its history. Tell no one of the filthy past! If you just soaked it all enough! That's what I was teaching myself. This was 2002 and Febreze and OxiClean were still new and it seemed they might be able to fix everything.

Morris's bedroom door, for a long time, stayed closed. We didn't need the master bathroom. It was filled with boxes and boxes of his junk, of collectibles and books and art. Every once in a while, Aaron went in there looking for something to sell and found it and closed the door again.

Slowly we formed a plan. We would stay in Florida for the year. Aaron would sell off the collectibles inventory, empty the storage units. We would fix up the apartment. We wouldn't gut it—we couldn't afford that—but we would give it a good facelift. And then we'd sell it. It was clear by now that Morris wasn't going to recover from his stroke. He'd never come back here again. Aaron had accepted that.

It was the way I got through the year, hating the apartment, waiting to be rid of it, telling myself, soon it will be gone. I was beginning to understand the hostile sense of possession Aaron had always had over his father's riches: that he was owed. It was a kind of passive aggression I was perfecting myself: I, too, felt I was owed, for the sacrifice of having left New York.

When I finally opened the door to Morris's room, I held my breath.

If I didn't breathe in the toxic dust, I would be safe. I crossed the room quickly, like a child afraid of the dark, and whipped open the curtains. Sunlight streamed in. It traveled across the ceiling and across the wall and to the bed, with its bare mattress, its rusting brass frame. It was where I had met the man, where he had looked up from his newspaper, sitting shirtless on that bed, and waved to me.

My disgust did not extend to Aaron. Aaron was, if anything, more beautiful to me, more precious; he was a child again, easier to love, easier to forgive. When you learn something about someone you love, something terrible, you find a room in yourself you didn't know you had, a new organ of understanding. I had a small key now for a very small, sticky lock. But when I could turn it, it made a kind of sense. *Ah yes,* I thought, *of course.* This is why he is the way he is. The key granted me a frightening sort of order.

Disgust is a breed of fear, though. And fear is a lack of understanding. There was disorder in Aaron, a chaos. Something had happened to him that was beyond solution, maybe beyond grace. It was a dark power let loose in the apartment. And that is what I feared.

He was sitting in the recliner in the TV room, as though we had just left him there that morning to run an errand. *General Hospital* murmured on the screen, one pink, airbrushed hospital inside another.

I didn't want to see him. I didn't understand how Aaron wanted to see him. But every few days, he drove to the VA hospital and visited his father. If Aaron could do it, I thought, I could, too.

Morris sat in a pink gown and pale-blue hospital pants, his hands gripping the arms of his chair. His mouth hung open, his head weighted back, his eyes resting on the place where the ceiling met the wall. A paper bib, leftover from lunch, was smeared with the dried crust of what looked like applesauce.

Was this his punishment? I wondered. To be trapped in this purgatory of old men in La-Z-Boys, year after year?

His steely eyebrows rose up, fierce. The wrinkles in his forehead had deepened. He was so weak, so fragile, his skinny collarbones were poking out of his V-neck.

Was it cruel to wish that he'd die? Or would it be too gentle for him, a gift? Was God drawing out his life on purpose?

Morris didn't believe in God. He'd told Aaron, When you're dead, you're dead.

Aaron put his hand on his father's shoulder. "Hey, Pop."

His eyes searched the room a moment before finding Aaron's face. He spoke one long, affirmative vowel. He touched Aaron's hand.

Before you can change your mind, touch his other shoulder, birdlike. Put your lips to his scalp. It's more out of curiosity than kindness, certainly not yet like forgiveness. Is this still him? Is he still there? He smells—your heart breaks—like Aaron. You know just what his skin will feel like when he's an old man.

Still, there was a kind of comfort in Florida.

It was a place I'd never wanted to return to, but now that we were there, it had its perks. I spent hours reading by the pool, watching the palm trees sway, watching my skin remember how to tan. I worked out in the women's gym off the pool, riding the ancient exercise bike. I remember reading all of *Middlesex* on that bike. Aaron and I revisited the hot tub where we spent so much time that first summer we'd met. We went out to eat at all the old restaurants and we hung out with old friends and we spent too much time at the Gardens Mall. It was so clean! Was there any place cleaner than the Gardens Mall? They had even banned smoking! I went there just to drink in the clean fountain air.

Now it was my parents' house we went to for dinner. Not every Sunday. Just when we felt like it. I helped my dad with a stir-fry. Aaron watched Westerns with him or helped him figure out something on his computer. I started substitute teaching at the middle school where my mom taught English, and we'd ride in together every morning, and I'd read her Alice Munro stories and we'd talk. She'd roll down the window to smoke her cigarette, and then roll it right back up.

There was a kind of acceptance required in living in Florida, an acceptance of ease, of idleness. I had fled such idleness. I was drawn, as we know, to difficulty. I craved change. Seasons. The windburn of winter. From our balcony, we could see the same old man tanning himself every day by the pool. He wore a royal-blue Speedo and royal-blue egg-shaped cups over his eyes and he was the color of roast beef. I was scared of turning that indolent shade of bronze. After spending hours dragging around a lounge chair to chase the sun, I would get up, sun-sick and disgusted, and go sit on the stationary bike, trying to pedal somewhere.

Aaron had his Range Rover back, its own little carport spot to park in, and he hosed it down lovingly and drove it all over town, to see friends, to go shopping, to go to the beach. He drove mostly to his friend's warehouse, where he practiced with his band. "How come I'm never allowed to see you play?"

"You are."

"Well, how come I haven't?"

"We're just practicing."

Mostly, I knew, he was hanging out and smoking pot. The warehouse was like a bar for stoners. It was his guy space. I got it. I was glad, in a way, he had it. In New York, he'd had virtually no friends. Here, he was with his people. It was like we'd never left. It was a perpetual adolescence he was choosing to live in, and I could kind of see why.

At home, he read an old copy of *Gray's Anatomy* he'd found in his bedroom. He told me he used to want to be a doctor. Also, it was the secret bible of metal lyrics. But now it inspired lyrics to a rap song he went around singing.

> *Yo, I live in my dad's condo*
> *My favorite part of the brain is the fissure of Rolando!*

In spite of myself, I laughed.

·   ·   ·

There was more.

More memories?

No. He'd found something. He hadn't wanted to tell me. But now here we were. It's hard not to think about it here, he said.

And I'd wondered why he wasn't having a harder time.

On his father's old computer, he'd found some stuff about incest. "Like, research."

Aaron had gotten rid of the computer. Wiped it, and then trashed it.

It was almost as creepy as child pornography. That he had known what he was doing, that he had a word for his depravity. And that Aaron was just the object within reach.

I don't want to know what he knows about my dad, he'd said about his father's psychiatrist.

Now I understood a little of that freaked-out look he'd given us, Morris and me, as we waited outside Dr. Delano's office during that first appointment. What a twisted thing, for your father to follow you on his scooter while you walked to the psychiatrist to seek antidepressants for the hell your father put you through.

I mean, I knew Aaron's depression—if that's what we were calling it—wasn't just his father's fault. You could only blame your father for so much.

Then there was your mother!

These were my thoughts while I waited for Aaron to come out of the psychiatrist's office, by myself this time, with another sample of Zoloft. I knew enough to know that Dr. Delano was probably only supposed to prescribe to vets. Maybe that was why he always gave Aaron samples, instead of writing a prescription. Maybe he did know what Morris had done to Aaron. Maybe it was his way of offering the amends that Morris couldn't, or didn't.

Had he confessed to the doctor? Did it matter? Would it have mattered if he'd told Aaron he was sorry?

I wondered what it would be like for me to find out before his stroke, while he was wandering around the world in his right mind. Would I have been able to look at him?

Well, Aaron was.

Then I wondered what it would have been like to find out after he was dead.

I closed my eyes. I could remember standing here with him as he sat on that scooter. He was anxious, too. I'd written it off to parental concern. I'd believed he was anxious because his child was suffering, and he wanted him to get better. I still wanted to believe it.

I couldn't stand still. Why was I waiting for Aaron?

I turned and walked down the corridor. Down, down, down. The hospital was the size of a small city. Morris wasn't in the TV room. He wasn't in his room. For a moment I thought: he's died. And my heart cramped with panic.

Then a nurse wheeled him down the hall. He was freshly bathed, the long strands of his combed hair silver and slick.

And I thought: Thank God.

And then I thought: I guess that means I still love him.

The incest stuff Aaron had found on his dad's computer—maybe Morris was trying to diagnose himself. Maybe he was trying to heal himself. Maybe it was a word Dr. Delano had used with him, and maybe Morris had accepted it, maybe he had cried, full of self-hate, a remorse so big he couldn't speak it.

On Valentine's Day, Aaron and I went to our favorite Thai restaurant, the one with the perfectly steamed tofu and the little flowers made out of vegetable peels, the little works of art my mother would sneak into her purse in her napkin, too pretty to waste, down the road from the Publix where Aaron had his first job, down the road from the Winn-Dixie where I had my first job, down the road from the strip mall with the CD Warehouse where Aaron and I had met, down the road from the entrance to Lake Shore Drive, where Aaron had lived and we now lived again. It had seemed a whole world, and much of it had taken place, our little story, on a few miles along US-1.

All through dinner, I'd had a feeling he was going to propose. He didn't.

Then, after dinner, we drove back to the condo and, in his childhood bedroom, Aaron grabbed my hand. In it he dropped one of those candy hearts, yellow. MARRY ME, it said.

My first ridiculous thought was to pop it in my mouth.

"Yes!" I cried.

"Why did you eat it?" Aaron said, aghast.

"I don't know! I was nervous! Are you really asking me?"

From his pocket he took the ring box. It was a very pretty and modestly sized diamond. He pointed to the long diamonds along each side. "They're called baguettes," he explained.

"I love it," I said. "Yes."

We were standing on the pee-colored rug in his disgusting bedroom, but over his shoulder, as I kissed him, I could see the ocean.

It would be a short engagement. We'd been together—practically married!—for almost six years already. We were just making it official.

Our mothers were thrilled. Aaron had driven over to ask my dad for my hand (a somewhat gross tradition now, we both acknowledge) and he'd cried. Happy tears!

The same week I got engaged, I received a call from the University of Virginia. My first grad school acceptance, and I was invited to compete for a Jefferson Scholarship. I flew to Charlottesville and did the interview. I didn't get the scholarship, but it was okay. A photographer took a picture of me in my one and only black suit, my engagement ring gleaming. "Nice ring!" he said. By the time I left Charlottesville, I'd gotten more calls from more schools, including schools in New York City and Cornell in Ithaca, New York, but I'd already made up my mind. We didn't have to return to New York! None of those schools were fully funded. We didn't want to go broke all over again. Besides, I liked Charlottesville; it reminded me of Burlington. "I'm in love," I told my fiancé. Aaron was happy for me. We would start our married life in a new place, in Virginia. We'd be in between my two brothers in D.C. and North Carolina. Online, we rented a townhouse that was brand-new. In the pictures, the tape hadn't even been taken off the kitchen counters.

I spent the next four months doodling pictures of wedding dresses and making lists in a notebook while my middle school students did worksheets and watched videos. I'd never really wanted to wear a white dress. Yellow, I'd thought, was sunnier. White was repressively virginal! Now, though, after a year of living in this urine-colored apartment, I really wanted a pure white dress. I wanted white everything. Cream-colored roses and cream-colored napkins and cream-colored invitations and a cream-colored wedding cake from Publix. We weren't fancy!

We booked the yacht club downstairs. We had never set foot in it before, let alone on a yacht, but it was pretty, and it was there, and we could practically spit on it from our balcony. The ceremony—it would be short and sweet—would take place in the community room off the pool. It was used for things like knitting club and bridge club and it had a broken coffee machine and flowered wallpaper that looked like a Laura Ashley dress circa 1989. But it was $25 to rent! My parents offered to pay for the reception. For months they put their groceries on one credit card to keep the other one clear for the wedding. Sandra helped with the groom's dinner. Aaron and I covered the rest. When we needed to put down a deposit—for the band, or the judge—Aaron went into his father's room and took out a coin or a baseball card and sold it on eBay. My mother was delighted to learn that a panda figurine covered the photographer. In this way, Morris helped pay for our wedding, too.

A few weeks before our wedding—in time to include it on the invitations—Aaron changed his last name.

He'd been talking about it for a long time. He'd been thinking of last names. He thought of Henderson for a while. I liked the idea. I wasn't going to change my name, I knew. But he didn't want to be absorbed into my family, just as I didn't want to be absorbed into his. He thought of Morrison. Son of Morris. It was direct. But also indirect. Was it indirect enough? The whole point was to drop his father's name, to chainsaw that limb from his family tree.

What he settled on was his mother's last name. "Italian as fuck" was how he put it. It sounded like an obscure pasta eaten only on the island of Sicily, and it would take our children a long time to learn how to spell, but it was his choice.

I didn't pretend to understand it or love it. It was a lesson in the kind of acceptance we would have to practice again and again in marriage. I was happy for him, that he'd shed a part of his identity he'd long wanted to shed, that he'd never have to see that name on an envelope again. I went to the courthouse with him to file the papers. And then we went to file for our marriage certificate.

He didn't invite much of his family to the wedding. I asked him about each of them, in case he changed his mind. Your sister? Your brother? Your niece? Your cousins? Your aunts and uncles? He didn't want them there, he said. "My family's complicated." Your dad? But I knew before he answered that he shouldn't be there, not in the state he was in. What was the point? His mother and her boyfriend would fly in from New Mexico, where they'd moved, leaving New York shortly after we did.

Months later, one of his cousins expressed disappointment—not that we hadn't invited her to the wedding, but that Aaron had changed his last name. "I know why," she said sadly. Other family members had changed their last names, too. She believed, I realized, that Aaron had changed his last name simply because it was Jewish.

The morning of the wedding Aaron saw a person hit by a car.

I'd woken up in a sleeping bag on my dad's office floor. No seeing the bride before the wedding and all that. I'd get ready at my parents' house with my aunts and my mom. Anyway, the showerhead at our stupid apartment had broken, and I didn't want to shower at the gym by the pool, not with all the setting up happening there.

Aaron was picking up his rental at the tux shop and saw the woman try to cross Northlake Boulevard. She was hit by a Buick going forty-five miles per hour and went sailing across two lanes of traffic. "A couple car lengths at least," Aaron told me on the phone. "Nell, it was so crazy." He'd had to stop and wait for the police, give his report.

"Oh my God," I said. "Do you think it's a sign?"

He gave a shallow laugh. "I hope not."

But he didn't know if the woman lived or died. She'd been taken to the hospital.

"Well, I hope she's okay." I was worried about something else. "Dude," I said, "I have my period."

"What?"

"I know. I planned everything around it! But I've been so distracted I forgot to take my pill for like three days!" I'd started bleeding that morning.

"Another sign," Aaron said.

"Shut up. I'm so mad. I don't want my period on my wedding."

"It'll be fine," Aaron said.

"Aaron?"

"Yeah?"

"Please don't forget to shower."

We were late getting to the venue and later still, as I had to run to the gym bathroom to blot my armpits. "Come on!" Jen, my maid of honor, handed me my flowers. I saw her scoot ahead of me along the pool to take Derek's arm, the best man, and together they ducked into the room. My dad and I followed. For the short walk down the aisle, he handed off his cane.

Aaron was already at the end of the aisle, waiting for me, shaved and smiling.

"Oh my goodness," Jen's mom told me later. "He just looked so in love!"

We didn't write our own vows. Embarrassing, to announce your love in a room full of people! Instead, my friend Ursula read First Corinthians, its pale, palatable loveliness. "Love is patient; love is kind." My cousin Darlene read an Apache wedding blessing, the one that starts, "Now you will feel no rain, for each of you will be shelter for the other." I liked it, and it sounded like something that should be read at a wedding, and hadn't yet heard of appropriation. I had not yet read Khalil Gilbran's *The Prophet*, the popular wedding reading that started "Let there be spaces in your togetherness." If I had, I might have included it. Instead: no spaces. All togetherness. Our moms came up to light candles. Aaron fumbled the ring, trying to put it on the wrong hand. Everyone giggled. It was over before we knew it. The organ started up, and we headed for the same door we came through. There was my eleventh-grade English teacher! And all my friends and their moms! And all the guys from Aaron's band! And my aunt Gretchen and my aunt Brenda and my cousins! And Aaron's weed dealer! They threw rose petals at us and we dodged them and laughed, and I started to cry. We didn't know what to do, or where to go, so we just stood by the pool and hugged and kissed and laughed, the two of us alone for a minute, the evening light so pretty on the water and the marina and the distant boats.

"I love you," he said.

"I love you, too. We're married!"

"I have something to tell you."

"What?"

He leaned in close. "I haven't showered in five days."

I smacked his lapel. "Aaron!"

"And I'm wearing an Anthrax T-shirt under this tux."

He lit a cigarette and held my train as we walked along the water, and the photographer snapped pictures of us as the sun slowly fell. If it felt strange to be there, to look up seven stories and see our balcony and beyond it that place I hated; if I felt like a teenager who still had no idea what she was doing—I was two weeks shy of twenty-four—it also felt magical and tropical and special and sweet. After the pictures, we walked to the yacht club, and everyone toasted us and cheered. For the first dance, the band had learned our song, "Everything I Have Is Yours," which the white front man in the keyboard tie sang with a kind of loungey spoken-word bravado. *I would gladly give the sun to you / if the sun were only mine.* Aaron and I laughed. Then he danced with his mom and I danced with my dad. We did most of the things that were done at American weddings. We cut the cake. I tossed the bouquet. "We know what a wedding is," our wedding said, "and this is one." A part of me knew it was for other people. Our wedding said, in the fine print, "We know we are an odd couple, but maybe if our wedding is totally by the book, you won't notice!" The cake wasn't even vegan. We didn't even eat it. The top tier sat in our freezer, which was what we were supposed to do, waiting for something, I don't know what. When we moved to Virginia, we threw it away.

Here is what I didn't want: to take the elevator upstairs and spend my wedding night in my husband's childhood bedroom.

So I'd booked a room in a fancy hotel on Palm Beach. My groom drove me over the bridge to the island. It was all symbolic, I was beginning to see, all a bit of a show. But I didn't really mind. What else was there? We were exhausted and drunk, my up-do had turned into a mullet, and I was bleeding. We made jokes about deflowering and I gave my husband a blow job. "I just gave my husband a blow job," I announced to him, and fell asleep. In the morning, he drove us back over the bridge to my parents' house, where our family and friends had gathered for brunch. "You don't look like virgins anymore," my mom joked as we stepped out of the car, and everyone stood on the lawn and clapped, and from then on we were married.

WAXING GIBBOUS

Spend the summer in waiting rooms, on hold with doctor's offices, writing your husband's health history on intake forms. He still has to look at the engraved date on the inside of his wedding ring to remember your anniversary, but you memorized his social security number long ago. When calling psych hospitals, a good thing to do is pace the deck, where he can't see or hear you from his bed. This one requires a local intake first. This one requires the patient to call. This one has no beds but may have a bed on Saturday; this one has no beds, but the state hospital may have one on Monday. This one takes your insurance but maybe not, it depends. Your husband is too sick. Your husband is not sick enough. Try to time the whole thing so you don't have to take him against his will. Try to time it so he is psychotic enough for them to take him, but not so psychotic that he refuses to go. Enlist the psychiatrist, the therapist, the doctor. He says he doesn't want to live. Cancel your appearance at the writers' conference. I mean, you can't leave him. Also, you can't leave the kids with him. Don't refill the lithium. It might as well be a Flintstone vitamin. But what is he if not bipolar? Chart the cycle in your little green notebook. Watch the pattern emerge like a sine wave. A weeklong flare, and then a weeklong crash. He is raging, sleepless, rocking, wild; then he is complacent, remorseful, and tired. He sleeps, and he heals. Sometimes suicidal, sometimes flirty, sometimes an asshole, sometimes cracking jokes over the eggs he's cooking while imitating Louis Armstrong, or Braveheart. Sometimes he doesn't even wake to eat, just sleepwalks to the kitchen in the middle of the night.

In the morning, there is a slice of Swiss cheese on the kitchen counter, empty cracker boxes he denies having opened. "That's not mine," he says.

"Yeah, okay," you say.

You manage to laugh together, looking at the mystery cheese melting a little, hardening at the edges as cheese does.

Watch him emerge from the coma. Enjoy it while it lasts. Stop calling the psych wards for a few days. Give yourself a break. Watch him shower and shave and wipe the grassy shake from the shelf in the bathroom, where he's arranged the shards of his skin like a kid with a rock collection. Sometimes you clean it before he does, because it is just so gross. *I didn't sign up for this.* But he's clean now and he's wearing pants with a zipper. Kiss him on his smooth jaw. There he is! You knew he was in there. He takes out the recycling. He walks the dog. He takes out his Pashto workbook. He is teaching himself how to speak Pashto! He boils an artichoke for your strange artichoke-loving child, and shows him how to eat the leaves, raking the flesh with his bottom teeth.

But it's as predictable as the recycling truck. Every two weeks, it arrives.

Slowly, first, like a cold. Then he starts disappearing into the bathroom again. The snakeskin bread crumbs on the bathroom shelf. He takes a four-hour bath. He knows better than to show you his skin now. You hear him talking to himself in there, until he's not talking at all. He's been in there an awfully long time. You knock, and he doesn't answer. You slide open the pocket door, your brain flashing red to all the haunted-house possibilities. What you see instead: your husband lying flat on his back on the bathroom sink, naked, holding up his phone to the back of his left hand. Looking, looking, through the magnifying screen of the camera.

He says he wants to be close to the outlet. His phone keeps losing its charge.

You find a therapist. You are smart enough to find a therapist. Someone for *you* to talk to. You haven't had one of your own since Charlottesville.

This one, like your last one, is a redhead, but she wears Birkenstocks. Your theory that the Birkenstocks with three straps were specially designed for therapists is, you are pleased to discover, actually really true. She wears flowy pants and has a big purple backpack at her feet at all times. She fights to keep her hair out of her eyes. Where was that folder, her pencil? Into the purple backpack she plunges a searching arm. You love her immediately. She is the gentle-voiced, grandmotherly version of you.

You tell her about the midnight trips to the hospital. You tell her they won't keep him. Or you don't want them to. You're not sure! She listens, nods, coos her sympathy. You both write things down in your notebooks. At the end of each session, she says, "I realize we haven't talked much about *you*." You both laugh.

What you have is more important, in the meantime. Concrete advice. Phone numbers. Little articles she rips out of local magazines. If you have to take him to another psych hospital, she says, don't go to Elmira. Go to Binghamton. You write it down.

One night at the dinner table, Aaron's having trouble breathing. He's been in a down period—depressed, tired. Now pain clutches his chest. Last night he was up tossing and turning, soaking the sheets in sweat. You've spent two hours making eggplant moussaka, and it sits untouched in front of him. Your dad gets out his blood pressure cuff, and the first number is low: eighty-something. It's eight thirty on a Saturday night, so your dad puts the boys to bed while you drive Aaron to Urgent Care.

You've barely walked in the door and they're already ushering him to a room. A white man says "chest pains" at any American check-in desk, and he'll be greeted with the fastest-walking nurses you've ever seen. Two nurses are attaching metal disks to his hairy chest. Another wheels in the EKG. Another tries to get her computer to cooperate. Then the doctor bounds in. The EKG checks out, but still, she's worried. "The fever, the disorientation, the pain in his jaw"—he has pain in his jaw—"you need to go to the hospital, and you need to go in an ambulance. We're good for a broken finger."

Before long, two paramedics wheel in a stretcher. One is short and rotund, one is tall and lanky, like a cartoon couple. The tall one recognizes Aaron right away. "Do you all live on Aurora Street?"

You do. Well, you did.

"I was there that night. The false alarm?" He smiles a friendly, toothy smile. He has a crown of very curly strawberry-blond hair. "You signed off, so we didn't end up taking you. I was glad you were okay."

Aaron nods, a little stunned. You are not used to such casual disclosures. One of the cops who was there that night is the father of one of Henry's classmates, and every time you see him, at a birthday party or field trip, he smiles blankly, his lips sealed by some AA-level respect for privacy.

"I'm Leaf," the paramedic says. "We'll take good care of you."

Leaf rides in the ambulance with Aaron while you follow in the car, and you choose to believe him. The casual way he's brushed over the incident—understandable, happens all the time, you did what you thought was best—makes you feel vindicated, understood. Someone is keeping track of Aaron, a goofily tall guardian-angel paramedic. The doctors will see him, at least. You know he's not having a heart attack, but still: maybe this is what it takes. Maybe they will keep him, look at him, listen. Maybe an ambulance will get their attention.

In the hospital where twice in the last four months you've waited six hours for a psychiatric evaluation, they test Aaron's blood, run an EKG, take a chest X-ray. Never have they taken such swift care of him. They are worried about him. He is out of it. Can't keep his eyes open. "Is this normal?" the nurse asks me.

"Well, it's not *normal*," you tell her. "But it's normal for him."

After a couple of hours, the tall silver-haired doctor comes into the room and moves your giant handbag from the seat beside you so he can sit. Good sign. Maybe he is one of the good ones.

"We don't know what's wrong," he admits. "Everything's checking out."

Aaron is sleeping, or almost sleeping. The hope drains out of me like a fluid.

"Look, he's very sick," you tell the doctor. "He may not die tonight, but something is slowly killing him."

He shakes his head sympathetically. "I'm good at figuring out what's going on with the heart," he tells you. "This—this is beyond my expertise."

You have your little book out, your pencil poised, but what to write down? *Nobody can help.*

"What does it take to get someone like this checked into a hospital? To monitor him for a while?"

"It doesn't really work that way anymore, unfortunately," he says.

He leaves the room. The gentle way he slides the curtain aside sounds like an apology. Aaron is moaning in the bed, grinding his teeth. His eyes are doing that thing where the lids lie half open, the whites staring at me in accusation.

"I tried," you say. "I'm sorry."

"Ask him about parasites," he says softly, barely able to open his jaw.

"You ask him," you say. "He was just here!"

"They'll send me to the psych ward," he says. "Please. Ask."

What are you so afraid of? Taking up the doctor's time? Ending up in the psych ward yourself? You go back out to the nurse's station and ask for the doctor to look in Aaron's ear. "His ear is hurting him," you say, "and his jaw."

Kindly, he comes. He looks in Aaron's ear. All clear. All fucking clear.

"I know this might sound crazy, but we're just trying to rule stuff out. Could it be"—you take a breath—"parasites?"

Again, the sympathetic shake of his head. "We don't really see that." If it were parasites, the whole family likely would have them. "Well, there's Babesia." He crosses a leg. "But unless you've traveled to a tropical country in the last thirty days, we just don't test for parasites."

F/U with GP, the discharge papers say.

It takes you a minute to realize that *F/U* stands for *Follow up* and not something else.

Together you do the midnight walk of shame through the dim waiting room, empty but for the blue glow of the TV.

.   .   .

The next time, you'll be prepared. You won't leave the hospital without having him admitted to the psych ward. You won't leave without answers. Be strong! Nerves of steel! Don't back down! You remember the way you let your firstborn cry it out when he was a baby. You probably wouldn't have been able to do it for long, but the volume was muted on the baby monitor and you didn't realize he'd been crying—for how long? Never mind; he survived. Your husband will survive, too. It's for his own good.

Two weeks later, when he's breaking out and freaking out, you convince him to let you drive him to the hospital in Binghamton. Maybe they'll have more beds, you reason, more resources, in a bigger city, maybe you can start fresh in a place where he doesn't have a chart a mile long. But you forgot to ask the therapist *which* hospital in Binghamton. Was this the right one? When you arrive at the ER, while Aaron uses the bathroom, you walk to the desk and whisper, holding back tears, "My husband has delusional parasitosis. He needs help."

The nurses escort him to the only empty bed. It is clear right away that you have made a mistake. Everyone in the ER appears to be in worse shape than he is. This makes you feel comforted and also deeply disturbed. Patients crowd the room in their beds, in their gowns, talking to themselves, talking into their phones, begging for help. One woman is trying to reach her father; she needs a ride home; won't he come pick her up? A police officer who looks no older than twenty-one is sitting at a desk reading a newspaper. Another man, in his street clothes, is sitting up on a bed rolled into the hallway. There aren't even *rooms*, per se, just a bunch of beds with curtains drawn around them in various states of enclosure, screeching along their rods. You feel at once shocked and sympathetic and stupid—that your privilege extends to your access to the Ithaca hospital, which in hindsight seems absurdly elite, with its organic vending machine in the waiting room.

"Are you always so . . . restless?" the nurse asks Aaron, taking his blood pressure. He's just nervous, he says. He tells her he has parasites. He says it kindly, a warning, but he is crawling out of his skin, can't stay still, gets out, paces, rocks, until she guides him back to bed. When she leaves, Aaron begs you, "Do *not* tell her I'm on Seroquel." He wants a clean slate; he wants them to look at his skin, not his brain. Wait with him; assure him; talk to him; try to keep him calm. He is talking to you about bugs, and the patient behind the sheet beside him, no more than six feet away, begins to talk back. That shit is for real! she tells him. Those bugs will get you. He is with it enough to give you a look that says *That woman is bat shit crazy*. Where is the nurse and what is wrong with this place?

You stay with him until you can't stay anymore. Then you run to the parking lot and call Jen. Jen is a therapist! She is tough as nails, she takes no shit. You are in a part of the parking lot that looks like the sad place behind a grocery store, where the trucks come to deliver the food into giant doors. Cry into the phone, "I can't do it! I can't leave him here." Listen as she says, "Yes, you can."

When you try to get back through to the ER, the doors are locked. "You're going to have to wait," the receptionist tells you. "We have a coronary situation." Through the glass panels of the swinging doors you can see an enormous man lying on his back on a stretcher, half a dozen people swarming around him with oxygen and paddles and beeping machines. Does this hospital have no proper rooms? It conducts its coronary procedures in the middle of the entrance? The man lies un-moving. There is no way around him. Sit in the waiting room and wait. Close your eyes and breathe, try not to panic, try not to worry about what's happening back there. If you leave, and they sedate him, he will never forgive you.

Finally, you're allowed back—what has happened to the man?—and your husband is in the same state you left him in. The nurse pulls you aside and says, "Let's have a chat." You duck around the corner and, when asked, give her the full list of your husband's meds. How can you not? They need to know about interactions; they need to know his his-tory. "He needs to be evaluated," you say. "There's something very, very wrong with him. He wasn't always like this. Look at his skin, look at his head, test him, scan him. Please." But as you say it, you feel it: you don't want him here. This place is scary. In the hallway, the man in his street clothes is still yelling from his bed. "Who called me a pedophile?!" he demands. He looks at you and yells, "Did you call me a pedophile?!" Do your best to ignore him. Ignore the fact that this place can't help you. "I'm sorry," the nurse says to you. "We can't help you. We're full." *Maybe* if he was admitted, they could transfer him to a state hospital. But they may not have any beds, either. The man demands again to know if you have called him a pedophile. The nurse, arms folded, again apologizes to you. You are not one of them. You are, like her, one of the sane ones. "Full moon," she explains.

In twenty minutes, you'll be discharged, driving your husband home with an antibiotic for "cellulitis." You'll be crying from relief and whatever the opposite of relief is. He'll be sitting in the passenger seat, peeling off his sock, hiking his bare foot up on the dashboard. He is wiggling, twisting, worrying the sores on his ankle, on the back of his legs. Nothing has changed, except he does not know that you have tried to betray him and have failed.

Ten minutes from home, his foot presses against the windshield with such force that the glass cracks. You shriek, skid a little, right the car. "Holy shit," he says. "I'm sorry. I'm so sorry." The spiderweb looks like a stray rock has struck the car from the outside. Later, the insurance company will ask you to measure it, will ask you to explain. How to say that the pressure is coming from the inside, that something terrible wants to get out?

IRONY 5

n the other waiting room, back in Ithaca, while I am still waiting for
Leaf to fetch me and tell me Aaron has arrived in the ambulance,
while I am still nursing my cautious hope, a commercial plays for an
NBC drama. It's a new fall show I haven't heard of before, *New Amsterdam*. A handsome young doctor in a white coat tells a room full of
handsome doctors in white coats: "You know, we all feel like the system
is too big to change. But we are the system. And we need to change.
Let's be doctors . . . again."

I snort at the empty room.

"They're not going to let you come in here and just . . . help people,"
says another handsome doctor.

The handsome doctor winks. Is he winking at me?

"So let's help as many as we can before they figure us out."

IRONY 6

Driving the kids to the trampoline park in Syracuse, I spot a billboard on the unfamiliar highway. Above the airbrushed face of a sultry brunette are the words:

PARASITE FOUND.

The car hurtles forward. My eyes adjust. Just as we are about to pass, the letters fall into place:

PARADISE FOUND.

A gentlemen's club.

From the backseat, Henry asks, "What are you laughing at, Mom?"

SEVEN-YEAR ITCH

t's been seven years, you both realize. It has come to a head, in a way. For a moment, he's there, your husband, looking you in the eye, as amazed as you are: seven years.

Then he is lost to his own reflection. His eyes hang inches from the bathroom mirror. He is waiting for something to move, in his eye, his eyebrow, his sideburn. He strips down, displays an armpit to the glass. He says, "I feel like my hair is not my own."

The thing is: for a long time you thought they were unrelated, what was happening in his body, what was happening in his mind. They were like wars being fought on different continents. Now you see them with the full rush of historical hindsight. Both armies are battling the same invader.

You have no more time to waste. Check out books at the library. Check out real books and audiobooks and e-books, about the brain and about skin and about infection and chronic illness, books that promise you will get your life back if only you read every page. Read articles. Articles sent to you by friends who swear by their dermatologists' advice and articles found on Wikipedia and WebMD and in the black hole of midnight, on Tripod pages made in 1998. Develop no system for organizing the articles whatsoever. Keep at least seventeen tabs open at all times. Email yourself the articles, with cryptic subject lines and lots of question marks. Stay up so late you feel sick. Oh well! The kids aren't in camp because you can't afford it. You all sleep in. Your sick house family will survive. The children eat a lot of toast and watch a lot of *SpongeBob*. Your dad is there, thank God, watching *SpongeBob* with them, eating toast.

This is the summer people are talking about Lyme disease. You read about it in *Total Recovery*, again and again, which, really, is a good book. In the case histories, there is always something invisible underlying: toxic mold, an amoeba in the gut, the trauma of a car crash, Lyme, Lyme, Lyme. Your child's friend gets Lyme. Your friend's child gets Lyme. They live in Syracuse and Connecticut, Vermont and Long Island and Maine. More and more in Ithaca, right here, children absent from summer camp, friends cancelling their summer trips. One child is bitten by a tick while hiking, a friend while picnicking in a downtown park. They feel terrible. They're achy and tired, their brains fogged. They're on antibiotics, all of them, some for a week or two, some for three or four. Some get the red bulls-eye rash, some don't. Most get better, some don't.

Read *Sick*, Porochista Khakpour's new memoir. Make avocado toast—toast is really all your family eats—and read it on the deck. Dog-ear all the pages that give you goosebumps. The drugs, the pain, the insomnia, the racing thoughts, the feeling of being lost in one's own house. Remember the time your husband said he felt his brain was like a slot machine? "Meanwhile, no one knew what it was that was physically wrong exactly, just as they could not pinpoint what was wrong mentally. My anxiety and depression seemed to scissor each other in ways that mimicked bipolarity." Yes! you think. Yes! The diagnosis, finally? Lyme disease! Her doctor told her that "you hear a lot about the joint pain and muscle aches, but that the first symptoms of Lyme for most are anxiety, depression, and insomnia. The sort of insomnia that does not let up. The sort of insomnia that does not respond to conventional medication. Lyme attacks soft tissues in the body, and the brain is one of its favorite organs to feast on." Squeeze your eyes closed, pound your feet on the deck in recognition and fright. Picture it: the bacteria devouring your husband's brain. If this isn't it, what is it?

Go to a NAMI meeting downtown. National Association for Mental Illness. You've been to Al-Anon meetings; it can't be so different, right? Aaron knows you're going; he is, amid the chaos, grateful for your concern. The people there talk about their grown children, mostly, children lost or nearly lost to schizophrenia, overdoses, suicide attempts. Should they call the police for a welfare check? Should they call the police for a restraining order? You want to gather them all up and let them gather you in their fleece vests and flowing skirts. When it's your turn, describe your husband's symptoms. "I thought it must be bipolar disorder," you say. "It comes out of nowhere, then goes away, then comes back." You are trying to get help. You can't get him admitted anywhere. You don't know where to begin. They listen—they are, as at Al-Anon, mostly sixty-year-old women—and they nod in solidarity over their Styrofoam cups of coffee.

Afterward, one of the women hands you a mint-green booklet. "I just happened to pick this up. Would you like it?" Take the booklet and read the title: *Lyme Disease and associated diseases: The Basics.* "I've heard," she says, "that Lyme can mimic bipolar disorder."

"You know," you say, "I've heard that, too."

You did not expect to go home from the NAMI meeting with a Lyme pamphlet. But at home, you get into bed and find yourself reading it cover to cover. It is published by The Lyme Disease Association of Southeastern Pennsylvania. It does, indeed, say that Lyme is the great imitator. Another thing you didn't expect: there, on page thirteen, in a list of "co-infections" and "associated diseases," are the words "Morgellons disease."

> Morgellons disease is an emerging disease that causes strange symptoms. It is the least understood and most controversial of the tick-borne diseases. One unique characteristic of Morgellons is the appearance of fibers growing out of the skin, accompanied by severe itching. Morgellons patients often experience sensations of something crawling under their skin, which leads many doctors

to conclude that the patient has a psychiatric problem. However, experiments have shown that dogs can have the same fibers and symptoms.

New organisms such as viruses and microscopic worms are being discovered in ticks. Their role in human illness is not yet known.

"I think you have Lyme disease," you tell your husband. "And I think you really do have fucking Morgellons."

He waves his hand. Morgellons is bullshit, he says. He still thinks Morgellons is the invention of paranoid people.

But people think *you're* paranoid, you point out.

"Do *you* think I'm paranoid?"

Show him the booklet. "I think Morgellons is real."

He's not so sure. What about this? you ask. What about this? What he has come to believe he has, simply, are parasites.

Why is it so difficult? Like convincing someone purple is blue? And who's to say your blue isn't purple? Who's to say you're both not right?

It's a contradiction you can't quite get your head around. You have caught up to him, to his reality—*there is something real inside me*—but now you have moved past him, into some other dimension of righteous, persecuted belief. Now *you* believe more than he does. But according to him you're believing in the wrong thing.

You'll wait for a better time, a time when he's more receptive. Leave the booklet in the bathroom for him to read on his own, one of your dad's pipe cleaners tucked between the pages, marking your spot.

Buy the Morgellons book on Amazon, the only book on Morgellons, by Dr. Ginger Savely. *Morgellons: The Legitimization of a Disease.* You cringe a little to see the giant margins and glaring misspelling (*Part One: Truth is Stranger Then Fiction*), the fuzzy grayscale photos. But the writing is good. Dr. Savely isn't an M.D.; she's a nurse practitioner with a Ph.D.; her dissertation was on Morgellons research. And the photos could be of your husband. Underline the passages. Star the symptoms.

Disfiguring, spontaneously appearing, slow-healing lesions.

Blue, white, red, and black hair-like filaments extruding through the skin or seen just under the epidermis using magnification.

Filaments that look like "feathers" because of the many fine projections from either side of the filament.

Occasional black tar-like exudate from the pores.

Metallic "glitter" on the face and other parts of the body.

Crystal-like exudates from skin.

A change in the texture or color of the hair.

An awareness of tiny flying insects around the body.

Fine markings on the skin that appear spontaneously but look like cat scratches or paper cuts.

Slightly raised, linear "tracks" on the skin.

Systemic symptoms including profound fatigue, anxiety, insomnia, joint and muscle pain, headaches, loss of balance, dizziness, and cognitive disturbances such as loss of short-term memory, and inability to concentrate or comprehend.

The constant and unnerving aggravation of feeling as though there are bugs or worms crawling through one's body, biting, stinging, and causing unbearable discomfort.

Check, check, check, check, check, check, check, check, check, check, check, check.

Underneath this list:

> As if the symptoms of the disease were not challenging enough, patients are forced to endure ridicule and abandonment by family, friends, and health care providers. Typically patients have futilely consulted as many as twenty to thirty different clinicians. With no hope in sight, it is no wonder that most Morgellons patients have depression, anxiety, and/or suicidal thoughts and many have ended their lives.

It's kind of like reading a novel and seeing in its pages a narrator who has felt the same feelings and thought the same thoughts, which you've never recognized as your feelings or thoughts until now. Except now it's not a novel but a reality, a science fictional universe: it *is* a world, that planet does exist, the horror is happening. Knowing that it's not a dream, or at least that others are having the same nightmare: it makes the horror holdable.

You choose the right time. A righter time. You're in bed, he is showered and clean, sketching in his sketchbook. You read the passages slowly, with curiosity but short of conviction.

My back felt like it was alive, living a separate life than my own.

He raises his eyebrows.

Interestingly, whenever an MD patient sustains an injury to intact skin such as an abrasion or even a paper cut, before long the injury becomes a new site of filament proliferation.

"Wow," Aaron says. This is why he doesn't shave for long periods, avoids using sharp knives.

"Now listen to this." The clincher. *"My hair is not my own" is something that I frequently hear from MD patients.*

How many times has he said these very words to you?

Here he lets his sketch pad fall to his lap. "Holy shit."

"Right?"

He says, "Maybe."

"Daddy's sick," I say to the kids.

"I'm sorry Daddy's so sick."

"I hope Daddy will be better soon," I say.

My dad helps Nico with his math homework. My dad reads Henry *Dog Man.*

The summer wanes.

"I can't do this anymore," he says.

"I can't do this anymore," I say.

We say it to the doctors, to Stu, to friends on the phone, to the suicide hotline, to each other.

There are two old Adirondack chairs out behind our house. Untreated wood, heavy and weather beaten from spending too many winters in the snow. I have taken to taking a baseball bat to them, when the knot in my chest needs releasing.

Then, another appointment. This time it's with a functional medicine health coach named Laura recommended by a friend of my friend Katie. "A miracle worker," the friend said. At the miracle worker's office, we are to remove our shoes. In the waiting room, our children tap the iPad, sharing a pair of earbuds. Laura wears a jean jacket. My bare feet sink into the plush carpet. In my hands, the paper cup of tea is warm.

Aaron describes his symptoms, a song he's long ago memorized. Anemic. Disoriented. Falling. Can't concentrate. Can't sleep. The flare every two weeks. The skin crawling. The stuff coming out of his hands. He shows her the purple scars of his lesions.

He knows how to say it now. He doesn't say, "I have parasites." He says, "I feel like I have parasites."

Laura looks at him, shrugs. Later she will tell us that her son didn't speak until he was five and a half. She learned functional medicine to learn how to heal him. Now, at twelve, he has a 98 average.

"You probably have parasites," she says.

I meet my husband's eyes.

You think you have pretty much memorized Google, and then you learn something new. The life cycle of a parasite? Two weeks. Every new moon, and every full moon, they lay their eggs. It is the first time anyone has ever been able to explain it.

Also, this. "Have you heard of Morgellons disease?"

I look back at Aaron. He's already looking at me. Our look is like a swear word, like a dare.

WEBLAND TERRACE

2003

There is a ritual in the life of many American newlyweds in which they must test the marriage rites by sleeping on an air mattress. The mattress must be made of velveteen polyvinyl, no more than six inches in height, and it must be designed with at least two, and perhaps hundreds, of invisible holes. The only tools at the young couple's disposal are a sticky denim-colored patch and a battery-operated pump that sounds like a helicopter taking off. For over the course of each night, the mattress deflates steadily, almost imperceptibly. Slowly, the young couple sinks. Their bodies pitch toward each other, as though on an uneven sea. Some might stare at the ceiling, or close their eyes against the force of gravity, or get up to resuscitate the lifeboat once, twice, three times in the night, or reach out for the other's hand. They might negotiate a balance: each of their bodies occupying just the right place on the marriage bed, a gap between them, so that they might buoy the other. No matter. By the morning, they will both be touching the floor.

We slept four months on that mattress, having left most of our furniture in Florida. Most of it belonged to Aaron's father, and none of it was dear to us. We had our books, our CDs and records, bulky desktop computers we set up on the floor of each of our offices. Our own offices! We had an enormous television and a coffee table, which we sat cross-legged in front of on the wall-to-wall Berber carpet while we ate meals and watched the TV. We had all we needed.

My new friends found it strange, our extended period of

furniture-less-ness. I kept promising to have them over as soon as we had some. They directed us to the secondhand furniture store in town, where they'd appointed their own apartments. For some reason I was set on buying everything new, from the IKEA two hours north. When we sold the condo, we'd take the check and go to IKEA and make the most of the delivery fee. I dog-eared the whole catalog. The MALM bed! The EXPEDIT bookshelves! The EKTORP couch or the KIVIK? Now I see that we were performing a regeneration.

I was determined, too, to undo the social exile of my college years. At Middlebury, I'd observed a short window, a kind of courtship period, in which students met, matched, and promised to be friends for life, appearing together in ten years, holding the MIDDLEBURY banner (where did one procure such a banner?) in the alumni magazine wedding pages. This window was no more than three weeks long, or approximately the span of time I survived on campus without my boyfriend. This was a mistake, of course. I saw that now. I hadn't tried hard enough.

So, in Charlottesville, I went to the parties, all of them. I went to the bar after workshop. I went to the professor's house. I went to the poets' apartment. I went to a friend's room on the Lawn, the parties spilling out onto Jefferson's brick-manicured campus, a few doors down from Poe's restored room. Another friend, Sean, had a bunch of us over to watch *Hedwig and the Angry Inch.* He also had no couch yet, so we all sat on the carpet against the wall, eating pizza, and afterward, upon realizing he had no napkins, he offered us a beach towel to collectively wipe our mouths with, and from then on we were bonded.

Aaron went to some of the parties. He was friendly with my new friends, and to our delight, he wasn't the only trailing spouse. Most of the students in my cohort were married. A couple even had kids. Many of the parties featured copious breastfeeding, and on one occasion, a drinking game that involved breastmilk. My friend Meredith had been married even more recently and had been with her husband even longer than I had. When we finally filled the house with furniture, we had them over for dinner, and I upped my culinary game, making gnocchi and not just potatoes, though I had to microwave them in the end.

We wouldn't sell the condo yet, we decided. It was a place for Aaron to stay when he visited his dad. It was, maybe, I see now, a way to hold on to Florida, to leave a door open. Instead, we sold the house on Ixora Circle, the house where Aaron had lived when I met him. It was an abstraction to me by then. Aaron signed the papers, and then it was gone, and then we had another abstraction in our bank account, a big lump of money. We drove straight to IKEA.

There is a ritual in the life of many American newlyweds in which they must test the marriage rites by assembling a house full of IKEA furniture. This was a challenge we passed with ease. We'd had practice. We were no slackers. We were committed. We were in it to win it. This was what we had in common: we didn't like to admit defeat. The badass stubbornness that was in us, the parts of us that were at various times vegan and straight edge, the part of us that married young and would be married forever just to show everyone we could, manifested itself in marathon evenings of hardcore furniture assembly. Marriage was like dating, except with even more Allen wrenches.

At the close of the first semester, Aaron and I threw a Christmas party, and in preparation I made pesto and cut my bangs and bought a tree, and everyone played with our cats and drank PBR and admired the two khaki love seats. It was all maybe a little square, but our house was warmed. I felt full. But also scared. Like the Christmas tree and all its artfully arranged ornaments could come crashing down, if they were to see what a farce it all was, a life ordered out of the IKEA catalog. "Is it even real furniture?" my friend Sean asked.

I wanted Aaron to go to therapy.

"I think you're depressed," I told him.

Oh, he was, he admitted. But he wouldn't go to therapy. Every few weeks we had the same conversation.

"Don't you think you'll feel better," I asked him, "if you tell someone?"

We both knew what I was talking about, but neither of us said it.

"I'm never telling anyone," he said.

He was a dark cloud. He was angry and isolated and he cried at car commercials. He was also fun and funny, and funnier when high. On most days I couldn't really tell if he was high. I mean, I just assumed. He had found a source through Sean. Part of me, the part that had taken the D.A.R.E. program very seriously, was afraid to talk to him or to ask. I was worried and ashamed and also glad when he was soothed, when the cloud was calmed. I was like a mother from a hundred years ago with a colicky newborn: just a thimbleful of whiskey in the formula . . .

Then I went to all the parties and occasionally I took a toke of a joint going around a coffee table. I didn't really like it but I guess I was trying to close the distance.

Another way to close the distance: I was writing a novel about him.

Well, not about him, exactly. But about New York, and straight edge kids, and drugs and hardcore and teenagers getting into trouble in the eighties on St. Marks Place. I lifted the stories he'd told me like he'd lifted Star Wars figures with his friend Ashmat, slipping them into my sleeve to resell on the street. If asked if the toys were stolen, Aaron and Ashmat would deny it up and down. These are mine, Aaron would say. And so they would be.

That year, I wrote and wrote. I submitted chapter after chapter to workshop. My readers were eager, and kind, then bitter and bored. The pages piled up. In the spring semester, one workshop mate wrote on the back sheet of a chapter: "Dear Eleanor, What can I say? You are writing a novel, and it is going well."

After I got married and started grad school, I had stopped going by Nell and started going by Eleanor. It felt like a real name, a perfectly good one just languishing on my driver's license, and the one I hoped to see on the cover of the novel I was writing. But I suppose it was also another way in which I wanted to hit restart. Aaron had a new name, and I did, too. A name is a kind of story. I wanted to rewrite mine.

I wanted also to rewrite Aaron's story. I could say the novel wasn't his story because it wasn't: it was the one I wished for him.

I had broken my hero's heart in ways my husband's had been broken—by years of drug use, by the failure of his parents, by the tragic loss of his best friend. But in my book, the boy's estranged parent returned. The family was reconstructed. It was a redemption song.

I pretended to myself that the only thing I was borrowing from Aaron was his record collection. I would cross the hall and knock on his office door and ask, "What band would have toured with Verbal Assault in, like, the fall of '88?" And he had the answer.

"What does Aaron think of your novel?" my friends would ask. They had read the same paragraphs over and over again, axed adjectives, skated through pages of his reimagined history.

"He hasn't read it," I'd say, shrugging. "Yet."

My friend Callie was seeing a therapist; she said it was the best decision she'd made in her twenties. She had, from all appearances, a very nice life! I did not know at that time a lot of people who went to therapy. I had a thought: *I* could go to therapy.

Going to a therapist for the first time is like visiting a new country for the first time: How will they speak? Will you look stupid? Will you be transformed?

The therapist's office was over a garage. I climbed the outdoor stairs. Inside, he sat at a desk in shorts and Birkenstocks and a golf shirt that strained against his big belly. I sat, very far away, on a couch, and immediately cried. Why was I crying?

"I'm sorry," I said. "I don't know why I'm crying."

In a kind voice, he reassured me. He asked me to start from the beginning. Childhood, family, early relationships. I had a great childhood, I said. I had a great relationship with my parents. I was privileged! I was lucky! All of the things in my life, I told him, made me happy. My work, my school, my friends, my new city—I was right where I wanted to be.

"Except"—here I began to cry again, gesturing helplessly with fists full of Kleenex—"my marriage."

It was the first time I had said anything of the sort out loud.

They were guilty tears, I recognized. I felt my mother's stoicism flow out of me. Saying my husband didn't make me happy felt the same as saying my child didn't make me happy. It was the grossest betrayal.

I didn't say this to the therapist. I told him I loved my husband. But he was so far away. So very far away from the rest of my life. He seemed as far away as this therapist was, across the room in his office chair, the wide flat field of an Oriental rug between us. How was I supposed to close that distance here?

MERCURY RISING

T he first day of October again. This year, in our new house south of Ithaca, it chokes the forsythia fields with fog. Over the French doors in the bedroom hangs a *Battlestar Galactica* bedsheet. We have forgone mirrored closet doors for hollow wood, and there is a hole in one of them the size of a fist.

The day is spent sorting test kits on the kitchen island. Each comes in a little wax-board box, the instructions folded with a silky FedEx envelope inside. I would like to get a pair of pants made out of these FedEx envelopes. The blood will be shipped to California, the saliva to Illinois, the stool to North Carolina, the urine and more stool to the parasite lab in Colorado. The vials wait empty in their bubble-wrap beds. For the stool, there is a plaid paper tray, the kind that might cradle an order of curly fries at the state fair. We tuck the saliva tubes into the freezer against the waffles. These tests will cost us around two thousand dollars.

"It was better before, when I didn't know what it was."

We don't yet exactly know what it is. The test results will take weeks. But two months ago, Laura, the health coach, recommended an herbal antiparasitic. Sage, clove, black walnut oil. How strong could it be? When we got home from his appointment, he took one drop of the foul-tasting tincture on his tongue. All night, all bad night, he sweated and swore and moaned. His nose ran; his head hurt; he was delirious with fever. He felt, he said, like he had the flu. Laura had warned us about Herx symptoms, the painful die-off of toxic bacteria that often occurs after an antibiotic regimen is begun. Short for Jarisch-Herxheimer Reaction, named for two doctors who were in fact dermatologists. The same idea applied here, Laura said. Herx was terrible, but it meant the antiparasitic was working. It meant it had things to kill. When I emailed her Aaron's symptoms the next morning, she replied, "I know it's going to be a road."

Now, almost two months later, the Herx symptoms have eased, but still Aaron takes the tincture, three drops three times a day, followed by an activated charcoal pill to absorb the toxins. For a week before the tests, though, Aaron must abstain from it. He must allow them to infest him again, undeterred. He feels them crawling through his socks, through the pads of his thumbs, through his scalp. I see a worm, an inch long, pink-gray, no wider than angel hair pasta, squirming in the bottom of the bathroom sink. Did it come from inside him? This I don't know. But it is, unmistakably, a worm.

The health coach leads to the psychiatrist—a functional medicine psychiatrist, which is a thing—who works in the office across the hall. Dr. Pascal. Aaron hasn't seen Dr. Friedlander for six months, after she went on vacation and he didn't reschedule an appointment. Dr. Pascal works as a team with Laura, the health coach advising us on the whole health picture, the psychiatrist writing prescriptions. Dr. Pascal is petite, middle-aged, with a blondish pixie haircut and sleeveless shell blouses, and we go shoeless in her carpeted office, too. Aaron is nervous; he wants me to go in with him. "Do you have an Ativan?" she asks. When he produces his little silver vial, she says, "Just chew on one, honey, while we talk." She isn't sure if he has schizophrenia. She is pretty sure he has ADHD. *Maybe*, I think. She is kind and understanding and nonjudgmental; she is the kind of doctor who wants to be on his side, them against the world. If we are in the world of *Stranger Things* (are we?), and all of the other doctors we've visited so far are the white-suited Hawkins Lab scientists who insist that no evil lurks under the surface, then the health coach and the psychiatrist are Murray Bauman, the eccentric, Russian-fluent conspiracy theorist/private investigator who is so out there he just might be right about the world: it's out to get you. They have that kind of outsider authority, with better grooming habits. I am not sure, though, if Dr. Pascal really comprehends the degree to which my husband is losing his mind on a biweekly basis. She re-ups his prescription for Ativan and Seroquel, and I write her a check for $225—she does not accept insurance—on a glass coffee table.

Laura doesn't accept insurance either, but she charges us only fifty bucks a session, which leaves me in awe. For her part, she has provided Aaron with the name of a medical marijuana website. "I don't like the alcohol," she says when Aaron tells her the drinking helps. "I'd rather you have cannabis." He schedules a phone call with a doctor—this is one doctor he will gladly call himself!—tells him his symptoms, and in ten minutes is emailed a certificate. The medical marijuana office is in a plaza in Binghamton next to a travel agency and a Papa John's; we present our IDs and are given an orientation by the "pharmacist" (*This is someone's job,* I can't stop thinking), who displays a color wheel and points out the best spectrums for Lyme, the recommended blend of THC and CBD. In the car, Aaron tries out the oil in his new glass vape pen, and I am relieved and confused, tallying the number of hours I've spent over the years trying to get him to stop smoking pot.

The health coach and the psychiatrist lead to a semi-famous Lyme doctor downstate, Dr. Bernard. He has treated the psychiatrist, and the health coach's son. He's written books with his semi-famous doctor brother. Ithaca is the kind of place you'd think would be crawling with Lyme doctors, but they are few and far between. This one's a quack, one friend warns, that one has no openings until December. So after we drop off the kids at school, we drive the three and a half hours to a little town outside Woodstock, where there is a little farmer's market and purple flowers hanging from the awnings outside the shop windows. In the medical building, we walk down a long, skylighted hallway, under giant colorful mobiles that look like Calder knockoffs, and I take a picture of Aaron standing there against the yellow and red and blue, thinking I will look back at this picture someday; someday it will be the *Before,* the beginning of the *After.*

We (by which I mean I) have had three hundred pages of Aaron's medical records—the size of a novel manuscript—forwarded to the office from a half-dozen doctors in Ithaca. We sit across from Dr. Bernard as he flips through them at his glass desk. He seems neither interested in nor impressed by the pages. He looks like a doctor. White man, white coat, white hair, metal-framed glasses. When I try to summarize helpfully, he just nods. I look around at the red Oriental rug, the modern mall inspiration-art, little stone-colored Buddhas, a long banner featuring a quote from Thich Nhat Hanh, another a quote from Bob Marley.

"You've heard of Morgellons disease?" the doctor asks, eyeing us over his glasses.

"We have," Aaron says.

"We are concerned also about parasites," I am sure to say.

We are shown to an exam room, where I take notes in my green notebook and the doctor looks, a little, at Aaron. We leave with a lot of orders for tests, which we need to complete ourselves, and a little white gift bag of medicines, except they are not gifts; they cost $400, and the appointment itself is $1,300; I take out my debit card once, then again.

Down the street is a vegetarian restaurant where we eat lentil soup and tofu steaks and think thoughts of wellness, of spring, though it is fall. Aaron looks like he has been shoved over while sleepwalking and is trying to stand up.

The smoothie Laura has recommended is mustard-yellow, and I make it every day in our Ninja blender, pouring it into what looks like a milk bottle, which I have bought for this purpose, a blend of papaya, pineapple, coconut water, cashew yogurt, sunflower seeds, and turmeric. It is a natural antiparasitic. I am healing my husband, I think. Dropping in the three ice cubes feels like love. I bring it to him and leave it on the bedside—he is in bed, in the darkened bedroom, almost all the time. The boys crawl over the bed, nuzzle his neck.

"Careful," I say. "Daddy's sick. He's getting better."

His eyes are closed; he reaches for them, pets them. He doesn't look like he's getting better. He is still breaking out, freaking out. He's just doing it in this bed.

When I fill the prescriptions, old and new, there are twelve of them. Antibiotics, antiparasitics, an antidepressant, an antipsychotic, probiotics, an adrenal lotion Aaron is to smooth onto his wrists in the morning, a different adrenal lotion at night. A watermelon-flavored gel he squeezes into his mouth from a tube. Four or five different powders he is to stir into water, to balance, detox, cleanse. It is a curious assortment of medicines: the strongest of Western medicine (some would say brutal), the most delicate of natural medicine (some would say feckless). The orange bottles stand on display on the white desk, a little pharmacy in a corner of the bedroom. The backup is stored in our closet in an old green reusable grocery bag: I LOVE MY CO-OP. In the middle of the night, if needed, I can reach into the bag in the dark and before long I can recognize the feel of each plastic cylinder in my hand, its circumference and height, which is the Rifampin, which is the Gabapentin, the Azithromycin, the Seroquel, the Fluvoxamine. I am proud of this skill, my ability to identify what my husband needs and give it to him.

Soon, though, the system requires more order. I buy a plastic pill case the size of a laptop, the kind with four openings for each day of the week: morning, noon, afternoon, night. I drop the pills in one by one; together, they make a colorful rattle. Aaron has a white board, a fancy one with a glassy surface and a stand, like an 8 x 10 picture frame. Where did it come from? It's the kind of thing Aaron has. I wipe it clean and with the dry-erase marker, in capital letters, I list the name of every medicine. To the left of each name, along the margin of the board, I Scotch-tape a single pill. They are tiny white tablets and blood-colored gel caps, fat ones and long ones and the big kind my dad calls "horse pills." It is a beautiful list, and this, too, I am proud of. I set it on the desk and sit down on the bed next to Aaron. I say, "Just so we can tell them apart."

Aaron nods.

"Isn't it nice?"

"It's nice," he agrees, but his eyes are closed. He looks like hell.

"Aren't you impressed?"

"I'm impressed." Without opening his eyes, he says, "Thank you."

It wasn't supposed to be like this. I have done the research. I have gone to meetings, checked out books, made appointments, I have figured out, more or less, what the fuck is wrong. I have solved the case! We just need to wait and see what the test results say. I have stuck with him. He should be grateful.

"I am grateful," he says. "But you have to understand. No one believed me. For seven years, no one believed me."

It becomes a refrain, sometimes muttered, sometimes sung, sometimes spit. Sometimes he cries. Sometimes he hurls it with a fist through a door. I try to remind myself that I am only the recipient of this anger, this sadness, I am the only other person in the room. I just have to sit it out. He is mourning the last seven years, time he can't get back. There will be more time, a future where he is something other than the long-suffering patient, where I am something other than the long-suffering wife.

Sometimes he tells the kids. It comes back to me, like a boomerang.

"No one believed Daddy had parasites," Henry tells me. "For seven years, no one believed him. That's as old as I am."

"I know," I say.

"The doctors didn't believe him. You didn't believe him."

"Yes, I know, Henry. It's complicated."

"I believed him," Henry says.

Stu doesn't believe him, Aaron says.

I don't know about that, I say.

This is an old refrain, pre-illness: Aaron says someone doesn't like him, looked at him funny, said something rude. I say: *I don't know about that.* I try to understand this as the safety measure of a child abandoned by his parents: Trust no one. Leave them before they leave you.

Now, though, the stakes are higher. One Wednesday afternoon we go in for our weekly appointment and Aaron is manic again, rocking in his seat, getting up, pacing. He keeps crossing the room to show Stu the pictures on his phone, as though Stu needs proof to see that something is very wrong. It's almost a comfort, Stu's calm witnessing. I can sit in my armchair and watch. I am not alone.

"Aaron, let's put the phone away," he suggests.

It's not until days later, after he's gotten some rest, that the insult sinks in. "*Let's put the phone away, Aaron!* Fuck that. Like I'm some crazy person. I'm done with him."

"Aaron. You *were* acting crazy."

"Well, fuck you both then."

"Great. Let's just throw away seven years of therapy."

"I am. I'm done."

"He's *Stu*. You love him more than your parents!"

"Fuck all of them. He's the one who dismissed *me*."

One of the problems is we still don't really know what we think of Morgellons. I don't, Aaron doesn't, and together we definitely don't. We don't understand how the disease is said to work, how it relates to parasites. The Morgellons diagnosis feels as flimsy as a hologram, but it is the firmest thing I've had my hands on in years. In the right light, it makes a kind of sense.

"I believe you," I tell him.

"Do you really believe me?"

"Yes," I say, which is to say, *I believe that something in your body is making you sick.* Which is to say, *I'm sorry, I was scared, I trusted the doctors.* What we are agreeing to is a shifting raft; it floats away; flips over; it isn't strong enough to carry both of us. Aaron accepts a Morgellons diagnosis provisionally, as part of a larger system of illness; he insists that what ails him is alive inside him.

According to the book, Morgellons fibers are not parasites; they are abnormal productions of keratin and collagen. Many patients mistake them for worms, though, because they feel movement in their skin, because a kinetic charge sometimes seems to send the fibers stirring. Laura tells us that a parasitic load could be unrelated to Morgellons, but could be a factor nonetheless. We all have parasites and bacteria in our gut, she tells us. When we are sick, when our immune systems are weak, our gut can become dysbiotic. People with Lyme often have other lingering health issues, a cocktail of symptoms that compound each other and slow the healing process: toxic mold exposure, gluten intolerance, physical or emotional trauma in the past. I watch a news video about a parasitologist who claims to have found the cure for Morgellons: a replacement of the mercury fillings in their teeth. Other, more reasonable sites confirm this theory: it is believed that heavy metals keep the immune system from fighting illness. I find Aaron in bed and ask him to open his mouth. His molars are filled with metal, that silvery gold—we count twelve teeth capped with mercury amalgams. He reminds me that, as a child in the nurse's office at school, he once accidentally bit into a thermometer, spilling liquid mercury into his mouth. The image of my husband, poisoned since childhood, speaks to me.

I find a holistic dentist—which is a thing—in Syracuse and make an appointment. What else are we to do, while we wait for the results? The dentist is kind and gentle. He will remove the amalgams, three at a time, over a period of months. If we have to, I think, we will take Aaron apart and put him back together again.

It is easier to direct my anger outward, outside of my house, at Them.

"Morgellons," the Wikipedia entry reads, "is the informal name of a self-diagnosed, scientifically unsubstantiated skin disease in which individuals have sores that they believe contain fibrous material. Morgellons is not well understood, but the general medical consensus is that it is a form of delusional parasitosis. The sores are typically the result of compulsive scratching, and the fibers, when analysed, are consistently found to have originated from clothing and other textiles."

The entry is filed under "pseudomedical diagnosis."

This makes me so mad I actually scream.

I scroll all the way to the bottom, rage-reading. There are forty-five sources cited for this article, but none of them has the name

Middelveen, the primary researcher who has confirmed the presence of filaments. The only mention of those who believe the disease is real: "An active online community supports the notion that it is an infectious disease, disputes that it is psychological, and proposes an association with Lyme Disease. Controversy has resulted; publications 'largely from a single group of investigators' describe findings of spirochetes, keratin, and collagen skin samples in small numbers of patients; these findings are contradicted by much larger studies conducted by the CDC."

The whole history of the work of Morgellons researchers reduced to a series of passive-aggressive semicolons.

This is unbiased? This is an encyclopedia?

I have never edited a Wikipedia article before, but I click on the "Talk" tab at the top. "The subject of this article is controversial, and content may be in dispute," I am told, and also, "Content must be written from a neutral point of view."

I have read a thousand Wikipedia articles, but the format of this underworld is foreign to me. Isn't anyone supposed to be able to edit Wikipedia? Isn't that the whole idea? But the only thing that seems editable is the Talk page, not the entry itself. I type into the textbox links to Middelveen's studies, with a request that they be added as sources for a more balanced, "neutral point of view."

Within a few hours, a response:

> please search the archive pages of this talk page as the paper you are citing has been brought up here multiple times and rejected

I feel slapped. Rejected.

I imagine the smug little gatekeeper behind his computer. Has he seen a lesion erupt before his eyes?

It is a small comfort that I am not the only reader who has attempted to change this page. Again and again, there are little blazes of rebellion. An entry by one user, for whom I feel something akin to love, says:

Reminds me of the old adage that 'absence of proof is not proof of absence.'

"Motherfuckers."

That's what Aaron says when I tell him. This is what gets to him the most. The people who are standing in between him and his dignity. The people with the power to control the story of the disease that is ravaging him.

It's what gets to me the most, too. Because I know that the internet, the world we all live in, has been for us the greatest source of our information and the greatest source of our doubt. It has led us to the answers, and then cruelly questioned them.

In the end, I think this is what turns Aaron, what brings him, on his knees, to my side. It feels like a slippery victory. Because our team— team Morgellons—are the underdogs, or the losers, depending on how you look at it.

We have been drowning, for years, in the ocean of the internet. I want to find dry land. People who understand. I want to look at them. And I want them to look at my husband.

So when I find out in the ocean of the internet that the first International Medical-Scientific Conference on Morgellons Disease will take place in October in Augsburg, Germany, I know we will attend. The annual Morgellons conference happens every spring in Austin, I know well, from Leslie Jamison's essay. But this is a conference for doctors and researchers as well as patients. Many of the people at the center of exposing this disease will be there. And Aaron, angry and exhausted, agrees to go.

Maybe I spin it into a vacation. We have flight vouchers! A couple of days in Munich after the conference. We will outsmart this disease, outfly American bias, and enjoy our first trip to Europe together all at once. We hire a sitter to help my dad with the boys. We order European chargers, pack all of Aaron's meds. We will be gone all of five days. I understand that my motivations are symbolic. I book the tickets anyway.

We fly into Munich and take a train to Augsburg, a cab to the hotel. The hotel feels adequately foreign, with dark, wine-colored rugs and curtains, a curved staircase with a gold banister. We take another cab to the highest-rated vegan restaurant in Augsburg, and eat too much food, satiny soups and smoked vegetables and pickled salads, everything garnished with pubic nests of herbs. For dessert, cashew cheesecakes and lavender lattes. Aaron is wearing his leather jacket and a buoyant black-and-white checked scarf and his black-framed glasses, and with his two-week scruff of a beard he looks very handsome and, I dare say, somewhat European.

Afterward, heading back into the hotel, I spot a familiar-looking woman smoking a cigarette outside the lobby. Middle-aged, in a dress and platforms. "That's Cindy," I whisper to Aaron.

"Who?" Aaron whispers.

"Hi, Cindy?" I ask, approaching and extending my hand.

Cindy Casey-Holman. She is the executive director of the Charles E. Holman Foundation for Morgellons Disease. There must be a name for this, the kind of celebrity spotting where you're the only one who knows you're in the presence of a celebrity.

We introduce ourselves. We've come to the conference from Ithaca, New York.

Wow, Cindy says. I saw your names on the list. So cool that you've come all this way!

There's another American, she says, from Virginia.

We chat a little about Aaron's Morgellons symptoms, Cindy's. She is doing better, she says—the before-and-after legs featured in so many of the foundation's materials are hers—but she has been diagnosed with a co-infection. I've read her story—in the *People* magazine feature posted on the foundation website—and I know that her husband, Charles "Chas" Holman, died of unrelated causes while fighting for recognition of his wife's illness. She worked as a critical care nurse for years before Morgellons disabled her. A dermatologist diagnosed her with Delusions of Parasitosis (DOP), but Chas wasn't buying it. On the foundation website are a series of archived "rants from Chas":

I hear from so many Morgellons patients, "He thinks I'm nuts . . . !" Or, "She doesn't believe me . . . !" And my all-time favorite, "My whole family agrees that I'm delusional because the doctor said so!" And I really do understand how difficult this situation can be. I've been through it.

The trailer for the in-progress Morgellons documentary, *Skin Deep*, features Cindy walking in a suit in slow-motion toward what looks like a federal building, and footage from Chas and Cindy's wedding video, and her voice cracking as she says, "He would say, 'I will get Morgellons disease recognized in my lifetime or I will die trying. Well, he died trying but I'm going to do it.'" It's hard for me to watch without tearing up in outrage. It's also hard for me not to feel a longing for the simple and straightforward love and trust that seems to have bound them: he believed her. He fought for her. He died a martyr for his spouse's pain. If I'm honest, I can admit it: I want a foundation named after me, too. I want my husband's voice to crack as he remembers the sacrifices that I made for him. This is why we've come all this way, a grand gesture, an international flight on a Boeing jet skywriting, *I believe you, okay?*

Thank you, I tell her now, outside the hotel, as she stubs out her cigarette. Thank you for your work in bringing light to this disease.

It's terrible, isn't it? she says. You're going to find a lot of hope tomorrow. A lot of information. Glad you guys are here.

Upstairs in our room, where the bed is two single beds pushed together, and the light switches feel like a new language, we look at each other.

"We're practically the only Americans here," Aaron says.

This means we are special, or stupid, or both.

The conference is a one-day event held in a conference room the size of my high school biology lab, white and windowed, arranged with tables-for-two and burgundy chairs facing a giant screen. We sign in, take our name tags, a folder with handouts and an agenda and a notepad with the name of the local clinic on it, a holistic clinic that focuses on vector-borne diseases. It is the Lyme clinic in Augsburg, founded by Dr. Carsten Nicolaus, that is co-sponsoring the event, with the Charles E. Holman Foundation. We find a seat.

It feels, I think, like the first day of college, waiting for the professor to begin, checking out the other students, taking stock of the room. Only one woman in a lavender short-sleeved blouse has a constellation of lavender lesions on her arms, daintier than Aaron's, but familiar.

What I'm wondering is, do we belong here? Are these our kind of people? We are dressed in the same kinds of clothes: blazers and belts and scarves and boots. Our hair is brushed. We sip our coffee reasonably. We all say good morning to each other in English, though we are in Germany and the breadth of our homelands, which Cindy points out as she welcomes us with her opening remarks, is substantial: Italy, Wales, Poland, Brazil—twelve countries in all, among the roughly forty humans in this conference room. There is something embarrassing about this small number, and something touching, that we have all found our way here, by bus and plane and train, across the globe.

Latitudinally, Augsburg is only a few degrees north of Ithaca. I imagine a band connecting us—a vector. Lyme disease is as common here, in the lush, temperate forests of Europe, as it is in the northeastern United States. Many of the morning's presentations ground the research in the Morgellons connection to Lyme disease. Indeed, Dr. Ginger Savely, who is, according to the cover of her book, "the world's leading clinical expert" on Morgellons, came across the disease because a small but consistent percentage of her Lyme patients were presenting with lesions, slow to heal and filled with filaments. That was around 2003, shortly after biologist Mary Leitao chose the name "Morgellons" to describe the suffering of her son Drew and founded the first Morgellons Research Foundation. Two years later, Dr. Randy Lymore began research on Morgellons at the University of Oklahoma State Center for Health Sciences. In 2011 and 2012, Marianne Middelveen and Dr. Raphael Stricker began to break ground with new studies of Morgellons, just as the CDC was releasing its long-awaited study. In my memory, warped by Wikipedia, the study concluded that Morgellons disease does not exist, that delusional parasitosis is the only explanation. When I look at it now, though, I see something slightly different: what it concluded was that it was an "unexplained dermopathy" that may be delusional parasitosis—or may be a "new condition." Inconclusive.

There were problems with the CDC study from the start, Dr. Savely wrote in her book. More than a hundred patients were studied, but they were not identified in accurate or responsible ways. Had the researchers encountered *her* patients, she believed, there would have been very different results.

When Leslie Jamison visited the Morgellons conference for her *Harper's* story "The Devil's Bait" in 2012, the CDC study had just been published, and the attendees were lathered into disgust and insurgence over its results. The only physician who made an appearance in the essay was an Australian doctor whom Jamison likened to a "swashbuckling Aussie alligator wrestler" who called the CDC report a "rocking horse dung pile." The rest of her focus was on the patients, the human-interest stories of the sufferers.

So I'm surprised then by the parade of researchers at the front of the room in Augsburg. It is after all not just the first European conference but the first one deemed "Medical-Scientific." With their PowerPoints about spirochetes and cell walls and etiologies, they are revealing a story of the science. This is what I've come for. I want the source. I want the treatment. I watch them all proceed through diagrams and charts and photographs, through antibiotic protocols and herbal ones, through a lot of medications that end in-*dazole,* through a lot of medications that end in *tincture.* I fill my notebook, a new purple one, with notes. "Treatment of the tickborne disease BARTONELLOSIS (whether patient tests positive for it or not) is hands-down the best approach for treatment of Morgellons Disease patients." When Dr. Savely gets to this slide, I abandon my pencil and take notes the way my students do, the way the other attendees are doing now, by raising my cell phone and taking pictures of the screen. In some patients with severe disease, one slide says, antihelminthics are effective, when combined with antiobiotics. We don't really know why this is, Dr. Savely admits. I don't know what antihelminthics are until one patient in the audience raises his hand and demands in a German accent, "What about helminths?"

He's talking about worms, I realize.

Dr. Savely seems practiced at answering this question. Morgellons filaments aren't worms, she insists. They're not parasites.

The patient shakes his hand angrily. "How do we know? How do we know?"

Middelveen intercedes to remind him that Morgellons filaments are known to be made up of keratin and collagen.

They may *feel* like worms, Dr. Savely says gently, but we have no reason to believe they are parasitic in origin.

After this little skirmish, we adjourn for lunch, the tension spilling out of the conference room. In the hotel dining hall, Aaron and I fill our buffet plates, and, like every kid on the first day of school, look for our kind. We find the American. She is a forty-something woman named Adrienne, slender and tidily dressed in a sleeveless blouse, with high-lighted hair and tasteful jewelry, braided in silver and gold. We chitchat over our meals. She is retired from the military, lives in Virginia not far from my brother, and is a devoted patient of Dr. Savely. She tells us about her years of suffering with lesions. Her dogs also developed Morgellons symptoms, she says. What brought her outbreaks to a halt was a radical change in diet: she eliminated gluten. She slides her fork around her plate. On Aaron's plate and mine are pasta and giant hunks of baguette. When she has even a little, she says now, the sores come back, around her mouth, then everywhere. She's here to tell people, she says, though the doctors say that Morgellons doesn't have a gluten connection. It strikes me that each of these patients has formed their own little medical team of one: running their own experiments in their bedrooms and bathrooms and kitchens, making their own observations, developing their own treatments. The half-solutions are as various as the patients.

In the lobby outside the conference room, while we wait in line for coffee, a doctor from Austria strikes up a conversation with Aaron. In his red shirt and shorts and suspenders, with his snow-white beard and glasses, he looks like Santa Claus on vacation. He asks Aaron to open his mouth, and he does. The doctor, looking resigned, says, "None of these treatments is going to work until you have that mercury out of your mouth." He doesn't say it like a snake oil salesman. He says it reluctantly, like a jaded mechanic who is sorry to tell you that you're going to need a whole new transmission.

The man who exploded over the helminths, also with glasses and a white beard, stands sipping his coffee by himself. Months later, when we visit Dr. Savely's office in D.C., Aaron will bring up the man's outburst, and Dr. Savely will shake her head sadly. There's always one who gets upset about worms, she'll say. You can't really convince them. You just try to nip it in the bud. Now, standing here watching him in the lobby, I wonder if he has spoken what more of the patients are thinking, what Aaron, perhaps, is thinking. Why are antihelminthics effective for some patients, unless there are helminths present? I remember the words from the mint-green Lyme booklet that propelled us on our journey here: "New organisms such as viruses and microscopic worms are being discovered in ticks. Their role in human illness is not yet known."

I have never been to a medical conference before, but I'm fairly certain this one is out of the mainstream. There is something punk rock about it, a DIY ethos, with its PowerPoints that might have been made by teenagers cutting up zines and its audience the size of a straight edge matinee at CBGB. And yet even here, in this outsider's refuge, there are keepers of power and authority, paradigm protection. There are people deemed too crazy for a Morgellons conference.

In the afternoon presentations, I start to drift off. Maybe it's my carb-heavy lunch. Maybe it's the exhaustion of trying to read every gesture, every specimen, every slide, for signs of subterfuge. I feel as though I'm back in the Wikipedia archives, and my defenses begin to melt. I long to have a white-coated doctor stride into the room to finish off the schedule: someone from Johns Hopkins, someone named John, a clean-shaven doctor, his neck strung with medals, with a book published by an academic press, a feature in the *Times*, and articles cited in PubMed—all of the status my stubborn biases demand.

And yet we have known many white-coated doctors. We have read many Wikipedia articles. That is why we are here.

At the bottom of one of the veterinarian's slides, under a glaring graphic of a cloudy sky, is the phrase *"in dubio pro reo." When in doubt, favor the accused.* Believe patients.

What about the timing of breakouts? is the question I ask, one of a dozen written in my notebook. Is there research that shows that stress brings them on? Or any other patterns or cycles you're noticing?

Oh yes, says Dr. Nicolaus. They've certainly observed that stress contributes to acute presentations. There is a strong stress-disease relationship.

I copy this in my notebook, not fully satisfied.

When the presentations are over, a small collection of boxed scopes is passed around. They are light microscopes, at least 200x magnification: the real thing. Eagerly, attendees open the boxes and begin to examine their own skin and others'.

"Let's get one," I whisper to Aaron. This is what we've been waiting for. But he shakes his head. He doesn't want to perform a self-examination here, in front of all of these people. There is something desperate about it, he must think. But what are we if not desperate?

So out of the corners of our eyes, we observe other people examining themselves. The researchers mingle about, assisting, observing. If it weren't so sci-fi, it would feel like a scene out of a high school biology class. Behind us, a young couple is scoping each other. The man is examining a spot on her neck. Then, giggling, she examines a spot behind his ear. We strike up a conversation with them. She is from Czechia, he is from Brazil, and they both live together in Prague, from which they have traveled by bus. They tell us about the long, taxing trip.

"You both have it?" they ask us.

Aaron and I look at each other. "I do," he says.

They offer to share their scope. "No, it's okay," Aaron says. "Thanks. You both have it?"

She does, she says. But she wonders if her boyfriend has it, too. He smiles shyly. He isn't so sure. I don't want to stare, but I don't see any lesions, at least not from a few feet away.

"You guys want to get a drink after this?" I ask. I've been kicking myself that we didn't ask Cindy to have a drink with us when we ran into her last night. I don't want to miss our chance to connect with others here.

There are six of us who meet afterward—a new, spontaneously assembled "us"—at the hotel bar. Then Adrienne, our American friend, joins us with two others, and we are nine people crowded around pushed-together tables in the loud lobby. Tourists come through to check in, pushing through the red velvet curtains, rolling their suitcases across the rustic tile floor. Aaron and I sit in the tall, throne-like chairs, order giant German beers and drink them slowly, listening to each person share their story. It feels like Al-Anon with alcohol, the kind of immediate intimacy that happens when strangers walk into a room, form a circle, and admit their shared trauma.

There is our young couple from Prague, a gray-haired man from Wales, a neuroscientist from Amsterdam. Some of them have had lesions, but I'm surprised to learn that some of them haven't: that their skin produces painful fibers and other materials without the presence of lesions at all. There are aches and pains and brain fog, fatigue for days and days. There is shame and disbelief, frustration. There is the same DIY philosophy that so many have had to cultivate, figuring this thing out themselves. The neuroscientist, who will send us emails afterward, will have to go to Bulgaria to treat himself with the antibiotics, according to Dr. Savely's recommendations at the conference. Aaron shares his war stories, too, from the rash that appeared one day to the latest cycle of breakouts. My heart slows down, calming with a certain relief and pride, as though I'm a mother watching her kid make friends on a playdate.

There is some other feeling, too, I try to pay attention to. Disappointment, that these other patients don't match Aaron's profile exactly. I was looking for the kind of recognition I found in the Morgellons book, Aaron's agony mirrored back to us. Instead, everyone's story is a little different. But this is a comfort, too, I guess—that their suffering is unique. Perhaps this is what they share more than anything—not the specific symptoms but the specificity of their symptoms, their aloneness in their disease.

"You can't turn it into a war," the neuroscientist says. He has all kinds of theories about the way the disease affects the body and the brain, and all of the multisyllabic scientific words to convince me, but in the end, he seems to say, there is only one's attitude about living with it. "If you're not fighting it all the time, you can't lose." He shrugs.

This, more than anything, is the wisdom Aaron will carry back with him. "I like that," he'll tell me later. "I need to channel that guy."

From the lobby, a ruckus, and we look up from our beers to see a group of thirty young men in Lederhosen flood the room, rowdy as a soccer team—maybe they are?—and begin to check in all at once. We all crack up, take photos with our phones, for which the men pose gamely. It is the answer to all of our German vacation dreams.

After that, six of us adjourn to the hotel restaurant, order rich wood-fired pizzas and bottles of red wine, talk late into the night. We pass around my purple notebook, write down our names and emails. I stop taking notes. I let myself drink too much. There is the pleasure and ease of getting drunk with a group of new friends, of putting aside my worries. Aaron's shoulder is warm, his scarf is soft.

We return the day before the full moon.

The day after that, Aaron's sores just beginning to light up, we drive the three and a half hours south to Dr. Bernard, the Lyme doctor. He confirms it: Aaron has Lyme disease.

"Really," Aaron says.

Well, it's up for some interpretation, the doctor says. The Western blot test, which looks for antibodies to *B. Burgdorferi* proteins, is considered positive by the CDC when at least five of ten specific Immunoglobulin (IGg) bands are present. Aaron's test shows four positive bands, and one indeterminate. ("41?" Laura will ask us later. When we confirm, she says, "41 is usually the problem.") But to Dr. Bernard, given the test results and the symptoms, the diagnosis is clear.

We tell him what we learned in Germany, present the slides I've printed out from Dr. Savely's presentation, the exact combination of medicines to fight Morgellons. For a moment the laconic doctor is interested. He adjusts Aaron's prescriptions. We make a follow-up appointment for six weeks.

Remember, the doctor warns. The treatment can take a while to work. Months. Sometimes up to two years. It will get harder before it gets easier.

Sometimes, when the moon grows big and his skin glows red, when he turns back into the fearsome thing, I want to be the werewolf that gets to howl at the moon.

Sometimes we go out into the car parked in the driveway and yell at each other, so the kids and my dad can't hear us.

It feels like we're watching ourselves fight. There is the terror of not knowing what we are capable of saying to each other.

We go around and around in circles. We go around the world, and come back, and we're in the same place, locked in a Nissan Rogue in the driveway.

"Why didn't you believe me?"

"I was scared."

"Why were you scared?"

"I was angry."

"Why were you angry?"

This time I know this will be a fight I will remember, this one will stand above the rest. I know he's not just talking about the last few months, even the last few years. He asks me again, slowly, and this time he is using the present tense. "Why are you so angry with me?"

We are both crying now. It's true, I hate us both. I am trying to think of the answer to his question. I reach back. Way back to the beginning. When I was a stupid kid and he was a stupid kid, and we got together and stayed together because no one believed we could. When we lay in that Colorado bed and he told me what our life would look like, and I believed him.

"Because you let me down, too." Maybe I'm shouting it.

He looks at me, like he knows what my next sentence will be, and is scared.

"You said you'd take care of me. And you didn't."

He doesn't need to ask for more. He closes his eyes. He rests his head against the window. There is the relief of having said it, a thing I haven't known I wanted to say.

"I'm sorry," he tells me. "I'm so sorry."

THEORY 7

have made him sick.

I have asked for too much. Or I haven't asked for enough.

Either way, he can't give me everything I need. (Does anyone give anyone everything they need?) The stress of not living up to who you said you'd be: if that's not enough to make you sick, what is?

People give each other heart attacks and hernias and ulcers. It happens all the time.

I scold myself: I'm not the center of the universe.

But I think of his parallel life: where he might be without me, if we'd never met. On a beach, in a band. On the balcony of his father's condo, smoking a bowl and watching the sun rise. Healthy. Carefree.

IRONY 7

"Why don't we talk in private?"

The last six months have been a blur of waiting rooms—in Binghamton and Syracuse, in Wilkes-Barre and Woodstock—but here I am again, in the Ithaca ER, in the hospital where Henry was born. Down the bright, busy corridor, the social worker will come for me. It's always a gentle-voiced, older man. This one I recognize—a big man in glasses and a golf shirt, his ID hanging from a lanyard around his neck—though he doesn't recognize me. "I'm sorry. Did we meet before?"

"In the summer." I settle into a chair. It's kind of a conference room, kind of a waiting room, off of the main ER waiting room, where a few months before I watched the commercial for *New Amsterdam.* Tonight there is the same *People* magazine I've read in two other doctors' waiting rooms this week, Jamie Lee Curtis and her triumph over opioid addiction. It's early November now. Through the window, bitter bites of snow are testing the dark.

"I'm sorry. Can you refresh my memory?"

"It was the same thing. We talked in the café." I point through the double doors to the next wing. "He was super manic. Agitated. I couldn't calm him down. We waited I think six hours that time for a psych eval. In the private waiting room with the bed?"

He shakes his head sympathetically. "Is that why you'd brought him here? For a psych eval?"

"It was the same thing. He wanted someone to look at his skin."

"He was seeing bugs at that time?" He looks at his clipboard. "Parasites?"

I nod. "*I* wanted him to get a psych eval. I can't tell you how hard I tried to get him into the psych ward." I laugh a little and shake my head, but I don't even feel like joking with myself. "I mean, unless you're a danger to yourself, it's impossible."

"But we didn't take him?"

I cried that night in front of this man, sitting in the darkened café, begging him quietly for help. "There never seems to be a bed."

Now I'm too tired to feel desperate. I am nowhere near tears. What's closer to the surface is anger, for the hours I'm wasting in this hospital, for the doctors who don't have the time for us, for my husband and whatever is inside him.

"I see he was on the behavioral ward before," the social worker says now. "Suicide attempt?"

I nod. "Five years ago."

"Do you think he's a danger to himself tonight?"

He's a danger to himself every day, I want to say. But that doesn't mean he's suicidal.

"No."

"Do you want him admitted again?"

"Honestly? I don't think you can help him."

"What do you think he needs?"

"I didn't want to take him here to begin with. I know how this works by now. I knew the doctors would see one thing and dismiss him. But he *begged* me. He was desperate and scared and in pain. What was I supposed to do? *I* know he's out of his mind tonight. But now I know more about why. That doctor in there? She put him in the crazy pile the moment she laid eyes on him."

The social worker looks helplessly at his clipboard, then back at me. "What's changed?"

"We finally have a diagnosis. But that doctor doesn't want to hear it. I *told* him, 'You don't want to go to the ER. You'll end up in the psych ward.' If he ends up in the psych ward, *now*, after all this time—"

"Do you think he has bugs infesting his skin?"

Through the door to the main waiting room, I can see half a dozen college students in sweatshirts numbed out in front of the TV.

I think carefully about the words.

"There's something infesting his skin. There's also something infesting his brain."

The social worker makes a few notes on his clipboard. Then he rises and asks me to wait in the other waiting room, for another social worker. I rise with him, a little unsteady. This is not part of the drill. Usually the social worker places a call to the staff psychiatrist, who makes the call, having never seen the patient: Should he stay or should he go? We've been here four hours already. All I want to do is pay the copay, drive my husband home, and fall asleep, he with the help of a couple milligrams of Ativan. In the exam room, he'd refused it. I'd convinced him to take half a dose.

"There?" I say, pointing to the main waiting room.

He nods. "He'll be right out to meet you."

I find a seat in front of the TV with the college kids. I am reading a graphic memoir about bipolar disorder, a book I bought months ago, when I thought Aaron had it. It seems like a long time ago. Knowing what it isn't doesn't help. And knowing what it is doesn't help as much as we thought it would. It has not saved us from the ER. Anyway, I can't concentrate on the book.

Tonight, the TV is playing a game of football. The clock says it's close to 9:00 P.M., but in the ER, time feels theoretical. It's Friday night, and tomorrow daylight savings time will come to an end, but I've been in this waiting room for six months.

Something is different tonight. Too much time has passed. Where is this guy, this other, mystery social worker? Has it been twenty minutes? More?

When I left Aaron's room, he'd been so restless that the fitted sheet had sprung up and curled under him. He writhed on the bare mattress, pulled the EKG disks from his bare chest.

I'd been climbing onto the exercise bike at the gym when I'd received his text. *I need to go to the fucking hospital now.*

I rushed home. Tried to rationalize. They can't help you there. You're on the right meds now. We just have to let them work. The doctor said it would get harder before it gets easier!

"If you love me," he'd said, "you'll take me to the hospital."

I sit up, look around, shake myself out of my dream. Already I am mourning the quiet comfort of the waiting room, the few minutes of peace I have while someone else is taking care of him.

But something is off. I can feel it. I stand and walk to the desk. I ask to be let into the back. They buzz me in. A few paces later, in front of room sixteen, I see a flurry of activity. *Good,* is what I think at first. They are paying attention to him. Then, a few steps closer, I can hear his voice. "You can't do this to me! You can't do this to me!"

This is not part of the drill. Now you've slipped out of time. By the moment you're at the door to his room, you've left your body.

"Don't *do* this! Don't *do* this!"

There is an intimacy in his voice, a lover's plea, a hurt. Your husband is standing by the door, trying to force himself from the room, and then he's lifted to, slammed on, the bed.

"Don't do this! Please don't do this!" It's your own voice saying this now, strangled with shock, and now the tears come. "Please don't."

They are strapping him down, though, nurses in their scrubs, order-lies, security, each of his limbs encircled by a leather cuff. "Don't touch me! You're going to get the parasites! Don't touch them!"

"Aaron," you say, and then he meets your eye.

"Nell," he says. He is afraid.

"Honey."

"What the fuck! What they fuck are they doing?"

"Honey, you have to calm down."

"Fuck this! Fuck all of you! Don't touch me!" He fights their hands, then relaxes, then flails, then falls against the pillow. There are ten of them. Count them. What else can you do? When he lifts his head, he recognizes someone else at the end of the bed: not a paramedic, but a security guard. "I know you, man," he says, and something about the man's presence jars awake his humanity, his manners. "Hey, man," he says. "You're cool. I've got nothing against you. But fuck all the rest of you. Fuck this hospital! It's not personal. Just fuck you all!"

The nurse at the head of the bed says, "That's fine."

"That stupid fucking doctor? Who *laughed* at me? Who wouldn't *look* at me? What kind of fucking place is this? Fuck him. Fuck this place."

"Okay now," says the nurse.

"I should never have come here," he says. "I should have gone to fucking Denny's."

The nurse holds back a laugh, then thinks again and lets it out. He is strapped down now. "I'm sorry," she says, and she must be talking to you. "We have to sedate him."

"Please don't," you say, standing over the security guard's shoulder. But it is happening. Here comes the big needle. Haldol, you will learn later. You will write it down in your notebook. You will learn about the scene your husband threw, yelling at the doctors, demanding to be let go, and you will learn that aside from attempting suicide, adding belligerent to delusional is a good way to get a seventy-two-hour hold in the psych ward.

"I didn't do this," you say to him, because you know what he is thinking.

But how you have wanted to strap him down. And how you have wanted to free him.

"Aaron," you say. "I swear. Listen to me."

Already his eyes are starting to close, but he levels them at you once more.

"Who is that?" the security guard asks him, still holding his feet, trying to get him to focus on your voice.

"Aaron, I'm here."

"Is that your wife?"

Your husband laughs. He closes his eyes. "Depends," he says.

THEORY 8

The ER doctor has curly hair and glasses and purple scrubs; she looks tired and pissed. We stand with our arms crossed in the hallway. "This isn't Lyme." Her voice is firm. "It's psych."

WELLFORD STREET

2004

Kissinger, Morris's tabby cat, was dying.

The townhouse we'd lived in, our first home in Charlottes-ville, had gone condo, so we'd moved into a real house in a real neighborhood, a little brick ranch with a carport and grass that Aaron cut while listening to metal. I stood by the very tall oak tree in the front yard telling my friend Penny on the phone that Aaron couldn't attend her wedding in Florida because our cat had cancer. A pot sat in the driveway; popcorn burnt black. I'm certain these are separate memories, but this is the way memories present themselves, fused by images. The years are stored as one dull day, heightened by smoke alarms.

Aaron's father had pneumonia. At the VA hospital, he had been moved from the nursing home to the ICU. Morris was a few months shy of his eightieth birthday. We could tell from the doctor's voice on the phone that when an old man caught pneumonia, it was serious.

"Are you sure you don't want to go down with me?" I asked Aaron.

"I'm sure." He wanted to stay with Kissinger.

By the time I got to Florida, at the end of August, Morris had re-covered from the pneumonia and was released from the ICU. I went to visit him in his regular room. As I stood by his bed, I tried to think of him as the guy who owned too many cats, who watched *Airplane!* with Aaron, who chaperoned a Cub Scouts camping trip, who took him to gun shows at the fairgrounds, who drove him to school with the hatch of the car up, embarrassing him, who drove him to the comic store in Lantana, who drove him and his friends to concerts at the West Palm

Beach auditorium. In the final years of his life, he had driven a high-tech minivan with a hydraulic lift for his scooter and hand controls for driving. When it was clear he would no longer need it, Aaron had shipped it to his mother in New Mexico, a gift. She had had the equipment removed. I tried to think of what he was leaving the people who had been in his life: a lot of weird junk but a lot of wealth, too. I tried to think of it as a gift. I kissed my father-in-law, who did not recognize me, and said good-bye.

I went to the wedding with my mom. As Penny danced by me, she asked, "Your dad isn't here?" Apparently my mother's RSVP indicated that he would be. I realized Penny had paid for his plate. I cringed, apologizing. My mother was accustomed to leaving her husband at home for nebulous reasons not easily explained on a dance floor, and so was I. Ahead of me was a lifetime of enthusiastically vague RSVP comments: "We'll both try to make it!" My father was old and tired and it was hard for him to be on his feet. Anyone who saw him with a cane could deduce that. But I wondered if there were times when they were younger when my mother had left him behind, made up excuses, when his physical weakness was a convenient camouflage for a social anxiety that was equally crippling. I didn't ask her this, but what she modeled through her silence was a certain willful unconcern. She coped through smoke breaks. We had our own antisocial streaks, anyway. When the Electric Slide started, we exited the ballroom and took a walk down by the water while my mom smoked a cigarette in the wind. We took a selfie with a digital camera, and in the blurry picture she is fixing her hair and laughing.

By the time we were ready to put Kissinger down, in September, Morris had contracted pneumonia again. The hospital called and left a message.

"Do you want to go down?" I asked.

He didn't. He couldn't run to Florida every time his dad caught pneumonia.

We brought the cat to the vet. We petted the little lump of his tumor, the dark stripes on his head. We kissed him. We were not brave enough to stay in the room while they put him to sleep. Aaron was already crying, though, when we left the vet's office, and he cried all the way home.

We were sitting in the living room one evening in October, sharing a khaki love seat with Blue and watching *The Weakest Link,* when the phone rang. I answered it. It was the VA hospital in Florida. I handed the phone to Aaron. He took it and stepped into the hall. I sat in front of the muted television and by the time he was off the phone a few minutes later I understood that his father had died.

Aaron didn't cry. He went outside to smoke a cigarette. When he came in, he moved around the house in a dull daze. There is not much to do on the night a faraway father has died. We called the relatives, the children of Morris's three dead brothers. We called Aaron's mother and my parents.

"Are you okay?" I asked him.

He said, "Yeah. I just want to go to sleep."

We put ourselves to bed and Aaron lay on his side with Blue tucked under his arm like a teddy bear. This morning a man lay in bed a thousand miles away, breathing. He was the reason my husband was breathing beside me, and also the reason for his restless dreams. Now he lay somewhere, in the morgue, in a freezer, no longer breathing. He had been dead to us for almost five years, a body whose brain had shut down. Now his body had shut down, too. What did that mean for Aaron? What did it mean for me? Sadness? Anger? Guilt? Relief? I watched his eyelids, trying to figure out if he was asleep. I tried to locate an organ to emit a feeling that made sense, but this death was an abstraction.

The next morning, I shifted into gear. I would take care of the logistics, give Aaron space. It gave me something to do with the tie-dye swirl of feelings I couldn't name. I called the VA hospital, a crematorium, and Arlington National Cemetery, where he'd long wanted his remains buried. It wasn't possible to schedule the funeral for another month. Morris would be cremated in Florida, and his remains would be shipped to Virginia.

Aaron was grateful for my help, and stressed out and stoned and sad, and withdrawn into what seemed to me a new state of brittleness. Usually he dealt with death by joking. He'd inherited his dark sense of humor, in fact, from his father. I was thinking of this, hoping for a moment in which we might connect over the absurdity of death, the absurdity of these long-distance logistics we were navigating, when I made a terrible joke. I was trying to arrange for the postal shipment of his father's cremains. I remember feeling a little flame of satisfaction upon conceiving it: a death-dark, Aaron-style riff. I put on my best post-office-clerk voice. "Is there anything fragile, liquid, perishable, or potentially hazardous in this package?" Aaron had been asked this question hundreds of times, each time he mailed off an eBay sale. Each time, he answered no. This time, I joked, he'd be able to say yes.

He looked at me, pained. I had made a grave miscalculation.

"That's a terrible thing to say," he said.

The funeral took place on a chilly but sunny fall day, American flags whipping in the wind. Aaron and I wore black suits and black gloves, and scarves that also whipped in the wind. Over his suit, Aaron wore his father's long black wool coat. A handful of relatives had flown in for the service, Aaron's two cousins and their families. We stood in a cluster on the green grass. The white headstones spread around us like too-straight teeth. They were the most beautiful and frightening thing I had ever seen. Under them were the ashes and skeletons of soldiers who had been killed on battlefields far from home, and those who had lived long enough to suffer strokes on their scooters at the zoo.

We sat under a small khaki tent. A group of military officers stood in salute, straight as the gravestones. Another group of officers held out an American flag, flat, four men preparing to make a bed. Beyond them, more officers discharged their rifles, piercing the gray sky. I startled in my chair. I felt it in my chest. I heard the rifle of a teenage boy discharged in the snows of the Hürtgen Forest. Then the bugler played "Taps," the saddest song on the earth. It loosened something in me.

Did anyone want to say any words about the deceased? asked the officer in charge.

Aaron did not move.

His cousin Ann stood. "My Uncle Morris was the most wonderful man," she said. He had always been so kind to her and her sister and cousins, welcoming them to his big house on the bay. She had swum in his swimming pool, visited his upstate farm. On the website where the obituary I had written appeared, she wrote, "My Uncle Morris was my best friend."

Months later, Aaron would tell Ann what Morris had done to him as a child. She was the first person, beyond me, he had told. Had he ever tried anything like that with anyone else? He wanted to know, now that his father was gone.

No, Ann said. Dear God, no.

After that, for a while, they didn't talk much. Ann tried to contact Aaron. He didn't respond. Months later, Ann emailed Aaron. You tell me this about your father, and then you disappear?

It was almost, Aaron said, as though she didn't believe him.

Well, I said. You did kind of disappear.

Years later, it would be clear that Ann had believed him, and that being believed was important, more important than he thought.

At the funeral, though, I was the only one who knew. The flag was folded by the officers into a triangle. One officer knelt before Aaron, the next of kin, and presented the flag to him. It was a gift he hadn't expected, hadn't asked for, but he took it. I had never seen his face so solemn, though I imagined the sorrow and bitterness and confusion the mask concealed. It was the face of a good son accepting the flag of a good father.

In the same house, months later, Aaron got the call from his brother's social worker. David had died. Also of pneumonia.

There was no funeral for David. His brother would be buried, we were told, in a cemetery behind the home where he lived.

Years later, after we move to upstate New York, we'll drive through Rome, knocking on doors, looking for his grave. The kids will be napping in their car seats. But the place has moved, or we have the wrong address. There is no record of him here, as though he didn't exist at all.

Q NORTH

The morning after Aaron is taken to the psych ward, a Saturday, I do the only rational thing, which is to descale the Keurig. All these months I've been putting it off, waiting for the perfect time. I scrub the reservoir, replace the filter, run twelve cups of vinegar through the machine until the water smells clean. I stand alone in the kitchen and drink my perfectly pure cup of coffee.

Where's Dad? the kids want to know.

The hospital, I say. They kept him overnight.

I'm sort of disappointed and sort of relieved when they don't press for more. Henry wants pumpkin pancakes. Nico wants to start a fire. Aaron is allergic to the smoke from the fireplace, so we don't usually light it. But he's not here. So we do, somewhat guiltily at first, then enjoying it, my dad happy to have a job, pulling up a chair to stoke it, the boys dazed in front of the flames.

At nine o'clock, I call the hospital. Press two for Behavioral Health.

"Q North," someone answers. The phrase knocks against some metal plate in my memory. Q North. What does the Q stand for?

When are visiting hours? Twelve to two. Can I bring him anything before then? Yes, but I can't see him until twelve. Can I talk to his doctor? There are no doctors in today. What do you mean? Well, the head of the unit will check in on him in the afternoon when he makes his rounds. But he won't be assigned his own doctor until Monday.

Monday.

When I text his psychiatrist, Dr. Pascal, to tell her what happened, she says. "Worst time to go to the psych ward is a Friday night. *Nothing* happens on the weekends." She adds her customary sunflower, which almost makes me weep. It's the same way I felt the night before, after they wheeled him away, and I stood there helplessly with the plump young nurse with the green eye shadow, one of the ten people who had held down my husband. "I'm sorry about this," I found myself saying to her. I knew Aaron was the one who deserved the apology, but he had yelled and sworn and caused a scene, and there I was, sorry for the disruption. She gave me a hug, and I fell apart. On the way home, I called Ursula, and Jen, and fell apart some more. I came home and sat at the edge of my dad's bed and fell apart some more. So many nights he'd stayed home with the kids while I took Aaron to the hospital, and this was the first time he hadn't come home with me. My dad held me while I cried.

At eleven thirty, I leave the kids with my dad and drive to the hospital. I walk past the fountain in the lobby Henry and Nico always want to put their hands in, the café, the wall of the main corridor with its life-sized photos of the hospital's smiling patients, their lives restored after hip replacements, physical therapy, bariatric surgery. Hang a right at the end of the hall to the new maternity wing, built after Henry was born here. Hang a left to Behavioral Health. I ring the bell beside the steel door and after a minute an orderly lets me in. I sign in, get my Visitor sticker, wedge my giant handbag in the bottom drawer of the file cabinet. I hand over the paper bag I've packed for Aaron with a change of clothes, toothbrush, all his meds, some books and pens and drawing pads, but I can't leave the pens or drawing pads because, oh yeah, he might impale himself or someone with their sharp parts. It's all coming back to me.

I walk through the second door and look down the long hall. There is the murmur and smell of lunch down there somewhere. But there he is—right there, in the first room to the right, the door open, lying on a bed under a pale-pink blanket. On the floor, wedged up to the bed, is a blue tumbling mat. "Nell!" he says when he sees me, sitting up and throwing off the blanket. There is gratitude in his eyes, and fear.

I crawl into the narrow bed and hold him. There he is again, my husband. The Haldol has worn off but it has chilled him the fuck out.

"I didn't know if you'd be glad to see me," I say.

"Of course I'm glad to see you."

"I thought you'd think I put you here."

He shakes his head. "I know you'd never do that."

He's in the same clothes as yesterday, a long-sleeved waffle-weave shirt the same pink as the blanket, a pair of sporty gray shorts. White socks. He's cold. I rub his forearms through his shirt, the way my mother warmed mine. And I remember the way his head rested against the bare, eggshell wall—so bare, this room, nothing but the twin bed and a giant, sinfully empty bookshelf—while he told me here, five and a half years ago, how he was going to save his own life.

"Have you had lunch yet?"

He shakes his head, shivers.

"Let's get you some lunch."

The psych ward is full of a lot of people who—like Aaron last time—did not get suicide right. Now they are in a purgatory of failed suicides. Or are there others who—like Aaron this time—aren't suicidal but psychotic? I wonder how many of them have been here in both states. It seems to me this feat should earn recognition of some kind, two Webelo badges. Either way, the sadness and shame smell the same, like the starchy rice pilaf they are serving in the lounge. An irresolute pink punch swishes around. There is decaf coffee only. Plastic forks and spoons, no knives. A young Asian woman in socks and flip-flops and a Cornell sweatshirt pads around the lounge without making a sound. An old white woman in a wheelchair is tucked up under a table, and two men—one young, one old—square off at another, newspapers in their hands. A woman in a hairnet hands Aaron a tray with his lunch. A lump of chicken rests on the nest of pilaf beside a pile of ribbed carrots. "He's vegetarian," I tell her. She tongs off the chicken, and Aaron takes the tray.

The chairs are hard plastic rockers, purple and blue, something you might see in a preschool classroom, but when we try to move them, they are heavy-bottomed, practically bolted to the ground. Too heavy to throw across the room. Aaron and I lower ourselves into them. How cruel, I think, these chairs, the embodiment of the pain these patients must try to lift.

What happened? we ask each other.

We say what we know, which is not much. Aaron picks at his rice.

What do you want? I ask him.

To go home, he says.

And so it is what I want for him too.

After Aaron puts away his tray, before he leaves the lounge, the young man at the next table stops him. He's wearing a button-down shirt and slacks and carrying a gray hooded sweatshirt. "You cold?"

Aaron's hugging himself, shivering, but he says no, he's fine.

"Here." The guy extends the sweatshirt. Has he just been carrying it around, ready to lend it out? Is he a family member? An orderly?

"Aw, no, man, that's okay."

"Take it," I say. "Yes, he's cold. Thank you so much."

Aaron accepts it, checks the tag. XL. The guy is skinny, with curly strawberry-blond hair and glasses. He looks not unlike Leaf, the guardian angel paramedic who brought Aaron to this hospital months ago.

"Thanks, man. I'll get it back to you."

"It's too big for me." The guy shrugs. "I think it's yours."

I come back again for evening visiting hours. Just after dinner—it's the end of daylight savings time; tonight we'll turn back the clocks—the clouds are hanging over the lake in such a way that there is a fine curtain of light falling across the yellow trees. "It looks like a spotlight," says one nurse, with delight. "Did you see it out there?" The girl in the flip-flops pads over to take a look, then walks on.

On Saturday a doctor—but not Aaron's doctor—comes in to check on him. Aaron asks for his regular meds, but the doctor won't give them to him. "How'd you get those marks?" he asks, pointing at the bloody lesions on Aaron's legs.

Aaron is calm now, the opposite of manic, almost dead. He does his best McMurphy, a well-behaved robot.

"I scratched them," he says.

"You did this to yourself?"

He nods.

The doctor writes something on his pad.

A few months later, Esmé Weijun Wang will publish *The Collected Schizophrenias*. In her essay "On the Ward," she'll say: "a primary feature of the experience of staying in a psychiatric hospital is that you will not be believed about anything. A corollary to this feature: things will be believed about you that are not at all true."

"Why'd you do that?" I ask him when I visit.

Aaron shrugs. "Told him what he wanted to hear."

"Proclamations of insanity," Wang writes, "are the exception to the rule."

He keeps his head low, sits by himself. He walks the halls in his socks, nodding to the other hall-walkers like regulars walking around a lake. He gets moved to a room with a roommate in the middle of his second night, and the one thing his roommate says to him is, "Lunch, man," and Aaron says "Thanks." Aaron is rereading *The Bluest Eye*, which he found in the lounge. I wonder if reading *The Bluest Eye* is a good idea. He sleeps most of the day. Is it the Haldol, still coursing through his system? Or is he just tired? Or just trying to disappear?

At home on Saturday, I dial the hospital number. Press two for Behavioral Health. "Q North." That dreadful pang of déjà vu again. I leave a message for the head of the unit, asking why my husband hasn't been given his regular medications. Then I look on my phone, at the hospital website where I have looked up the number, and I pull up the hospital map. No Q North. I search for it. Q North does not exist on the map, nor on the Web, nor does Q South, nor any other letter. I wonder if I have made it up, if my ear is mishearing.

At visiting hours on Sunday, I wait for ten minutes outside the ward for someone to answer the big metal door. I wait with a guy delivering what smells like cheeseburgers from Grubhub. I wonder who has ordered food in there—an employee or a patient? I wonder if I'm pressing the right button. "I been pressing it before you got here," the delivery guy says. Finally, someone comes to the door and lets us in.

"Sorry," the orderly says. "A little action around here."

I find Aaron in the lounge, but quickly he ushers me into a quiet hallway. Ten minutes ago he was sitting in the lounge at lunch when another patient yelled at an orderly that he was being kidnapped. "You can't do this to me!" He threw his cereal bowl at the TV, punched a male nurse in the face. All the orderlies and nurses rushed him, took him down, shot him up with Haldol. There is still a flurry of aftershocks around the ward. Orderlies speed-walk around the halls, their keys hopping on their belts. Can I talk to a nurse about Aaron's meds? No, it's not a good time.

Aaron is shaken up, holding back tears. "I'm sorry you had to see me go down like that," he says.

Amidst all this, in the lounge, a new patient, androgynous and light-footed and slim, is dancing. The dancer has long, dark hair, glistening, and black painted nails; the dancer wears sneakers and hospital scrubs, the top pulled up around a flat chest and knotted to reveal a flat white belly. The dancer twirls from corner to corner, weaving through the tables where people are eating their dinner, smiling, singing, unceasing.

"I'm going to kill that guy," Aaron says, his voice low. He shields his eyes with a hand.

"Or girl?"

"I'm going to kill that person." The dancer has been singing outside Aaron's room all day. The happiness is enough to drive a sane man in the psych ward crazy.

"Please don't get in a fight," I say. "Then they won't ever let you out."

"I know," he says, "I know."

Still, the incident has put everyone on edge. As I leave the ward, one of the hall-walkers walks ominously close to the nurse escorting me out.

She finds the right key on a fistful of keys. "Joe, if you touch me again," she says, "I will make you very sorry."

This time I call the hospital from the hospital parking lot, sitting in the car as it warms up. "Q North." A shiver shoots from my ear to my shoulder. Through the defrosting windshield I can see the whole of the building, a sandy concrete square, wings and wards pinwheeling off the sides. I wait to be transferred to the doctor. And as the dial tone stretches on I see another building, sandy concrete, massive against a blue Florida sky, imposing as an institution. A condominium, thirteen stories, gently curved against the shore. Quay North. Across from it, a twin. Quay South. "Quay," as in "key," but we pronounced it with a "Q." A key turns in my ear. This is what I've been hearing, not the echo from five years ago, but an ancient echo, a different haunted house, the one where Aaron grew up.

When I visit again that evening, during dinner, the ward is calmer. The dancer is still twirling but has stopped singing. The hall-walkers have paired up. A cheerful dietician is making the rounds, asking how she can help accommodate Aaron's vegetarian diet. Wonderful, we say. Thank you. Is the cashew burger still available? It was the first meal I ate after Henry was born and we used to joke about having another baby just to eat one again. She will look into it. When she's gone, we produce an empty laugh together. We are more confident about getting the cashew burger than we are about getting the meds.

Across the lounge, under the big window with the view of the lake, the doctor—the head of the unit—is talking to a family. I recognize him from the website. And I recognize the Cornell student. Her parents—I assume they're her parents—are listening and nodding. I wonder if they've traveled far to come fetch her, if this is the first time they've come for her in the hospital or if it is already the fabric of their parenthood. It is almost too much to see their expressions of restrained concern. But I don't have time for empathy: I need to talk to that doctor.

"How do I make an appointment to talk to the doctor?" I ask one of the orderlies.

"You just have to kind of catch his eye. He makes his evening rounds until six."

There is a line of other families, it seems, here to talk to the doctor. Aaron and I stalk him from corner to corner, then to the conference room. You do the talking, Aaron tells me. He is too tired, too demoralized to advocate for anything. It's just after six when the doctor emerges from the room, says good-bye to another family, and locks it. "Excuse me, Doctor," I say. "I left you some messages? About Aaron's meds?" I grip Aaron's elbow. We know his rounds are over, but will he please give us a few minutes?

"Oh. Yes." With some reluctance he unlocks the room again and invites us inside. He takes a seat across the conference table from us. We might be giving a job interview or applying for a mortgage. He's a small man with rimless glasses; his name tag rests on a prim little belly. He looks not unlike Henry Louis Gates, Jr.

"You do know I'm not your doctor," he clarifies.

"Yes, we know."

"You'll see the doctor assigned to you tomorrow. He's the one with the power to release you."

We know. But what's urgent is that Aaron is given his regular medications right away. The doctor explains that the medications were stopped to ensure that Aaron's psychosis wasn't drug related. It's common practice, he says, to cease all prescriptions when a patient enters the ward.

Okay. That makes a certain sense. "But the antibiotics. Those are essential. The Seroquel I can understand, but—"

"There's the potential for an interaction between the Seroquel and one of the antibiotics." He flips through some pages on his clipboard.

"The Rifampin. Yes, we know. It can reduce the effectiveness of the Seroquel." The doctor gives me a level look. Perhaps he is deciding whether to be impressed. "But his psychiatrist raised his dose to 700 milligrams."

He takes some notes. "I left a message," he says. "For a Dr. . . . . ."

"Bernard," Aaron says.

"It's the weekend. He's not going to call back until Monday at the earliest. He needs his antibiotics before then."

"And for what condition were the antibiotics prescribed?" He flips through some pages on his clipboard.

I don't want to say Lyme. I definitely don't want to say Morgellons. Aaron has been given a booklet of patients' rights. Our primary goal is to keep you safe, it says, from hurting yourself or others. It does not say: we're here to help you figure out what's making your brain sick. I'm not here for a diagnosis anymore; I'm here to get him out. The only thing that has cured my determination to see my husband hospitalized is seeing him hospitalized against his will. "Dr. Bernard is a Lyme specialist," I say.

He agrees to resume the other antibiotics. The Rifampin will have to wait.

In her essay "John Doe, Psychosis," Esmé Weijun Wang writes about the ways her collected mental conditions clash and compound. On top of schizoaffective disorder, she has been diagnosed with chronic PTSD as a result of a rape by someone close to her. "There are still nights when I feel myself on a knife-edge, when the terror of PTSD mingles with the trickiness of unreality. It spreads through me like ink-blotting paper." One day her husband shouts out after burning himself while frying eggs, and, terrified, she flees into the bedroom closet. Years after her sexual trauma, the memory consumes her. Still, the subject that persists in *The Collected Schizophrenias* is the damage done to her psyche over the course of three involuntary ten-day hospitalizations. In "On the Ward," she writes, "I believe that being held in a psychiatric ward against my will remains among the most scarring of my traumas."

Months later, getting the mercury fillings removed from his teeth, the dentist's chair cranked flat, Aaron will panic, swimming up for air, jumping to his feet. "Sorry, man," he says to the dentist. "I just can't be held down like that."

In the urgent care waiting room, where I'll take him when his face is pulsing with Bell's palsy, he'll jump to his feet again when the nurse sneaks up behind him and hands him a clipboard. This time he'll walk out the door. I'll have to coax him back inside, like a scared cat hiding under a car.

Never the hospital again. "I don't care if my head falls off," he says. "Don't ever take me back there."

He was already a person who couldn't sit in a room without facing the door. "I like to be able to see who's coming up behind me," he shared in a twelve-step meeting once. Others in the room nodded at their laps. "Like John Wayne."

The truth is, I left. On Friday night at the ER, while we waited for him to be seen, while he twisted and turned in the bed, I left Aaron alone to go to Wegmans. I said I had to pick up a prescription for my dad before the pharmacy closed, and I did. But I also bought myself dinner. I bought myself forty-five minutes. I needed any excuse to get out of there. What happened to him happened while I was waiting in the waiting room. But it could have happened while I was buying myself a tabouli salad and a green smoothie.

The next day, Monday, when I arrive during lunch, the dancer is still dancing. I remember the dancing patient in *One Flew Over the Cuckoo's Nest,* the white-mustached man performing the perennial waltz with an invisible partner, forever lost to the music in his head. The pay phone is ringing in the lounge. Our friend who has gifted Aaron the sweatshirt answers it, cheerful as a receptionist, though he is, I have gathered, a patient like the rest of them. "Are you Nick?" he asks Aaron. He puts the phone down and travels around the lounge, asking every man he sees: "Are you Nick?"

Aaron is still wearing the sweatshirt. I am wearing my brown tweed blazer with the elbow patches. "I'm so ready to get out of here," he tells me.

What it takes to get him out of here is five minutes with his doctor, a South Asian man in a brown suit. He and I are wearing the same uniform of the nonthreatening expert. The three of us sit in the corner of the lounge on the couch that lines the room, side by side, as though we're watching the TV together. I cross my legs. I put on my professor voice. A complication of Lyme is how I put it. It affects his skin. It also affects his mind. I don't say "Morgellons." I say, "We just returned from a medical conference in Germany." The doctor nods with approval. We will follow up with his Lyme doctor, I assure him. We will follow up with his therapist. This is what they want to know: what can they put on the discharge papers? What sane person will be responsible for this insane person?

"Are you willing to take him home?" he asks. "To receive him into your care?"

Across the lounge, our friend is still looking for Nick. I'll think of him every time I see the sweatshirt, heavy and hooded and stained with my husband's blood, and I'll remember the best in people and the worst in people, until Aaron can't stand seeing it anymore and throws it away.

"I am."

Nick has been found. It's the very last person our friend thought to ask: the dancer, who, without missing a step, dances his way over and takes the phone.

PATTERSON MILL LANE

2005

We organize our histories into houses. It was, we say, a chapter in our lives. We say: that chapter is over. It was a long chapter, the longest, five years in one house. It was a house with a name, Walnut Grove, for the black walnut trees that shaded the acre around it. But we called it Chez Crozet, for the name of the town we'd found ourselves in, this rural dot off the Interstate fifteen miles west of Charlottesville.

Built in 1800, it was more of a cottage than a house. It was the kind of house you could stand in the center of and imagine the shack it once was, the way it must have grown outward, awkward room by awkward room, over the generations.

We had lived in a number of houses before, but it was what they call a starter house: our first mortgage. My father warned us it was too much money. I'd just graduated with my MFA; I didn't even have a job yet. But we knew that we liked Charlottesville and we wanted to stay. We wanted to be close to my family. And Aaron had cashed in an insurance policy of his father's, enough for a down payment. It was 2005, the height of the real estate market, the age of the no-doc loan, when white people could buy houses they couldn't afford.

We walked through the house with the Realtor, eyeing the wraparound porch, the not one but two claw-foot tubs, the separate shower with not one but two showerheads, the six-burner gas stove salvaged from a New York City restaurant. The beadboard walls, thick with coats of paint, had seen plenty of their own stories. We felt it was a good place to begin ours, to begin again.

You could, I realized in Crozet, write a story with a house, with three strategically hung ferns along the porch, with a glass cake stand full of lemons on the dining room table, with my parents' rickety old dining chairs, which I painted lime green, then antiqued with sandpaper, making the old new and then old again. The story said: We are people of taste. We are good country people. We threw a housewarming party. The story said: I hand-squeezed all the lemons in this lemonade.

There were good memories in that house. Dinner with friends on the patio, and all my nephews squeezed onto the red porch swing, and the stray cat who wandered into our yard and didn't leave. She was fat for a stray, so fat we thought she was pregnant. Aaron named her Prego. The stray deer that wandered into our yard and didn't leave. Aaron named her Sheila. He would sit on the porch and smoke a cigarette with her.

At the Vegetarian Festival in Charlottesville, in the same park where more than a decade later white supremacists would protest the removal of the Robert E. Lee statue and spark a deadly rally, we spotted a black and brown rescue puppy. He looked more beagle than anything else. They told us he'd be maybe forty pounds, but he would grow to be eighty, with the strong, coarse-haired body of a German shepherd. Usually the rescue agency required a few days' waiting period for a background check, but we looked like such a nice young couple. Aaron held him wiggling in his lap while we drove home, where we crate-trained him in our bedroom, watched him bound through the tall wet grass until he was so tired we had to carry him. We named him Zabka, for William Zabka, the actor who played the blond villain on *Karate Kid*, because that was Aaron's mostly inexplicable sense of nostalgia and humor. It meant "little frog" in Czech. We called him Zabby.

I called my mom. "I got a job."

"Fabulous!" she said.

"Waiting tables."

"Oh," my mother said.

I was happy about it, though. Crozet was tiny but there was a little Mexican restaurant called La Cocina with decent guacamole and good Mexican beer and a festive little patio strung with lights. I was happy to spend the day writing and then go in for the dinner shift, coming home late, my apron pocket fat with tips. I just wanted time to enjoy our new house, our new dog, to work on my novel. I'd finished a draft that summer, but now I had to scrap it, more or less, and start again.

Next door to the restaurant was the post office, where Aaron mailed his eBay packages. He was deep into his business then. The only room on the upper level of the house, like a little square hat, was his office. The stairs creaked as he climbed them. He spent a lot of time up there, the room choked with weed smoke.

Meanwhile I read books on the patio and filled the flower boxes and on the six-burner stove, prepared elaborate vegan meals, stacked and stuffed and garnished, tiny white beads of aioli drizzled seductively at the edge of the plate. I picked mulberries from the tree in the backyard, though they were more trouble than they were worth, my hands stained purple for a small bowl of them. I collected black walnuts from the grass, black walnuts that were really green, and washed and dried and stored them in baskets in the tub. They always grew moldy before they dried out properly. I tried so hard to get the fruit of those trees to yield something.

It was a good family arrangement. My brother Pete was four hours south in North Carolina, a straight shot down I-81. My brother Sam was two hours north in Alexandria, along with my parents, who lived in the basement apartment. I did that drive so often I memorized every turn. One day, Aaron and I arrived at Sam's house just after Keri had put their baby to bed. "Go on in," she said. "Maybe he's still awake."

I tiptoed into the nursery. There was still light in the windows. My nephew lay on his back in a white sleep sack. He was awake and looking at me with his round blue eyes. I leaned over the edge of the crib, wanting badly to pick him up but knowing I shouldn't. Something in my stomach kicked.

"I want a baby," I whispered to Aaron, crawling onto the pullout couch with him that night.

"Me, too," Aaron said.

"No, like I really want to have a baby. I want to start trying."

"Really?" His whole face smiled.

I had gotten a job, to my mother's delight, teaching composition. It was an adjunct position, forty-five minutes away. For a while, I still kept some shifts at the restaurant. I commuted with my friends Meredith and Sean, who had gotten jobs there, too, each of us alternating driving weeks. Meredith and I shared an office in a crumbling building at the edge of campus and in our new blazers we talked about the novels we wanted to finish and the babies we wanted to have. The next semester, when I got a full-time contract at the university—with a salary and health insurance and my own real office—I told Meredith that I'd thrown out my birth control.

"Why not?" She sounded surprised to hear herself say it. "You have the job. You have the house."

"Why not?" I agreed. Maybe she was thinking about Aaron, too, or maybe only I was. Her husband was getting his MBA at UVA. They were waiting to start a family until he was done with school. They had made the wise decision to stay in their one-bedroom apartment with their hand-me-down couch.

"Nothing helps someone get their shit together like starting a family, right?" I said.

I was joking, because I felt I needed to joke. But I believed what I said, that a baby would bring about a new chapter for me and Aaron. I was twenty-seven. He was thirty-four. We had been together for ten years. He had wanted to be a dad since I met him. Getting pregnant would ignite in him, I was certain, the spontaneous desire to (1) see a shrink, (2) quit smoking, and (3) get a job. I would will the life I wanted with my womb.

.   .   .

I went about trying to get pregnant with the determination, organization, and superstition that my father had put into trying to win the Florida lottery. When I was growing up, he kept a binder full of all of his pink scantron-bubble sheets, a record of all the winning numbers, line graphs charting frequency, form, design: an attempt to de-randomize the random. My father's daughter, I owned graph paper, clipboards, fine colored pencils, with which I charted my cycle month by month. I took my temperature every morning. I learned the rather humiliating list of abbreviations in the fertility chat rooms. I bought the giant and famous book *Taking Charge of Your Fertility*. I bought a little ovulation predictor kit with a tiny microscope that lived in a velvet sack in our bathroom drawer; it required spitting on test strips and watching the pattern of my saliva, noticing the way it ferned or didn't fern. I couldn't see anything in those strips, but it gave me a strange rush of power and wonder, that my body, without my knowing, was producing signs and symbols of its mysterious utility.

There are people who struggle with fertility for years, whose stories include drugs and donors and IVF and loss. I heard those stories in my chat room. Compared to those, my story was small.

But it was still painful. A few months into the process, I started having terrible cramps. Periods unlike I'd ever had before. And sex started to hurt. When you're trying to get pregnant and sex hurts, and then you get your period and not only are you not pregnant, but you feel like your whole body will shatter, it sucks.

I went to the doctor. A young internist who I later learned was pregnant with twins. This detail would sting: that she had interfered with my having a baby, and she was having two. I explained my symptoms. I'd done some Googling. "Could it be endometriosis?" I asked. I was embarrassed to ask it, as though my illness might inconvenience her.

She gave me a paternal smile. "What does it feel like?"

I didn't know to say, "It feels like uterine tissue is growing outside of my uterus." I said, "It feels like really bad gas."

"Then it's probably gas," she said.

I cried a lot those months, in pain and in frustration, in shame over my false hopes, in my wildly misinterpreted symptoms, a phantom boob pain, an abdominal twinge. I cried on the phone to my mother as I dusted the dressers. "It's the only thing I've never been able to control!" My house was very clean in those months. I got my period, I lay in agony on the couch, and then when it was over I got up and cleaned and cleaned.

My mother understood. She hadn't been able to get pregnant for a long time, either. I had known in my bones that I might have inherited my mother's diminished fertility. Maybe that was why I'd thrown my-self so scientifically into trying to conceive. There was little my mother could do to comfort me, though, and little Aaron could do.

Of course, he did his part, happily. When my temperature rose, he did his part two, three, four times a day. Afterward, he helped me slip a pillow under my hips. He shared my excitement, and my disappoint-ment. But the project was my own, and it was not a romantic one. The charts, the books, the test kits were my own. I retreated into my chat rooms, spent hours there speaking a language of mourning and hope Aaron could not decode. *Praying for a positive LH for you and your DH!*

Perhaps, it is easy to say now, if I had put a little more effort into our marriage as it was, I might not have needed to force a fantasy upon it, might not have needed to narrow our odds to one solution. *Things will be better when we have a baby.* We might have tried talking about what was really on our minds, the resentment and fear and isolation that had crept into our house like mold. We might have tried some therapy.

Aaron himself had agreed to see a psychiatrist. There was that. He knew he was depressed. He was ready to try a new medication, to get some help. I called the same doctor Callie had recommended when I was looking for a therapist and this time we were referred to a Dr. North. I dropped Aaron off for that first appointment at a second-story office in a brick building above a music venue downtown, and I picked him up. "He's a good guy," he determined. Older fellow, gray in his wavy hair, experienced, mellow, respected in the community. Dr. North pre-scribed him Lexapro. In time, Aaron came to trust him enough to tell him about his father's abuse. He was the first mental health professional he'd ever confided in.

What else they talked about inside that building I didn't know. What

was Aaron's story about those months? Was he sad that we weren't getting pregnant, or was he just sad that we'd become a fertility factory?

We flew to Mexico, swam in cenotes, zip-lined through the rain
forest. Aaron threw up on the ferry to Cozumel, and then on the ferry
back. We sunbathed and drank and bought weed on the street, and I
thought *Jesus, can't he go one week without weed,* thought *Maybe we're not
getting pregnant because he smokes too much weed,* then *Maybe he has the
right idea,* and for the first time in a long time I smoked some with him,
out on our hotel balcony. *Relax,* I thought. I tried. We tried.

I had read all of *Taking Charge of Your Fertility,* but when we returned
from Mexico, I read it again. This time, I stopped at the description of
endometriosis. Pain during menstruation, pain during sex, back pain,
excessive bleeding, infertility. Now, that last symptom leapt off the page.
It had been eight months.

This time I went to an ob-gyn. "I think I have endometriosis," I told
her. She told me, "I think you do, too."

The word rang a bell for my mother. Endometriosis, I told her, ran
in families. Maybe, back in the early seventies, the doctor had just said
"blocked tubes," not explaining what those tubes were blocked with.
"Who knows," said my mother, "if I passed it down to you?"

My mother came for the laparoscopic surgery. She and Aaron were
there when they put me under, and they were there when I woke up.
How sweet their friendship was. I imagine that they got a snack in the
hospital cafeteria while they waited, smoked a cigarette or three.

In the course of the surgery, endometrial tissue was in fact discovered in my fallopian tubes and removed. It made sense. A decade of
hormones from birth control pills had suppressed the disease, and then,
set loose, it had roared back. A flare.

You kept trying. Your body, a machine put back together, wept a rusty
blood. You might have let go of the charts and graphs, now that you
knew what the problem had been, but still you minded the calendar.

When your husband made a plan to go to Florida, you made sure he went in between cycles.

Why did he go, and why didn't you go with him? Now you can't remember why. His father was gone, but he was still going to Florida, to retrieve things from his father's storage units to sell, to have hurricane shutters installed at his father's condo, to see friends. You weren't teaching that summer. You might have gone along. You might have done a lot of different things. Maybe staying at his father's place didn't sound like a vacation. Maybe trying to get pregnant had exhausted you both, and you needed some time apart.

Tell it fast, like ripping off a Band-Aid. Your husband was gone nearly a month. You were sad, desperate even, lonely, confused, your hormones made you a person you didn't recognize. These are all the reasons why, when you attend a two-day conference at work, a department assessment of academic writing—is there anything less sexy?—your attention is captured by the guy sitting across from you. A colleague—how that word will be corrupted for the rest of your marriage—you'd never met before. He complimented your shoes. He drank tea from a mason jar, had another full of homemade trail mix. At the end of the second day, a beer with other colleagues. You had so much in common! You were both writers! And teachers! He laughed at your jokes! He asked about your novel! Six years you'd been writing this book, asking your husband to read it, leaving the half-finished manuscript on the coffee table, like you used to leave the Help Wanted ads, a passive-aggressive stack of demands: *Read me.* And here was this guy you'd known for two days, asking to read your book. He paid attention to you in a way you did not know you needed.

Look, it didn't take a lot. You were not a girl to whom many guys paid attention. In the seventh grade, sitting in the courtyard before homeroom, the jockiest jock in school had laughed at your boyfriend in front of you. This is her? he asked, and laughed. You and your boyfriend sat in a quiet puddle of shame, and the next day you broke up with him in a note, even though he was a nice guy, because who wants to be someone's laughable girlfriend?

Excuses. It was flirting. You didn't act on any feelings. But the feelings—they were there. They had you by the neck. They scared you. You paced the house. You walked the dog. That the beautiful house you built, the marriage you built, might explode: you felt sick to your stomach. You had that Sylvia Plath line in your head, from "Lady Lazarus." *What a trash / To annihilate each decade.*

You called Ursula. "I feel sick to my stomach."

"Tell him," she advised.

"He'll die," I told her. "He'll want to die."

"Maybe he'll understand. Maybe you can work through it."

What did you want to work through? What did you want? You couldn't tell up from down when he came home. He parked the car, came through the gate, big smile on his face. It had been a long drive, a long time. You met him on the porch, heart beating. How many times had you wanted to have a talk? To say, We are in trouble. To say, We need help. How many times had you backed down?

"Let's sit," you said.

His face fell.

You were on the verge of ovulating. He was supposed to be carrying you inside. But on the red porch swing, you told him you'd met someone. You liked him. You didn't know what it meant. You didn't know what you wanted.

His face fell. Then hardened. "You want to be with this guy?"

"I don't know," I said. "I don't know."

Part of you knew it already: it wasn't about the trail mix guy. There were a thousand trail mix guys out there just like him. Who knows if he even wanted you? Before long you wouldn't feel anything for him but embarrassment. He will be a series of cartoonish details—your husband will ask for all the details, and you'll give them—that will trigger you both for the rest of your days. It wasn't about him. It was about the hole he revealed in your marriage, gaping, a silent chasm. It was about the part of you that you'd silenced or stored away, the part that wanted more than the perfect house and the job and the dog and even more than a baby: the part that wanted more. What, exactly? More connection? More common ground? *We don't have anything in common anymore,* was how you put it. Cutting out the words for him with children's safety scissors, not wanting to harm. Did you want him to make his own trail mix? To read your novel? To do something with his talent? To take an interest in his health, in literature, art, the future, life? What you really wanted—was it for him to be, simply, someone, something else?

No, no. He had simply gone away, and it had taken his going away to understand just how far you were from each other, just how far you'd drifted apart.

Perhaps a regular kind of marriage, then, a regular kind of problem. But it was not mended in a regular way. You didn't go to couples counseling. You didn't start talking about your problems or saying what you wanted. And you didn't even consider trying to stop getting pregnant. You did what you always did: backtracked, sewed up, soothed. And after many unbearable hours on the porch, as the sky darkened and you'd both talked yourselves dry, you took him into the bedroom and made peace.

There's this dark, secret stanza in "Everything I Have Is Yours." It can only be found in the early versions of the song:

> *My love is yours alone*
> *You came and captured*
> *A heart that was free*
> *Now there's nothing I can call my own*

The opposite of everything is nothing. "I Have Nothing." "Everything I Do, I Do It for You." Those were the songs of two of your middle school friends and their boyfriends. You always wanted a boyfriend, if only so you could claim a song, too. What could you expect, growing up with these ballads on the radio, but this totality of sacrifice? Your heart didn't get to be free.

In the coming days, he began to turn into stone. Stopped talking. Stopped eating.

"Come back," you told him. "Let's work this out. Come back," you said, "I love you."

"We'd be breaking up, wouldn't we?" he asked. "If we weren't married."

"No," you told him, "of course not."

But you said you didn't know what you wanted, he said.

You said, "I was confused."

And then, a few days after his return, you went to Vermont. He was supposed to go with you, for a friend's wedding. But he could not go to Vermont. He could not leave the couch. You were scared to leave him again, scared of what he might do. Scared that he would not be there when you returned. Go, he said. You could have stayed. Would it have been better to stay, to work on your marriage? Or was that the problem, always staying, always taking care of him, when you wanted to go to weddings in Vermont?

You went. Got in the car and drove north in the rain. You didn't get far. A half hour out of town, on the wet, dark road—you were talking to Ursula on your cell phone, already crying, it was before hands-free laws!—a deer appeared in your headlights. You turned the wheel, braked, screamed, pinwheeled, fishtailed, how many times, across the opposite lane, across the median, thought you were dead, came to rest against the barricade. Alive. But totaled.

You called AAA. They towed the car. And, of course, you called him, and of course he came to pick you up.

Maybe it was a sign. You were so shaken. You could have been dead. In bed, you cried on his shoulder. Come with me, you said, please. So many times, you'd tried to coax him to you.

The next day, you rented a car and made the drive to Vermont by yourself. At your friend's wedding, in the misty Green Mountains, you watched the whole beautiful ceremony as if you were made of cardboard. After it, while everyone else filed into the tent, you crouched behind a tree in your coral-colored dress and cried.

At home in Virginia, you returned to find your husband had not resumed eating. He was a husk.

Was he punishing himself, or you?

Eat, you told him. Please. You have to eat.

He had looked up the guy while you were gone. You had told him his name when he asked for it, and then he wanted to see his face. He had seen the guy's face, the slender cheekbones, and now he would be skin and bones, he would make you want him again. At least that's the way you saw it. But it wasn't like that. You told him, He's no one. You told him, You're beautiful to me, and meant it.

He had also gone to see Dr. North, his psychiatrist. It was one of the reasons he'd wanted to stay, to make his appointment. He had bonded with the man, whose wife, it turned out, had cheated on him. Your husband told you this. You pointed out that you had not cheated. You felt a little cheated on yourself, felt the loyalties shifting, the loyal men against the unsatisfied women. You could hear in his voice the new love he had for his fellow man.

You told him, patiently, I'm sorry.

You told him, angrily, I didn't do anything wrong!

You yelled—you were beginning to yell—For fuck's sake!

You didn't yell, Get over it.

You remembered a recent visit your parents had made to Charlottesville. All of you sitting outside at a restaurant. For some reason you had mentioned an old boyfriend of Mom's, a *college* boyfriend—here she was, a woman in her sixties—and she kicked you, hard, under the table. Don't go there. An almost imperceptible nod toward your father.

You thought, Jesus, did your mother have an affair or something?

But maybe she hadn't. Maybe it was enough to say another man's name. And that was enough to undo him.

I was wrong, of course. When I told my mother that getting pregnant was the one thing I couldn't control, what I wasn't saying was that getting pregnant was an attempt to rewrite my story with Aaron, to guide us toward some new and promising future, and that he, more than anything, had always been beyond my control.

Of course, I wanted a baby, badly. I wanted to be a mother. My mother talked about the dolls I'd had as a child, a new life-like baby I demanded every Christmas. I gave them serious names, like Jonathan and Sebastian. It was a want that preceded any man. But now I wanted a baby with this man, and I couldn't have one.

After a year of trying unsuccessfully to conceive, a woman is officially deemed infertile. We didn't waste any time. We had hoped that the surgery would clear my tubes enough so that I could get pregnant on my own, but four months later, it hadn't happened. We were still on the clock—the endo could come back at any time. We'd invested so much! Can't stop now! We went to the fertility clinic. We did some tests. It was recommended that we try intrauterine insemination. We made an appointment. I was prescribed Clomid, to stimulate my hormones before the procedure. I picked up the prescription, ready to start it at my next cycle. I was ready to log it all in my notebook.

I'd like to think I relaxed a little that month, but I was probably just tired. Distracted, looking the other way, toward the next month, and the next. I wasn't thinking about the non-medicalized sex I was having with my husband that month. It was still make-up sex, the only kind of communication we seemed capable of, our wordless way of trying to repair the damage. My own body, it was repairing itself, building its own scar tissue. On my belly were the three little scars from the surgery, two under my bikini bottoms, one in my navel. I watched them heal and fade and then all but disappear. I brushed them with my fingers, my secret battle wounds, tiny talismans of hope. And after I got pregnant—to our amazement, on our own, in that thirteenth month—I watched them stretch across my growing belly, bright and proud.

It was a beautiful time.

The day the two lines appeared on the test, we got Bodo's Bagels and took our bikes to the park and had a picnic and basked in the autumn sun, vibrating with joy. The universe was trying to teach me about patience, powerlessness, the present, but I felt that it was a happiness I'd earned through my own efforts. My obsession with getting pregnant became an obsession with pregnancy. I read the books, subscribed to the magazines, researched the gear. I painted the nursery, designed and decorated, posed every little bunny and burp cloth and frame, every-thing a creamy oatmeal color, the color of the tiny Seventh Generation diapers I lined up in baskets. I loved being pregnant. I felt powerful and purposeful and in perfect communion with my baby. Perhaps it was the kind of communion I wanted with my husband. Or perhaps it was the kind of communion a mother can have only with her children, a pure and primal belonging.

Underneath the joy, a worry, like a strained muscle. My belly grew, stretched. Time was running out to get our shit together. I told Aaron what I wanted, more or less. He was already seeing a shrink. He was on an antidepressant. I guessed it was working? That box was checked. Now I wanted him to get a job. And I wanted him to stop smoking. Cigarettes, pot.

A baby in the belly is womankind's oldest instrument of persuasion. I argued, joked, nagged, cajoled, flirted, pushed and pulled. *I hope you're enjoying that bowl because it's going to be your last one.*

He assented. He smoked the last of his weed. He smoked his last cigarette. He knew it was something he needed to do. He had quit be-fore; he could do it again. If he was resentful of being coerced, he kept it to himself. I cheered him on. *I'm proud of you! I know that wasn't easy.*

I helped him put together a résumé, some cover letters. In the spring, just as we started our birthing class, he got a job.

I had read about the company in our local alternative weekly, a wry joke about how hard it was to score a job there. It handled fan mer-chandise and concert ticketing. Aaron would be doing customer service, fulfilling orders over the phone. It was a glorified call center, but it was a respectable job, and it was at least adjacent to the music industry. I didn't care that he could only attend the first birthing class because he had to be at work. My mom and my friend Gina filled in for the rest of the classes.

A job is many things. It's a paycheck. It's stability. It's groceries and insurance and a roof over your head. It's also a social identity. A busi-ness card, real or not, that we hand to our family and friends; *My shit is together,* the card says. *What do you do?* is still the first question we ask people after their names, in a culture that pretends not to equate our worth with our work. What does your father do? What school did you go to? What is your role in our market economy? To work is to do, is to be. To not work is to not do, is to not be. What might we ask each other instead? *Who are you?*

I knew this, on some level. I resented the expectations capitalism and classism and sexism had enforced upon my freedom to make the life I wanted. I had wanted to push back against those forces. I had fallen in love with a man who hadn't finished high school because he was warm and loving and adorable and played guitar and made me laugh, and I married him. "We'll make it work," I said about just about everything back then. We'll wait tables! We'll live in a tent! We love each other! What did it matter?

But it was a piecemeal and provisional rebellion. I had always given the system one middle finger while hiding my face in the other hand. It turned out I wanted a roof over my head, an expensive metal roof with exposed bespoke beams, and all the social security that came with it. At least, I wanted other people to know I was capable of living the life that was expected of me.

There were problems with making it work. For one thing, it was a philosophy born of privilege. It was easy to tell the system to go fuck it-self when the system had produced money and property, your father-in-law's, that still sustained you. For another thing, it didn't always work. Not for long. Waitressing did not pay for the house with the expensive roof. Our money was running out, fast.

So when Aaron got a job, his first real job in years, I practically melted with relief and pride. "My husband has to work." They were the most comforting words I'd ever uttered.

If we wrote books about love without the trouble, the books would be filled with mothers staring at their babies, hours and hours of descriptions of their babies' blank beautiful faces as they nursed, the milk pouring into their mouths the shrewdest sort of market exchange, and the most steadfast sort of love: I will feed you if you look at me that way forever.

Nicolas—Nico—didn't nurse well, though. The first few weeks, I agonized about it. I wanted so badly for it to work. Then, my bloody nipples decided for me. I bought a pump. For six months, I pumped four times a day. My body kept trying to fail me, but still I felt like I had fairy-tale-level powers, Rumpelstiltskin spinning straw into gold. I started each day by going into the nursery and sitting on the plush oatmeal-colored carpet while Nico kicked happily beside me in a bouncer, the music of his bouncer mingling with the music of the pump, then feeding him a fresh bottle. Aaron fed him the midnight bottle, warming it on the stove when he got home from work. And he fed him many of the daytime bottles, too, when I went back to work. When we moved Nico into the nursery to sleep in his crib, and he cried for us, I started sleeping on the floor in his room, and then Aaron joined me, and for weeks we slept there, huddled in sleeping bags. We laughed at ourselves. What are we doing? We were too tired to be logical, but we were happy.

I loved my baby with the fullness that I felt my parents had loved me. It was the kind of love I felt *could* mend our family. We had not been short on love, Aaron and me, but look, we had done it, something magical, we had produced a new kind of love, we had produced something in common. It was a love that raised our stakes, made me love him in a new way: the father of my child. And because I felt that it was the kind of love Aaron had been denied as a child, it felt like love with a vengeance. Aaron's parents, too, had tried to improve their odds with a child. But had they tried hard enough? Had they slept together on the floor of their baby's nursery?

Our shit, from all appearances, was together. Nico was a beautiful and happy baby, with curls like his father's. While I worked, Aaron was the one who fed him, diapered him, swung him back and forth while beatboxing his name, sending him into giggles, dressed him in his little sleep sack, readying him for his nap, before handing him off to me when I got home and he went off to work, leaving me with a kiss, ships passing in the night.

He liked the job. Lots to learn, but his coworkers were nice. There was the stress that comes with every job. The stress of getting to know new software, of people yelling at you on the phone, of meeting a certain number of calls per hour, of apologizing to your boss for being late. A job, too, is a place to go. A gym, a vending machine, a coffee station, lunch at the Subway next door, a bathroom you don't have to clean, an ergonomic desk chair that molds to fit your body, work friends in their matching cubicles. Work friends! Over breakfast, Nico in his high chair, Aaron would tell me about them, silly things they'd gotten into at work, different ways they'd told customers to fuck off. There was the boyfriend-girlfriend couple who liked oxy, the couple who liked heroin, the guy who supplied the call center with weed, the guy who supplied the call center and much of Charlottesville with coke. That many of Aaron's stories about his new friends revolved around drugs was not lost on me. But he spoke about them as though they were a different species: young, crazy, carefree. Aaron was the old guy with a kid. He was past those days.

On one particularly stressful day, he joined a friend for a smoke break, the guy who sold weed. He wasn't smoking anymore, but maybe the guy saw the need in Aaron. He said, "You know what you need, dude?" and got him high in the bathroom. That was the way he put it, "got him high," like a middle school video on peer pressure.

I laughed a nervous laugh. It sounded like the kind of pot-smoking that responsible people occasionally indulged in: a wacky thing to do at work, a one-time deal. "It was a one-time deal," he said. I was happy that he told me, and happy, above all, he had friends. So many friends! He was so well-liked! He had become again the boy at the record store I had fallen in love with.

One morning when Nico was six months old, between Christmas and New Year's, I dropped Aaron at Dr. North's, parked the car downtown, and bundled Nico into his stroller. For the last couple of years, more often than not, I would tag along while Aaron was in therapy, driving into town with him, never getting close to his building but occupying myself a few blocks away, writing and drinking coffee at Mudhouse, or after Nico was born, pushing him around in his stroller. Afterward, we'd meet up for lunch. He wouldn't talk about what he'd talked about in therapy. He went, and then we moved on.

I had barely steered the stroller onto the brick expanse of downtown when Aaron called. Weird. Maybe he had the appointment time wrong. I answered my flip phone.

"He's dead. North, he's dead."

"What?"

The downtown mall was still decorated for Christmas, the lampposts hung with wreaths, the giant Christmas tree lit up outside the Paramount, though it was an unseasonably warm day, sixty degrees. Everything seemed wrong, inside-out.

"There was a note on the door. He died a week ago. It just says he died suddenly."

"Oh my God. How?"

"It doesn't say. It just says to call this other doctor's office for more information."

"Call," I said.

When I hung up, I walked toward him, and he walked toward me. I walked quickly, maneuvering the stroller around a construction site. Men were working, building something, machines moving. A bright and normal winter day. I thought, how terrible, his family, right around Christmas. I thought, heart attack, heart attack, please say it was a heart attack. "It's okay," I said aloud to Nico, "It's okay, we're going to meet Daddy." We met on the corner where downtown met not-downtown, alongside a concrete barrier. His jacket was off, tied around his waist. He looked like he was sleepwalking. He was hanging up his own flip phone.

"He killed himself," he said.

He had to raise his voice to be heard over the construction. I reached out and touched his jacket, grabbed his waist.

"At the office." He hooked a thumb over his shoulder. The earthmover rumbled. "He shot himself in the head at his desk."

Go to the memorial. Pay your respects. Stand in the back of the packed funeral home, in the lobby. The lobby, too, was packed. He had been a well-regarded practitioner. He had held positions in state organizations. He had worked for the university. Stand by the door, the baby strapped to your chest. How many of the people standing around you had been his patients? Think of all the things they'd told that psychiatrist, all the secrets that died with him, and with them, their trust. It must feel, you thought, like a theft.

When the person who is supposed to keep your husband alive, who has been teaching him to get past his distrust, betrayal, abandonment, who has been helping him endure his suffering, decides to leave the planet, you should probably be worried. But you were too busy being angry. Not judgmental. The guy had his own world of pain. It made you sad. But also angry. You were the one who finally got your husband to go to therapy. He was finally making progress. Then this?

You had a baby, and you wanted to give your husband space to grieve. If you were scared, you shoved it under the bed. La la la la! Don't let yourself think it. Forget that suicide is a contagion, an invitation. Look, the baby was standing! Look at the way he pulled himself up. Maybe his father would pull himself up, too.

He was seeing another doctor right away. There was that. All of his psychiatrist's patients had been assigned to other doctors, colleagues going through their own grief. *I want you to know I won't kill myself,* the new psychiatrist told your husband, and she wouldn't be the last to have to make that promise.

It became a secret of his own. "Don't tell anyone," your husband told you. Why? Don't ask. To protect the man's family? No. You could see he was protecting himself. He was trying to wrap himself up, ward off the world.

A new person for you to blame, then. First it was his father. Then, the closest thing to a father.

Ignore all the signs. When he stays out all night with his coworkers, be grateful that he has friends. A distraction. When he comes home feeling like hell, try not to notice. He has had headaches his whole life. Freeze the washcloth, like you learned. One night in April he came home looking worse than you'd ever seen him. All night he moaned in pain. Washcloth, Advil, water. You tried to soothe him, stayed up with him, rubbed his sweaty back. The next day, he could barely get out of bed. It was your parents' fortieth anniversary. You'd cleaned the house to a shine. One of your brothers and his family arrived, then another, their dogs and children bounding toward your dog, your child; it was spring in Virginia and everything was in bloom. Then your parents! Surprise! They were surprised, and moved, and they drank champagne on the porch and chased after their grandsons and posed with them for a picture, the whole family. You roused Aaron for the photo. It still hangs in your hall, and in your brothers' halls—your parents, silver-haired and jubilant, all of the smiling babies, all of the smiling young parents, and your husband, handsome, sunken-cheeked, in a wrinkled white T-shirt. Then he went back to bed. *Aaron's got a terrible headache.* It barely needed to be said, even then.

Tell it fast. But you are slow. Would you even have found out, if he hadn't told you? It wasn't until a couple of weeks later that he came into the bathroom. The baby was sleeping in his crib. You were shaving your legs in the gleaming white claw-foot tub. He had to tell you something. His new psychiatrist had urged him to tell you.

"Okay," you said, pausing your razor.

He leaned against the sink. He said, "I've been using heroin."

Everything you'd been shoving under the bed—more!—came flying out of you then. All the rage came flying out of your mouth, out of your hands. You threw everything in the bathtub at your husband, the razor you were shaving with, the pumice stone, the bar of soap, the soap dish. *Are you fucking kidding me What the fuck is wrong with you Great Fucking great Aaron Fucking beautiful You've gone and inserted in your son's story in his tenth fucking month of life fucking heroin Fucking heroin Are you fucking kidding me You can't undo that Aaron! You did that! You did that!* You were murderous. You wanted to undo it. You wanted to kill what he told you.

He cowered. He was calm. Stop throwing things at me, he said. Please. He said, I wanted to tell you. I wanted to be honest. I'm sorry, he said.

You rose from the bath, a wet, hunched, furious beast. Wrapped yourself righteously in a towel. Marched into the bedroom. Began getting dressed, slamming drawers.

"How many times."

"A few. Like three or four."

"Who."

Not the heroin couple from work. Someone else.

"Did you drive."

"Yes."

"Did you—"

"I didn't shoot up. Never. I snorted it."

A little wave of relief. Then it passed. Then disgust.

You have stepped into a pair of underwear, a T-shirt. You look at the bed from a different time and tense, like it's someone else's bed, a showroom bed with its microsuede headboard; you have stepped out of the age of microsuede into a time travel machine that allows you to view all of the dramas that have played out on this mattress. It is not the mattress you hauled together onto his Pathfinder at age eighteen, but a newer one, firmer, built for a grown-up life, where you made hundreds of attempts at reproduction, lying afterward with your legs raised up against the headboard, feet tingling with hope. It was in this bed where you brought him the pregnancy test with its two pink lines. It was in this bed where your water broke, and this bed where you pulled the bassinet as close as it could get, so you could sleep with one hand on your swaddled newborn. You have enough distance in this moment to think this is the worst, to mourn the ways he has fouled the marriage bed. They are not the ways some marriage beds become fouled, but he has found his own. You do not yet know that your next mattress will be soaked and stained with his blood, that you are not through soothing him through his feverish dreams. Now you stand on opposite sides of the bed.

"You were high that night you came home, weren't you. When you said you were sick."

Did he even really have headaches? It was the beginning of something poisonous, though you didn't know this part then: that you will distrust his symptoms, that you will always be suspicious that he is the one who has made himself sick. When he is sick again, really sick, the wrath will return. You will reach for the razor, ready to throw it.

He nodded.

"What is wrong with you. My parents' fucking anniversary."

"I wasn't trying to get high," he explained. He held out his hands. The baby monitor on the nightstand was quiet. "I was just kind of trying to die."

You didn't call a rehab. You didn't go to Al-Anon. You didn't yet know that you have failed a test, that you have reacted in exactly the wrong way when an addict tells you he's been using. Blaming, shaming, sarcasm, martyrdom, not to mention physical harm, like a woman in a movie slapping a man across the face. How many times have you seen that scene play out? How could you claim any of it, when you didn't know that an addict is what your husband was?

Instead, you opened the phone book and called a marriage counselor with a pleasingly alliterative name.

From the beginning, it was a threat: we're going to therapy, or else. Your husband agreed. Did he have a choice?

The therapist, Madeleine Minter, had flame-red hair and wore floral hoop skirts and tottered around on tiny little heels. Your husband thought she didn't like him, that she sided with you, and he wasn't wrong. You spent two weeks laying it all out, both of you. Even then, the story felt long. The drugs, the guy, Dr. North, trying to have a baby, the extreme imbalances of work and school. "Look, you're both very intelligent," she said. "If I gave you both an IQ test, you'd probably score around the same." It was one of her few kindnesses, something you didn't know you needed to hear. Aaron nodded, gulped. "But your lives are so radically different, they're incompatible." By the end of the second session, Madeleine Minter concluded that if things kept going the way they were going, you—you, only you—would be "vulnerable to an affair."

What the fuck does that mean? your husband asked.

You did not want to have an affair, but to feel uniquely entitled to one—it made you shiver with a terrifying power.

Maybe she knew that he wouldn't hear anything after that. Maybe she saw how deep in delusion you were. Maybe she sensed that the two of you weren't ready for couples counseling. At the end of the second session, she pointed at you. It was you she needed to see, she said. Alone. Your husband had his own psychiatrist. You needed to focus on what you wanted, what you needed. You needed to find your voice. You needed to do some work of your own. You felt pinned to the back of your chair by a knife.

Was it work you were doing there in that office over the next year? You spent a lot of tearful solo sessions talking about your husband's moods, his anger, his depression. You talked about how you didn't feel connected anymore. You talked about how you hated fighting in front of the baby. You talked about what it would take for you to pack up the baby and leave. They were things you'd never said to anybody on the earth. It was important that you said them, that they moved outside your body into the room. You felt lighter, and also guilty, and scared. You reported one week that when you went to the mall your husband got so mad at something that he punched the concrete wall in the little vestibule between the two entrance doors, and she looked at you with such disdain that you felt carved in two—horrified at what you tolerated, and also protective of your wall-punching husband. You could see that she had already dismissed him, that in her eyes he was irredeemable.

When you sat him down on the porch swing that night, you felt sick to your stomach.

"She says it's abusive. Your behavior. When you get so angry—"

"That word." He actually put his hands over his ears.

"I know. I know you don't like that word."

"Okay," he said. Like, I heard you.

His psychiatrist, for her part, was taking her own sides. His psychiatrist said you should have been more understanding when he made his confession. That you shouldn't have lashed out. Maybe that was what therapists did, why people paid them. Instead of being in couples counseling, you reported back your own private revelations, lobbing them like grenades.

One time, another day after parking at the mall—what was it about the mall?—you opened the glove box and found a pack of Marlboro

Reds. You were like a spooked horse. You didn't wait for him to explain. You got out of the car and slammed the door and marched into the mall alone, leaving your husband with the baby. You wanted to punch the concrete wall in the vestibule. Instead, you called Meredith and spilled it. She didn't quite get why you were so mad. It was just cigarettes. "Because he told me he was doing heroin. Fucking heroin. And I told him that if he kept anything from me again it would be the end." You had never said the word aloud to anyone but your therapist, but you said it as you speed-walked around the mall, your purse banging against your hip.

"Oh," Meredith said.

When you told your therapist, she looked at you with something like pity. Something like "I told you so."

When he told his psychiatrist, she told him you shouldn't have over-reacted. You shouldn't have left the baby in the car with your husband.

That did it. A little dart thrown at your mothering.

Fuck your psychiatrist, you said. *What, he wasn't safe with you? You're his dad. Were you high? Why wouldn't he be safe? Why do you get to get out of the car and walk away whenever you want, but I don't? Because I'm a woman? A mother? Why the fuck do I have to be the responsible one? Why the fuck don't I get to punch walls?*

A faucet had been turned on, a hose hooked up to an endless tank of resentment and rage. It was his fault, all of it.

You went to visit your parents. You needed to get out of town. Took the baby, drove to your brother's house, let yourself through the back gate. It broke you, the easy, peaceful way that gate always swung open for you. Your brother's chocolate lab came and nuzzled your knees. Was there a safer feeling? You didn't know how unsafe you'd felt until you came in that gate.

That night, while the baby slept inside, you sat with your mother at the patio table, back in that yard. That's when you spilled everything. Well, not everything. You didn't mention the heroin. But the fighting, the therapy. That's when she told you about going to therapy with your dad. You told her some days you thought about packing up the baby and leaving.

"Do you?" your mother said neutrally. With one hand she held a lit cigarette. With the other, she ran her fingers through her salt-and-pepper hair.

You nodded. You cried like a baby yourself. Your face was slick with snot. You said, "It's not my job to look after his mental health!"

Your mother ashed her cigarette. She was careful with her words. "Honey," she told you, "that's what marriage is."

Your mother has a younger sister who was married for years to a man not unlike your father. When their sons left for college, they divorced, and your aunt moved to Belize, where she opened an inn on the beach, wore a bikini, wrote romance novels, and fell in love with a younger man. Was it you, or was your mother a little annoyed by this? Meanwhile, your parents lived together in your brother's basement. For forty years, one would start the crossword, leave it in the bathroom, and the other would finish.

If instead of sponsoring your dysfunctional marriage, your mother had said, "Come stay with us for a while. Figure out what you want. You're young. You're twenty-nine, for God's sake. You have a baby to think about. We love Aaron, but it looks like he has some stuff to figure out, too. If you want to leave, you'll be okay without him. You're strong. You deserve to live the life you want." If she'd said that, would you have moved into that basement apartment with her? Would you have listened?

Or would you have done what you were determined to do anyway? Would you have just dug in your heels deeper? Would you have resented the implication that your marriage, your husband, was unsavable? Would your mother's words just add fuel to the fire, like every word from your therapist's mouth?

You went home. You kept going. Nothing had changed, except now he was smoking in the open.

"Aaron," Madeleine Minter told you, "is a limited person." She said it like, come on, we both know this to be true. It felt like a key, but a key to the gut.

True, went a voice in one ear.

Cruel, went a voice in the other. Was there anything crueler than to call someone *limited*? Was there anything that limited a person more?

It was a challenge. There wasn't much fire left in you, but that fanned it. You started scowling through your sessions. Arms crossed, like a moody teenager. That hose of rage, it could be turned on your therapist, too.

You'd lie to her, then, and to yourself. You'd stay in your marriage and quit therapy.

If she'd said, instead, "Look, your husband has been on and off drugs all his life, and he's never been to rehab. Maybe you should look into that," would you have listened? Or would you have balked at the word "addict," the way you balked at "abuse"? If she'd said, "Look, there's a great program called Al-Anon, and it might save your life and your marriage," would you have gone? Would you have been ready?

In your last session, when you broke up with her, she said, "I'm very sorry to hear that."

"We're trying to have another baby," you told her. It was what you knew, how you coped, how you kept on. And you knew she'd look at you like you'd failed her test. You had found a voice, but you didn't use it in the way she'd wanted.

She was exasperated. "It's entitled," she said. "To have a new baby, while you're in financial distress, while your marriage is in crisis, it's incredibly entitled." She flung her hands in the air, like, what more could she do for you anyway?

He was limited. You were entitled. Another key to the gut.

The financial distress. There was that. Do you need a whole separate book for that? How to describe the financial funk that filled the rooms of your beautiful house? The organic Pottery Barn crib sheets, the organic mashed carrots, the Bugaboo stroller, the giant shipwrecked sectional couch, the marriage counseling copays, the satellite TV, the phone, the other phone, the car, the other car, the gas in the car, the mortgage, the mortgage, the mortgage—it had added up, was adding up every hour. We watched our bank balance plummet. The down payment on the house had been Morris's money. We had sold the condo, his last property, for far less than we'd hoped. Now all his money was gone. All our money was gone. We got one month behind on the mortgage, then two. One morning, in order to get to work, I had to pay for gas with my parents' credit card number at the mom-and-pop station across the highway, reading the number off a Post-it while the cashier keyed it in. I held my breath as the gas flowed from the pump. The shame was like a too-bright day I had to close my eyes against.

Aaron was working two jobs—he'd picked up weekend retail shifts at the mall. That winter, into the spring, he worked and worked and I worked and worked. I applied for a tenure-track teaching job in Ithaca, and tried to finish my novel, and tried to get pregnant. *Entitled,* said Madeleine Minter in my head, again and again. But we didn't expect something for nothing! We were just trying to make something from nothing. Make it work.

Aaron, for reasons beyond my understanding, was becoming Catholic. He was taking classes at the Roman Catholic Church in Charlottesville, Rite of Christian Initiation of Adults. There was something vaguely embarrassing about it, something inaccessible. Hadn't the therapist said our lives were too radically different as it was, that what we needed was integration? But there was something beautiful about it, too. He was looking for something outside himself, bigger than himself, spiritual structure, belonging, a path. That was good, right? What did it matter if I wasn't on the path with him? He didn't miss a class. Not since he took the weekly classes at the NYPD had he been so disciplined.

His mother visited that fall, the one and only time. Flew from New Mexico to Virginia. It was a nice visit. She complimented my corn chowder. She read to the baby. Held his little hand as he toddled up and down the porch steps. Look at the baby walk! Look at the baby talk! Look at the baby say Da Da Da, chasing after him. We told her nothing of the drama, of course.

I thought maybe she would approve of Aaron's conversion to Catholicism. Maybe he thought she would, too. She'd been raised Catholic. Aaron had changed his last name from his father's to his mother's, and now he was changing his religion from his father's to his mother's. She was agnostic on the issue, though. She had parted ways with the church herself, something about being annoyed with the priest at her congregation in Santa Fe. It occurred to me that Aaron wasn't choosing his mother so much as choosing not-his-father. He was choosing another father, a Heavenly Father, and Father Geoffrey, who led the classes. He came home talking about him with the same respect and admiration he'd had for Dr. North.

When you get three months behind on your mortgage, you get fore-closure notices, and then the foreclosure notices appear in the newspaper. And then your Realtor calls you and says, "What happened?"

We went to a free financial counselor. She took down our income, all our expenses. I felt like I was in Madeleine Minter's office again, in the principal's office. At the end of the session, she said in the most neutral voice available to humans that she recommended we file for bankruptcy.

You dug in your heels. That's what you did under pressure: showed all those fuckers what you were made of. When the fire got hot, you sold the Subaru. A stranger sat at your dining room table in one of the lime-green painted chairs and wrote you a check for $10,000. You paid off the past due mortgage and with what was left over, bought a thirty-year-old Mercedes station wagon with 200,000 miles on it— *These things run forever!* Aaron said—with stiff leather seats and no power steering and an engine that needed ten minutes to warm up. Whatever. You had avoided, for now at least, foreclosure and bank-ruptcy. Made it work.

And then, you do. It does. Did. All of the work, tears, effort: some-thing from nothing. In a span of a week, you were offered a job contract and a book contract. One way out, then another. When your agent called to tell you, you sank to the kitchen floor, leaned your head against the cabinet, and cried.

Then your husband took your hand, raised you to your feet, and you danced.

What saved us then—our livelihood, our marriage, our self-respect— wasn't a great new insight earned in therapy—we'd earned little—but good news, fickle, with its sweat and luck. A survival instinct, the jungle cats in us clawing out of the cave. Our love for each other and for our child and our hope for a new one, for a new start.

That spring I rewrote *Ten Thousand Saints*. Went to Mudhouse with my manuscript, my editor's beautiful pencil scrawled on every page. I was willing to revise. I was writing a new story for us. It was a book made from Aaron, something we'd birthed together, an offspring of sorts.

The week before my deadline, I printed out a fresh manuscript. "It's your last chance," I told Aaron, "if you're going to read it."

The next two days, he went to Mudhouse and read my book. For nine years I had been building a fictional universe out of the scraps of his childhood. What if he hated it? What if he saw too much of himself in it, or too little? What if I'd gotten the whole world wrong? Toward the end of the second day, I drove Nico to the coffee shop and bought a piece of vegan chocolate cake and we sat down next to Aaron as he turned the last page.

"I like it," he told me.

I smiled. Nico, in his high chair, stuffed his mouth with cake. Sweet relief.

"Only thing is, Gorilla Biscuits would never tour with the Cro-Mags."

When Aaron finished his classes and was ready to be baptized, my parents came to visit for Easter weekend. They took care of Nico while I went with Aaron to the very large church, sat through the very long Easter Vigil by myself, and at the end, watched as Aaron stepped barefoot onto the stage in his long white robe, like a child entering from behind the curtain in a school play. I sat up in my seat to see him better. With a crystal bowl, Father Geoffrey poured the water over his head three times, in the name of the father, and of the son, and of the holy spirit, and then my husband was redeemed.

OLD BOYS

Aaron isn't out of the psych ward long before my dad starts dying. He needs to rest on a stool between the coffee machine and the dining room table. His feet begin to swell into cold blue balloons. We're at the doctor every week. The doctor employs his theatrical metaphors. He shuffles around his meds, orders more tests. Before a CAT scan, I help him strip off his undershirt and to lie on his side on the table. His long, ancient body is flat as an ironing board between my hands. I see the seventy-year-old scars that crisscrossed his ribs. I see the boy he was. He is still that boy, with the same body—how is it true?—that traveled from there to here, from south Georgia to upstate New York, and around the world in between, and now he cranes his neck to see the technician's screen, the cloudy picture of his insides. I want to see his insides, too. Where is the problem? How can we fix it? "How much longer do we have to do this?" he jokes at these appointments, but he also says, with relief, when the test results are good, "I thought I was a goner." I see that he wants to die and that he wants to live.

The CAT scan reveals emphysema in his lungs. Not a surprise, given his lifelong love affair with his pipe. "I didn't really inhale," he points out.

Mostly it's his heart, though. His heart has been failing for years and now his lungs are in the marathon, too, and there isn't much to do about it.

"How does it feel," Stu asks me, "to watch your dad get sick?"

I've started seeing Stu on my own. Aaron still doesn't trust any doctor, even Stu. "I love him," he clarifies. But trust is another matter. He is careful about these words. He loves his parents, for example, but he doesn't respect them. He says this so often that our children sometimes recite, as a means of understanding, "Dad loves his parents but he doesn't respect them."

Stu accepts this new reality with grace. In reply to his question, I cry. This seems to be Stu's strategy: get me alone in order to make me cry. In order to give me a space to feel my own feelings. To remind me I have other things, other people, to cry about and worry over, other than Aaron. He has a point. And I need it: I've stopped seeing my other therapist. My week has filled with so many doctor appointments, so many therapy sessions, for my dad, for Aaron, for the kids, that blocking off another hour on Google calendar is more stressful than it's worth.

"I want to do it right this time," I say. With my mom, I wasn't there.

"You have a lot to focus on. A lot of people to take care of."

"I don't want to regret not talking to him. Asking him questions."

"What kind of questions?"

I watched my dad watch Aaron return from the hospital. "Welcome back, babe," he said. "Thanks, man," Aaron said, and then they went about their days. What was behind that circumspection? Respect? Denial? Empathy?

"Like, about his mental health."

Stu nods.

"Aaron's dad was pretty unstable. He had PTSD. Aaron thinks he was suicidal. Now Aaron has this schizophrenia diagnosis. I mean, it still doesn't feel totally right to me. But it feels right to Aaron, at least a little. And my mom used the same word about my dad. I want to know—did he really have it? Does he? I mean, I have kids. Mental illness can run in families."

"Sure." He looks at me over the tent of his hands. "Ask him."

"Stu. We like, *never* talked about this in my family. I don't even think my brothers know."

"What do you want to know?"

I glance around the room. "Like, he was at Bellevue. What was that like? Was he ever on any medication? Why were he and my mom in therapy? There was this whole time when I was, like, eleven. He and my mom had this family friend who was a doctor, and they saw him for therapy. It was all hush-hush."

"A lot of times, when people are at the end of their life, they find it's a relief to answer questions. To set things right. It unburdens them. I've seen it with many of my clients."

"Maybe," I say.

"Ask him. You won't regret it."

November goes on with its slick chill. Dad hates the winter. He sits bundled on his couch in his bathrobe. I bring him coffee and ice cream and his favorite, biscuits and gravy, but he can only manage a few bites. He used to come into the kitchen while I was cooking dinner and we'd listen to Bob Dylan and drink wine, but now he stays in his room, kind of hunched over, staring at the floor between his feet. I wonder what he's thinking. I want to ask, but my jaw feels heavy. I am scared. I don't want to ask him how he feels about his own death. And asking about his schizophrenic episodes seems absurd. He is tired, confused. I don't want to bring him back to a place he doesn't want to go. I don't want him to bring me to a place I don't want to go.

"You okay, Daddy?" I ask him instead.

He nods, takes my hand. "Just weak."

I kiss his dry scalp. Then I go dump his pee bottle.

My brothers have been planning to come to Ithaca between Christmas and New Year's, but in the last days of November, he takes a steep dive. On Thanksgiving, I text my brothers a picture of Dad asleep at the table after dinner. We buy a Christmas tree and put it up the next day, in the living room, where Dad can see it.

"Maybe they shouldn't wait," Aaron suggests. My brothers agree. It was so fast with Mom.

They come up the first weekend of December. Pete and his wife, Cameron, and their two boys arrive first, from North Carolina, late on Thursday night in a snowstorm. Will there ever be a good time for them to come see our dad for the last time? No. But it's a bad time. Aaron is breaking out. The next day is a new moon. "I'll be fine," he says. "Don't worry about me. Take care of your dad." I feel the giant force of it all moving along without me, the moon orbiting the earth, the earth orbiting the sun, other people's bodies doing what they please.

Pete and his family come from the hotel the next morning to be there when the hospice nurse arrives to do the intake. As she's settling in upstairs, I check on Aaron in the downstairs bathroom. He is naked, distressed, raving with pain. He rubs his distended belly. A metallic ooze pours out of his navel, like silver spray paint.

"Aaron, I can't do this right now. I'm sorry."

"Please," he begs. "You don't understand what's happening."

"Hospice is here," I say. "I have to go."

And I roll the sliding door closed.

Upstairs, while the boys play in the snow with their cousins—it's novel to the North Carolina nephews, all this snow—Pete and I help Dad move from the couch to the dining room table. He sits in his smart green cardigan and the navy knit cap he's never without, trying his best to answer the nurse's questions, but he's slow, disoriented. Pete jokes that he could probably beat him at Jeopardy! for the first time in his life. Dad asks about morphine. The nurse assures him he will have plenty. She tells us about the drugs, the phone numbers, the equipment that will be delivered—the bed, the oxygen tank, the commode. I fill out forms. Family history. Heart disease. Diabetes. I pause at the box that says "mental illness." Then I check it. I don't specify that he's the family member who had it. What does it matter? He probably has days to live. Probably the nurse will be the only person to glance at this form. But I feel a quick flame of having righted something. I doubt he ever checked such a box in his eighty-six years.

I try to focus on my dad, my brother and sister-in-law, on the paper before me, on the nurse's gentle voice, but one ear is listening for Aaron, in the bathroom directly below us. I can hear him moaning, mumbling. I know they can, too. When the boys come in from the snow, I bring their snow pants and jackets and mittens down to the dryer and check on him again.

When I roll open the bathroom door, he's on his knees, sobbing, holding a rag in his hands. "I can't do this anymore," he cries.

"Shh! They're right above you." I'm whisper-yelling. "Please."

"You don't understand. I can't take this anymore. Please."

We both plead. Please please please.

"What is that?"

I try to take the rag from him. He holds it. I yank again. I recognize the old faded beach towel. It has been cut and fashioned into a noose. I yank harder now, and he lets it go. Then I whip him with it.

"Are you kidding me?"

He's kneeling, crying. Another day I might have held his hands, helped him to bed, given him some medicine, kissed his eyelids, and sat by his side until he was safely asleep. Today, I am furious.

"My father is up there dying. You want to die too? You both going to leave me?"

"I'm sorry," he says.

"Please," I beg. "Do not do this. Not right now."

"I'm sorry."

"I have to be with my dad."

"Go be with your dad."

"I'm sorry."

"You should be with your dad. Don't worry about me." He exhales a long cry, and is still.

"I can't," I say.

And I close the door again. I bury the towel under my jeans in a drawer.

Sam arrives from D.C. that afternoon with two of his three boys. His wife, Keri, is home with their oldest, who has a tuba competition. We all take turns sitting by Dad's bedside, in the hospice wheelchair. The boys admire the functions of the hospital bed. We feed him morphine and Ativan. It's a familiar ritual, sad in its ritual and sad in its familiarity. On Dad's eightieth birthday, when we all gathered at Sam's, we watched my mother's hospital bed delivered, learned how to operate the equipment. With her it was lung cancer, but there was morphine and Ativan then, too, the hospice paperwork scattered everywhere, the photo op of all the grandsons gathered around the grandparent wearing the oxygen cannula, the quick, ugly, merciful decline, the shrill joy of boys in the background.

By Saturday, Dad stops eating altogether. I make him a cup of coffee in the morning, pour in a half cup of French vanilla creamer, the way he likes it, in the clear glass mug. I hold it to his lips. Gently, he shakes his head. I burst into tears. I have made him a cup of coffee every morning since he's been unable to do it himself, at five thirty, when we were the only ones up. He'd take a sip and say, "Boy, is that good." Now the coffee sits untouched on the hospital-bed table, growing a cold film on top. I can't bear to pour it into the sink.

We make Christmas cookies and do the handmade Christmas tree puzzle we've done every year since we were kids and Pete tickles Nico and Henry until they scream. Aaron has recovered enough to shower and get dressed and entertain the nephews with the little electronic noise-makers they love. I try to keep them out of his office, but they marvel at it, all the music equipment and monitors, the bow and arrow and Fushigi ball and Rubik's cubes. There is junk stacked in plastic bins up to the ceiling and blood smeared on the walls, but they don't seem to care.

Pete and Cameron leave that afternoon in order to avoid a freak snowstorm that will drop ten inches of snow on North Carolina shortly after they arrive home. They say good-bye to Papou. On Sunday, Sam and I take our kids out to lunch and for a walk down the gorge near Collegetown. The sun has come out, and it's a warm day for December. We leave Dad and Aaron alone at home, Dad sleeping, Aaron sleepless. We bring Aaron a sandwich. Dad still won't eat. He can barely take a sip of water.

When we get home, while Dad sleeps on, Sam helps me clean up the kitchen. He'll be leaving that afternoon. We collect all the empty bottles and juice boxes and cans.

"I'm worried about you, Nellie," he says. "You're taking care of everyone."

"I guess." I jiggle a juice box and take the last slurp. "I mean, Dad took care of us, too."

Sam knows what I mean. Dad lived with him and Keri for twelve years, the first six of those years with Mom. He's been living with me and Aaron for only ten months. Our parents helped care for their grandchildren, and in turn they were given a home. We know that we're mostly caring for our parents, not the other way around, but as parents ourselves now we know there's no balance sheet. Our father worked for forty-five years to care for us. Our mother made us twenty thousand forgotten meals. And even in the last weeks, nearly every night, Dad called Henry into his room to slide next to him on his couch, hair wet from the bath, to read him *Peter Rabbit*. "What's that rascal gotten into this time?" We know we've been lucky.

"I know," Sam says. "But still. You're doing everything. You going to be okay?"

I've resented it, sometimes, taking care of all these boys. The feeding, the cleaning, the ferrying to doctor appointments. Recently I emailed Meredith a list of all the fluids I cleaned up that day. Blood, shit, vomit. Aaron's, my dad's, the kids', the dog's. We agreed that the piss of our sons' friends on the toilet seat was the worst.

Then the creatures I was taking care of started dying. In October we lost our dog, Zabby. Shortly after his twelfth birthday, he collapsed on the concrete floor of our bedroom and couldn't get up. "Time to put that old boy down," my dad said. The vet came to our house and gave him the shot while Nico and Henry bravely petted him. I wanted my kids to be there, and they wanted to, too. We watched his eyes close. I was thirty-nine and had never seen anybody, any animal, die. I felt I was being given some rite I'd been denied. We all cried and held each other and held Zabby, the shocking eighty pounds of his lifeless body. Even the vet cried. "We love you, Zabby," we said. Henry was practical. "He can't hear you," he pointed out.

Now I tell Sam, "I'm scared of him dying in the house." It's an illogical thing to say. What else might happen, except our father dying in this house? Our mother died at the hospice center in Alexandria, shortly after arriving there. Some people want to die at home. She wanted,

I'm sure, to die in a hospital, where she would be out of the way, not any trouble. What I mean is that I'm scared of our dad dying when I'm alone with him, that I won't know how to recognize death, or what to do about it. It's the same way I felt about other life passages—sex, childbirth—what if I just didn't know how to *do* it? I wish for the traveling vet, her gentle syringe.

"I know," Sam says. "Look, I can stay if you want."

I want him to. I want both my brothers to stay and never leave. "I'll be okay," I say. They have their own lives, and I've chosen this one.

"But how's Aaron, dude?"

I toss the bottles we're collecting in a paper bag. "Not great. I'm sorry you have to see him like this."

When something happens that will embarrass you, that will expose you, that is out of your control, the shame is like a puddle of piss you stand in. There's the terror of peeing in your pants, the shock of the hot piss on your cold leg, but then there's the relief, the warmth.

"What's going on with him?"

I give him the broad strokes of the story. Lyme, Morgellons, co-infections. The hold it has on his body and his brain. The cycle we've been trapped in for the last year. The mania, the hallucinations.

"He was watching this spot on the wall in his office," Sam says. "He was like, 'What is that? Is that thing moving?'"

"Yeah. He does that."

I tell him about my attempts to get him into the psych ward, then his getting forced into the psych ward.

"Jesus, Nellie."

"Yeah. It's been kind of nuts."

"How was Dad with all that?"

I take a sip of an almost-finished beer. "Great. Understanding. Like, they *got* each other." I realize we're using the past tense. "They kind of took care of each other."

"Yeah?"

It's hard to describe. Dad has been neither approving nor disapproving of Aaron's illness, or the way he handled it, or the way I handled it. If he was concerned, he kept his concerns tightly buttoned, except to occasionally suggest that Aaron not eat so many eggs. It's as though he recognized Aaron's helplessness, his inability to be anyone but himself, and accepted it. I wonder if he saw my own worry, my panic, my need to fix, and saw my mother. If he did, he accepted that, too.

"I don't know if you ever knew this." I can hear the kids' voices from Nico's bedroom, the Darth Vader sigh of the oxygen tank from Dad's. I can feel the now-or-neverness. I lower my voice, lower my body over the counter. "Dad tried to kill himself once."

"What?" Sam drops to his elbows across from me. "When?"

"Before we were born. When he lived in New York. He took a bunch of pills after some girlfriend left him. His friends found him days later and took him to Bellevue."

"No shit."

I tell him everything else I know and have never said about our father. It comes tumbling out. I tell him about Dad telling me he was going to move out, about Mom telling me, years later, that they'd been in therapy, that she'd chosen to stay with the family rather than visit her dying brother, that Dad had had "paranoid schizophrenic episodes."

"What does that mean?"

"I'm not sure. I asked Mom and she said, 'I would never say.'"

"I think I know," Sam says. Then Nico comes into the kitchen and all the other boys follow him. Can Henry and Cormac play *Batman: Arkham Knight*? What's it rated? No, they cannot. Well, can they watch Nico and Will play it? Fine. Sure.

I nod toward the back door and Sam and I gather the recycling in our arms. Outside, he tells me, "I only remember one time where Dad was crazy like that. At your softball game."

"My softball game?"

"You don't remember this? You were probably like ten or eleven. Dad had picked me up after school and we were meeting you and Mom at the field. It was kind of lightly raining and when we pulled up we could see Mom was sitting in the bleachers next to some guy under his umbrella."

"Who?"

"I don't remember. Just like the dad of one of your friends, I guess.

I'd seen him around. It was really obvious he was just being nice and letting her sit under his umbrella."

"Oh, God. I don't know if I want to hear this."

"Dad saw them and just jumped out of the car. He marched over in the rain and was like, 'I see what's happening here. I'm not a fool.'"

"Oh, God."

"Mom was like, 'Bill, don't do this.'"

"No."

"He was just out of his mind, yelling. Mom had to calm him down and get him out of there."

We've dumped the recycling in the bin, and we are standing behind the house in the snow now, no jackets, hands stuffed in our pockets. I wonder if that was the "paranoid schizophrenic" episode, if there were more. Surely there's more we don't know. My kids don't know everything about Aaron's episodes, but they know enough. I want it that way. I don't want them to grow up with secrets and silences.

I asked Stu if I should talk to the kids frankly about Aaron's mental illness. I worried about what they'd think when they learn about it someday. He said, "It won't be a surprise to them. They've lived through it."

For me, though, standing in the cold beside the recycling bin, it is a surprise. My mother pretty well contained the fire of my father's episodes. That was the way she wanted it. I suppose now it was a kind of gift. We knew our father, for the most part, as a healthy and capable adult. It was only partially a fiction. I needed that fiction of my father, whole and sane, even as he lay dying. Maybe I even needed my mother to craft it for me.

I have some answers now. They are enough.

There's the rush of relief and regret, of sudden emptiness, that comes after throwing up.

"Sorry to dump all that on you," I say to Sam.

"Me too," he says.

"Jesus."

"Damn."

Before Sam leaves, he helps me change our father's diaper. We lift his narrow body, fragile as a newborn's. We try to clean a bit of shit off his groin. It is a birthmark, we realize, large, not handsome, but beautiful. We never knew it was there.

That night, I drag the beanbag into my dad's little room and sleep on it beside his hospital bed. I sleep the sleep of the new parent, waking every half hour to check if he's still breathing. He talks and grunts in his sleep. He sounds as though he's working out something difficult. Who is he talking to? In the morning, he doesn't drink his coffee. He barely wakes up. When he does, his blue eyes settle on me like a baby's and his face blooms into a smile, as though he's been somewhere far away, and is surprised to find himself here, and me with him.

Henry wakes up with a fever, so I let him stay home from school. He's still in his footed reindeer pajamas, playing downstairs with Aaron in our room, when the hospice nurses arrive for their daily visit. While they change the sheets and clean him up, I take my first shower in days. I come out in my bathrobe, my hair wet, and stand near the head of his bed while they finish. He's in his bathrobe, too, bright red. The nurses tuck the blanket up to his chest. He opens his eyes wide enough to see them: the nurses, they're here. It's safe to go. "It's okay," I say. "I'm here." His breath is wild and ragged, trying to get out. I have heard about the death rattle. "Is this it?" I ask them. They don't answer, but retreat, slowly, toward the doorway. My hand is on Dad's shoulder. The nurses draw the door closed. I lean close to his face. He takes a big, brave breath, and then he lets it out. His tongue rests against his teeth.

For a few moments I stand with my head on his shoulder, quietly crying. I kiss his wrinkled forehead, his snowy white hair.

Through the door, I hear one of the nurses ask, "Do you want us to get your husband?"

"No," I say. "Thank you."

I don't want him here yet. I don't want him to intrude upon this space. I climb into bed with my father and I cry into his bathrobe. I tell him, "Thank you," again and again. I tell him, "I'm sorry" and I tell him, "I love you."

After a few minutes, I step out of the room. The nurses are

standing silently in the kitchen. I hug them. They help me make the next arrangements—the undertaker, the social worker, the cremation service. I thank them.

When they're gone, I go to the bedroom. Henry is jumping from the bed to the floor. Aaron has his foot propped on the bed, looking at something on his leg.

"I have something sad to tell you," I tell them. "Papou just died."

Aaron is wild with grief, loud with it. Henry wants to see him. "You don't have to," I say, but already he's running past me and up the stairs to Papou's room, bursting through the door. There Papou lies, half-propped up in the bed with his eyes closed and his mouth open. He might have just fallen asleep, as he did every night watching TV, but he looks like he's made of stone.

Henry takes one look at him and howls. He leaps into my arms. Aaron comes up the stairs behind me, crying. He goes to Dad and touches his arm. "Oh, Papou." Henry watches him cry.

We call the boy's school and ask for Nico. Does he want to come home? Yes, he does. Aaron puts on his shoes, puts himself together, gets in the car, and goes to pick him up.

But Henry is scared to be close to him. "Papou looks freaky," he cries. He runs up to the loft, and I go after him, and while we wait for Aaron and Nico to return, we sit on the floor and we cry. I let him climb inside my bathrobe like he likes to do, and belt him in. He lies curled against me in his pajamas, our faces wet with snot, our glasses steamed with tears, Henry looking up at my face to see my crying, to show me his.

When Nico comes home, he, too, cries over Papou. We stand with him and watch him.

Henry's cries have slowed to a whimper. "It was weird when Dad kissed Papou," he declares.

"Well, I love him," Aaron says. He has calmed, too. He puts one hand on Henry's shoulder. I reach for his other one. "And I respect him more than anyone." He makes a chuffing sound. He has realized something. "I didn't cry for my own parents when they died."

Something sometimes happens when someone dies, though. You're crying for the loss of that person, but for all the people you've lost before that, too.

"We have no more grandparents now," Henry says. "It's not fair."

Maybe Aaron is crying for his parents. I am crying for them. I'm crying for my mother. I'm crying for death, because our fear of it has made freaks of us.

Orphaned, we're the grown-ups now. We have survived, and it's time for lunch.

SOLSTICE

The morning of the last full moon of the year, I wake up to rain. I'm braced for it, the Cold Moon, though it's warm enough to be raining. The last twelve nights, I've slept on the mattress in the loft, one child nestled under each arm. "I need them," I told Aaron, and he said he understood. But this morning they're not there. I go down to the kitchen. The flowers are everywhere, and dying. The Christmas tree's white lights have been on for a very long time. My father's ashes are in a white cardboard box on the shelf, next to my mother's ashes. Hers are in the wooden box my father brought with him when he moved in with us. In the funeral home, my father had balked at the expense. He would have been pleased to know that I'd found a discount cremation service that didn't require a wooden box. Only half my mother's ashes were in that box. The other half had been scattered in the mountains of Vermont. The plan was to have a memorial for Dad in the summer, in Vermont, and to scatter half his ashes there with Mom's. Then we figured the rest of his ashes could share Mom's wooden box.

"It's the way they would have wanted it," I said. "The economy edition." Why take up more space than you had to?

Other than the rain, the house feels haunted with quiet. It's a Saturday morning. Winter break. On the kitchen island is a note from Aaron: *Took the boys to Denny's!* With a cartoon face. Full moon, and Aaron feels well enough to drive.

In my dad's room, his desk is still scattered with inhalers, an unused bed pan, his navy cap. His bifocals, spotted with fingerprints. Everything has changed; nothing has changed.

And then it occurs to me, as I look up at the crooked Christmas tree, its dumb, patient wings: the reason why I feel so strange in my body. I have never been alone in this house.

By the time the moon is out, Aaron's skin is glowing that eraser-burn pink, and it's raining parasites out of every orifice of his body. Little moth-colored shells spill from his mouth. From a distance they look innocent as sunflower seeds. He digs in his pointer, pulls out a fingertip full. Collects them in a little clear plastic box he used to keep baseball cards in. They make a dry sound when you shake them. Others are larger, the size of a pumpkin seed. Under the lens of an iPhone camera, they are shaped like an oblong blade, or a fish. And then, in one video, in the bathroom sink chalked with our kids' toothpaste, the thing leaps like a fish in a frying pan. "Play it again," I say, and for once, I'm transfixed. It leaps, shakes, struggles in the sink.

"Flukes," Aaron says. He is calm. He has done some research. "At least that's what they look like." I pull up Google. A kind of tapeworm. It's worse with the full moon, when they spawn. But they're there, all the time. "I've been puking and shitting these things for *weeks.*" I don't ask to see these pictures.

It's the Alinia. Arguably the most powerful antiparasitic on the market. So powerful our insurance wouldn't cover it. When I first called the pharmacy to check on the prescription, the woman on the phone gasped.

"What is it?"

"Oh, my." I could hear her tapping a keyboard. "The copay is . . . quite high."

"How much?"

"Eight thousand dollars."

I shouted out a laugh. "I love my husband," I said, "but not that much."

The doctor switched Aaron to Flagyl instead, which our insurance would cover. Not my favorite drug, Laura told me. It doesn't kill the eggs. But it will do.

But then, a few weeks later, picking up his other meds at the pharmacy, there was the Alinia, waiting in its little plastic baggie. The insurance company, apparently, had cleared it. No copay. I didn't ask questions. I signed for it.

And it worked. Oh, it worked. The next day, Aaron hands me his phone and plays a video of a bug. There's no other word for it. A two-year-old would look at the thing and say: "bug." It is roach-brown, segmented, legs kicking, antenna swimming, and it has come from my husband's testicles.

Hundreds of them, he says. "They sting like you wouldn't believe."

I hold the lonely bug, the size of a garden ant, in a Ziploc bag. Still it faintly moves, just enough to say "I am alive."

Between Christmas and New Year's, we have two phone consults—one with Dr. Bernard, the Lyme doc; one with Dr. Savely, the Morgellons specialist we met in Germany. Aaron describes the parasites. "There's, uh, a large amount of stuff coming out." Interesting, Dr. Bernard says. We'll retest for parasites. Dr. Savely diagnoses him over the phone with babesiosis and neuroborreliosis. I drive to campus to take care of the paperwork, email one office the release form to send records to the other. In the car, last rainy days of December, I listen to a Radiolab episode on parasites. It is jokey and voicey, with an intro about *Alien* and fake horror music. But then: there is a parasite called a blood fluke. I turn up the volume. In certain rivers in Sub-Saharan Africa, it burrows into a human ankle, then swims through its blood. Then the male fluke will wait for a female fluke. They will mate. This is no one-night stand. Parasites are generally monogamous, and they stay with their mates for a lifetime. The male fluke will form a groove the length of its body, and the female will fit into it. The male will feed her and keep her safe and warm. They will stay in that position, the

Radiolab scientist says, for perhaps forty years, spooning in the tide of a human's heart.

In January, we drive to D.C. to visit Dr. Savely. We stay with Sam and Keri. We bring Sam Dad's good loafers. Keri, bless her, watches the kids. The morning of the appointment, Aaron and I get in a fight in the car over the GPS. I yell at him to turn it off—it's interfering with the directions on my phone. Aaron throws an open bottle of medicine into the back of the car. Pills spill everywhere. We're driving through the lettered streets, yelling at each other through yellow lights. I miss the turn. We're tense.

We find a parking garage, a Starbucks. Aaron takes a walk. We make up on the street corner, slushy with overnight snow. "I'm sorry," he says.

"I'm sorry," I say. "I just want this to go well."

Does it go well? I think it does. Dr. Savely spends two hours with us, going over the records, taking Aaron's history, asking after symptoms. She takes out a scope—a bigger, corded version of the scope that we didn't ask to use in Germany—and presses it to Aaron's arm, and on the monitor a giant, graphite-colored filament blooms. Oh, yeah, she says. That's a good one. She adjusts Aaron's meds, adding another antibiotic, another antiparasitic, and three new meds for sleep. You can't get well if you can't sleep, she says.

She looks at the photos on Aaron's phone. The electric red and green filaments. The black flake. The creamy hands. She nods, impressed with Aaron's photography but not moved. I don't mean to sound jaded, she says, but you can't show me anything I haven't seen before.

I take this as comfort. We're in the right place. Aaron takes it as a friendly challenge. What he remembers most about the Morgellons conference is that man asking about worms, Dr. Savely's insistence that Morgellons isn't parasitic. He scrolls through the hundreds of photos on his phone until he reaches the recent ones: the fluke, the bug. Tell me that isn't a bug, he says.

She shrugs. It sure looks like one, she says. But Morgellons takes lots of forms.

Before we leave, she gives us an armful of free samples of Mepron, the new antiparasitic. She may not think that bug was a bug, but for some reason, she says again, Morgellons patients respond best when antiparasitics are in the mix.

This isn't quite enough for Aaron. The ride home is as tense as the ride there, but tense with quiet. It feels like an immense waste—not just the trip to D.C., but the trip to Germany, too. "Seriously?" he says after a while. "She looks at that picture and doesn't see a bug? Why is everyone so afraid to say parasites?"

"Does it really matter?" I'm still clinging to the hope we can frame this as a new chapter. At least a new page. "She gave you the parasite drugs."

He says, "I just want to be *seen*."

"She looked at you!"

"She looked at me," he says. "But she didn't see shit."

A week later, the Super Blood Wolf Moon. On *Saturday Night Live,* they make a joke about it. Aaron is in a jokey mood, too. The morning of the moon, he comes upstairs and takes a seat at the island on a stool. He tells me he started to bleed from his stomach in the middle of the night. Blood just appearing on his skin. He thinks parasites are dying inside of him. He has made peace with them today. "I don't even care anymore." He addresses them, his unruly roommates: "Just don't put fish in the microwave and be in bed by nine."

He carries around these little electronic music makers, gadgets that look like calculators but make arcade sounds. In another life, he says, he would write music for *Miami Vice.* He starts to make up a song about Fluke Skywalker.

"What will my tombstone say?" he wonders. *"He meant well."*

The next day, he can't get out of bed. The coldest day of the winter so far, and he feels it. Pain shoots through his feet. He sleeps all day, and the next. He calls the hotline. His tears are hot on his face. Our room has begun to smell like the cafeteria at the VA hospital. He's forgotten his meds; he's spilled ink on the bed. "Jesus, Aaron," I say. "Get it together."

"Leave me alone," he tells me. His eyes are dark with disgust.

So I do. I give him space, rage-wash the dishes, rage-wash the laundry. I don't want to be anywhere near that room, anyway. It has become his room, not our room. Worse, it has become his father's room. It is the room of a sick old man. All it's missing are saucers of dried cat food on the floor.

"I'm sorry," he tells me later, stumbling from the room. He's been stumbling lately. Falling. His balance is shit.

"Okay," I say. I float past with my laundry basket, the boys' clothes stacked in two towers. I don't want to talk about it now. The boys have come home from school on the bus, and I need to make them a snack. Nico's best friend is with them. He's recently moved back into our school district after his mother, our friend Demitra, separated from her boyfriend, and she found herself needing afterschool care. The boys are buzzing with joy. I rage-butter their bagels. Then they play *Fortnite* while I work on an article in my office. All I have to focus on is the screen, the words appearing line by line.

I don't realize how much time has passed—an hour? two?—until Demitra texts. "On the way."

"OK!"

Not much later, from an upstairs window, I see the SUV coming up the long, snowy driveway. It's not the usual white SUV, though; it's maroon. I'm downstairs by the time it's at the top of the driveway and my husband, who I thought was sleeping, steps out of the passenger side in the bright yellow parka he bought in Germany. He thanks the driver. He comes to the door.

"Who was that?"

"Oh, that's Samantha," he says, a polite cheeriness in his voice. He kicks off his snow boots. "She was nice enough to pick me up."

He's been out walking. How long has he been out walking?

"I went that way," he says, pointing away from town. "I must have gone four miles!" He sounds proud of himself. His teeth are chattering.

I close my eyes. "Aaron, it's literally zero degrees outside."

He shrugs. "I needed to walk."

"Why didn't you call me to pick you up?"

"I didn't have my phone."

"You didn't bring your phone? While you were walking four miles in zero degrees? You can barely walk up the stairs, and you thought it would be a good idea to take a fucking *walk*?"

"You didn't want me here." His voice is small; it could fit in a box.

"What?" I want to wrap his shaking body in my arms. I want to smack him.

"You didn't want me here. I tried to apologize. You just walked by me like—" He makes the face he makes, cold and angry, when he's imitating my face.

"Don't do that," I say. "I have to check on the boys."

I knock on Nico's door. The boys are sprawled over the beanbag, intent on the TV screen, oblivious. "Your mom will be here in a minute," I say to his friend. "Start packing up, okay?"

Aaron is coming up the stairs, still in his puffy yellow coat, when I start going down. He says quietly, as though telling me that the dishes in the dishwasher are clean, "I just took a fatal dose."

He walks into my father's old room and lies down on the couch.

"Aaron. What does that mean?"

His eyes are closed. He won't answer me.

"Aaron. What did you take?"

He shakes his head.

"Don't do this. Don't do this." I whisper loudly in his face. "The kids are right here. Right here! Don't do this. What did you take?"

He shakes his head. I pull out my phone.

"What are you doing?"

"Calling 911."

"Don't."

"Of course I'm fucking calling 911. You think you can tell me that and I won't call 911?"

"Don't."

"I am."

I make the call. My husband may be overdosing. I don't know what he took. He won't tell me. I give the address. I hang up. What I feel is fury, disbelief, panic. My brain is expanding, shooting out of my ear, that part of my brain watching the scene on the couch.

"Call them back. Tell them not to come."

"No."

"It might not be enough," he says.

We are in the room where, a little over a month ago, my father lay dying, where for days I lay beside him in the hospital bed. I thought he was barely conscious, but one day as I cried into his shoulder, he patted me gently on the back. "Oh, honey," he would say if he were here right now. He would pat me on the back.

I stood outside the door when the undertaker came for him. I remember the loud zip of the body bag.

"It was just four Ativan," Aaron says. "And four Aleve PMs."

"That's all?"

"And Ambien."

"How many?"

"Maybe four."

"Anything else?"

"Maybe."

"I don't know if that's fatal."

"Well, I'll let God decide."

"Aaron."

"Call them back."

"I'm not calling them." And yet I do call them, somehow, for some reason, I call them back helplessly and say, "My husband says he didn't take a fatal dose after all."

They are still sending the ambulance. "Just let them check him out," the operator says reasonably.

I manage to convince him to walk downstairs, to lie on the little love seat in the family room near the front door. Aaron is deranged and scared. I am afraid he will hurt himself or hurt one of the officers. It is two months since he was strapped down at the hospital. "This isn't the hospital," I say. "I won't let them hurt you."

I pray that the ambulance and our friend won't arrive at the same time. Above all I pray that the kids won't see or hear the ambulance. It seems futile. It is in motion. My brain is still outside my body, and the shame is out there, too, leaving me through my pores. You can't un-piss yourself.

Except something lucky happens. Up the driveway comes the white SUV. Demitra. A little over a month ago, she placed her own suicide calls. She said good-bye to her mother. In the background was her son, yelling, "Mom! Mom! Where are you?" It was his voice that brought her out of it. She told her mother where she was. A Rite Aid. The police found her out back, by the Dumpster, and drove her to the hospital. She was in the psych ward, Aaron's psych ward, for two weeks.

Now I lean out the front door and wave Demitra inside. She sees the urgency in my wave. Zero degrees outside, but she bundles up her baby and comes into the house.

I explain the situation. "I'm so sorry to say this but Aaron may be overdosing on something. The ambulance is coming any minute." He watches us from under a blanket on the couch.

"Hey man," she says, not blinking. "I get it."

What I want is for her to help draw him out of it, the way her son's voice did for her. I want her to speak to him in their language. I want him to see the beautiful baby on her hip and want to live.

"You want me to take the kids so you can deal with this?"

Relief like a river of piss. Yes, yes, that would be great. I run upstairs to get the kids. "I've been where you are," I hear her say to Aaron.

"Yeah," he says.

When the kids come down, they are elated to learn that they're going home with their friend. "You guys want to do pizza?" Yes! Quickly, quickly, get your shoes, don't worry about your car seat. Daddy's sick. Go have fun! Thank you so much!

"Thank you," Aaron tells her, and his face is more open now, not a dark and jagged thing, only scared.

Twenty seconds after her car leaves the driveway, the police car comes up it, followed by the ambulance. It's been perhaps seven minutes since I called 911.

I try to talk to the cop outside, warn him that my husband isn't in a good place, that he was held at the psych ward, that he can't be forced there again, but it's zero degrees. "Can we talk about this inside?" he asks.

The paramedics trail wet puddles of snow onto the concrete floor. They talk to him in calm voices. They call Aaron "man" and he calls them "man" back. They just want to check him out, make sure he's okay. This is exactly what I want. "Okay," he says. He sits up and lets them take his vitals. They ask what he took, and he tries to remember. Meanwhile I leave Stu a message, and though Aaron hasn't seen him in months, he calls back within a few minutes. I repeat the same combination of drugs into the phone. "Doesn't sound fatal," Stu says. "Can I talk to our friend?"

By the time I hand Aaron the phone, he's making jokes about 1970s TV stars with the paramedics.

"Neat house," one says, packing up his equipment. "I saw them building it. Always wondered what it looked like inside."

He has an appointment with his therapist tomorrow, I assure them, and though I am not at all assured Aaron will go, they leave him talking to Stu on the phone. They make him promise not to take any more winter walks. Aaron lifts a hand in good-bye. "Thanks, fellas," he says, and then, a little later, with some warmth, "Thanks, Stu. Thanks for being there." And hangs up.

An hour later, when we pick up the kids, they are still shrill with excitement, playing with the baby, taking pictures of their distorted faces with an app. They are almost wholly uninterested in what has happened tonight, or maybe they don't want to know. "You okay, Dad?" Nico asks, not looking up from the iPad.

"Yeah, I'm okay." Aaron eats three slices of pizza. We each give Demitra a giant hug. Here she is, proof that you can be at your lowest, behind a Rite Aid Dumpster, and then what feels like five minutes later, prepping your coffeemaker for the next morning, planning to live another day.

"Cannot thank you enough," I whisper. Her son will be coming home with my kids on the bus again tomorrow. "If you don't feel comfortable—" I say, but she stops me.

"Girl, please. If anything, I trust you guys more now."

It feels like a week has passed when we get home. It's long dark. We put the kids to bed.

"What did she say?" I ask him when we're in bed ourselves. "When I went upstairs."

His skin is still cold to the touch, but his face is his again.

"She said I was lucky to have a wife who cared."

I like this, of course. I hold his icy hand in mine.

A few days later, while all the boys watch *The Simpsons,* eating the fried rice I've made them, I sneak upstairs and read the Donald Antrim essay in *The New Yorker* that's just arrived: "A Journey Through Suicide." Antrim writes of suicide as a force that resides in a living person. "I believe that suicide is a natural history, a disease process, not an act or a choice, a decision or a wish. I do not understand suicide as a response to pain, or as a message to the living. I do not think of suicide as the act, the death, the fall from a height or the trigger pulled. I see it as a long illness, an illness with origins in trauma and isolation, in deprivation of touch, in violence and neglect, in the loss of home and belonging. It is a disease of the body and the brain, if you make that distinction, a disease that kills over time. My dying, my suicide, lasted years."

The words bring me some comfort. Here he is, having survived, alive for now. The suicide speaks.

Mostly the words bring me dread, because I know them to be true. They provide the clarity of a good diagnosis. What does your husband have? Suicide.

It was a disease Aaron says started in childhood. When he was a little boy, he found a jar of silver beads in a kitchen cabinet. He thought they were bullets. He ate them one by one, then lay down on the kitchen floor to die. He found out later they were cake decorations. He'd overdosed on sugar.

When I was a little girl, I had dreams of calling nine-one-one. What a thrill it would be! That girl married the boy who'd swallowed the silver bullets. I wanted to be close to that desperation, that sharp edge between life and death.

I had been deathly afraid of death. Aaron's courtship of it emboldened me. He was so close to it. Perhaps his lack of fear of it would help me to be less afraid.

But of course I misunderstood his proximity to death for fearlessness. He was fearful. He was fearful because he was so close to it.

It's like the people who jumped from the burning towers, Aaron told me once. That's what being suicidal feels like. They didn't want to die. They were just trying to escape the fire.

You want the suicide attempt to be the climax, because nothing is worse than suicide, but it's not the end, it's a chapter in a ceaseless story, and there is something worse than suicide. Worse that suicide is hallucination. Suicide, the long disease of suicide, is manageable, familiar. You like your sad husband more than your crazy husband. You like him forlorn, in bed, supine, drained of energy: you can climb on top of him and take some of his heat. Or you can wake him up, revive him. And you recognize him: you know this guy, the guy you have lived with for twenty years. The psychotic one, though. You don't know him. And what you don't know, you fear.

Aaron's body is covered in sores, more than I've ever seen. Old sores, new ones. They mottle his thighs like the flesh of a blueberry scone. One on his side, under his armpit, I accidentally graze while giving him a hug, and he howls in pain. I don't touch him again for the rest of the day. It looks a little like Ohio, but I don't say so. Last week, after several nights of no sleep, his brain on fire, he saw all kinds of things in his sores. Just one kind of thing, actually: athletes. "Doesn't this one look like a golfer?" he says. That one, a basketball player.

"Don't even start," I say.

I don't know then that this is better, this is good: that the things he sees and feels are on, in, his own body. I can simply say, "I don't see that, babe."

It starts with a string of texts. They arrive while I'm driving home one night, the car full of groceries. I don't see them until I'm inside.

"Did you see them?" Aaron says, taking my grocery bags from me.

"See who?"

I check my phone.

> Please hurry. Seriously. I'm hearing cars And the people are on that lot next to us with flashlights again I'm not kidding. scared
>
> I'm worried. It also might be police. do not invite them in. Seriously
>
> They can't come in unless invited
>
> If it looks sketchy call the cops

I ignore the contradiction: call the cops on the cops. "I didn't see anyone out there, babe."

"Will you look with me?" he says. "Please?"

We leave the groceries on the floor. He puts on his boots, his jacket, grabs his heavy-duty flashlight with the broken button, which needs to be pressed with a paperclip to turn on. The driveway is slick with ice; the night sky is still mostly blue. He bounces the light across the field. Next door, three acres away, I can see the weak lights of our neighbor's house, the wisp of smoke from its chimney, the black square of the barn. In the field between, nothing but snow and scrub, and the camping tent and horse trailer left behind months ago by the people who bought the land. They have been in the field before, on a handful of days, walking the property, truck parked in the grass. But now the tent is collapsed with snow. Cars come and go on the road. The flashlight bounces off the Adopt a Highway sign.

"I don't see anyone out there, babe."

Aaron drops the flashlight. "Oh, good." Hand to chest. "They're gone."

THEORY 9

Sometimes I just don't get it. How the formication, the wriggling, the itching, can bother him so much. How it can *scare* him so much. So there's something, a parasite, in his body. So what?

It takes him spelling it out for me. When your body has been violated, anything that's in your body without your permission is another violation.

NEW MOON

like listening to Dad play his music," Nico says, falling asleep one April night. "It's so soothing."

Aaron himself hasn't slept in days. From the living room, the sound of his keyboard climbs the stairs, slow and eerie and electronic, part horror movie score, part love song.

"Me, too," I say.

"I don't know why he doesn't *do* something with it," Nico says. Without his glasses, his eyes are a painfully beautiful gray-blue. I fear he's repeating my own words back to me.

The music spikes now, tendrils, skates over a glass lake. Pac-Man meets Brian Eno meets Edward Scissorhands meets Vic Chesnutt's "Speed Racer." Maybe he's recording it and maybe he's not. Probably no one else will ever hear the song, if a song is what it is. It is notes without a beginning or end. Every day the song is a little different. But mostly it's the same.

"It's for him," I tell Nico. "It's for us. Lucky us."

Thing is, he doesn't want to take his meds. They are making him miserable. They exacerbate everything, making his agony only more agonizing. They force everything out: a reckoning. "They're killing me, too," he says.

He says, "I don't have the strength."

He says, "I can't do it anymore."

Abruptly, he drops all of them.

It makes no sense to me. He wants to stop trying just when we have answers?

"Please don't do this," I say.

I say, "I know it's hard."

I say:

"It's not forever. Maybe just a few more months."

"They said it would get worse before it gets better."

"What's your treatment plan, then?"

"You're so brave. You're amazing. You can do it."

"'Nothing' is not a treatment plan."

It goes like this for a few days. Time stretches out, all the little orange bottles untouched, the pill chart standing there on the desk like a fool, and the panic reaches into my throat. It's the kind of adrenaline that comes with trying to give medicine to a very scared and angry cat. How to get the medicine into the cat? If I am clever enough, I can do it.

When I was four years old, I was prescribed an antibiotic for an ear infection. The medicine was a viscous liquid the color and taste of chemically produced banana. It was horrible. I refused. My father drove to Mike's Bookstore in downtown Gainesville. Mike's sold books and pipe tobacco. It was our favorite place. He brought home *Old Mother Hubbard*. I remember the thrill I felt seeing him slide it out of the familiar white paper bag, the thrill of a new book and the thrill of understanding how a bribe worked. Okay. It was an easy choice. I took the medicine.

This is the desperation that leads me to promise to have sex with my husband every day that he takes his meds.

It's a joke, ha ha, but then it's not. We make it light, flirty. Oh really? Why not? Well when you put it that way. I rationalize. What's wrong with sex? He's in agony; I can help relieve his pain. I can reward him for his obedience.

April moves on. Our plan is carried out cheerfully. There is a certain afternoon when the clouds clear and the snow has melted into the distant fields and we sit on the deck in our shirt sleeves, feeling that spring might come.

It lasts eleven days. Not a bad run. Then it comes for him and brings him to a place even sex can't touch, where he's lost to me again, and he is in one room, and I'm in another. He is on the couch, drinking. I am in the bedroom, where the medicine bottles sit like neglected children, and I cry in defeat and shame, because I have lost.

He has lost more weight. He's one-forty, skinny as a sickle, a Demogorgon. "There's not much left of me," he says. He drops his pants and shows me his testicles. They are red, swollen; they look as though they've been scraped on a sidewalk. He holds them in his hands fearfully. And then his testicles move. Something is inside them, moving. Like a baby's foot across a pregnant belly. Like a wind across a plain. They move.

On a video conference with Laura, he'd complained about his testicles. He was frantic. I was embarrassed. "Hold on," she'd said. She'd put on her reading glasses. She typed something into her keyboard. We were sitting on our bed. "That sounds like Bartonella," she said.

It made a kind of sense. He was already on Bartonella meds. We knew that Morgellons patients responded well to Bartonella treatments. He'd all but been diagnosed with it, even though he'd tested negative for the bacteria. But there I was, ashamed, and he was suffering, and it was real.

Now I watch his testicles move. Is this Bartonella? Something wants out. In fact, something will get out. *Things* shed from them, cells, fibers, flakes, flukes. Who knows. He reports it when he leaves the bathroom. He looks like he's just seen someone killed.

He flares; he crashes; he heals. He drinks. We wait for the next time. He breaks up, over email, with Dr. Savely. It's a friendly breakup, but still, I have to swallow my disappointment.

And then something unexpected happens. In early May, the new moon passes. And for the first time in over a year, Aaron doesn't break out.

A week later, Aaron turns forty-seven. In the morning, the kids present the cards they've made for him. From Nico: "Happy Birthday Dad. You don't suck." From Henry: "Happy Birthday Dad. You are a stinky ass. You smell like beans and cheese." He opens his presents: a summer bathrobe, pajamas, boxer briefs (size small—the mediums I bought him last month are too big). He models everything for us, twirling around.

It's a rainy, gloomy day, and after the kids are at school we go back to bed together. The bed is in the closet. "Let's put the bed in the closet," he said last week, joking, and then we measured it and realized it fit snugly, a queen-sized bed in a walk-in closet. We rolled out the hanging clothes. We'll turn the closet into the room and the room into the closet! When we close the doors, we're in a little nook, a cave. I've strung up little globe lights above the bed. It makes me absurdly happy, this secret bedroom within a bedroom, the weird magic of it.

"Forty-seven," I say. "You're the oldest guy I've ever slept with." It's a joke, every year.

"Oh yeah?" He climbs over me. His arms and chest are firm, but he has lost so much weight so quickly that, in this position, his belly sags with extra skin. "I look like an old man," he laughs, screwing up his face.

"You look so good," I say, pulling him closer. My own belly sags with extra skin, the flesh of pregnancy I don't seem to have any hope of shedding. "You've spent nearly half your life with me."

"Is that all?" And then he kisses me, and we're belly to belly. I fit my fingers to his bony spine like piano keys. Inside the circle of my limbs are all the warm, aging organs that keep him alive.

Afterward, I tell him, "You don't fuck like an old man. Or a sick one."

But already his smile looks a little strained. By the afternoon, little candle-tips of red burn through the skin on his arms. We'd planned to go out for a birthday dinner, but he spends the evening in the bathroom, chipping away at his skin. This was not part of the plan. We're in the safe hammock between the new moon and the full moon. But the tide is finding him here.

He emerges in his new bathrobe, still in its tags. One half of his mustache is coated with what looks like a creamy sawdust. "Your mustache is blond," I inform him. He puts a hand to his face. His hands are coated with it, too, like a lotion he hasn't rubbed in. We barely blink. All the husbands I might have had, I think, are here in one body: a dark-haired one, a fair-haired one; a big one, a thin one; a sick one, a well one; gentle and rough, moody and sunny, hopeful, hateful, fearful, loving, tender.

I say, "I'm sorry this is happening on your birthday."

He puts his forehead to my forehead. "I don't want to do this again," he mumbles.

"I know," I say. "I know."

At the end of May, it's our turn to go to the couples retreat on Owasco Lake, our third. Every year now, we trade childcare with our friends in the RCA program. We drop off our kids with their bags of groceries and sleeping bags and then we drive an hour north, through farm country and lake country, cow dung and canoes and what reminds me and Aaron of the sea grass of our Florida youth. Lilacs and wisteria bloom along the road. Last May, when we stayed home, Aaron was on lithium. He was puking in the school parking lot. Our world has been around the sun since then, and we can feel it.

Last time we were here, two years ago, we opened the retreat as the speaker couple. We were so nervous we were shaking. We sat around the circle of fourteen couples and shared every detail of our story, an hour of it, reading from the script we'd written together—the drugs, the suicide attempts, the childhood abuse, separation, recovery. Afterward, the other couples surrounded us as though we were a bride and groom, hugging us, thanking us, sharing their own stories. "It was remarkable," one man from our home group said. "It was almost too much," he admitted. "Like watching surgery."

One couple was from another upstate group. Theresa and Steve. She was a little older than me, with dark curly hair she tamed into a neat braid, and had a calm, direct way of speaking that made me want to be at ease. He was a little older than Aaron, with a neat haircut and a penchant for board games. We asked them to be our sponsor couple at the end of the retreat, sitting on the porch. "Wow," she said admiringly. "You just came out and asked, like a prom date."

They thought about it. Then they said yes.

After that, every two weeks, we spoke on the phone, saying the serenity prayer together, the unity prayer, meditating, sharing, working on our steps. They listened, validated, challenged, soothed. They were like our coupleship fairy godparents. Sometimes just hearing their voices through the speakerphone made me sit up straighter, slowed my breath down.

Now, at the retreat again, in the big wood-paneled room Aaron says looks like the library in Clue, Theresa and Steve are leading the icebreaker. We pass a ball under our legs, over our shoulders. We guess which famous person we are. Then, on a piece of paper, we write down a regret. We ball it up and throw it into the middle of the room. Anonymous. Then we grab one and, going in a circle, read it aloud. Missed opportunities, uncontrolled anger, unmet needs. The chemist in our home group reads mine.

I can't tell if Aaron flinches. Part of me wants him to acknowledge it. Wants him to need this and only this to heal, a public amends in this place of recovery.

Afterward, Aaron skips the bonfire—the smoke makes his chest close up. It's just me and Theresa and the chemist left when I remember the bag of balled-up regrets. Together we feed them to the fire, watch them disappear. It feels pretty good, in that way that manufactured rituals feel good, though I wonder if Aaron should be the one doing the burning. I feel unsettled. Is he mad that I stayed at the bonfire? Does he resent that I aired such a sore subject? When I get back to our room, after ten, he's already asleep, facing the wall. In past years, we've always pushed our beds together, but tonight I fall asleep in my twin bed across the room.

The next morning, when I come back from the early meditation, he's gone. I find him taking a walk down by the water. He's got that look on his face, says he's fine but I know he's not.

In the next session, led by our sponsor couple's sponsor couple, we struggle. Aaron's not feeling well, can't sit still. His hands are turning blue. He says he feels like his blood isn't flowing. He leaves the session, and I cry. People bring me tissues. I clear my tears, try to focus. The session is on acknowledging our universal human needs.

In the afternoon, Theresa and Steve invite us to their cabin. Most of us stay dorm-style in the main house, but they won the lottery this year and have a separate place down the road, with a private porch overlooking the lake. The air feels thinner here, silkier. We sit in our rockers and talk.

The morning's quarrel seems like it happened last week. We try to explain what it was all about. Mixed signals, cold shoulders. We both felt abandoned. "It's hard for me to see him get up and leave," I say. Theresa reminds us that, at her first retreat, she almost got in her car in the middle of a session and drove away. We laugh, imagining the sight.

Steve is sharing a porch swing with me. "Are you powerless over Aaron?" he asks. And for the tenth time that day, I cry. I nod. Aaron smiles at me from his rocking chair.

I used to think retreats were cheesy. The ice breakers and nametags and craft table, the gratitude meditations. But we've come to find some ease here, even some transcendence of our wretched selves. Some higher power.

It isn't until that night, lying with Aaron in bed, that I think to ask him if he heard my regret read at the icebreaker. He didn't. He didn't feel great that night, couldn't focus. I tell him what I wrote. *I regret not believing in my partner's pain.* He pulls me close to him. All night we hold each other in our pushed-together twin beds.

The week after we get home, Aaron announces he wants to take his meds again. Not the antipsychotics, but the antibiotics, the antiparasitics. Even the liquid stuff that looks like egg yolks, that once made him say, "I'd rather die than take this." He takes it. By himself. Then he settles on the couch and closes his eyes. I tell him, "You're the bravest boy I know."

He says, "Fuck right I am."

He takes it as long as he can, when he can. Which is not long, and not often. But there's something else going on, he says. There's something this medicine isn't touching. In the middle of the night, in the middle of a flare, I check on him in the living room. He's doing something in his bathrobe. When he sees me, he nearly jumps out of his skin. He closes his bathrobe. The next morning, sitting on the couch, he tells me, calmly, firmly, that there's something inside him. He shows me the video on his phone. "Just wait for it," he says. In his distended navel, on the screen, something is breathing. Seething. If I ask myself, *Could that thing be a giant worm, could those pointy pores be a lamprey's suction teeth trying to break through the skin,* the answer is *yes.*

"I see this thing with *hair,*" Aaron explains. He's said this before, but his tone is different now. It's Aaron saying it, not some scary-eyed stranger. "At least it *looks* like hair. Black hair. It darts out of my skin, and quick as it comes out, it's gone again."

The internet is no help. Look up "Parasite + Hair" and what you will get is the same skin-tingling story about a parasitic twin discovered in the belly of a teenage boy in India. The story says, WARNING: GRAPHIC CONTENT. The growth, which is still technically alive but not technically human, resembles a rock implanted with Halloween-costume teeth, sprouting a rope of black hair six feet long, that has been growing for eighteen years. It looks like it belongs in a Ripley's museum. The parasitic twin, absorbed through the umbilical cord, has been living in the boy's abdomen since birth. "That evil has been tormenting him for years," his father says.

Aaron says, "That is the most horrifying thing I have ever seen."

There have been only two hundred such cases reported worldwide, the article says. So rare! Impossible!

Do we suppose that Aaron has a parasitic twin inside him? Odds are: no. But do we believe, at this point, that whatever is inside Aaron is as rare and as evil as this twisted hulk of brain and bone? Absolutely.

He's been saying it for months—for years—and I've been telling him, telling myself I believe him. Mostly, I've been thinking, *Maybe.* Mostly I've been thinking, *I don't know.* It's not just the video on Aaron's phone. I've seen a dozen videos like this, explained them away. It's his end-of-the-rope, you've-gotta-be-fucking-kidding-me voice. It's the fact that no doctor we've come across can explain the insane cycle of symptoms except for Laura's full moon theory, and that no patient we've come across has a parasite load big enough to trigger it. It's that thing that was in his lung, and now isn't. How to explain it? I'm lining up all the cards still, trying to use logic to justify this conclusion, but now they're not just cards dealt by others. It's what they're leaving out. It's a hole. It's a feeling. "There is Still. Something. In. Me."

The day of the Strawberry Moon, we drive down to meet Laura in her office for the first time in months. In the car, we agree our expectations are low. How can they be otherwise? But there's something reassuring about her office, with its essential oil diffuser, the little rack for our shoes. Laura is freshly blond, her toenails royal-blue on the plush cream carpet. "Well, you look great," she says to Aaron. He does: he's in a smart plaid button-down with a peach T-shirt underneath, peaking out of the collar. He's thin. He's got a few days' beard. The lesions on his hands have healed for now.

"So. What's been going on?"

Aaron asks me to tell her what I've seen. I tell her. There's something inside him. There's still something very wrong. At first Aaron sends me pictures to show her; he can't do it himself. But the Wi-Fi isn't working, so reluctantly he tilts his phone to her. The flukey things. The flies. His distended stomach. Her eyes go big. "Send that one to me," she says again and again.

She takes notes, does research, bouncing between her notebook and her laptop and her phone. Could it be cutaneous leishmaniasis, a parasitic infection spread by sandflies? It causes skin lesions that look not unlike Aaron's. She shows us the pictures. Could it have been transmitted by a tattoo needle? When was Aaron's last tattoo? About five years ago, he says. He pats his right shoulder. Underneath his shirt is a half-sleeve of Keith Haring people, dozens of little figures spilling to his elbow. She turns up some articles about NIH research on parasites introduced by tattoo needles. She says, "I have a lot of reading to do."

Whatever it is, it doesn't seem to be affecting the other people in our house. "This is something that was transmitted directly to you," Laura is certain. This puts Aaron at some ease. "Either that, or your immune system was so compromised that they were able to fight off what you weren't."

She puts her pen down. "I have a client who just saw a parasitologist in Manhattan. He's the only person on the East Coast who tests live in the office." A Dr. Caine. She will call him after we leave.

"I have to tell you, Aaron," she says, tapping on her phone. "I absolutely believe you."

I think Aaron might cry. "Thank you," he says.

After the appointment, we stop at the medical marijuana office in Binghamton to pick up some oil. Aaron vapes it in the car like a madman on a full moon trying to ward off a parasitic infection. He once created a fake Facebook group called Vape Dads, before he'd ever vaped, with a logo and everything. *Don't judge my path until you've walked my journey!* Like some of his public attempts at humor, this one either fell short or flew over most people's heads. Most of his friends thought it was serious. Now, in the car, I say, "Let's go home, Vape Dad."

He has stopped taking his meds again—what can I do?—but he drinks and he smokes, smokes and drinks. Beer, whiskey, vodka, downing it in shots like medicine. He doesn't like the vape pen, so he takes to smoking the oil on a sheet of foil out on the deck, like someone who knows what he's doing. Catching sight of it shoots me in the heart with a dull little Nerf dart. "I'm sorry," he says. "I wish I didn't have to do this." I'm sorry, too. I wish I didn't have to see it. I wish it didn't work so well. Four days after the full moon, he's feeling the crawling all over his body, and he's bearing ten new pounds, but he's not breaking out.

"I can't go through it again," he says. When I tell him, "That whiskey might kill your liver before the flukes do," he says, "Then at least I'll be out of my misery."

Meredith visits. She sees the fifth of whiskey on the floor by the couch. She raises both eyebrows. Later, over tacos and margaritas, she brings it up. "Trust me," I tell her. "I wish alcohol were the only problem."

I don't worry about it much anymore, I tell her. The alcohol helps with his symptoms. He drinks when he's in pain.

"Alcohol doesn't really help with pain," she says.

I shrug. "He says it does."

There's nothing moderate about Aaron's drinking this week. But he's not drinking like a man trying to kill himself, either. He is drinking like a man trying to outrun God. Outrun death.

Plus, he's present when he drinks now. He doesn't even seem drunk, and he says he isn't. I don't tell Meredith this part. Who would believe it? He's happy, goofy, jokey. He snuggles Henry on the couch. He goes to Nico's fifth-grade graduation. He's Vape Dad. If he weren't drinking, I know, he wouldn't be at graduation. He'd be home, on fire.

Eventually, we know, it will catch up with him, and he'll stop, at least for a while. Is this messed up? Of course. Is it more messed up than the horror that's happening to his body? I'm not sure. Was alcohol put on the planet to suppress the horror of nature, or is it a horror of nature? How can it be anything but both?

"Don't be mad," Meredith says. "I just worry about you."

"I know," I say. "I worry about me, too."

"I just think that, look, maybe he'll be cured of whatever this disease is, but you'll still have a lot of problems on your hands."

I shake my head. I sip my margarita. I can't remember what those problems were, before he was sick. I don't want to remember.

ETNA ROAD

2010

t was a dump. An old country house, built in 1850, without all of the charming renovations of our Virginia country house. Peeling, sloping vinyl floors I could never get clean, and that sagging AstroTurf porch, and industrial-blue carpet up the steps that were so steep and so narrow we couldn't get our bed upstairs. Layers upon layers of ancient wallpaper. We didn't have the time or money to gut anything, to get to the bottom of the rot. We just carpeted and papered over everything, swept it all, literally, under the rug.

It was a dump, but it was our dump. One way to outsmart a mortgage is not to have one. With the money we got out of our first house and with the first installments from my book, we were able to buy the house outright. We had gone to Ithaca to hunt for houses and found one at the cheapest end of the cheapest range on the market. We were going to live within our means! It even had an accessory apartment, which we thought one day my parents might live in. For now, it would be a little extra income. The apartment opened onto a little deck and a nice flat lawn with a clothesline and the relic of an old wooden fence that bloomed with sunflowers. And on the other side of the fence was a squat little duplex with a shake roof and a satellite dish. It did not take long for someone to tell us that the duplex had been the site of the Christmas murders. What Christmas murders? We were new in town.

This was not quite true. In 1989, days before Christmas, in an eerie echo of the Clutter murders, a family of four had been bound, shot, and burned. That house was miles away. The duplex next door was where the killer had lived. When the police had found him, he was sitting on his bed with a gun under his chin. He fired a shot at the officers, and they shot him dead.

At least we don't live there, I reasoned.

Our move to Ithaca had been decided by the fates of the labor market, but it had been sanctioned, pre-approved, by Aaron. *Go for it,* he'd said when I applied for this one and only job. Neither one of us had set foot in Ithaca. It was just an idea.

"It's awfully far," my mother said.

That he wouldn't look for work in Ithaca had also been settled with little conversation. Perhaps there was some unspoken math involved: a sacrifice for a sacrifice. He did a little eBay on the side. "He's a stay-at-home dad," I told people when they asked, and he was. Aaron stayed home with Nico while I worked, potty-training and making oatmeal and taking him on long drives for his naps and watching *Yo Gabba Gabba* and making up songs that should have been on *Yo Gabba Gabba,* singing them in his robot voice. "Don't—Pick—Your—Nose!"

If we could ignore the smell of sulphur from the well water, if we could keep our gaze from the neighbor's house, it did feel like a fresh start. I loved my new job. I loved my new friends. I loved Ithaca, the waterfalls and the lake and all the playgrounds, every weekend a new playground for Nico to explore, with their elaborate wooden bridges and rocket ships and rope webs Aaron and I stood under, wood chips in our shoes, saying, "We're right here, you're fine!" If I think hard back to that first year in Ithaca, I think I can remember that Aaron loved it, too.

After another surgery, after almost another year of trying, I got pregnant again. I found out in a hotel halfway to Chicago, where Aaron and I were driving to my friend Jen's wedding. My parents were in Ithaca with Nico. I went to a roadside pharmacy and bought the test. At the wedding, Aaron drank enough for both of us and we dirty-danced and had hotel sex and dreamed our new life into existence, the way you can really only do when you're in another place. The foreignness of Chicago gave us city-sized sights. We got home just before Christmas. My

parents stayed with us, our first holiday in Ithaca. I wrapped the pregnancy test and gave it to them, and my mom howled with joy. "Did you
pee on that thing?" my dad asked.

In January, we put the accessory apartment up for rent. The first call
was from a woman named Emily. When she arrived that night to look
at it, she had a one-year-old baby on her hip. *Single mother,* I thought.
Her long red hair was piled on top of her head, a scarf wrapped up
to her chin, her glasses foggy from the cold. She was maybe a little
younger than I was, but that night she had the look of someone older,
someone who had five minutes ago fled a war. It was a look I recognized, and that I would remember when I was the one, two years later,
looking for apartments for me and my children. She didn't smile or chat
as I made faces at the baby, as she looked around at the little kitchen,
the living area, the bed and bath. She did some math in a notebook, first
month plus deposit. She's not going to take it, I reasoned. It was too
small; she didn't like it. I was disappointed, perhaps because I wanted
to help her—save her!—to be in proximity to whatever trouble she had
been in, to watch our babies play together and to see her transform into
a person who smiled. Ridiculous, that I was a landlord, yet I liked it,
liked that it was a position that afforded me grace to give.

She called a couple days later, though, and said, "I'll take it."

How does any mother raise a family without another woman and her
baby next door? Well, having a husband who stayed at home helped.
We were all in it, our little village. We took care of the kids together.
She took Nico to her place so Aaron and I could go on dates. We took
her daughter to our place so she could go to meetings. She came over
to do her laundry while we all watched *Yo Gabba Gabba.* Some nights,
she came over to watch a movie while her daughter slept on the other
side of the wall and Nico slept upstairs, two baby monitors posed on
the coffee table side by side. We played *Just Dance* and sat for hours in
the playroom and Emily made the most amazing desserts, cookie dough

balls frozen in chocolate, full of fat and not pretty. Her apartment was messy, clothes everywhere, little crescents of construction paper scattered across the floor. I loved it. Our side of the house was messy, too, the vacuum cleaner standing guard at the front door next to the bag of kitty litter, sippy cups abandoned in the couch cushions. My colleagues had kids, too, but I still had not invited any of them over. I was ashamed of our little house with its trash-heap porch and thrift-store kitchen. But when Emily knocked on the door, we did not clear the clutter. She was a compatriot.

When the weather got warm, as my belly grew, we frosted the kids in sunblock and picnicked in the grass and they chalked the stone steps and licked Popsicles while we planned their wedding. We laughed. They were one and two years old.

"No, I'm serious," Emily said.

I stopped laughing. "Me too." Then we laughed again.

The two of us pushed the kids in strollers down the shady country road, past the murder house, past the house with all the dogs, past the abandoned house with grass growing out the windows, past the rusty trailer with the rusty swing set hiding behind the fence, the sick smile of the clothesline that made me shiver. I told her some of our history, skimmed the surface like a lake, leaving the muck at the bottom. Emily told me about her marriage, though I could sense there was much she was leaving out, too. She told me about her husband, the man she'd followed to Ithaca for his Ph.D. at Cornell, only to find out he was having an affair with a woman back home. He came over now and then to pick up their daughter. He was a nice enough guy. Aaron helped him move. They had worked out custody while the lawyers worked out the divorce. Emily was a lawyer herself, licensed in California but not in New York. She was working at the Gap for now. A gap. She had a dark sense of humor that rivaled Aaron's and a disgusting sweet tooth and knew everything about musicals and needed saving from no one, I was chastened to learn, least of all me. If she had been saved, she had saved herself.

One day a delivery of flowers came to our door. We signed for them. When we handed them over to Emily, she blushed a little. They were from her mother, she told us. She sent her flowers on her sober anni-versary every year. That year, I think, was seven.

Some days, we heard her singing through the wall. Madonna. Top of her lungs, shrill as the ceiling.

Before I left for my book tour, I had Aaron take a picture of me stand-ing with my new book—my book!—balanced on my head, my belly big in my pink maternity top. *Look at me doing everything and having everything I've ever wanted. Look at me balancing it all. Dare it to fall.* The picture was taken in front our new shower curtain. I cropped out the moldy bathroom tile.

I was across the country putting on mascara when the text came through: *I have this weird rash.* It was the first in a series of photos. I did not know that there would be a ceaseless stream of them. That in the future, my phone would be an objective archive of irreconcilable images, no buffer or blindfold, no trigger warning. A birthday party, a field trip, blood and bugs and bruises, a Saturday at the lake.

You've seen those pictures before. Swipe past them.

ME IN FRANCE

n Toulouse, we eat baguettes with fig jam. A breakfast of it, the four of us each with our own, *oui*, just a baguette, *s'il vous plaît*. It is hot. By noon the bricks of Place du Capitole burn through the soles of our shoes. I listen to middle-aged French women ask me questions in a library, then in a bookstore, and think, Thank goodness for middle-aged women who keep libraries and bookstores open in every country, nod, listen to the translator translate their words to me and mine to them. I feel immeasurably lucky.

We are here at the invitation of an international literary festival. A few days in Toulouse, then a few days in Paris, then nearly a week in London where I'll be doing another conference. Two weeks in Europe, because we haven't been to any of these places before, and because I'm almost forty and other people are paying for part of it and who knows when we'll get the chance again.

Two weeks. The rhythm of our lives. We have done our best to prepare for the worst. What if Aaron breaks out—inevitably, on the full moon, won't he break out?—what if he goes mad, needs a hospital, in a country whose language we don't speak? What if he needs me when I'm working? Will he even be able to walk around, see the city? I imagine him and the kids stuck in the hotel for two weeks, while Aaron sleeps, the kids zoned out in front of European TV.

But in Toulouse, the sunshine, the novelty, the stately brick beauty, the ubiquitous cafés where beer and wine are drunk all day, are a shock to Aaron's sick system. While I am driven to events by middle-aged women in European cars, he ventures out with the boys for sandwiches at the vegetarian place they've found, to the record store, the toy stores, before returning to the AC of the hotel, battered by the heat. At night, after the sun goes down—9:30, 10:00!—we meet under the big white tent strung with lights, entering through the courtyard that is neither inside or nor outside, eating dinner at long tables with other authors on tablecloths held down in the wind with half-full bottles of wine. We eat baguettes with fig jam. Henry asks for more, and more.

By the third afternoon, a Saturday, it's 104 degrees. The boys have ridden every carousel in the city, crouched in the shade of every statue. We walk to bookstores, cafés, a church, any place we think might be cooler than the streets, though there is no AC here, nearly none. It's the summer of 2019 and cities across France are readying for a weekend of Yellow Jacket protests, and though we don't see anyone in yellow jackets, we see hordes of police in riot gear, shields and helmets and guns, head to toe in thick black clothing that looks as though it's made by Marvel Studios. We feel sorry for them and are vaguely on edge, mostly because we don't know how on edge to be. This is not our country. In a square we see an ambulance and a cluster of people, hustling police, and for a moment fear a flare of violence, but it is just a woman who has fainted in the street of heatstroke. We retreat to the hotel. I don't know how on edge to be because I am on a family vacation, and my husband is sick, and he is drinking, because it keeps him from being sick, and because he hasn't gotten really sick on this trip, not yet. All day and night we come in and out of the hotel. Aaron loves a hotel more than anything and he loves this one. If we might just always stay in this air-conditioned hotel, the white marble lobby with its glass water jugs, one with slices of lemon, one with lime, perhaps he will never be sick again.

In Paris, our hotel is decidedly less comfortable. We spend the first hour in our room chasing flies with a rolled-up magazine. From the balcony we overlook Gare du Nord, which at night is beautiful in its glassy light, but by morning is as romantic as Penn Station, with its honking cars and desperate cabbies and men selling cigarettes on the street. The sidewalks smell of piss. One morning I wake early to sneak out for coffee at the Starbucks in the station, and on the couch in the lobby, the night clerk is snoring, his hairy stomach hanging out of his shirt.

In the identical bistros along rue de Dunkerque, we eat baguettes with jam. "So many baguettes here!" Henry remarks. We take taxis, rent Lime scooters, ride the Metro, to the Louvre, the zoo, Notre Dame with her scaffold sheath. On the train, Aaron makes a game with Henry, touching his nose when the alarm buzzes each time the doors open, then releasing it when the alarm stops. Henry laughs and laughs. In the Metro station, the boys want to take a picture in front of a *Stranger Things* season three poster, the characters hanging upside-down. We are in Paris and all you guys can think about is *Stranger Things*! Aaron makes another game, posing for pictures as though he's capturing a landmark between his thumb and forefinger, the way tourists do, except he's off, way, ridiculously off. He laughs and laughs. The kids do it, too. I can't take you guys anywhere! Henry and I climb the stairs to the first platform of the Eiffel Tower. Aaron and Nico are scared of heights, and I realize as I am climbing the stairs of the Eiffel Tower, I am, too. When we come down, we all cross the street and buy crepes and ride the carousel, and Aaron is drinking a green slushie that tastes like Listerine, and laughing as the sun sets, as we try and try to take a family selfie in front of the tower. It makes me want to cry, my hunger to get us all into the frame, to live inside this memory, the goodwill and good health, to make it last.

On a corner not far from the tower, a news column. Aaron pauses, slurping his slushie. It is the kind of old-fashioned column you see all around Paris: the round green pillar with a fancy hat, slapped with news bulletins and ads. Later, when I look them up, I will discover that they are called Morris columns.

"That thing gives me déjà vu." Aaron points. "I have a picture of myself in front of one of those."

"Here?" I ask.

"It must have been at Epcot." He shrugs. "Weird."

On our last night in Paris, we find the vegan restaurant we wish we'd found the first day. We walk until Aaron is too weak and the boys are whining, and then we take a cab. It's late by the time we get there, ten o'clock. The couple at the table one foot from us is smoking, and we don't care. We have become so Parisian! What is bedtime? We order pizza and waffles and burgers and little mugs of puddings and soufflés. Aaron orders gin and tonic and I order wine. From the table, at the threshold of inside and outside, we watch the full moon rise over rue Montmartre. It hangs like a clock tower over the cobblestone street. Aaron turns pale. His forehead sweats. His belly grows big. Our dinner lasts an hour, two hours. It is nighttime, summer, midnight. Dinner is so good we order it all over again. Aaron grows into an old man. Earlier in the day he was young, his chin stubbled, his waist slim. He posed for pictures in cafés, on the streets, in sunglasses and shorts, faking the Frenchiest faces he could make. Now his stomach stretches against the fabric of his blue Oxford shirt. Between the buttons, I can see the staring eye of his belly button; it's as sudden and violent as if I can see into his guts. "Whoa, Dad," the kids whisper, in awe. It is not the weight of two dinners, of two gin and tonics. But he flags the waiter and orders a third.

On the Eurostar to London, the boys don their enormous headphones and begin their season three binge of *Stranger Things*. No spoilers, I say across the aisle. I love *Stranger Things* but I don't want to spend my European vacation watching TV. I know enough from the trailer to know that the characters are sickened by a dark parasitic life force. Aaron doesn't want to watch anymore. Too close to home. Season three can wait. By the time I work up the courage to watch it, months from now, Brexit will have come, finally, and gone.

For nearly a week, we have an Airbnb apartment in Fulham. The ad doesn't mention that it's in a housing project, but the old brick building is lovely, with the laundry hanging off the balconies, the wrought-iron gates, and the stray cats crossing the courtyard. In the back is a wooden play structure that the boys take to, and I watch them play from the second-story kitchen window as I hand-wash the dishes in the cast-iron sink and pretend I am a housewife in post-war London, that all I need are these four small rooms, the washer with its powdered detergent, the toilet with its fussy pull-chain flush. Around five thirty each evening, the song of the ice cream truck can be heard from down the street, and by the time it's pulled behind the playground, the kids have run downstairs with their fists sweaty with pounds. The four of us eat Popsicles on the wooden bench in the shade, and by then it is our house, our park, we have written ourselves into these summer evenings, our chins sticky with sugar.

My husband's antipathies are smug and well-advertised. His list includes almost every place we have lived, every house, every city, none more than Ithaca, which has let him down fundamentally, first by making him sick, then by failing to cure him.

So, to see him fall in love with London, the kind of love he once had for New York, for Florida, makes me a little breathless with hope. He loves our little neighborhood with the Pizza Express on the corner, the convenience store that sells liquor!, the coffee shop with perfect foam cappuccinos and vegan banana bread. He makes a habit of walking there on his own first thing in the morning. One afternoon, he takes the boys there shortly before closing, then comes home with a bag of goodies. "Guy gave me all these free pastries! Nice guy. Good dude."

"You always say that," Henry points out. He imitates him: "'He's a good guy.'"

"Yeah," Nico laughs. "Why isn't everyone just automatically a good guy?"

"I always say that," Aaron says, "because everyone's a good guy. I'm a good guy. I love everyone. Everyone's great."

"You love everyone *here*," I say.

"I know!" Aaron says. "It's weird."

We take the tube to Hyde Park, London Bridge, Big Ben with his scaffold sheath. We walk along the Thames from Borough Market to the London Eye, finding benches for Aaron to rest on along the way. "Like Papou," Henry says. On one bench, he falls asleep for ten minutes, then wakes up, disoriented, and moves on. Can you go on? He can go on. At the Natural History Museum, we visit the Museum of the Moon exhibit. A giant glow-in-the-dark moon hangs from the center of the room. Henry tries to hold it in his hands, the way everyone is doing. Aaron does not want to think about the moon. He leaves the room and goes to look at the petrified animals.

He should have broken out by now, is what we think but don't say. We are pressing our luck.

Still, as the week comes to a close, we dare to dream about what a life could look like here, outside Ithaca, an ocean away from our problems. What if he hasn't broken out because there's some copper balm in the river air here, or some axial proximity to the moon? I don't want to believe it's just the alcohol. I don't want to admit it has that power.

"London is stupid expensive," our cabbie tells us on the way to Heathrow. "You don't want to live here."

Nico is riding in the backward jump seat. It's the boys' favorite spot in London cabs, but not wise, we'll later realize, while playing a Nintendo Switch and eating a package of Sour Cream & Onion Pringles. We're almost to the airport when he vomits all over his lap. When we park, we change him into new clothes, clean the seat, and leave the cabbie a big tip. "I'm just going to go home now," the cabbie decides. In the airport bathroom, we throw out the soiled clothes. The dream is over.

Throughout our trip to Europe, in a black billfold in Aaron's backpack, tucked among pounds and francs, are five American hundred-dollar bills.

On the morning after we land at Newark—we have stayed the night with my cousin Butch in New Jersey—Aaron and I take an early Bergen line train to Penn Station. The boys are sleeping when we slip out of the house. They will spend the day building and painting their own skateboards with Butch in his workshop. They are happier perhaps than they have been on the whole trip to Europe, happy enough that they're not sad about not coming into New York with us.

Besides the five hundred American dollars, we have almost no money left. We have spent it all on our trip. So instead of taking a cab or the subway we walk from Penn Station across Manhattan.

Dr. Caine's office looks like it has not changed in fifty years. In the sublevel waiting room, already full at eight in the morning, the midcentury end tables are cluttered and clustered with magazines and sculptures and braided mahogany lamps. The frame around the current receptionist's window is painted toothpaste green. Here in New York, I think, the doctor could make a lot of money renting out the space for a movie scene in a doctor's office circa 1969.

He already makes a lot of money, though. When the receptionist calls Aaron's name, I take out the billfold and count out the five bills. The office accepts no insurance, and only cash. How many patients does he see a day? Ten? Twenty?

The internet gives the doctor mixed reviews. One five-star reviewer calls him a "genius." A one-star reviewer calls him a "quack."

So I am in a heightened state of my usual state of alertness when the doctor appears in the waiting room and hustles us into his ancient-looking, high-ceilinged office. He is a small, old man with a blunt face and a full head of silky white-blond hair. He has received no records (the office neither emails nor faxes), knows nothing about Aaron's history, so Aaron fills it in, the abbreviated version. The only other parasite testing he did—the stool sample we sent off to Colorado—came back rather inconclusively, showing a very small amount of two types of protozoa.

How long have the symptoms been with you? the doctor wants to know.

"Eight years," Aaron says.

Nothing else could cause those symptoms for eight years, the doctor says. Nothing bacterial. Certainly nothing viral. Some parasites can live, very contentedly, for up to twenty years inside of us.

I see Aaron actually gulp. It is exactly what he wants to hear and the last thing he wants to hear.

Dr. Caine reaches—he doesn't have to reach far—for a book on his desk. It is his own book, on tropical medicine, though parasitic infections are not limited to the tropics, he tells us, paging through the book. We nod. We know, but it is good to hear it from him. Then he reads us a paragraph from his book. I can't really focus on the words he's saying.

I can only pay attention to the fact that he is reading to us from his own book.

In the exam room next door, Aaron puts on a gown, open in back. Is there a sweeter and more vulnerable sight than a man in a hospital gown? I sit in the corner, holding his clothes folded in my lap. We make jokes about the anal swab to come, because when you're about to get an anal swab, there is nothing to do but make jokes. When the doctor comes in, he puts on a pair of gloves and asks Aaron to turn to the wall.

"Which wall?" Aaron asks.

The doctor laughs. In all his years of doing this, he says, no one has asked that question.

Bravely, he turns over. My husband who does not like to turn his back to anyone. He's had colonoscopies before, but he's been blessedly unconscious. What I think of, cringing, is a pap smear. The speculum, the gel, the specimen, the strange feeling of having your cells scraped from some hollow place inside you. I hold my breath while the doctor narrates what he's doing. The only reliable way to test for parasites, he says, is to look for evidence in the rectal mucosa. By the time a stool sample is processed, parasites and their eggs are often dead.

"What are these?" the doctor asks, looking at the purple scars on Aaron's thighs. "Injection sites?"

He says it casually, as if he's not really curious, just making conversation. He says it while his hand is inside my husband.

Aaron lies still. He couldn't move if he wanted to. He says, "No."

"No," I say, sitting up straight. "No, they're scars. From lesions. From the skin disease we mentioned?"

Why don't I tell him that half the doctors we've seen look at Aaron's skin and ask if he's using drugs, that it is the last possible question he needs to hear, with or without a hand up his ass? Why don't I explain that it's not the accusation that he's a drug user that's so insulting, but the accusation that he has somehow caused this disease himself?

When the doctor is done, he leaves the room, and Aaron sits up slowly, as though waking up from a sedative. I don't even want to acknowledge the question that has just been asked, the question that erases every step we've taken toward this office, every one of those five hundred-dollar bills. None of it matters. Now this doctor will be in a pile with the rest of them.

On the walk back to Penn Station, Aaron grows heavy. He shuffles slowly, as though into a wind, but it is not windy; it is a beautiful July morning in New York, still early, the city still waking. All along Central Park South, we walk arm in arm, and I remember our time here eighteen years ago, this path I walked every evening that summer, the joy I felt putting my new cell phone to my ear to call Aaron after a day at work. That summer before the world went wrong, the park was full of magic. The yellow construction cranes reminded me of wild animals, giraffes reaching up into the treetops. Now Aaron stops to rest on street corners, on benches. For a while, we don't speak. Then the light turns. We pause on a corner. "Did he really say that?" he mumbles. "Did I make it up?"

I hold him around the waist. The yeasty heat of his body rises. His body tenses. "He said it," I say. "I'm so sorry."

The rest of the walk, I have to hold him tight to keep him upright, to keep him from stepping into the street. I can feel his body muscling toward the traffic.

Come on, I will him. Let's keep going.

When we return to Ithaca, a package is waiting for Aaron. His uncle, his mother's brother, has sent him a batch of family photos and letters. Aaron thumbs through them, holding them at an arm's length. There are photos of newborn Sandra, Sandra at her first communion, Sandra with her first two children, Sandra hugging Aaron's father in a park. There are class photos of Aaron and one of Aaron and Ashmat sneaking into a room where the grown-ups are clowning, out-clowning them.

Then, there it is: the photo of Aaron in front of the news column! He looks to be twelve or thirteen. He wears sunglasses, a baseball cap, a tight polo shirt, short shorts he calls "nut huggers," and the tall striped socks every American boy wore from 1980 to 1985. He leans with one foot on the ground, one bent back against the newsstand. On the back, in Aaron's preteen handwriting, are the words "Me in France."

He shows me, mouth dropping open. "I *was* in France."

He must have sent the picture to his mother, we conclude. Which probably means he went to France with his father. There is no one to ask, to confirm.

"How could you forget that?" asks Henry. We have just spent two weeks in Europe precisely to "make memories."

How can he have no memory of this trip? What explanation is there, other than the tricks his brain learned to perform at this very age, to survive?

I suppose it was kind, the beast, to let us have our trip. The moment we return, it does, too.

Aaron is sick and I am sleeping when Dr. Caine calls the next week and leaves me a message. I catch the words "inflammation" and "crystals" and "negative serology." What I gather is: evidence of a parasitic infection, but no particular parasites identified. He prescribes a new antiparasitic.

I call back, leave a message. Should he continue to take the other antiparasitics? Is this new one supposed to better than the others?

The next morning, at 5:32 A.M., he leaves another message, this time, for some reason, on Aaron's phone. "I can't really answer your question about medicine," he says. "One of the problems we have with parasites is we don't have the technical capacity to know which medicines are better." He goes into a brief lecture on strep throat, bacteria, cardiology, efficacy rates. All of it sounds very familiar, and then it comes back to me: it's the paragraph he read to us in his office. I wonder if he is sitting there on the phone in the dark of Manhattan, reading again from his own book, a little script he repeats on autopilot. "I can only say that with the amount of medication that you're taking, it's going to be very difficult to define what is working or what is not." The recording garbles a few words. "I think you should stop the medication that you're taking, even three-four days off, then take the other medications, you might well be resistant to the other medications you're taking right now, so that's my answer. I see patients very early, I'm sorry, I call very early, but that's the nature of my practice, so hopefully that will give you a path forward, stop the Ivermectin and Alinia, etc., wait three-four days, start the drugs which I prescribed, and I don't know if they're going to work any better!"

The click is loud. He doesn't say good-bye, take care. He is of course hanging up a real rotary phone.

Aaron saves the message on his phone. Later, listening to it again, we'll laugh at the absurdity of it. Much later.

I'll fill the prescription, but Aaron won't take it. He's done with meds. It will sit in the cabinet, next to a big bottle of vodka.

On my fortieth birthday, Aaron wakes me up to ask me to look at the sores that are blooming over his body. He is naked and manic, standing at the end of the bed, talking to himself. He is standing in his own little weather system. I can almost see its borders around him, the way you can see the edge of a rainstorm from far off. I lie in my bed. I look. I know that, if I lie here, the weather will pass. When he leaves, I turn over and go back to bed and sleep until noon. When I wake up, the children are fed; Aaron is clothed. It's not that I don't feel guilty; it's that I've shielded myself with a poncho for the day, waterproof. "What I want for my fortieth birthday," I say, figuring it out as I go, "is to sleep until noon and go to the pool by myself." Later, when I ask him, he will not remember waking me up. He will apologize.

At the college pool, I lounge on one of the good lounge chairs, under a hat with a book. I swim the breaststroke like my mom, keeping my head above the water. I don't have to take anyone to the bathroom or coax a clinging child to swim to the stairs. The worry is a gentle nibble in my ear. "You guys good?" I text Nico. "Yes," Nico replies. I turn over on my belly to sun my back. It is a dizzyingly sunny day. In Ithaca, I tell myself, such days are not to be wasted.

What I want for my fortieth birthday, I decide, is to throw myself a party. I text my friends. On Saturday, Aaron is moody and sick. His skin has erupted. We get in a fight in the afternoon. He does not want to be at the party. Fine. He spends the day in the bedroom. I spend the day scrubbing the house, then put on a black jump suit. Aaron emerges from the room to say, "You look nice. Have a good party." He gives me a kiss.

One friend brings sangria, another guacamole, another a bottle of prosecco, which burps lavishly when we open it and makes us laugh. Amy Winehouse is at the top of the playlist and Henry dances with me while Nico gives VR tours in his room. The house is warm with bodies, none of them Aaron's, and my happiness is almost enough to fill the house.

I know it before I admit I know it: Aaron's not coming to Vermont. The trip has been there on the calendar, first week of August, for months. Three days at our family camp, three days in Burlington for my dad's overdue memorial.

"You have to understand," he says. "I have to protect my health."

The trip to Europe: he rallied for it. But when we got home, he crashed. The stress of taking another trip, of seeing my family, saying good-bye to my dad, camping at the lake with no privacy, no provisions: it would be too much.

I do understand. But I'm disappointed. "I'm saying good-bye to my dad, too. I need you there."

I do and I don't. I wake the boys early and we drive the six hours to the lake. I haven't been there since my mom's memorial seven years ago, and the kids don't remember it. When we get to the dirt road, I roll down the windows and the smell of the woods floods into the car, the branches brushing the windshield. I'm practically standing in the driver's seat, a kid on a bike. In the road, my nephews greet us wet-haired in towels. Nico and Henry tumble out of the car to greet them. There's Sam and Pete and Cameron and Keri and Aunt Marty, who looks so much like my mom I have to try not to cry when I hug her. Where's Aaron? Not well? Their faces are sad; then we move on. The old cabins my grandfather and uncles built are shells of their former selves, but there's the beaver dam, the stone fire pit off the deck, the old wooden raft we threw rocks at, where another aunt got married in a white bikini. There's the loon on the water, its plaintive howl; only one this year; where's its mate? Sam has strung a new REI hammock in the place where the rope one used to hang. He's brought a new forest-green canoe. The path to the privy I can still navigate with my eyes closed, my bare feet finding the same root steps and moss carpet that were here thirty years ago. We set off on a hike before we can even settle in. Watch for nettles! Where's the old Long Trail cabin? Didn't this streambed used to have water in it? Mom, have you ever seen a bear? Pete gives Henry a boost. Sam and I quote *Stand by Me* and *Goonies* and *The Never-ending Story*. When we get to the caves, the temperature drops: a new space here in the woods. The stone walls rise above us. The boys scamper ahead with their cousins into the ravine. Mom! Look at this! The oldest cousin appears wearing a grisly mask: a skull with antlers. Is it a deer? A moose? Was he dragged here by a bear? Did he slip and fall? Later, when we get cell reception, Nico and Henry will tell their dad about it. They'll tell him about scaling Bare Rock, about chasing frogs and playing poker and swimming to the raft and whittling wood. Now, there is no way to contact him. He might as well be on a different planet. Sometimes the ghost of him hikes behind me, a brush in the bushes, an empty space. My worry, though—there is no space for it here.

For three days, I walk the dirt road around the lake. I paddle out into the middle of it. I swim in it. I bathe in it. I follow the path down the Point between the blueberry bushes where Henry is picking blueberries to the place where the same pair of thirty-year-old snakes are mating on the rocks, past the place where the moss gives way to slippery rock, where the rock gives way, gives out, so the only thing to do is push off into the water, all of you. Underneath the dark surface are fish and frogs and who knows what? A lake monster? I wouldn't say no. Once, swimming together in this lake, my parents passed directly over a beaver. My mother screamed, jumped onto my father's back.

When my mother was a teenager, she complained to her father about not having been baptized. He walked her to the Point, dunked her in the lake, and said, "Look—there's God in the sunset."

Now I am here, treading water, forty, safe, surrounded, alone, in the church of the lake.

At Bare Rock, looking down at the lake, Sam and Pete and I scatter some of Dad's ashes into the wind. We try to make jokes, about the ashes scene in *The Big Lebowski,* about Dad's ashes being eighty percent tobacco, but our voices catch. In the canoe, Nico and Henry and I scatter more, a little here in this corner, on that shore. Mom is here, her ashes, too, and her brother's, and her mother's. When Dad's ashes meet the water, they dissolve, a chalky spirit. Fish food. The boys are a little weirded out. *Shh,* Nico tells Henry, and they let me sit and cry in the bow.

When we get home from Vermont, Aaron is okay.

He has not broken out. He's meditated, exercised, cut his own hair, eaten from the garden, washed the dishes, fixed the upstairs toilet. In that bathroom, on the mirror, are a dozen yellow Post-it notes he has affixed, notes about letting go of resentments, about self-care and solitude and serenity. "Very Al-Anon, babe," I compliment him. I don't want to take them too seriously. I can't let myself. They are the same kinds of notes, I try to remember, that I saw on his mirror his first time in the psych ward. Still, they're elevated. If those were the notes of a man telling himself to live, these are the notes of a man telling himself *how.*

"I'm sorry I wasn't there," he says. "I'll always regret it."

I close my eyes. "Don't tell me that," I say. But I don't really regret it, not completely. I can see he needed the space as much as I did, that he didn't waste it.

One more thing, Aaron says. While we were in Vermont, he took a Seroquel. Just 200 milligrams, a third of his regular dose. An experiment. "I freaked out so bad. Nell. It was insane. I was seeing things, hearing things. I'm telling you. That drug was making me psycho."

It's still afternoon, but I'm tired after the drive, so we get into bed. The new sheets are white. A risk. Is it stupid to invest in white sheets? Or is this how we choose to live in the present, to stop waiting for a cure?

Aaron is tired, too. He can't catch his breath; his stomach is distended. His eyes roll back in his head for a moment. He struggles to get under the covers, puts on a dumb voice, makes fun of himself. I laugh hard. I tuck the duvet up over us. He says, "You make me feel like a person."

Immediately I start to leak mascara on the white pillow.

"What?" he says.

I shake my head. He rests the tissue box on the nest of our bodies. The late summer light taps through the window. We half-sleep for a while, two mismatched spoons in a drawer.

SINGULAR MONSTER

No more doctors, Aaron says. Then, okay, he'll see the neurologist. His name is Dr. Queen. We've been referred here by the doctor at Urgent Care, who told Aaron "I really feel like you have Bell's palsy" a few weeks ago, hours before we boarded our flight to Europe.

He has an East Texas accent and a kind face that has seen too much sun, though he looks about Aaron's age. He shines a light in Aaron's eyes, watches him walk up and down the hall. I mention the lesions, trying to ward off the doctor's inevitable question. But he doesn't ask about drug use. Instead, he nods knowingly. "Morgellons?" he says.

I look at Aaron. I swallow a laugh.

How to answer this? I'm not sure if this word now lives somewhere on Aaron's chart or if this doctor actually knows and accepts Morgellons. For a long time, all I wanted was to find a white-coated doctor who would speak that word. But now, I don't even know if Aaron believes in Morgellons anymore. He longs for the language of Western medicine, and speaks the language of metaphor, but seems to have time for little else.

"Maybe," I say.

Dr. Queen says, "I'm trying to get a read on you two as a couple and I'm having a hard time."

We laugh, loosen up. "We've seen a lot of doctors," Aaron explains. "We're a little cautious."

"I understand," Dr. Queen says. "Look, it's clear there's a psychiatric component and a physiological component. What's harder to tease out is how they're related. Which is driving the other?" He points at me. "What do *you* think?"

I look at Aaron. Does he want me to answer? Is it the last thing he wants? Doctors have been looking to me to read Aaron since the beginning. I want and don't want to be asked. But there is a sincerity in the doctor's voice. He wants my opinion. And Aaron's face is open.

"That's the question," I say.

Dr. Queen nods. He understands the bigness of the problem. Maybe this is all we need today: someone to acknowledge its size, the work we've put into it together. He smiles. "A few things are clear to me." He counts them off on his fingers. "One, you're not crazy. Two, you're suffering. Three, you're honest. And four, you want to get better."

Aaron nods. He agrees!

"We'll start with an MRI," the doctor says. "Eliminate some things."

"Is that at the hospital?" is Aaron's first question. "I can't go back to the hospital."

It's at the imaging center affiliated with the hospital. But not at the hospital. Aaron lets out a breath.

Dr. Queen is worried that it won't turn up anything. Then what? Maybe a spinal tap. His concern is that Aaron will be shuffled along from doctor to doctor, medicine to medicine. He's seen it, chronically ill patients who undergo the same testing again and again, and end up in the same place in a year. He is bracing Aaron and apologizing.

Aaron waves a hand. He hasn't come here expecting a diagnosis. That would be a bonus. "You're refreshing, man," he tells the doctor.

Then we push through the double doors into the summer heat and walk to Gimme! Coffee next door. Aaron tells me about the *Neijing*, the bible of traditional Chinese medicine he's reading. Huang Di, the Yellow Emperor who reigned five thousand years ago, lays the foundation for holistic medicine by telling the story of the patient he cares for. Aaron says it's so beautiful it makes him cry, and he starts to tear up here in the coffee shop, waiting for his double espresso.

The full moon comes, the Sturgeon Moon, electric orange and fierce. It's been a year since Aaron's first appointment with Laura, when we first learned to wait for the moon. But the moon comes and goes. Aaron's skin does not break out. He pours himself little plastic cups of alcohol all day: vodka with an olive, red wine, a golden honey whiskey. "I'm sorry I'm drinking so much," he says. We stand on the deck beneath the moon.

"So am I."

He says, "This stuff is going to kill me. I feel it."

"Then stop," I say. "Or at least cut back."

He says, "At least this way I can see it coming."

Maybe it's the alcohol that's keeping the fire inside. Maybe it's the meditation. Maybe it's the mercury, or the Seroquel, that has been cleansed from his system.

But the alcohol is its own kind of fire. He feels it burning as it goes down. He closes his eyes, hangs a fist against his chest.

And just because the fire isn't breaking out doesn't mean it's gone away. It's just inside now, a contained flame. At the back of his neck, on his scalp, at the place where his ear meets his jaw, a white cream froths. It looks like foam from a fire extinguisher, the scum of ocean tide. He looks like a clown who's washed his makeup off and missed a spot. This thing that's happening to him: it's a sickeningly endless gag bag of metaphors.

Aaron doesn't like to talk about it anymore. He tries to keep it to himself. It's a gift to us, I know, to me. But I can feel him seizing up, bracing himself against the current inside. Over the side of the deck, he vomits violently. Has he had too much to drink, or is it something else? Maybe both.

Aaron is worried he'll freak out during the MRI. Being so confined, having to be still for so long.

But instead he falls asleep. His own snoring wakes him up, and then he's laughing.

My husband's belly grows. He is growing something in there. Something biblical, something unholy. It's October again and he is showing the children all the horror films of his youth, *It* and *Evil Dead* and *Nightmare on Elm Street,* and they shriek with fear and delight. Nico is going to be the Joker for Halloween; Henry is going to be Pennywise.

Aaron approves. In his belly is a small child in a raincoat, or a Gremlin, or a nest of worms, the brainy noodles of Halloweens past. Touch it—"feel," he says, lifting his sweater—and it's hard as a beer belly but it's not a beer belly. He's had those before. It's taut as a raft, the membrane thick as a waterbed's. What it feels like more than anything is a pregnant belly, six months or more, a mass inflated inside an amniotic sac. It's irregular as a baby, a knee here, a skull there. "There's no more room," he says, which is what I said, too, when the babies' feet pressed against my lungs. Resting his forehead on the kitchen counter, he leans over and rocks his hips. He moans. Awake, asleep, he moans. On the couch, in the shower, he moans. The contractions come every few minutes, then closer together. A tightening. A bracing. I rub his back, if he'll let me.

Four days in, he admits it: He's on the antiparasitic that the parasitologist prescribed. The one I filled and left in the cabinet, just in case. He didn't want to talk about it. He didn't want me to know.

It's the way it is these days: he can't talk about it, won't, until he can't *not* talk about it. "Some crazy shit is happening," he says. "I can't tell you what it is."

It feels like years, but it's only been months since he stopped spending whole days in the bathroom, reckoning with the horror movie of his body. Now he reckons with it by lying flat on his back, eyes shut against the pain, or standing upright at the kitchen counter, alternating between shots of whiskey and shots of tea, which he pours into a sweet little glass that looks like it might hold a tea-light candle. "How are you feeling?" I ask him twelve times a day. "I'm fine," he answers, hand to chest.

Then, the thirteenth time: "Okay. I have to tell you what this is."

"You can tell me. What is it?"

"It's my nipples."

"Your *nipples*?"

He lifts his sweater higher.

"The foam," he says. "It's coming out of my nipples."

The foam. It's been pouring out of him. It built up in his head, weeks and weeks of headaches every day, until we finally went back to the neurologist. His MRI is perfect, Dr. Queen said. No problems.

"You didn't mention the foam," Aaron pointed out after we left the office, defeated.

"You told me not to!"

But I've seen it, frothing off of him in the shower, the unruly remnants of it still clinging to the bathtub hours later, a beach after high tide. The shower is the only thing that helps with the pressure. It has to come *out*. It comes out of his eyes, his ears, through his skin, but this—his nipples—it's unreal. "It stings like a *bitch*."

"Oh my God." I cup my own breasts in sympathy pain. "Ouch."

"I have so much respect for you," he says. "Those things *hurt*."

"What the fuck."

"I'm *lactating*." He gives a sad laugh.

For days, when I go to hug him, to climb on top of him on the couch, he says, "Careful." I lift my head from his chest. He lifts his shirt again. His nipples have, in fact, scabbed over. They look like mine did when, after six weeks, I gave up on breastfeeding Nico. His lamprey latch had left my nipples chewed and bloody like sausages. Too late, we learned he was tongue-tied. I am a little proud of the scars, healed white now.

Later, I look it up. Men can lactate; it's rare but it's true.

Is Aaron yielding milk? Is it milk that seethes from every pore, hot human milk frothing from some secret duct? An evolutionary adaptation for the stay-at-home dad?

I try not to research. I go weeks without it. Then I get sucked in. I spend a day Gimme! Coffee, following the yellow brick road of

Wikipedia articles. Galactorrhea, milk production that occurs outside of regular breastfeeding, can be connected to high levels of the hormone prolactin, in the blood. Then this: it can be caused by certain antipsychotics, including Seroquel. Galactorrhea, says my screen, can occur even years after taking Seroquel.

My brain screen starts to stutter and flash. Too many tabs open. Galactorrhea. Intergalactic. Milky Way. I imagine the milk flowing out of my husband, a teapot of it.

In Karen Russell's short story "Orange World," a new mother breastfeeds the devil to ward off harm to her child. It's a rodent of indeterminate species, with sharp teeth that bite. I can't read the story without my own nipples wincing.

Aaron's devil isn't outside, though; it's still in utero. Does it want to be exorcised? Or does it want to keep him alive, to feed on him from the inside? The womb of parasites in his belly—what umbilical cord does it feed from?

The boys, like all children, want to know why boys have nipples.

"It's one of life's great mysteries," we agree.

Henry breastfed like a champ. A soft little mouth that knew what to do. Still, I dream I am nursing my babies. I miss it like a country I can't return to. Like many babies, Henry had slightly swollen breasts when he was born, from the hormone bath of the birth canal.

Galactorrhea can occur in newborn babies, girls and boys both. This is still sometimes called "witch's milk." It was said that the "familiar spirits" of a young witch—demon fairies that took the shape of animals, like rabbits—suckled the babies' milk while they slept.

Aaron is watching the silent movie *Häxan,* made in Denmark in 1922, about witches persecuted in Europe in the Middle Ages. It's perhaps the first movie to acknowledge the murder of thousands of mentally ill women—and perfectly sane women—under the justification of witchcraft. On the black-and-white screen, the naked women, crawling in a graveyard, look like they're made of stone. The devil dances in the night. The witches come one after another and kiss his behind. They feed him babies. "This is the best movie ever made," Aaron says, nearly weeping.

I'd be the surrogate mother if I could. I would nurse the devil to save my husband from this hell.

"Milk, milk, milk," Henry would say, clutching my breast. It sounded more like "Muck."

In Target, as a toddler, recently weaned, he wandered the lingerie aisle, pawing the bras. "Muck, muck, muck," he mourned.

Now we wander Target together, the four of us. "Milk!" Henry says, pointing at the bras, laughing at his former self. In a nearby cart, a child is crying.

"Watch out, guys," Aaron says. "I may start leaking."

For months, the package of family photos sent by Aaron's uncle has stood against a speaker in the family room. Now Aaron is cleaning up and he opens the box again.

In a manila folder, a word-processed document his mother has written, her life story. "The Painted Picture," it's called.

Aaron reads it. When he's done, he tosses the pages on the table and scoffs, "She knows how to paint a picture, all right."

Aaron is not in these pages much, it pains me to see. What's mostly in "The Painted Picture" are misadventures, famous people who ate in her restaurants, beautiful things in her home in Manhasset, and terrible things she endured at the hands of men, including being terrorized by her first husband and neglected by her second.

There are a couple of anecdotes about Aaron. Giving him a bath with a neighbor girl. Waiting for the rain to stop so they could board a plane, Aaron impressing the other passengers in the terminal with his wit. "I want to sit next to this kid," everyone said.

Were there other moments, quiet moments not worthy of remembering, let alone telling? Did she sit quietly in a dark room, rocking him in her arms? When he cried in the night, did she go to him? Did she delight in him? Did she love him?

In the box, there's a picture of Aaron and his mother on Halloween. He's maybe five. Soon his mother will leave, but now they stand on the elegant staircase. He is wearing a homemade Batman mask, a black cape, a black leotard, and black tights. She is a witch. She has made his costume, I am certain.

In the bathroom, a week before Halloween, I paint the boys' faces. Their hair is pulled back from their beautiful foreheads with my cloth headbands. Without their glasses, their faces caked in white, they are stone-faced dolls. Their eyelids crinkle when I apply the black eyeshadow. I teach them how to stretch their lips taut when I apply the blood-red lipstick. Nico gets a long red smile across his cheeks. Henry gets a red nose and a spear of red through each eye. Their white masks dry and crack, the shadow of my fingerprints still on their cheeks. Henry gasps when he sees himself in the mirror. "I look just like Pennywise!" He hugs me, spotting my cheek with red, and I have to redo his nose.

Nico tells me I should be a makeup artist.

"Really? Thanks, honey."

"You know why?"

"Why?"

In his sinister Heath Ledger voice, he says, "When you're good at something, don't do it for free."

I laugh. "What?"

"It's from *The Dark Knight*!"

When they fit on their wigs, one red, one green, they are transformed into perfect monsters. No store sells Pennywise costumes for children, so I've bought a craft-store tutu for Henry and fit it around his neck, a perfect clown collar.

Aaron has signed up to chaperone Nico's first dance. He is in bad shape, unsteady, tired, in pain. "You don't have to do this," I say. "You can cancel." But he says he's not missing it. He dresses in his black Fred Perry and the only jeans that fit and his maroon, ten-eye Docs.

He asks Nico, "You won't be embarrassed if I bring my cane?"

"No!" Nico says, like, of course not.

I drop them off and watch them walk into the middle school, Nico going slow, holding on to his dad's arm. It's my dad's cane he's started using. For months it hung in Papou's room, and then Aaron took it off the hook.

The same night, Henry and I go to the Fall Festival at his school. I'm not really a costume mom, but for a moment I wondered if I should go as a witch. It's an easy mom thing to do; we have the makeup. Aaron saw me eyeing the hat at Target. "Yeah, please don't do that," he said.

Afterward, Henry and I have time to kill before we pick up Aaron and Nico, so he takes off his wig and we help clean up, putting away the folding chairs in the gym. Henry, forty-eight pounds, can barely lift one, but slowly, with determination, he carries them across the room. When I cross the gym to get more chairs, he runs after me, howling. "I didn't know where you were!" He bumps into me, his red nose now smearing my jean jacket.

"Henry! I was right here."

"Tell me when you're leaving."

"I'd never just leave you," I say.

Walking to the car, he stops and looks up at the dark sky. "Can we just look at the sky?" he says. When you're eight, the dark is a novelty. "We never just like look at the sky."

"Of course." But he's right: we never just like look.

The sky is a haunting Halloween sky, purple black, like the makeup in the Halloween makeup kit. A mummy's gauze of cloud hides the stars. My son still loves to find the moon.

"Can we play on the playground? At night?"

"Of course."

He swings on the swings, slides down the slide. We ride the seesaw together, but I'm wearing a dress and it's cold on my thighs, so I just balance on my feet. I video him running toward me. He is perhaps the happiest I've ever seen him. He is eight.

I think of the way I love my boys and the way my boys love me. I think of the wound I would leave if I picked up and left now. What perfect little monsters I'd make of them. I think it isn't that Sandra didn't love Aaron. It isn't that he didn't love her. It's that they did love each other, and then she was gone. And after that there was nothing else that mattered: it was the only part of the story he could hear.

Can you wish on the moon? I lean my head back and try it. I wish that our kids won't be possessed by their parents' story, the way Aaron and I have been by ours. That we won't be the wrathful gods they worship and curse. I want to tie off our story, like I've taught them to tie a knot in a balloon. I want them to see it, sealed and secure, float up and away from them. I want them to be free.

AURORA STREET

2013

Do you know about the four M's?" Kate asked me over coffee.
I shook my head. Being in Al-Anon meant admitting, finally, sometimes, I knew nothing.

"Manipulating, managing, martyring, mothering." She smiled gently, a mother's smile.

In Al-Anon, women spoke of their qualifiers' little triumphs with a careful sort of pride. Whether they were talking about their children or spouses mattered little. The wives who were like me always sounded like parents, full of fear, watching them toddle out of the nest.

Aaron went back to school. That first summer in the new house on Aurora Street, still in boxes, still in group therapy and outpatient rehab, he walked downtown to the community college campus. I felt the seasons in my limbs, learned the rhythms, the winter of our discontent having given way to a spring of near-death and rebirth, and now the Ithaca summer stretching before us, possibility.

A college writing class. The last time he'd attempted one, I was a college student, too. This time, a college writing professor, I did not help him with his papers. He still got an A.

In the fall, two more classes. Math, Spanish. He took the city bus to the more distant community college campus. Woke up before any of us, put on his backpack, and walked to the bus stop by himself.

That was when the rash returned.

By midterms, after more than a year of remission.

Did the stress of the classes bring it on? Was it that he wasn't drinking? Or was it in him, ready to return in any case? Would he have finished the classes if he hadn't gotten sick again?

What happens to the disappointment when you're not supposed to feel it anymore? When you've detached with love, let go of the outcome? Feel it coming up, a little vomit in the throat. Go to Al-Anon. Say, "I am so disappointed."

Okay, so he wouldn't go to school. He wouldn't work. Not yet. Not now. Soon. When he was better. If stress brought it out, then he had to reduce the stress. We went back to the dermatologists, more specialists. We went to therapy. We went to RCA. I went to Al-Anon. He went to AA. He took care of the kids. He stayed sober. These were full-time jobs, I told myself. We told some friends he was in rehab, but we didn't tell many.

Aurora Street was the main street leading to campus, and our house was just a few blocks from the boys' new school—Nico was starting kindergarten!—and a few blocks in the other direction from downtown. There were benefits to being in the middle of things. We took turns driving or walking Nico to school, or went together. We walked down the steep hill to the Commons, ate in the sidewalk cafés, let the kids play on the rickety wooden playground that would be torn down in a few years.

But at night, on the weekends, the neighborhood erupted in college-kid chaos, drunk students with fake IDs stumbling down the sidewalk under our bedroom windows, drunk guys chasing each other down the middle of the street, drunk girls woo-wooing from one corner to the next. On Saturday and Sunday mornings, we woke to beer cans in our yard, Solo cups, vitamin water bottles, Doritos bags, lipstick, and once panties. Change went missing from our car when we forgot to lock it. Once, someone stole the lug nuts off our tires. Once, someone simply slashed the tires. Once, at midnight, a guy rang our doorbell and asked for a drink of water for his girlfriend. Aaron closed the door in his face.

We invested in new double-paned vinyl windows, and double-helix window shades, to soften the noise.

Okay, so it wasn't exactly a refuge. It was an alcohol-soaked neighborhood. There was no hiding from it. There was no hiding from anything.

Sometimes, during those years, Aaron would leave the house, sick or angry or depressed or desperate, and I would run out to the sidewalk and yell for him to come back, hoping none of our friends were driving down the street. Sometimes he came back. Sometimes he disappeared downtown. I worried about him going to a bar. They were nearly indistinguishable fears, as though having a drink might be the end of him, the end of us.

Al-Anon told me I wasn't supposed to run after him. Not far, anyway.

When it was Henry's turn to start kindergarten, in the fall of 2016, Aaron interviewed for a job. He had been without a flare for a few months. He felt ready. It was for a housing assistant at a local nonprofit, helping people get their housing benefits. A worthwhile job with decent pay. In his interview, he impressed them by talking about the history of poverty and the origins of the education system. Every step of the hiring process—the background check, the references, the W-9—I thought, it's going to fall through. I kept the disappointment at an arm's length, ready to grab it before it could grab me. But he was hired, and his first day was the boys' first day of school, too, and I took pictures of all of them standing on the front porch, the boys in their backpacks, Aaron in his tie. It was his first job since Virginia, when Nico was a baby.

Every morning we drove him to work, then picked him up in the evening. Sometimes, at the end of the week, his coworkers gave him a few items from the community pantry and garden that were unclaimed, ears of corn, a baguette. Once, when I had a meeting, the boys went to work with Aaron, sitting on the floor behind his cubicle. Such well-behaved boys, his coworkers said. There was a framed photo of them on his desk, and his energy bars in the drawer, and a turmeric stain on the carpet where he had spilled it trying to make tea. On Fridays, we cashed his check at the grocery store on the way home, then bought groceries. We needed the money badly. He was happy that the cash he was handing to the cashier was his own. It was a kind of lifeblood, those green bills.

Most of his days were filled with paperwork, filing the various forms associated with the two hundred people in his case load, answering phone calls from people who were being evicted, who were waiting for housing. He told them he was sorry, he was doing everything he could, there were eight people in line ahead of them. There was math. There were systems. Some days he made visits to the sites to do inspections with his coworkers, seeing the grave conditions people lived in. He felt overwhelmed, powerless to do much good, and yet it was important work. It made him feel needed, and connected, and proud. He was the first to arrive at work in the morning and the last one to leave.

My pride was a full breath in the lungs I was afraid to release. There was my husband! Kind and smart and bright-eyed, sharp in his blue blazer, sober, healthy, productive, well-liked, drinking turmeric tea. His teeth were so white! His desk was so clean! Once, I surprised him on his lunch break and we drove to the waterfall nearby and held hands watching the water rush and absolutely nothing was wrong. *This is the man I married,* I thought.

I remember making the bed one day, asking myself, is this really it? Is this the way it's going to be? Is it too good to be true?

Then, in November, the election.

We were thrown. The world was thrown. I cried for days, struggled to get out of bed. He went off to work. He was thrown, but undeterred.

And then his mother called. She was sick. COPD. She was on oxygen. Didn't know how long she had.

My own mother had had COPD for twelve years, but once her cancer diagnosis came in, she was dead within weeks. We didn't want to waste any time. Aaron was nervous about taking time off his new job, nervous about seeing his mother, but I pressed him. "Talk to her," I said. "Make peace. It could be your last chance."

"I'll go for the kids," he said. "Just for the kids."

So, the next week, for Thanksgiving, we all flew to Santa Fe. It was our third and final visit. Sandra was living in her recliner, sleeping there. It was the only way she could breathe, sitting up. The boys crawled into her lap and she hugged them and uttered sweet words. To be fair, she didn't have much energy. She wasn't herself. We stayed at a hotel. We went to the children's museum. We went to the little toy stores she'd taken us to when she was well. We drove to her house three or four times, never staying more than an hour or two. Aaron didn't exactly feel comfortable there. He didn't say much to his mother and she didn't say much to him. Had she been well, she would have been cooking with the boys and showing them all the flowers in the yard and her boyfriend would have been doing tricks for them, pulling quarters from their ears. But her boyfriend was the one doing the cooking now. On Thanksgiving, we weren't invited to stay for the meal. They had Sandra's French club over. We ate at a vegan Indian restaurant. It was delicious. We went back to the house just once after that, to say good-bye. "I love you, Ma," Aaron said to her, and she said, "I love you, sweetie pie," to Aaron and to each of us, and then we left.

Aaron liked to drink in airports, on planes, liked airplane bottles even when he wasn't on an airplane. But he'd quit drinking. Instead, he took an Ativan, settling into his seat.

"I can't believe we took three planes to New Fucking Mexico and we weren't even invited for Thanksgiving dinner."

I tried to reason. We were vegetarian. His mom's boyfriend was stressed out. He didn't need to cook for a couple of picky kids.

It wasn't the point. The point was he didn't feel welcome. He didn't know what it felt like to be part of a family, but he was pretty sure that wasn't it. I remembered a Thanksgiving years ago, when we lived in New York, his half-sister calling, the yelling that ensued. It had never been great, even when it was good. Was it a coincidence that both her other children no longer spoke to her?

By the time we got back to Ithaca, Aaron was already getting sick. No, I told myself, no, no, nope. It's something else. It's just stress. Just trauma and grief and a bad headache. He called in sick to work one day. He was sent home sick the next.

The day after that, his boss called him into her office. There had been some mistakes, she said. Miscalculations. She showed him some of the forms he'd filed. In the original versions, he'd gotten the numbers right, but then he'd corrected himself, and they were wrong. "It's like you second-guess yourself," she said. It was a pattern. He would be on a kind of probation period, to give him a chance to get it right. They liked him. They wanted to keep him on. But these were dollars, people's lives.

Aaron thought about it for a day. His body lit up like a match. And then he quit.

"You're quitting because you're afraid you'll be fired," I said.

"Yeah," he said. "So? I'm going to be fired anyway."

"They're giving you a chance. Don't pass up a chance."

He held his arms up, red with a fresh rash. "How am I supposed to work like this? I can't fucking do it. My brain doesn't work. My body's falling apart. I'm not good at this shit."

I let him let it go.

Was it the stress of seeing his mother? Or the stress of losing his job? Maybe he'd been right. Maybe we shouldn't have gone to New Mexico. Maybe, if we hadn't gone, he wouldn't have gotten sick. It was like a virus, all the cold indifference in his mother's house. He'd caught it and brought it home.

She hung on for a few more months after that. He spoke to her on the phone in her last hours, told her again that he loved her. His half-brother, when Aaron called him, wanted nothing to do with her. His half-sister, estranged nearly as long, came to her death bed and was there in the end. There was a memorial for her in New York, but Aaron chose not to go to. He said he couldn't stand to be around all her friends talking about how great she was.

"How's that going to look?" I said. "Us not showing up at your own mother's funeral?"

"I don't give a shit how it looks," he said.

The only thing that kept me from being consumed by disappointment was that Aaron was already consumed by disappointment in himself.

He was disappointed enough for both of us. His body was enacting it, engulfed in flames, the self-pity battling the self-loathing. I could only make room for it. He sat on the couch and he lay in bed and he went to therapy and he didn't hide it: he said he'd been knocked down and he was afraid he'd never get back up.

Get back up! I said.

Get back up! Stu said.

This was a setback. Everyone had them. You're not so special. Send out your résumé again! It had a nice new line on it, and he was pretty sure he'd get a good reference.

You're smart! Capable! That math was hard!

Stu made recommendations to his doctor, mixing and matching his meds. Let's drop the Depakote, let's up the Wellbutrin, let's try Seroquel, Ativan at night.

Meanwhile I felt like stabbing a small innocent creature with the silverware as I unloaded the dishwasher. Maybe not the forks or knives. Maybe a spoon. Maybe not a creature. Maybe just a big bag of jasmine rice.

I had spent nineteen years desperate for my husband to find work that would validate us. Nineteen years of writing cover letters for him. *Please find attached . . .* He'd stop me there. "That sounds weird. 'Please find attached'?" "That's what you say!" I'd scream.

Everyone else's husband was an engineer or an analyst or an exporter or did something else I didn't understand but that meant a lot of money and a 401K. This was where my mind went while I threw the silverware in the drawer, the shiny, spotless blades hot from the dry cycle. I knew my friends' marriages weren't perfect. We talked shit about their spouses too, our Bluetooth earbuds picking up all the clatter of the dishes we were doing. The one whose husband played online video games with teenagers all weekend long. The one whose husband was addicted to porn. The one whose husband did not understand her needs. The one whose wife did not understand her needs. Almost always there were problems with work. There were the husbands who worked too much, the husbands who traveled too much, the husbands who got jobs that required them to move across the country. There were the husbands who lost their jobs. This was perhaps the most destabilizing marriage problem of all. Almost all my married friends had seen marriage counselors at some point, and no matter the chronic issues—sex, money, kids, communication—they were often brought to crisis, to instant instability, when their husbands lost their jobs. When will he get a new job? became the consuming question of my friends. They watched their husbands go out on interviews and I understood their worry and I hated them for it. Because their husbands always got another job. I would have given anything for my husband to get another job. I would have given anything for him to text, *Sorry babe, I'll be home late again.*

But what was it for, who was it for, my longing, my lamenting? Why did I need him to work so badly? I would be slamming the glasses into the cabinets by then. They were the same questions I'd asked in Virginia, pregnant with Nico, desperate for him to get a job. Was it so I could tell my friends? My family? Was it so our kids could be proud of him? Was it just because we were broke all the time and needed the money? We were; we did. But that was just part of it. What I wanted a job to give us, I was beginning to admit to myself, wasn't just financial capital but social capital.

There's the man I married, I thought. It was the same sentence, now inspired by panic instead of pride. It didn't really matter. Either way, I felt responsible for him, felt that he was responsible for me, that we manifested each other's worth. And that was the messaging, wasn't it? Ask more of your man! Don't let him drag you down! Women did not, should not tolerate indolence. Women worked hard enough as it was, inside the home and out of it. Women should work and men should work; we should be equals; we should do the same thing.

But wasn't demanding that your husband work also the opposite of equality? Wasn't that assumption also rooted in primitive models of marriage and, like, toxic masculinity? In repressive models of labor? Women should make a good marriage, so others know they're good, too? Fuck that, right? Why were we still asking our men to go out into the woods and kill and drag home our dinner, in a time when people of any gender are capable of preheating an oven for an organic frozen pizza? Didn't modern feminism need to include sympathy for male weakness, and to imagine masculinity in various forms? Wasn't there strength in vulnerability, and all that? It seemed like a lot of things, or maybe just a lot of things that were happening in my house, were the epitome of American feminism and the exact opposite. I was confused and angry and tired of reading the *New York Times*'s Vows column— why did I keep reading it?—the crowns of roses, the rented barn behind the happy couple. Maybe none of the people in Vows had problems or maybe as a culture we had created a language to talk around all of the things we didn't want to put in print.

My dad lost his job when I was fifteen. He was let go from his position as head designer at an architecture firm he'd been with for years. The office was moving to another city and he was too old, sixty-two, to move with them. The phrase we used was "early retirement," and then, when he tried to pick up work here and there, "consulting." "He's consulting," I told my friends, trying on the word. What I felt was a need to use language to make a painful thing less painful for a man I cared about. I heard my mom say it, and I said it, too. Meanwhile my mom had gone back to school to get her teaching certificate and she got a job teaching seventh-grade Language Arts. She went from homemaker to breadwinner, not because she wanted that title but because she wanted to pay for our college, for the Nikes my brothers kept growing out of.

My dad didn't last long in those consulting positions, and it wasn't until I was an adult that I suspected it had been a pattern all along. My parents moved several times when my brothers and I were small. The work dried up, was how my mother put it, but I wonder if my father's short fuse, his fragile ego, was to blame. When he was a young man, after seven years in New York working for I. M. Pei, Pei reprimanded him for some work poorly done, or an attitude problem. Probably my dad's feelings were hurt that Pei hadn't shown sufficient deference to his designs. Pei told him to take some time off. My dad drove to Vermont to visit a friend, and he never went back to New York. He met my mom and married her. To try to save his self-respect, he quit before he could be fired.

The euphemism we'd used for Aaron, "stay-at-home dad," wasn't a lie. Our progressive friends in Ithaca were impressed by it, or pretended to be impressed by it. *That's great! The most important job there is!* Or they pretended to not be impressed by it. *Cool,* like it was the standard thing. It wasn't exactly standard, but there was a Friday dads group that met at the baby store downtown, the one with the cloth-diaper delivery service, and they all gathered around the little germy indoor bouncy house, watching their toddlers topple one another. You should go, I told Aaron. No, he said.

It seemed like the title "stay-at-home dad" expired when your kids started elementary school, though technically Henry had been in preschool practically full-time until then anyway. Still, Aaron picked them up from school, gave them a snack. It wasn't like they could be alone. That was still his job, wasn't it?

How much time did I spend doing this, mentally constructing acceptable narratives to present to other people about what life looked like in our house? Hours upon hours. How much time did other people spend worrying about what life looked like in our house? Minutes, maybe. I'm sure we were a passing fascination, maybe a concern. *What is up with them? Is he sick or something? Where do they get their money?* What did it matter? What did it matter if I told them "He lost his job" or "It was too hard" or "He quit before he could be fired"?

Some people I told one of those versions. Other friends, our friends in RCA, Stu—I told something that felt more like the truth. All of those versions, plus "His mom got sick" and "He got sick" and "He panicked" and "He's supremely depressed" and "We're really struggling" and "I don't know if he'll work again." I named it. And the shame, old-fashioned, ugly, a little of it left my body through my mouth.

There were times when I could name it, could choose a euphemism or choose the truth, and there were times when I was so frightened by the truth I didn't have any words for it at all. One evening a little before Christmas, I came home from work and Henry was crying and Aaron couldn't handle it and by the time I took off my snow boots and jacket he was rushing to the bathroom, the little half-bath off the kitchen, struggling to find his meds, any meds, something in a little crushed white box, and when I realized what he was doing I ran to him and fought him for it, both of us pulling on it, me crushing half of it in my hand, trying to wrestle it down to the toilet and him down to the floor, to reality, both of us pressed up against each other, his ear in my face, my chin in his neck, and through gritted teeth he was saying those words again, *I'm going to do it,* a monster turned not on me but on himself, and I thought, this isn't happening again, and the fear and rage whipped out like a third arm and I hit him on the ear, *I'm boxing his ears,* I thought, and then I bit his ear, until he released the box or I tore it from him and it went flying into the toilet bowl. It wasn't the romantic cascade of pills that could be flushed. It was a wet pasteboard box of generic medication, floating like a pitiful raft. This was when I realized that Nico was standing in the kitchen watching us.

"He's okay," I said. "We're okay."

Aaron caught his breath. "I'm okay, Bubba," he said, and I fished out the box and bagged it and hid it and then later threw it away, after hiding all of the rest of the pills in the house, too. The only pills I didn't hide I gave to Aaron, made him take, made him lie down in our bed and tell me what was going on, what was he thinking, and he said it had come out of nowhere, the urge to put his lights out, the crying, it sent him back to being a little kid himself, it sent him over the edge. I listened. I apologized. He apologized. As quickly as it had come on it passed. I looked around the nighttime chill of our narrow room. I breathed. The college kids were gone; the neighborhood was bathed in a snowy quiet. We had not yet repaired the ice dam-damaged ceiling, or replaced the closet curtain with mirrored doors. I focused on the wall behind the bed, which I had painted denim blue, and on that wall hung a painting my mother had done years before I was born, two figures without features, a couple posed on a bed, the man lying on his side, head propped on an elbow, the woman sitting cross-legged, leaning in. My heart slowed. I sat cross-legged on the bed, our blood-stained white sheets, Aaron on his side, I ran my palm along his ribs. Close your eyes, that's it, it's over now, and I waited until he was asleep before I closed the door and went to Nico's room and sat next to him on his bed. Henry was downstairs watching *Teen Titans Go!*

"What were you and Dad doing?" he wanted to know.

I sighed. I wanted to be honest. But I didn't want to scare him. I definitely didn't want to tell him his dad had been trying to take an overdose of pills. "Dad was having a hard time, honey. Sometimes when Henry cries, I guess he gets panicked. Why was Henry crying?"

Nico narrated the squabble, a small matter. Henry had hit Nico and Nico had hit Henry back. "But why did you hit Dad?"

I froze. "You saw that, huh?"

He nodded.

"He was really upset. I was trying to calm him down."

"You hit him to calm him down?"

"Yes. I know. I shouldn't have hit him. I apologized." I cringed. "I actually bit him, too."

"You *bit* him?"

"On his ear. It's not okay to hit. Or bite. I know, your brother bites and hits! It's hard to explain."

Nico gave me his too-wise-for-an-eight-year-old look. Like he had my number. Like he was the one here to advise, correct, and comfort me.

"Listen. You know what depression is, right?"

"Kind of."

"Your dad, he's what we call clinically depressed. He takes medicine to help him feel less sad. But sometimes he still struggles."

"He's sad he lost his job," Nico pointed out.

"Yeah. That, too."

"I don't care if he doesn't have a job. I mean, I know other dads mostly work." He still had trouble with his *R*s. "I just don't want him to be depressed."

"I know. I don't either. But he might always be depressed. It's a disease, like anything else."

"And he's sad he's sick. I mean, I'd be depressed too, if I was sick."

I laughed a little. "Yeah, me too."

"I just want to know one more thing."

He had his arms crossed now, his negotiation pose. He used it to lobby for more allowance, for a new video game, for another item on his Christmas list. Please ask for another Christmas gift, I thought. Do not ask me about suicide. Anything but that.

"What's that?" I asked.

He said, "I want to know if Santa's real."

I laughed again, then gasped. "Nico. Really?"

He was firm. "I want to know. I want you to tell me the truth. I can take it."

"Nico," I said. I was practically crying already. I had not expected this question so soon. I was three years older when I had begged my mother to tell me, and then when she had, I had felt stricken, angry at her, embarrassed that I had extended my childish belief for so long, betrayed by the lies parents got away with telling, all of it an elaborate hoax. That was the year my own parents had been enduring a difficult time—my uncle's death, my father's breakdown, their near separation—though it wasn't until I was older that I understood the size of it, and though I had sympathy for them there was anger too, that I had been kept in the dark. That I hadn't been trusted. I didn't want Nico to be angry at me, not tonight. I couldn't take it. But I didn't want to look at him and lie. I believed him, that he could take it.

"Okay," I said. I put my hand on his back. "Santa's not real."

He nodded. "I knew it." A smile grew on his face. "So it's just you and Dad? You leave us all the presents?"

"Yup. You mad?"

"No. I kind of figured. It's okay."

"I'm sorry. I know it's kind of like lying. But it's kind of a fun thing to pretend. And now you can help us keep the story alive for Henry."

Nico liked that—a chance to exert maturity over his brother. He had been initiated into a rite of adulthood. He had needed it tonight, this little bit of authority, of control. Still, I cried, from grief and also from relief. "I didn't want to tell you yet!" I pulled him into my lap. I wrapped my arms around him and hugged him and cried.

"I'm okay, Mom. I promise." He patted my shoulder. "You'll be okay."

It was a mark on our clean slate. A relapse of sorts. It was as painful as if he'd fallen off the wagon—that he'd wanted to kill himself again, had gone through the motions, however briefly. I knew I wasn't supposed to tally, but I tallied, I despaired. I knew having suicidal thoughts, even acting on them, wasn't a moral failure on his part, just as I'd learned that having an alcoholic relapse wasn't a moral failure. Mental illness was a disease and alcoholism was a disease and morals had nothing to do with it. I knew it wasn't a failure on my part, either. But it felt like a failure on someone's. Our higher power's, maybe. It felt unfair. I felt we deserved more. I had told my brothers and my dad, in the email after his suicide attempt, when we'd gotten into recovery, when we were giving it another shot, that I was seeing a new Aaron. *Maybe not Aaron 2.0*, I joked, trying to be realistic. *But maybe Aaron 1.5.*

Sometimes he was Aaron 1.5 and sometimes he was Aaron 1.0 and sometimes 2.0 or 3.0 and sometimes some negative number, in the crib, in utero, bathing in his mother's nutrient-deficient amniotic fluid. Sometimes he was just Aaron and I was the one relapsing, reversing, so scared of his regression that I saw it everywhere that I brought us there all on my own. Sometimes I told myself that maybe we were past it, that maybe recovery was a crutch we no longer needed. The sweet smell of normalcy beckoned, and I wanted to just fucking be like everyone else.

It was that summer that we were at Sam's new house in Alexandria, sitting at the black brushed granite island, big as a queen bed, while Keri mixed mojitos. Van Morrison on the ceiling speakers, our kids running around the house with my nephew's new pet bearded dragon, my dad pointing his cane saying, Whoa, slow down, fellas! It was a new kitchen, and the old, adjacent kitchen had been transformed into a bar, with a wine fridge and a liquor cabinet and a petite sink where Keri squeezed limes and mashed mint so strong we could smell the juices from across the room.

Aaron had been flirting with alcohol. He flirted with it, I thought, like he flirted with suicide, making jokes about it to ease the tension—a temptation he thought about but wouldn't go near. But now he was maybe going near this one. He kept poking it, poking me. He'd stopped going to meetings. He'd stopped meeting with Rich. He even mentioned it to Stu.

"Do you think that's a good idea?" he asked Aaron.

"Probably not," Aaron said, shrugging. "But I'm fucking dying anyway." He held up his scorched arms. "It keeps coming back. For three years, it's been back! The last time it went away, I was drinking."

"Why do you think that is?" Stu asked.

"I don't know! I wish I knew. I'm already drugged up on all these fucking meds. They fuck with me more than alcohol does. Depakote? Seroquel? I don't even know what that shit is. Alcohol I know."

"True," Stu said. "But they're carefully calibrated drugs. Their use is monitored. And they're not addictive like alcohol."

Aaron waved his hand. "I don't know if I even believe in that anymore."

I didn't know if I believed in it, either. I knew I was losing faith in finding a cure for Aaron's illness. I knew his sobriety made me feel safe. But it also made me feel scared. I was as scared of alcohol as I was scared of suicide. I was scared he'd try one or the other again. Maybe it was a kind of deal I made with him, with myself, his higher power: if he drank in front of me, not at home, not alone, just when we were out, if I knew just what and how much he was drinking, if he didn't hide it, it would be okay. I told myself it was his choice, but the truth was I still felt it was within my control. If he drank with my blessing, it wasn't a relapse.

I knew it wasn't my blessing to give, or Keri's. She presented the offer without pressure. Aaron raised his eyebrows at me, and I said, detaching with love, "It's your decision."

And Aaron said, "Sure, I'll take one."

And I said, "Make it two."

And Keri presented us our drinks, and we thanked her, and we lifted the glasses cold and sweating and knocked them together, like two heavy heads.

Later he'd tell me that when we'd taken a trip to New York that spring, he'd already gone to a bar and had a gin and tonic while the boys and I were at the hotel. Just one drink, he admitted. Just to tell himself he could do it and stop.

Who understands the power of alcohol, what it does to the body and the brain? It does something, magical and merciless. Aaron's demons scattered, back to their cages. His skin cleared, his mind cooled. We told Stu about the drinking. We didn't tell our friends in RCA.

Well, I told Kate. She understood. Not everyone in the rooms would understand, she acknowledged. Aaron did not tell Rich, for fear that he might disappoint him, or trigger him, but anyway, they didn't meet up anymore. Rich and Kate had split up, actually, sort of—Kate had asked Rich to move out. Aaron helped him move. They still cared about each other, still attended RCA, still worked on their coupleship, from under two different roofs. A coupleship could look like anything, she showed me. Other people didn't have to understand it or condone it. You could make it work any way you wanted. Actually, "make it work," my favorite motto, wasn't quite right. "You have to change the sentence," Kate said. *"It can work."*

Later that summer, we got in a fight. Something stupid that had nothing to do with alcohol. I wanted Aaron to go to Movies in the Park with us. He didn't want to go. It was *Jurassic Park*. We liked *Jurassic Park*! Why wouldn't he go? I wanted all of us sitting under the stars, under the blanket, sharing that really good vegan curry from the food truck, making memories. But he was moody and stubborn and he didn't like mosquitoes and he didn't like crowds and he didn't feel like it. So what? Go without me. I was resentful, felt slighted. I ask for one simple thing! Come to the movies with us. Let's be a family! Let's do family things! I didn't say, Let's let other people see us do family things! Let's post a picture of us doing family things together!

We left, the kids and I. I huffed. "Is Dad coming?" How many times had they asked that? *Is Dad coming?* Nope! I loaded the beach chairs into the car and we were off. Aaron was wearing a black tank top we still called a wife beater. He didn't wave to us as we backed out of the driveway.

We weren't three minutes away, just down the hill, when my phone rang. Aaron's name came up on the ID on the stereo. For a moment, I was flooded with satisfaction. He had changed his mind—could we come back and pick him up? I had successfully guilted him into assenting. I answered the call through the Bluetooth speakers and his voice filled the car. Except it wasn't really a voice but a kind of high-pitched moaning. It sounded like someone having a panic attack, or possibly a heart attack, possibly because he had just swallowed a bottle of pills. He was crying.

"What is it?" I asked. "Aaron? Are you okay?"

"I'm sorry," he whispered through his tears.

Of course. Of course he hadn't changed his mind but the moment we had left him, abandoned him, he had tried to kill himself, and was calling to say sorry, sorry he had done it, he didn't mean to, sorry—

I hung up.

I didn't want the kids to hear.

"Mom? What's wrong with Dad?"

"Hold on, guys. It'll be okay."

I yanked the car over on State Street on the corner of the Commons, not a real spot but a loading zone, and I turned off the car so it wouldn't pick up my call. "I'll be right back." And I stepped onto the sidewalk and dialed nine-one-one.

I told the dispatcher that I thought my husband had just taken an overdose. Why did I think so? Because he'd done it before. Because we'd gotten in a fight. Because he called me in hysterics and I hung up so I wouldn't scare our kids. I gave her the address. They'd send an ambulance right away.

Then I called Aaron back. I prayed he'd answer.

"Why'd you hang up on me?" His voice was still weak, but he sounded more like himself.

"I didn't want the kids to hear. I called the police. They're on their way."

"What?"

"What did you do, Aaron?"

"Why the fuck did you call the police?"

"What did you take?"

"I didn't take anything. I kicked the suitcase against the closet! I broke the mirror."

I looked around. It was a summer evening in Ithaca. People were walking by in pairs, in shorts and sunglasses, drinking iced lattes. ·

"Wait. What? Why were you crying like that?"

"Because I broke the mirror and I knew you'd be mad at me and you're already mad at me. We just got those fucking closet doors and they were so expensive. Jesus! You called the *police*?"

"I'm sorry! You sounded so fucking freaked out!"

"I knew you'd think I did it on purpose, that I went in a rage and threw the suitcase at the glass. But I didn't! It was an accident! Oh, fucking Christ."

"I'm sorry. Look, just explain."

"*You* explain. Call them back."

"I can't call them back. They're like one minute away." The police station was around the corner from our house, even closer than I was now.

"Well, come home and meet me and tell them. They won't believe me. I'm not going back to the fucking hospital."

I plotted. My brain moved quickly, too quickly, apparently. "I don't want the kids to see. I'll bring them to Jaime's, and then I'll come right home."

I got back in the car and told the kids everything was fine and it was just a misunderstanding but I had to go home and check on Dad and did they want to hang out with Jaime for a while? I called her on the way over and of course she said of course bring them over and I was there in five minutes, saying thank you, thank God for you, and kissing the kids good-bye.

From the bottom of the hill I could see the cop car pulled to the side of our street, the ambulance with its silenced flashing light, another cop car around the corner, all of our chaos in the middle of Aurora Street, for the world to see on an August night. I pulled into the driveway. Aaron was sitting on the porch steps, calmly, barefoot in his black tank top and shorts. Three police officers and two paramedics circled him, and later he'd tell me how he noticed one of them stood behind him, to the side of the porch, in case he bolted. "You're the wife?" one of them asked. I was aware in a distant part of my brain, not the animal part that was still running through the woods, but the human part that made sense of things, that he was the father of one of the kids in Henry's class. Yes, I was the wife. I offered my version of events. My husband had been hysterical and I had overreacted. I could tell from the officer's voice already that the night would end in *No harm, no foul*. I could tell from their postures that they were all chatting amiably, and he had them convinced, maybe even charmed, and that they were just ensuring he wasn't on drugs or beating me up. We were lucky. We were so fucking lucky. And I felt sick with embarrassment. "Yeah," I said.

We talked for a while. "I'm sorry for jumping to conclusions." I said it to the officers, but I meant it for Aaron, too. "Sorry for wasting your time."

"Don't ever be sorry," one of the paramedics said. He was tall and lanky, with strawberry blond curls and a kind voice. "That's what we're here for."

As they drove away, another shame settled in: that I, a white woman afraid of my husband's madness, had taken three seconds to decide to call the police. I knew they would keep me safe. I knew they were likely to keep my husband safe. And I knew that other people in neighborhoods nearby might choose any gory probabilities of a mental health crisis before electing the gory probabilities of a police call.

I didn't go inside to look at the damage. "I don't care about the stupid mirror," I said. We got in the car. I said I was sorry and he said he was sorry. The adrenaline cooled in our veins. At Jaime's, the kids were watching *The Empire Strikes Back* on a shower curtain Jaime had rigged in the living room. Aaron and I went in for a minute and sat awkwardly on the couch. Then we thanked her and we all left.

"You okay, Dad?" Nico asked, buckling his seat belt.

"I'm okay, Bubba," Aaron said.

"Are we still going to *Jurassic Park*?" Henry asked. He was confused. We were confused, too.

I raised my eyebrows at Aaron. We had been to hell and back in twenty minutes. The movie had only just begun. "Sure," he shrugged.

And so as the sun went down we drove to the park and slipped into the back row and set up our beach chairs, and the stars came out over the lake, and the mosquitoes. No one noticed us but the moon.

STONE BABY

There's one other thing Sandra says about Aaron in "The Painted Picture." This one gets his attention.

"When Aaron was born, I was huge. It was actually twins, but only one developed. Twins run in the family, and my brother had twins, my grandmother was a twin, and genealogy-wise, I was really supposed to have twins. So only one developed and I felt, 'Thank God.'"

My mouth must be open, because Aaron says, "Right?"

"How did she know? Did they have ultrasound back then?"

He shrugs, eyes wide.

"Honey," I say. "Dude."

He agrees to see the doctor, the GP he hasn't seen in six months. "Just to get referred for a scan," he says. Aaron can never remember his name, so he calls him Dr. McLovin.

Aaron lies on his back on the exam table. The doctor palpates his gut. He touches, very lightly, the mass above the mass, as though cupping an infant's head. "You've got a little baby in there," he says.

We laugh. "That's the joke."

The doctor suggests an X-ray and an ultrasound. Then, on second thought, a CT scan. A CT scan should catch anything. It takes so long to schedule an ultrasound these days.

We schedule the CT scan for Monday.

.   .   .

Things have been better, no doubt. Long, lovely spans of weeks and weeks when my love is back, when he's *there*. He bakes us our favorite pastry, strawberries and cream cheese tucked inside croissants. He speaks sweet nothings to the cat. He hides a plastic grasshopper in the fiddleleaf fig plant, making us scream, and then laugh.

So when it happens, it's all the more painful, all the more clear: he's himself, and then suddenly he's not.

Half his face is purple now, deflating, the bloody nose collapsing into a bruised cheek. He opens his bathrobe to reveal the wings of his collarbone. Across his chest is a sprinkling of fresh lesions.

"Do you see the lettering?"

It does look like cuneiform, an ancient language tapped out on his skin. But I say, "Honey, it's not lettering."

"Or numbers." He runs his finger along the marks on the ridge of his fist.

"It's not a message."

"It's okay. It means I won't be here for long."

"Don't say that."

"It's okay," he says. "It means I'll be okay. I think it's from my dad."

I **read with** the boys before bed. Aaron's on the couch, delirious. "I wish Dad could be here," Nico says.

"I hope he can sleep," Henry says.

"I know. I'm sorry he's like this." From the other room, I can hear him talking to himself. "He'll be back to normal soon, okay?"

"The surface of this singular monster was covered with a quantity of sebaceous matter, such, in all respects as is often met with on the skin of infants recently born. When this was removed the creature appeared as rosy and as healthy as if it had been yet alive."

In 1808, George William Young described in detail one of the earliest cases of *fetus in fetu*, in a chapter titled "Foetus in a Boy." In the illustration plates, the parasitic twin looks like a yam-shaped organ folded in on itself. The twin has a penis but no anus, blood vessels but no brain. It has a foot. "It must be said," writes the doctor, "that to this foot belong eight toes."

One of the things that gets me about these parasitic twins: sometimes, their hair and nails don't stop growing.

Usually, the mass is identified in a baby or child. The oldest person discovered to have a parasitic twin is a forty-seven-year-old man from Italy, who had an upper abdominal mass and "a familial history of twinning." I do a double-take, reading the abstract. I request an interlibrary loan. When the article arrives, I read it for more signs. When the cystic mass was removed in 1989, it contained several ribs, some bones, an incisor, and two liters of "a viscous yellowish fluid with hairs."

The mass was visible from birth, though, and it didn't cause him any pain. Still, I imagine the Italian man is Aaron's twin. I stage the sick C-section, the surgeons lifting the singular monster from Aaron's body. I'll watch from the other side of the blue sheet, breathless as a new parent, waiting for the doctors to deliver him, for life to begin.

The article about the other forty-seven-year-old man concludes: "the patient is in good health and leading a normal life."

They say that twins have a connection, that one feels pain when the other feels pain. Twin telepathy.

This isn't limited to twins, maybe. My mother used to tell me a story. In the seventies, when she and her siblings were grown, she woke up in Miami in the middle of the night with the gut feeling that something was terribly wrong. Her sister woke in Philadelphia with the same feeling. The next day, they found out that their younger brother, the one who years later would die of AIDS in San Francisco, had been mugged, stabbed in the stomach, while cruising in Central Park.

On *Days of Our Lives*, the long-married couple Bo and Hope share this sense of intuition. It's like a spousal telepathy. Bo can sense when Hope is trapped in an elevator. Hope can sense when Bo has been in a car accident. When Aaron and I read each other's minds, we say we're having a Bo and Hope moment.

I'd like to say I feel Aaron's pain. I can sense when he's off, when he's in distress. When I'm away from him, at my desk at work, sometimes I think: he's not doing well. A gentle little pang in the belly, like a tug on the umbilical cord.

Sometimes, though, Aaron says, "If you could feel this pain for even a second . . ." He says, "You have no idea what kind of pain I'm in."

By Halloween, Aaron has turned a corner, crashed: the transition phase. He sleeps on the couch, in a sleep that seems both deep and restless, while I take the boys trick-or-treating in the rain. Pennywise in a frog raincoat and boots. The Joker with an umbrella. Aaron wakes up to text, *Don't forget to take pictures*, with a heart.

One of the kids we pass is wearing a long, black wig that covers his face. "I'm Cousin It," he tells me, and I say, "Oh, I know," but all I can think of is the *fetus in fetu* with the long, black hair, and then all I can think of is what a grotesque Halloween costume that would make. Nobody would know what you were and everyone would be scared. Fetusinfetu, cousin of Nosferatu (another of Aaron's favorite silent films from 1922). Fetusinfetu is your undead twin, haunting your abdominal cavity, sucking your blood from the inside. It is not fair that you were the one who got to live.

Dictionary.com lists three definitions for parasite:

1. an organism that lives on or in an organism of another species, known as the host, from the body of which it obtains nutriment.
2. a person who receives support, advantage, or the like, from another or others without giving any useful or proper return, as one who lives on the hospitality of others.
3. (in ancient Greece) a person who received free meals in return for amusing or impudent conversation, flattering remarks, etc.

.   .   .

For three days—not a week this time—Aaron sleeps on the couch. When he wakes, he sits but remains a stone. When I try to look at him, there is nothing in his eyes. There is very little more painful to me than this—not being able to find my love, who is right in front of me. Is this his pain I'm feeling, or mine?

I have a friend who is a physical therapist at a rural hospital not far from Ithaca. A few years ago an elderly patient was admitted with a huge, swollen belly. "Let's get you scanned," she told her. In the patient's abdomen, doctors discovered a stone baby. A fetus, grown inside the uterus, dead and calcified for half a century.

These are the words I think of when I look at Aaron on the couch. He is awake but unmoving. Trapped in the womb. My stone baby.

You don't have to have shared a placenta with someone to sense their pain. Some would say that empathy is what makes us human. But I think empathy was here, like parasites and the moon, before we were: a sixth sense, an intuition. The thrumming awareness that we are all connected to the smallest speck, the most distant stars, by the great umbilicus of the solar system, the orbits tossing and tearing us with the force of the tides. When we pay attention to things like parasites and the moon, we are paying attention to the fact that we are citizens of the universe. Most of being human is an effort to forget.

My next interlibrary loan is an article written in German and published in an Austrian medical journal. This time last year, Aaron and I were in Germany, where I downloaded Google Translate and marveled over my phone's ability to magically mutate the words on my menu into English. Now I use the app to take pictures of the article, then watch the text transform. The ancient Greek "parasitos," Dr. Andreas Hassl tells me, "possessed no fortune himself and no prospect of acquiring one." Considered "the house fool"—a kind of jester—he was also "a flatterer and seducer of his host." A sycophant.

("The jokes are a front," Aaron sometimes tells me, usually after someone tells him how funny he is. "If I were to act the way I felt inside, it would be a world of darkness." This makes me incredibly sad for the parasitos.)

The parasitos was also considered a storyteller. In the work of Homer and Aristophanes, they were "immortalized as intriguers." They spun long, comic tales. They were beloved for their entertainment, yet they were always apart.

The ancient Greek character of the parasitos resurfaced centuries later in Roman comedy, but the word "parasite" didn't come into use in English until the days of Shakespeare, who extended its first definition. "The renaissance of the ancient term Parasit, however, does not lack a noteworthy degree of irony." Hassl seems to ascribe the shift, with some exasperation, to poetically inclined scientists. "In a work written in 1646 by Sir Thomas Browne, there are folkloristic errors," he laments. Browne started to use the term too figuratively, describing some plants as "parasitic" because they lived at the expense of other plants.

The fact that Mary Leitao, the mother of the young boy with "harsh hairs" on his back, revived the word "Morgellons" from the work of Sir Thomas Browne, does not lack a noteworthy degree of irony. I suspect she, too, was making a folkloristic error. I suspect I am making a number of them now.

How lovely, how baffling the world must have seemed to Sir Thomas Browne through the lens of the newly invented microscope. I can't blame him for finding a metaphor there.

When Aaron wakes up from his ancient slumber, there is a kind of melting period, wherein he admits he is not made of stone. He says to me, in a who-am-I-kidding-voice, "I can't do anything without you." He hugs me in his size-small gray bathrobe, which can barely close over his big belly now. He corrects himself: "I don't want to do anything without you."

I'm relieved and moved by this small revision. This is the marriage I would sign up for: everything I have isn't yours, but everything I have is better when shared with you.

For his abdominal scan Aaron changes into a pair of drawstring shorts and the puffy yellow jacket he bought in Germany. He is to have nothing but clear fluids that morning. He drinks vodka. "Vodka is a clear fluid," he says.

The difference between a twin and a parasite is a parasite never wanted to be born. They want you alive so they can be alive. You are their safe and warm cosmos.

"Maybe we ourselves are organisms inside some cosmic superbeast," Kathleen McAuliffe writes in *This Is Your Brain on Parasites*. "What we call the universe is nothing more than a bubble of flatulence in its monstrous, gurgling gut, and we can no more comprehend its complexity and purpose than *E. coli* could imagine what makes a human tick or fathom the vast expanse of time that separates its lifespan from our own."

We call for the results of the CT scan. We are told to access the Patient Portal. From the couch downstairs, Aaron texts me a screenshot of the doctor's note:

> The report has a lot of small, incidental findings. Nothing of great concern.

By this time, the mass has receded. Vanished, like a twin. Aaron's belly is as flat as a lake. Above his navel is the healing blister of a sun. Under his right nipple, a patch of pink.

Some call people on public assistance parasites on the system. In his job as a housing assistant, Aaron defended them. Now, he does not qualify for one kind of disability benefits because he did not work enough in the last ten years. He didn't put enough into the system. He doesn't qualify for the other kind of disability benefits because he is married to me, a person with sufficient income. I feed him. I house him. I feed and house his parasites. Some would call him my parasite. Perhaps that makes his parasites mine, too.

Where does his body end and mine begin? We can point to the epidermis, but the epidermis is porous. If we were a different kind of twins, conjoined, forged from the same yolky egg in the ocean of the womb, we might be born merged, sharing an organ or two. What then?

Anyway, marriage is a parasitic arrangement. I can no more change that than I can stop the earth from turning, or exorcise the invisible beast from my husband, or outsmart God.

I prefer to think of him as my parasitos, selected partner, immortalized intriguer, bringer of joy, giver of jokes, compliments, rhymes, stories at the dinner table, drawings and love notes and heart emojis and half-recorded songs. Isn't this a kind of provision, a family nutriment? I like to think it's worth something. I like to think it's enough.

Still, there's the ancient caste system. If he's the intriguer, that makes me the intrigued. I'm the divine, the immortal, the one with the power. For his loyal entertainment I pay him with food and a roof and vodka. If I wanted, I could banish the mortal from my kingdom.

I prefer to think I'm the epic poet, immortalizing him, but maybe I am both.

If I shared this theory with Aaron, he would no doubt dismiss it on the grounds that the Ancient Greek social system also included pederasty, "the love of boys."

More romantic, maybe, to just say he is my moon, or my sun, or I am his. Or maybe one of us is the Earth—who is the primary celestial body, and who the satellite?

With Aaron at the library, I spotted a book on the new shelf: *The Moon*. In it, Oliver Morton writes of moon landings, gravity, moon myths.

"It is generally true that, when the Moon is male, the Sun is female, and vice versa—'Brother Sun, Sister Moon,' as the Franciscans have it. Often the two are siblings. That said, they are also often lovers, and not infrequently both."

We make metaphors of the moon, of the sun, in order to understand them, but they shine over their light-years back to our earthly relations: siblings, lovers. Metaphor tells us that everything is related, nothing is wasted, nothing alone, nothing beyond our measure. What to do then, with the excess? With the detritus of our home planet, the mistakes, the vestigial organs, the tumors and miscarriages and garbage islands, forests and bodies on fire? They are as manifest as the pockmarked face of the moon, which itself was a made thing, "born molten." Its craters were formed from fountains of lava. They remind us that no metaphor is stable, that the cool slice of blue cheese in the sky was once fire.

I am startled to learn that "too much fire," in traditional Chinese medicine, is simply another term for *yang*. When you are "on fire," you have too much yang, or masculine energy. When you are "taking cold," you have too much yin, or feminine energy.

Brother Sun, Sister Moon.

"Your face is so cold," Aaron used to tell me.

The opposite of too much is not enough. When I was in seventh grade, when asked in Spanish class to translate "too much," I wrote on the worksheet *demasiado mucho*. I had a feeling I'd gone too far, gone too literal, stuck in my English. I went to the front of the class to turn it in. My teacher smiled, stopping herself from laughing. Then she crossed out *mucho*. "Just *demasiado*."

Too much too much.

In seventh grade, like all the wannabe surfer white girls, I liked to draw yin yang symbols on my notebooks. I still feel like that girl,

Google-translating the world, stealing a phrase I haven't bothered to fully understand. Not enough.

A 2007 article in the journal *Immunologic Research* posits that chimerism, the presence of two genetically distinct kinds of cells in one person, plays a "possible role" in autoimmune disorders. The idea is that when a human is made up of more than one human—a vanished twin, for instance—his body rejects the Other.

In the upstairs bathroom, in a basket by the toilet, is a book by Dr. Gabor Maté called *When the Body Says No*. Little orange Post-it tabs poke out of its pages. "We want to describe human beings," one page says, "as though they function in isolation from the environment in which they develop, live, work, play, love and die. These are the built-in, hidden biases of the medical orthodoxy that most physicians absorb during their training and carry into their practice."

The body is connected to what's outside the body, just as holistic medicine insists that organs are connected within the body. They orbit each other in their own bloody galaxy: liver, kidneys, thymus, heart; pancreas, stomach, esophagus, lungs. The largest organ, the skin, is a kind of gravity, saying, we belong together.

"Some stories of the Moon's influence are baked into language," Morton writes in *The Moon*, "in words like *mania*, and *lunacy*, and *menstruation*. This does not make these stories true. Women's monthly cycles are close to the duration of the Moon's, but they are not synchronized to it. Nor is madness, at least as measured today, which shows no relation to the phase of the Moon."

But, Morton continues, "is there anything madder than a light that makes things look different and only comes in darkness? And if there is a cycle of the womb and a cycle of the sky, do they have to be in lock-step to be some sort of same? Stories can be true and untrue at the same time; they can mean one thing and also its opposite."

If the gravest harm has been done by human hubris, by the folly of attempting to play God, to control, conquer, cure, then I suppose it's humility I must seek, acceptance. Stop resisting. Stop fighting gravity. Let the earth, our bodies, be. Close the laptop. Put down the microscope, the telescope. There is no portal. There is no world better than this one. This is what my love is trying to tell me, if I listen.

"People are missing the point," he says, walking in the yard one evening. It's November. The trees have emptied, and the tall grasses have gone brown. "They should take a hint." We hold hands. The moon peeks through the clouds, a hint of it, over his shoulder. He says, "We're not supposed to live forever."

THEORY 10

He has all of it, or any of it, or none of it. Morgellons, Lyme, parasites, PTSD, schizophrenia, too much fire—all names for an unknowable thing. Not *or* but *and*. Nature and nurture. A boy was bitten, and broken.

Picture a planet in a galaxy far, far away. Undiscovered by human science. Picture tunneling the same distance, light-years, inside a human body. Then the same distance inside a tick inside that body. A worm inside a tick. A virus inside a worm. Something else, something smaller, nesting inside the virus, something subcellular we don't have lenses or language for yet. Will we ever? Does it matter? Does the something in the virus have a purpose other than to poison something bigger?

Feel sorry for the something. Don't bother asking its name. It doesn't feel the wind. Only the polluted atmosphere inside the body it has made sick.

QUARANTINE

Aaron's nose is bleeding. In the sink, in the car, little red drops that spot the kitchen floor, then the soles of our white socks.

He has an appointment with the neurologist, who refers him back to the ear-nose-throat doctor who did the surgery on Aaron's deviated septum last year. The ENT doctor recommends a saline nasal gel, which I buy at the supermarket.

Dr. Queen also refers him to a rheumatologist, whose office is in the floor above in the same new shiny building, a building that did not exist when Aaron first got sick, and I think maybe there will be a new building built in some future year that will contain the office of a new specialist, the right one. Aaron is superstitious of elevators in buildings with only two floors, so we take the stairs, even though his joints are aching and he's using a cane. The rheumatologist, Dr. Toscani, wears a bowtie with his white coat and uses "heck" in every other sentence. He gives us a full hour of his time, takes down all the symptoms. "I like to detectivize," he says. He asks Aaron if he has oral lesions. Aaron says he does. Dr. Toscani wants to test him for Behçet's, a rare autoimmune disease that causes inflammation of the blood vessels, joint pain, vision problems, neurological effects, and lesions. I allow myself to entertain the hope, Googling it as we wait to check out. *Ba-shetts.* Named after the Turkish dermatologist who discovered it. I imagine myself saying it at a dinner party, writing it down on a health form. "He has Behçet's." Those two syllables, how they might shape a rough structure we can live inside, a shelter of twigs and clay.

The labs must be done at the hospital. Aaron doesn't like this, but he goes. I sit in the chair next to him at the intake, then watch his blood shoot into the nine vials. *Labs* is the syllable that shapes us for now, the blood a thing we can see and know.

On the afternoon of the snow moon—it's February, on what feels like the day of deepest snow—we go to the Fire and Ice Festival at the Children's Garden. Ithaca, land of festivals. Aaron says he feels like he's in a Hallmark Christmas movie. Families parallel park their Foresters against the bank of snow, Christmas trees strapped to the top, then drag the piney carcasses to the bonfire and watch them bounce and blaze. Hot cocoa is ladled into earthenware mugs from a giant steaming cauldron. Toddlers in teddy-bear snowsuits toddle through snow up to their chins. The boys climb over the snow-covered tree stumps, through the snow-covered branch huts. On the giant snow-covered turtle, they reenact the finale of *Revenge of the Sith*, Anakin sliding into the lava lake, Obi-Wan standing on higher ground. Aaron laughs hard, steadying himself on his cane. He says, "I'm so happy right now." At the snack bar we buy vegan lentil soup and hand warmers, which we take turns sharing, but our toes are frozen a half hour in. By the time the sun has dropped and the fire dancers begin, we are sitting in the car with the heat on full blast. The full moon rises across the lake, above the distant ridge of Cornell. It's the color of a watchful eyeball, a little yellower than white, a little bluer. The kids use their mittens to clear a circle in the steamed-up window and watch the torches twirl in the settling dark.

At home, Aaron starts to fall apart. His ankles feel like they're being crushed, he says. His head throbs. I fill and refill his Nalgene bottle. "I feel really weird right now," he says calmly, leaning against the refrigerator. "You don't look right." He looks at me. "You don't look like you should be here." He says, "I don't know what I'm supposed to do." The boys help me help him to the couch, where he lies down, falls asleep, and then promptly wakes up, mumble-shouting, "I don't know I don't know I don't know!" This goes on for an hour or so. The boys take turns sitting by his side until they too have to go to sleep.

"He keeps waking up and falling asleep," Henry says, shrugging. They muffle their laughter, delighted and concerned.

"He'll be okay," I say.

The next day, he is. It's like he's slept off a bender, except he wasn't drunk. He laughs when the kids imitate him sleep-shouting.

"You smell like syrup," I say, suddenly alert to him, getting a whiff of it from his neck.

"Great," Aaron says, "thanks."

I've noticed it for a day or two now. I thought maybe my own sense of smell was distorted; maybe I was hormonal. I first suspected I was pregnant when I woke up and Aaron smelled powerfully of mustard. But the next day Henry says, "You do smell like syrup, Dad."

Aaron sniffs his own wrist. "God, I do."

I sniff again, near his ear, his overgrown sideburns; there is no other metaphor: he smells like syrup.

"This is what I need," he says. "To smell like an IHOP."

That night, as I'm putting Nico to bed, Aaron texts me from the couch with symptoms from a medical website. *What is Maple Syrup Urine Disease?*

> Omg. Did you google "Why do I smell like maple syrup?"
> Maybe
> I'm sorry I'm giggling
> No seriously read it

I read it. A metabolic disease. I am not totally sure what this means. Genetic. A problem with amino acids. Apparently it's mostly diagnosed in newborns, or even in utero.

> Untreated in older individuals, and during times of meta-
> bolic crisis, symptoms of the condition include uncharac-
> teristically inappropriate, extreme or erratic behavior and
> moods, hallucinations, lack of appetite, weight loss, ane-
> mia, diarrhea, vomiting, dehydration, lethargy, oscillating

hypertonia and hypotonia, ataxia, seizures . . . rapid neurological decline, and coma.

Wow, I text back.

You think you know some things about the human body by now. You
were not really paying attention during the unit on the endocrine system.

The next day, at Dr. McLovin's office, I say, "You're going to laugh,
doctor. It's okay. He smells like maple syrup."

The doctor nods.

"You know what I'm going to say?"

He does. It's rare, he says. But he once came across a family who
carried the gene. One baby died as a newborn. The next baby was diagnosed but survived. The next child was not diagnosed but developed
the disease at age ten. She had to be careful of what she ate for the rest
of her life. "It's definitely bizarre," he says. "It's a reach." He plays his
charade game, imitating the building blocks of proteins, of recessive
and dominant genes. The genetic test is complicated. But they'll start
by checking Aaron's amino acid levels. The next morning, he fasts and
I drive him to the hospital and they draw his blood. He can come here
now, to the hospital, without shaking.

We wait for the results. Every other night, it happens again. Evening
coming on. After an outing, some exertion, he'll sit at the dinner table
and fade away.

"I'm disappearing," he warns.

The next time it happens, he licks Nico's face. Aaron is the exact last
person who would ever lick anyone's face. The next day, he can't believe
it. He cracks up, shakes his head.

"I licked your *face*? Oh, Bubba, I am so sorry."

"Why are all these guns pointing at me?"

"I don't want to go over there." He wags a hand in front of him. Eyes
half-closed. "Please stop shooting. I don't want to but I'll kill you back."

"I'm scared."

"I don't know where I am."

"I don't want to go up. I don't want to leave. Why am I leaving?"

"I'm going into space."

"I don't trust you."

"What are you doing? Are you recording me? I told you not to record me."

He's like a parody of a guy having a bad dream, but the dream lasts for hours, and he's half-awake, waking to shuffle across the room, to collapse again on the couch, to look in the refrigerator, to ask for water, to cry. When I come into the room, he looks at me like I'm a stranger. He looks like he's trying to figure out why he hates me.

"It's okay, Dad," Henry says, petting his head. "You're in your home. You're safe."

"No one is trying to shoot you," says Nico.

I was recording him, though. Nico and I, aiming the barrels of our phones at him. We wanted it for later, when he was himself again. To tell him, this is what we saw. It was real.

We have decided to sell the house. The dream house we built in the country. The house I dreamed tile by tile, to distract myself from the nightmare.

Thing I've learned: The dream house cannot save you from the nightmare.

Thing I've learned: Magical thinking doesn't work on a mortgage. Or a marriage.

We can't really afford it, is the main thing. Every morning, beside my worry about Aaron, is another worry: How will we keep paying for this house?

Too much money, too much house, too far away. We feel isolated out here, the blank-faced mountains watching us like God. When we built this house, we didn't know Aaron would all but stop driving, that my days would be filled with shuttling him to doctor appointments ten miles into civilization and back, that the stairs would strain his knees, his lungs, that it would be the perfect sick house, keeping him stranded on the empty acres all winter, *a very dull boy*, while I carried on my life in town.

We start to look for a new house. Something in town, a neighborhood, with a garden someone has already started for us.

Thing I've learned: I can come up with a lot of reasons to move. To start the story again.

I guess other people have affairs. I guess this is better than that.

The results for the Amino Acid Screen Plasma come back via the Patient Portal. Aaron texts me a screen shot.

"This is a normal profile."

Not Maple Syrup Urine Disease.

Aaron is devastated, cries, says he doesn't want to go on.

I try to make him feel better. We go to bed and make each other feel better. When he withdraws his face from between my legs, I see that it is covered in blood. He looks as though he's been punched in the nose. Very red blood soaks his nose, his mouth, his very full beard. I think for a moment that it's my blood, that I've spontaneously gotten my period, a period I don't really get anymore. But it's his nose that's erupted, and his blood is on me, too.

It's not Behçet's, either.

Back at Dr. Toscani's, though, we tell the bowtied rheumatologist about the new symptoms, the syrup smell, the way the hallucinations come on like a cloud. He looks in Aaron's eyes and nose and mouth. "If it makes you feel better," he says, stethoscope to Aaron's chest, "I can smell it, too."

Dr. Toscani asks Aaron to lie down and he feels his belly. His belly is huge, pregnant. When the nurse asked him to get on the scale, the number was almost as high as it was years ago, during the bad time, before he gave up drinking. "It's kinda firm, isn't it?" he asks Aaron, concerned. Is it firm because it's soaked with alcohol, or firm because his body has ceased working like a body should? Casually, as though he's squirting mustard on a hot dog, he grabs a wand from the laptop cart beside him and covers it with gel.

"Is that an ultrasound?" I ask.

"Yeah. I'm not an expert radiographer or anything," he says. But he rubs the wand over Aaron's belly, in the place where he has the pain. Is it his liver, begging for mercy? Or something else, begging to get out? The screen is a black hole. "It's a baby!" Dr. Toscani says. "Just kidding."

He cleans off Aaron's belly and then sits down. "I'm an expert Googler," he boasts. He is literally looking at Google on his phone when he discovers that the maple syrup smell can also be the result of an "annoyed" liver. Annoyed by alcohol or annoyed by something else? He wants Aaron to get a real ultrasound, and some more liver testing.

Dr. Toscani says, "We gotta find out what the heck this is."

In the imaging center, we sanitize. The first Ithaca patients have just been quarantined on suspicion of carrying the coronavirus.

Aaron lies on his side on a hospital bed. The tech, tiny-waisted in scrubs airbrushed with pink and purple swirls, churns an ultrasound wand over his belly. I remember my dad on his side, getting scanned, the cardboard-thin slice of him. Aaron is big today, his beard overgrown, his belly wide and full; his head aches. It is a full moon, the first Monday of daylight savings time, the ninth day of March. On the wall, the calendar is still flipped to February, four Valentine's cupcakes perky with red candy hearts.

I had ultrasounds myself, of course, with each pregnancy, and the second time, to find out the sex of the baby. Once, during the months I was first trying to get pregnant, an unwelcome wand probed inside me for the source of my pain and infertility. It was during the first hours of my period, my uterus gasping with cramps. The ultrasound couldn't read the endometriosis that grew in my tubes; that would be confirmed later, through laparoscopy. The wand just tore around, a blind moon rover. It felt long enough to reach my guts; it stirred a little white light in my brain.

Which is to say, my empathy for Aaron has a source in memory, not just in theory. He closes his eyes and holds on to the railing of the bed, bracing himself, against his headache or the cool gel on his belly or the indignity of the procedure or his fear of medical buildings. Over his shoulder, I watch the gray images bloom on the screen, a Rorschach galaxy, a Loch Ness gallery, a crystal ball. Everyone knows you can't see anything on those screens, but if you look the right way, you can see everything: a hawk, a butter knife, a howling mouth, a flaming fish. The tech does not joke that she sees a baby, but I see it: the third baby we tried for, half-heartedly, wondering if we should, if our sick house family could hold another life, if the briar patch of my womb could. I see the tomatoes that didn't grow in the garden, the stillborn jobs, the dinners gone cold, the ashes of our parents, the malformed pillow of each morning. I see the things that were and things that weren't, the things that might have been.

The results of the ultrasound and the liver bloodwork come back fast, the next day. We get calls from the rheumatologist's office and the neurologist's office, nervous nurses reading his chart. For once, the results are not normal. They can't tell us much, though. Follow up with your GP right away, they urge him.

By the time we see the doctor that evening, the world has shifted a few inches. Our thumbs try to keep up with the news. Harvey Weinstein is sentenced to twenty-three years in prison. The World Health Organization declares COVID-19 a pandemic. In the exam room, we make small talk about the virus with the doctor. He wears the same half-laugh expression as when he told us he found a V8 in his in-law's pantry that had expired in the year 2000—and drank it. The local health department isn't ready, he says. But from what he's hearing, it might not be that serious. "Children get it, and it's like a cold," he says, showing us his palms.

Aaron's liver is enlarged. Dr. McLovin squints to decode the chart on his tiny laptop. Spleen also mildly enlarged. Elevated enzyme levels.

"How enlarged?"

Normally, he says, a liver is 8 to 10 centimeters wide and 10 to 12 centimeters long. When the liver grows, it grows vertically, never horizontally. Aaron's liver is 23 centimeters long. "So, basically, it's twice its normal size." Dr. McLovin says this as though it's unsurprising, natural, even, like a sourdough rising. He continues to translate the chart. It's non-cirrhotic: not scarred. Increased echogenecity: not necessarily fatty, but sort of grainy. He holds up an imaginary sack. "Imagine if you had a bag of different grains, and you can see the individual grains inside. That's what your liver looks like now." I picture the sack, millet and oat and amaranth, bloated with whiskey.

"Are we super concerned?" Dr. McLovin asks. "Not yet."

"Good," Aaron says. "I'm not concerned, either."

I raise my hand. "Can I be concerned?" It's not Aaron's behavior that concerns me. In a lineup of sober people, no one would be able to pick him out as the drunk one. No slurring, no stumbling, no aggravation. It's clear to me that even his blackouts aren't typical alcoholic blackouts. "It's these new symptoms that concern me." I remind them both what's been happening: the passing out, hallucinations, memory loss, nosebleeds. Yesterday, he vomited blood. "I read about hepatic encephalopathy." Brain damage brought on by liver disease.

The doctor nods. "Always activated through ammonia levels. His ammonia levels are fine."

Aaron nods, too, as though he knew this, and can take credit.

"Okay, your liver is *twice* its normal size. I mean, how much bigger can it get?"

"Oh, it can get quite a bit bigger," says the doc.

"But once it's damaged, once it's . . . fatty, the damage is done, right?"

"Actually, the liver can repair itself. It's quite resilient."

Aaron raises his eyebrows, satisfied.

Dr. McLovin refers us to a new gastroenterologist, since the liver is a digestive organ—who knew? The gastro will run some more tests to determine the source of the enlarged liver. They can even do a liver biopsy. The source! I don't know whether to be grateful for the circumspection, or insulted, or just amused. I can tell you the source of the enlarged liver, I think but do not say. I'll save you some time.

"Obviously, in the meantime, you want to cut back on alcohol."

Aaron and I exchange tight little looks.

"It's complicated," I say.

Aaron admits it: he's been drinking heavily for nine, ten months. He doesn't say how heavily. I don't even really know, or want to know, myself. But he also hasn't broken out in five months.

"I understand," the doctor says, and for once I think he does. I am grateful for his lack of judgment, and also furious. Usually I'm angry because the doctors assume drug use; now I'm angry because this one doesn't. But if he's not going to tell my husband that his drinking is going to kill him, who will?

We check out, sanitize. It is hard not to confuse the world health crisis with my husband's rapidly expanding liver. We are all grains in a yeasty sponge of our own poisoning. *How much worse can it get? Oh, a lot worse.*

"See?" Aaron says in the car. "Not so serious."

I give him a look. "He doesn't think the coronavirus is serious, either!"

I remember Dr. McLovin's happy chatter with my father a week before he was dead.

Aaron is not concerned about his liver, but he is following COVID-19 with a disciple's devotion. He texts me updates from across the globe: infection rates and death rates, school closings and restaurant closings, each store shuttering in our little town, one by one, the world drawing down its metal doors. When he reads about the old people dying in Seattle, in Italy, he begins to cry, cradling his phone as though it, too, has lost life in his palm.

It is both abstract and concrete, the pandemic: you can't see it, and you can. Its terror is its invisibility, the way it transforms strangers, even loved ones, into carriers, everyone unsafe, everyone a threat. Yet we have all seen the images of the virus, sometimes a blood-colored planet with its gold crown, sometimes a gray foam ball with little pigtails of red yarn, something out of a cartoon about ocean life. It looks three-dimensional enough to touch, real as a Kooosh ball. The coronavirus has no cure, no vaccine, but by the time we heard about it, it already had a name, an origin, a history, a test. I imagine what this pandemic would feel like if it didn't, if we were still trying to trap it in the microscope.

We are attracted, Aaron and I, maybe all of us, to the chronicle of the pandemic, even as it frightens us, throws our days into disarray. The story is shaped by our newsfeeds. We wait for the next chapter. We cannot look away. There is something equalizing about this virus: anyone with lungs can catch it. Some are more vulnerable, of course. But the reality of the disease is experienced, in a way, by all of us—each of us susceptible, each of us a player, actors or athletes ready to be called. As Susan Sontag said, "Everyone who is born holds dual citizenship, in the kingdom of the well and the kingdom of the sick." Odd, to watch Aaron participate in the democracy of disease, when isolated with an illness so private it seems invented by the circumstances of his own body. His illness, whatever it is, is the opposite of a pandemic.

How neat, a virus: it is in you, or it's not.

For now, it's not in us. At least we don't think so.

It is out there. We can stay in here. Aaron wants us to stay in here.

He does not want to follow up with the gastroenterologist. He does not want to step foot in another doctor's office, not with sick people coming and going.

He does, however, want to stop at the liquor store.

We stock the pantry, swab our phones with alcohol wipes, install Zoom. We Zoom into the Recovering Couples meeting, where we haven't made an appearance in months. Aaron's been too sick to go most Sunday nights, and too uncomfortable showing up when he's been drinking—he feels like a hypocrite. But the pandemic has created the technical conditions that allow us to attend. We watch our friends' faces appear on the screen, listen to the rasp of their fingers trying to find the mute button. We have all found each other. We are here.

One friend, the chemist, thinks he might have the virus. He is quarantined in his basement. His wife leaves soup outside his door. They Zoom in from different rooms in the same house, take walks together on the opposite side of the road. Aaron's eyes fill with tears.

When it's our turn to share, he doesn't say that he's spent the last three seasons drinking his way toward liver disease.

"I've been in quarantine for the last year," he jokes. "Need any tips? Let me know."

The next day, our house is supposed to go on the market. The Realtor has already hammered the For Sale sign into the rocky earth by the road. I've cleaned every inch of the house, patched and spackled the holes in the doors. I have hung a new door in our bedroom closet, the hole—the size of my own fist—too big to patch.

But it's also the first day of lockdown, the first day my classes are cancelled, and the kids are home. Stores are closed. We are not to be within six feet of another human unless completely necessary. Is it completely necessary? Is it insane to try to sell a house in a pandemic?

We call the Realtor. We take the sign down. We do not want strangers coming in and out, we realize, not when the world is sick. Our sick house has become our safe house, something precious, worth preserving. The lockbox remains hanging from the doorknob, a reminder that one day this will be over.

Strange, to feel the sick *out there,* beyond. We have not eradicated illness from Aaron's body, but it has been eradicated, I realize, from the body of our house. It is not lost on me that this is because it has been trapped, like a bad spirit, in Aaron's body. He has helped make our house healthier by keeping his sickness inside. This is called a sacrifice, like the one we are all asked to make now, for public health.

"Of course we'll stay inside," Aaron says. He wants to protect the health of our family—Henry has asthma, and who knows what kind of shape Aaron's immune system is in?—but he also wants to participate in the greater good. It is a side effect of chronic illness, the practiced, selfless art of taking one for the team.

Before the pandemic reached us, we requested a referral to a local endocrinologist. We wanted to pursue more advanced testing, after the GP's preliminary tests came back negative. Aaron still smells like a maple syrup bottling plant.

Now Aaron gets a call from the GP's office, from a receptionist working from home. I hear Aaron's voice on the phone. When he hangs up, he tells me the endocrinologist denied our request. After reviewing Aaron's file, he recommended that he see a dermatologist.

Odd to live in a world where doctors have let down my husband again and again, and where doctors are saving lives every day. Some of them give their own lives. They are heroes, walking into hospitals as though into battle, poorly armored with masks and gloves. They are made for this, although they perhaps never meant to enlist in this war.

Every evening, in neighborhoods across the world, people are stepping out onto their porches, their balconies, to sing the praises of doctors and nurses; to sing, literally, their voices whooping and reaching. On my phone, I listen. It makes my eyes water. I do not live in a neighborhood. Our houses are too far apart to make any kind of music. But if I did, I would sing, and my voice would catch, joining the chorus of thanks and grief. Maybe I would just bang some pots and pans, beat them gently with a baseball bat.

One of our favorite *Seinfeld* episodes is the one where George pretends to be a marine biologist to impress a woman. When a beached whale is discovered as they stroll along the shore, someone shouts, *Is anyone here a marine biologist?!*

Now Aaron and I put on that voice, walking around the kitchen, acting out an emergency. *Is anyone here a dermatologist?!*

You think you've heard every story about your husband. Maybe you have; maybe you've forgotten some of them. Then they come back around, one night during quarantine when you're all sitting around the dinner table, and you hear them.

Once, in a Long Island pizza shop, Aaron choked on a mouthful of mozzarella cheese. His father stood up, threw him over a chair, and gave him the Heimlich.

"He saved your life," I say. It's almost a question: how can it be? I look at my two children, who wouldn't be here if my husband had died, a child himself, their age.

"What did it feel like?" the kids want to know. "Did you think you were going to die?"

"It happened so fast," he says. He didn't have time to think about anything. He just remembers not breathing, and then the feeling of the mass flying out of his throat.

It happened in the same mall, he says, where he first saw a Michael Jackson jacket. He really wanted that jacket.

It was the same mall where, once, Aaron and his father were separated. Aaron didn't panic. He knew what to do. He went to the info desk and reported that his dad was lost.

The woman behind the desk smiled. "You mean you're lost?"

"No," he said. "My dad is lost."

"I wasn't just being cute," he tells us now. "It was like, even then, I knew my dad was the one who needed help."

"What am I supposed to do?" he says. "I don't know what I'm supposed to do."

"You don't have to do anything," I tell him.

"They're not supposed to be here."

"No one's here. Just you and me."

"I hear someone else's voice."

"Who is it?"

But my husband is some kind of asleep.

In his morphine dreams, the night before he died, my father talked all night. I've heard the same from others who have witnessed their loved ones cross over, holding conversations with the dead. *What am I supposed to do?* they seem to be asking, and then pause for a moment, awaiting instructions.

In the hospital, on ventilators, COVID patients are beginning to go mad.

They become paranoid, agitated, reporting disturbing technicolor hallucinations. The doctors call it delirium. It happens because of a lack of oxygen to the brain, they say, because of sedatives, lack of sleep. But the virus itself may also cause changes in the brain. Blood clots. Neurological inflammation. After they recover from COVID and leave the hospital, delirium can have long-term, dementia-like effects.

Alone in their beds, patients believe they are being burned alive, attacked by cats. One woman says she turned into an ice sculpture. One man says his doctors, armed with guns, were trying to kill him.

What are you supposed to do?

There are moments, hours, when you cannot believe you have accepted this life as your own. When you try but can't quite remember being a girl with a body and a mind bound only to a family of origin, quarantined from the woman you would become. You remember the restless questions that bannered your days. *Where will I live? What job will I have? Who will my husband be? What will be my children's names?*

Now there is the restlessness of aging beside another body, living the middle part, living the answers. Now the questions are *What will we die of? When?*

On our anniversary—not our wedding anniversary, but the twenty-third anniversary of our first date, which we still count—I put on Billie Holiday and we dance in the kitchen. Both of us are in our bathrobes, our quarantine uniforms. We just kind of sway. I'm kind of holding Aaron up. His head is heavy on my shoulder. His neck smells like syrup. "Everything I Have Is Yours" was maybe an extreme choice for our song, we recognize now. *Everything that I possess, I offer to you!* We laugh at the lyrics. "Kinda codependent, Billie," Aaron says in my ear, though we know it's not really her song, that it was written by a man and recorded by men for twenty years before she ever sang it.

Still, we love the song. It's ours. We keep dancing.

"The rhyming is the part I like best," Aaron says. If he has schizophrenia, even a touch of it—he believes he does—then he is glad for the rhyming. It keeps him, us, entertained.

He and the boys change the lyrics to the White Stripes' "Blue Orchid."

> You've got an erection
> It points in many directions
> I think it's got an infection!

The boys laugh and laugh.

Across the world, families are on lockdown, trapped in their houses with one another. But how many hours like this one have my kids already logged with their dad? "My dad wasn't really around" is not something they'll ever say.

I roll my eyes. And laugh.

.   .   .

Aaron turns forty-eight. He is one hundred pounds heavier than he was on his last birthday. He says he thought he was forty-eight already. He says he's daylight-savings'd himself.

I bring home takeout for his birthday, and stop to get some groceries at the local co-op, and a few days later we learn that a worker at the store tested positive for the coronavirus. I go through our local drive-thru testing site, get my nostril swabbed, which feels like someone trying to aim a javelin at the back of my skull. It brings back, for ten seconds, the shock and discomfort of the ultrasound wand. While we wait for the results, I have to quarantine. "Quarantine" is from the Italian *quarantina*, a period of forty days. But everyone knows that COVID quarantine is two weeks. A fortnight. Aaron and I know exactly how long two weeks is.

A couple days later, on the day I get the negative result, Aaron's jaw begins to swell on each side. Is it just the weight he's put on? He shaves his beard, his massive, Unabomber beard. The kids can't stop staring at him. "You look so different!" His neck and jaw are huge. He looks like Robert DeNiro when he played Robert Mueller on *SNL,* with the prosthetic jowls. "I look like I'm storing nuts for winter," he says. He says, "Jesus, I don't want to Google this shit." But then he does. The first result that comes up is mumps.

Mumps! We laugh and groan. What's next? Maple Syrup Urine Disease? "Hot chocolate syndrome?" Aaron says. Did he catch it at the grocery store? Mumps, in the middle of a pandemic?

Mumps, or whatever it is, hurts. He can barely swallow. Sores appear on the inside of his mouth. His neck aches. When I call the doctor and describe his symptoms, the nurse wants him to come in that afternoon. Aaron is seen behind the building in a shed, an actual shed, that looks like it was purchased out of the parking lot of Home Depot. The doctor is an older man we've never seen before, and we don't really see him now: he is wearing goggles and a mask and gloves and a yellow get-up that is either plastic scrubs or a full-body poncho; it is drizzling outside. All we can see is the top of the doctor's bald head, sun-spotted and vulnerable. When the doctor's light won't turn on, Aaron takes out his cell phone and turns on the flashlight and aims it into his own mouth. I watch from ten feet away, standing next to our parked car. It is a strange world we live in. Aaron doesn't say mumps, but the doctor does, and takes his blood to test for it, though in all his years he has never seen it before. He also swabs his mouth for strep and asks Aaron to swab his nose for the flu. "I do it myself?" Aaron asks, taking the Q-tip. After the invasive gouge of the coronavirus test, after the ways both our bodies have been prodded and probed, this seems simple and infinitely humane: to allow a patient to test himself.

We watch the doctor undress himself carefully before he goes back inside, stripping off his poncho scrubs. How many times a day does he have to do this? "Amazing, what they have to do," Aaron says in the car, "putting themselves at risk like that." The next day, the doctor will call Aaron with the results: all negative. Of course. Aaron will take more tests, for old diseases and new ones. He will go through the ritual of blood draws and disappointment. What matters is that the doctor calls and says, "I hope you feel better," before gently hanging up.

"What a nice guy," Aaron says.

The extra hundred pounds, it's alcohol weight. He knows it. It's the same kind of weight from the bad time. He has pains in his liver, pains in his heart.

"It's going to kill me," he says.

He says, "I'm so scared."

"It's been seven months. It can't come back. I won't survive if it comes back."

"I know I have to stop. I will stop."

"I hate being this big."

"But when I'm this big," he says, "I don't feel anything." He has a layer of fat protecting him, like a polar bear. "I don't feel anything moving inside me. No sensations at all." Nico touches his back on the couch, and Aaron says he barely feels it.

"That's terrible," I say.

"No," he says. "It's fucking great."

He starts, stops. Stops, starts.

Usually Nico is the last to wake up. But one morning he wanders into the kitchen first, where I'm writing at the table. He is barefoot, in a sweater and sweatpants, his hair sticking up in all directions. "Can I interview you?" I ask, and he takes a seat, smiling.

"Do you remember that homework you did, the worksheet about feelings?"

He looks confused.

"You were in fourth grade, I think. It asked what you were anxious about. You wrote *sick house family*."

He twists up his face, amused at his former self. "Really? I don't remember."

"When I came to you with it, you balled it up and threw it under the bed."

Nico laughs. "I do *not* remember."

"Do you remember feeling that, though? Anxious about Dad being sick?"

He nods. He says he remembers a time Dad was really sick and I asked him and Henry to come into the bedroom and say good-bye to him.

Now I twist up my face. "I do *not* remember that."

It could have been any number of nights. Bad nights, when Aaron would say, "I don't think I'm going to make it."

"I don't think I would have asked you and Henry to do that, honey. Probably Dad said he wanted to say good-bye. He was probably really worried." I don't insist too hard, though, wary of pressing my version of events in lieu of Aaron's.

Nico nods.

"Do you still feel worried about Dad?"

He thinks about it, hugging his knees into his chest. "I feel a lot less worried." He's eleven and a half, and his *R*s are deliberate and sharp. "I mean, I wish he didn't drink so much."

"Of course."

"It sucks, when he can't pick me up from school 'cause he's been drinking." He flexes his toes back, palming the soles of his feet. "Then again, I'm not in school anymore."

"And you take the bus," I point out.

"Oh yeah." He smiles. "Can I ask you a question?"

"Of course."

"Why didn't you believe Dad? About the parasites?"

I sigh. It's not the first time I've answered the question. "It was complicated, honey. It still is. When you see someone you love become someone you don't recognize, it's really scary. You know what that's like, right?"

Nico nods.

"When the doctors said Dad was making them up, it was the only thing that made any sense to me at that time." I burrow a little deeper into my bathrobe. "But I will always regret not believing him."

"Okay."

"To be honest," I add, "I still don't know what's making Dad sick. But it's best to trust people about what's going on with their own bodies, to let them live their own lives. Don't you think?"

"Yeah." He is already thinking about something else. "Can I ask you another question?"

"Yup."

"Now I think I'm interviewing *you*." He points a finger at my face. "Did you ever think about leaving Dad?"

I wince. "Wow, you're really asking the tough questions."

Nico smiles an apology. I remember him at a year old, his blond curls and brown sandals and the pacifier he was never without. I remember carrying him on my hip into my brother's backyard. I thought it might be the two of us against the world. I was plotting my escape from the life I hadn't signed up for. I remember sitting with my mother in that yard, crying the burdens of taking care of my husband. "That's what marriage is," she said. She was telling me to stay. How to tell my son that she was right, and also that there's more? That marriage can mean plotting an escape all the time and choosing to stay anyway. That it's the dreaming of another life that makes this one worth living.

"Yes," I say. "There were times when Dad and I thought we . . . wouldn't make it. But I think most couples have hard times. And it was a long time ago."

Nico releases his feet to the ground, sits up straight. He is satisfied. "Okay. Good interview, Mom. Can I play Zelda now?"

I once thought that recovery was achieved only through purity—abstinence from alcohol, remission from disease—but our recovery, imperfect though it may be, has been defined by acceptance. "The point," our RCA book says, "is that we are willing to grow together along spiritual lines." Acceptance of our problems, our powerlessness, and our mortality. If my parents' Puritan-Boomer generation, with its children growing up under the alcoholic wings of the war and the Depression, was defined by silence and suppression and avoidance, I will accept acceptance. Maybe I'd go so far to say it's the most divine form of love.

Aaron might say he's not an alcoholic, not today. Years ago, when he was drinking to die, to sleep, sure. Now he is drinking to live, to stay awake against the nightmare of illness. I would say that the word "alcoholic" doesn't contain nearly enough nuance. But as I understand it, from my side of the room, alcoholics drink to ward off all kinds of nightmares. Aaron's is just a highly idiosyncratic one.

"He likes it cold," the boy in *Stranger Things* says, of the monster who tries to possess him.

Aaron's monster likes it straight, in a juice glass.

But none of the words I choose contain enough nuance. If our house has been sick with three diseases—addiction, mental illness, and what I have taken to calling, inadequately, "chronic illness," whatever has battled Aaron's body for the better part of a decade—it is their comorbidity that makes them so difficult to parse. These diseases have fed upon, made necessary, the other. Alcoholism is, for him, for now, the parasite of his other illnesses.

I don't have the cure I hoped for Aaron. Our recovery from the sick house has not been realized through medical intervention. Aaron is just as sick in some ways, in some ways less sick, in some ways more. I feel sad about this, immeasurably sad. But I don't feel the same pall of doom, the panic or rage. I no longer enter a room and fear I will find my husband's lifeless body. I no longer dread the bad nights. And if he leaves me again, leaves himself, I trust he will come back. And I trust I will stay.

Judith Butler writes in *Giving an Account of Oneself:*

> As we ask to know the Other, or ask that the Other say, finally who he or she is, it will be important not to expect an answer that will ever satisfy. By not pursuing satisfaction, and by letting the question remain open, even enduring, we let the Other live, since life might be understood as precisely that which exceeds any account we may try to give of it.

Sometimes we talk about renewing our vows. Sometimes I have dreams about it. A chance to revise our wedding. Aaron in a tux that wasn't tailored in 2003. Me in a dress I don't have to fast to fit in. Bubbles instead of rose petals. A vegan cake, the top layer of which we will eat all by ourselves. In my dreams, there are people gathered to see us, we are running late, my heart is pounding.

But if we did it again, I think we'd do it alone. We'd write vows, and no one would be there to hear them but us. They might go like this:

> "Can I know you?"
> "Sure. You can try."

DANBY ROAD

2020

You're home with the kids, making spaghetti, making ramen noodles, all the revolting cheap starchy foods the children demand. You like to make a big batch of mac and cheese, two boxes at once, and the orange powder never really mixes all the way through. No matter. You keep the children alive. You watch *Sponge Bob* and *The Simpsons* and the show where they eat ancient expired food, which Henry loves. You feed the cat. You water the garden. On the deck, with Henry, you blow bubbles. You both love blowing bubbles now. It helps Henry calm down. It helps you calm down, too. You stand out there smiling in the sunshine with your quarantine-long hair and say, like a wizened old man out of a folk tale, "It helps me see the wind."

The country is slowly coming out of lockdown and for the first time in months I haven't slept beside you. You let Henry sleep in our bed, on my side. "Sleeping with Henry is like sleeping with a kangaroo," you text me, "but otherwise I slept fine."

At the arts colony, I'm in the studio with the rocking chair and the red quilt and the view of the field. It's next door to the studio where you picked me up that morning while the kids were in school, when we hadn't seen each other in days, when no one was around, where we made love on the bare mattress while the sheets were in the wash, then walked the field hand in hand while we waited for them to dry.

This time, there is a basket of vegan treats, fresh baked bread and homemade granola and jam in tiny hand-labeled jars the size of a teddy bear's fist. It's all so sweet it makes my eyes sting just to behold it. In the fridge, meals in glass containers, polenta pie and strawberry rhubarb crumble and tofu marinated in something that makes it actually melt in my mouth. It's the kind of food meant to feed to a lover, the kind of food we ate in our honeymoon suite, and because a husband is someone to text pictures of food to, I do. "I never knew tofu could be like this. Better-than-sex tofu." You text me a picture of your dinner: a box of dried rotini.

Yesterday when I arrived I sat in the armchair next to the window and read *Darkness Visible* straight through. You handed it to me when you finished it not long ago. You told me it described things perfectly.

"Which things?" I asked. "Where?" I wanted the page, the sentence.

"It's all in there," you said. "You'll see. He describes how it's—indescribable."

I sat by the window and as I finished the June breeze came in and brushed my neck, and the pleasure of it as I read the story of woe sent me into tears, because for once you were the one telling me how it was, not in your words but not in mine.

Here in the woods the trees are denser than the wisp of trees in the cemetery behind our house. Those trees are old but younger than the crooked graves, a forest grown up from the fertilizer of skeletons. But the trees here are about the same height, strong and tender, and their branches rustle with the same sound, a distant applause, and their leaves look like busy little hands. In its sign language the wind says everything, *Hello, I love you, I'm sorry, I miss you, thank you, it's going to be okay.* It makes me happy to think that the wind where you're blowing soap bubbles might blow out here to where I am, not so far away.

Soon, we'll do our third step with our sponsor couple. A vision for our higher power. We'll laugh about it. We'll make dumb jokes. We're supposed to visualize it, an energy that keeps us together, keeps us safe. It could be anything, our sponsors told us—the ocean, the stars, the sun. I know you don't like the moon. To me, it's as good as any of them, just a symbol of the mysterious power we don't understand, a force that was here before we were. Mother Nature leaving the bathroom light on. But I think the wind might be the best face of our god, invisible but undeniable, sometimes placid, sometimes fierce.

When I get home and park in the driveway, you're above me on the deck, waiting. Romeo in reverse. You wave a wing of bubbles. The boys run out and hug my waist. Nico is nearly as tall as I am. Henry is still small enough to jump into my arms.

After dinner, after putting the boys to bed, we go down to our room. Soon, we'll move to another house, but this is where we are now. The bedside lamp is low. The air purifier hums.

"Where do you want to go when you die?" I ask. I'm lying back against the pillows, one bent arm behind my head. You're sitting at the edge of the mattress, elbows on your knees, back to me.

"I want to be a bird," you say, no pause.

"No, like, practically speaking." I put my hand on your T-shirted back. "You know I want to be cremated."

"You want your ashes spread in Vermont."

"Yes."

"I don't want to be cremated."

"I know. But where do you want to be buried?"

You think about it. "Not in the backyard," you joke. But you know I'm asking because I'm worried you're rushing yourself toward death. For a moment I can face my fright. I've spent so many nights trying to ease your suffering, so many years trying to stretch the distance before the grave. I've done that, I see now, because I didn't want to be alone. I didn't want to be without you.

"Long Island?" I offer, helpfully.

"Yeah, that sounds good." You say it like I'm asking how much money we should give the mail carrier for the holidays. You don't care, I guess, and I realize I don't either. What we agree to without agreeing is that we don't need to put our bodies in the ground together, or throw them into the same wind. That sharing a bed in this life is plenty. It is enduring. Maybe these are, after all, the only vows that matter, the ones we said to each other when we didn't know what they would mean: to have and to hold, in sickness and in health. We can't give each other everything, but I believe this is enough.

"Come to bed, honey," I say, and you lie down beside me, and I turn off the light. We face each other, foreheads touching, and your breath finds my breath. This time, this night, we fall asleep easily.

ACKNOWLEDGMENTS

It takes a village to write a book, raise children, and stay married. So many people have supported Aaron and me through the writing of this memoir and the living of it.

Ursula, Joan, Katie, Jaime, Joanna, Mary Beth, Jen, Jennifer, Penny, Anna, Emily, Demitra, Kathie, Callie, Kate, Rich, Theresa, Steve, Stu, Jennifer, Chris, Claire, Jen, Jen, Liz, Ed, Livi, Dave, Cory, Lisa, Julie, Jack, Raul, Jacob, Shaianne, Derek, Derek, Sarah, Sara, Gina, Emily, Rene, Nina, Nina, Adrienne, Margaret, Carol, everyone from Al-Anon and Recovering Couples Anonymous, and so many other friends: thanks for being part of my village.

Sue-Je: wishing you peace.

All the caregivers who treated Aaron with respect and compassion: thanks for being bigger than the system.

Ithaca College, the family of Robert Ryan, and the Constance Saltonstall Foundation for the Arts: thank you for the time and space.

My wonderful Flatiron team—Lauren Bittrich, Kukuwa Ashun, Sam Zukergood, Chris Smith, Mara Lurie, Henry Kaufman, and above all Megan Lynch: thank you for your faith in this book. Megan: thanks for holding my hand. Jim Rutman: thanks for holding my other one. I couldn't have written this without either of you.

All the writers whose voices are in these pages: thanks for making me feel less alone.

Peter, Sam, Cameron, and Keri: thanks for being my first family.

My parents, Ann and Bill: thank you for teaching me what radical acceptance looks like, even if we didn't have the words for it. I hope you're still sharing the crossword.

Nico and Henry: thanks for taking care of us and each other, and for sleeping late enough for me to work on this book. I hope it's a balloon and not a burden.

And Aaron: all my love and thanks for letting me tell our story. You're the bravest boy I know.

ABOUT THE AUTHOR

Eleanor Henderson is the author of the novels *The Twelve-Mile Straight* and *Ten Thousand Saints*, which was named one of the ten best books of the year by *The New York Times* and was a finalist for the Award for First Fiction from the *Los Angeles Times*. Her writing has appeared in publications including *The New York Times*, *The Wall Street Journal*, and *Poets & Writers* and in the Best American Short Stories anthology. An associate professor at Ithaca College, she lives in Ithaca, New York, with her husband and two sons.